Books between Europe and the Americas

Also by James Raven

THE BUSINESS OF BOOKS: Booksellers and the English Book Trade, 1450–1850

JUDGING NEW WEALTH: Popular Publishing and Responses to
Commerce in England, 1750–1800

LONDON BOOKSELLERS AND AMERICAN CUSTOMERS: Transatlantic
Literary Community and the Charleston Library Society, 1748–1811

THE ENGLISH NOVEL, 1770–1829 (*2 Volumes, with Peter Garside and Rainer
Schöwerling*)

FREE PRINT AND NON-COMMERCIAL PUBLISHING SINCE 1700 (*Editor*)

LOST LIBRARIES: The Destruction of Book Collections since
Antiquity (*Editor*)

THE PRACTICE AND REPRESENTATION OF READING IN ENGLAND (*with Helen
Small and Naomi Tadmor, Editors*)

Also by Leslie Howsam

PAST INTO PRINT: The Publishing of History in Britain, 1850–1950

OLD BOOKS & NEW HISTORIES: An Orientation to Studies in Book & Print
Culture

CHEAP BIBLES: Nineteenth-Century Publishing and the British and Foreign Bible
Society

KEGAN PAUL: A Victorian Imprint – Publishers, Books and Cultural History

SCIENTISTS SINCE 1660: A Bibliography of Biographies

Books between Europe and the Americas

Connections and Communities, 1620–1860

Edited by

Leslie Howsam
University Professor of History, University of Windsor, Ontario, Canada

James Raven
Professor of Modern History, University of Essex, UK

First published 2011 by
PALGRAVE MACMILLAN

Palgrave Macmillan in the UK is an imprint of Macmillan Publishers Limited, registered in England, company number 785998, of Houndmills, Basingstoke, Hampshire RG21 6XS.

Palgrave Macmillan in the US is a division of St Martin's Press LLC, 175 Fifth Avenue, New York, NY 10010.

Palgrave Macmillan is the global academic imprint of the above companies and has companies and representatives throughout the world.

Palgrave® and Macmillan® are registered trademarks in the United States, the United Kingdom, Europe and other countries.

ISBN 978–0–230–28567–5 hardback

A catalogue record for this book is available from the British Library.

Library of Congress Cataloging-in-Publication Data
Books between Europe and the Americas : connections and communities, 1620–1860 / [edited by] Leslie Howsam, James Raven.
    p. cm.
    Includes index.
    ISBN 978–0–230–28567–5 (hardback)
    1. Books—Europe—History. 2. Books—America—History. 3. Books and reading—Europe—History. 4. Books and reading—America—History. 5. Books—History—17th century. 6. Books—History—18th century. 7. Books—History—19th century. I. Howsam, Leslie. II. Raven, James, 1959–
    Z8.E9B66 2011
    002.094—dc22   2011004896

10 9 8 7 6 5 4 3 2 1
20 19 18 17 16 15 14 13 12 11

Printed and bound in the United States of America

Contents

Acknowledgements

Books between Europe and the Americas began as a conference entitled 'Connected by Books', held in February 2004 in London, under the auspices of the Cambridge Project for the Book Trust. The intellectual approach to the Atlantic and its relationships was reinforced by the first two settings of the meeting. The opening sessions were held in central London at Dartmouth House, international headquarters of the English-Speaking Union, whose Governors (including James Raven) are keen to promote the study of relationships among people who share a lingua franca. The following day the conference migrated down the River Thames to Greenwich, where the National Maritime Museum proved an equally welcoming and stimulating setting for our ideas. Following the success of these meetings, a second conference was convened, again at the invitation of the Cambridge Project for the Book Trust, at the University of Essex in December 2007.

For financial support for the conferences, the editors are most grateful to the British Academy, the Royal Historical Society, Magdalene College, Cambridge, the University of Essex, the University of Windsor, the English-Speaking Union of the Commonwealth and the Cambridge Project for the Book Trust. Chapter 5 is a revised translation of an article which appeared in the *Papers of the Bibliographical Society of Canada* 37 (1999): 35–58. The author and the editors are grateful to the council of the Bibliographical Society of Canada for permission to publish the translation and to the Université de Sherbrooke for funding the original translation made by Rod Wilmott. Other assistance given to individual contributors to this book is acknowledged at appropriate places in the following chapters.

Notes on the Contributors

Catherine Armstrong is Lecturer in American History at Manchester Metropolitan University. Her research interests include British and American print culture in the seventeenth and eighteenth centuries. Her *Writing North America in the Seventeenth Century* was published in 2007. She is currently working on the changing representations of the American landscape in various print genres between 1660 and 1760.

Aileen Fyfe is Lecturer in Modern British History at the University of St Andrews, and the author of *Science and Salvation: Evangelical Popular Science Publishing in Victorian Britain* (2004) and editor (with Bernard Lightman) of *Science in the Marketplace: Nineteenth-century Sites and Experiences* (2007). She is completing a monograph on W. & R. Chambers and the firm's uses of new technologies to reach a wider readership for its instructive publications.

Joyce D. Goodfriend is Professor of History at the University of Denver. She is the author of *Before the Melting Pot: Society and Culture in Colonial New York City, 1664–1730* (1992) and numerous essays on colonial Dutch and early New York history. She is the editor of *Revisiting New Netherland: Perspectives on Early Dutch America* (2005) and co-editor of *Going Dutch: The Dutch Presence in America, 1609–2009* (2008). She is also a member of the North American Editorial Board of *Urban History*.

Leslie Howsam is University Professor in the Department of History at the University of Windsor, Ontario. She is President of the international Society for the History of Authorship, Reading and Publishing, and a Trustee of the Cambridge Project for the Book Trust. The author of numerous books and articles on the history of the book, her 2006 Lyell Lectures at the University of Oxford are published by the British Library as *Past into Print: The Publishing of History in Britain, 1850–1950* (2009).

Phyllis Whitman Hunter is Associate Professor in the Department of History, University of North Carolina, Greensboro, and a former Fellow of the National Humanities Center at Research Triangle Park. She is the author of *Purchasing Identity in the Atlantic World: Massachusetts Merchants, 1670–1780* (2001). She is currently completing two books, *Sailing East: The Empress of China and the New Nation* (forthcoming 2011), a study of the first American merchant voyage to China, and a monograph provisionally titled *Encountering Asia in Early America*.

François Melançon is an independent scholar and former Lecturer in History at the Université de Sherbrooke, Quebec, in whose Department of French Studies he successfully defended his 2007 thesis on book traffic in colonial New France. His research has been assisted by fellowships from the Fonds pour la formation des chercheurs et l'aide à la recherche, the Social Sciences and Humanities Research Council of Canada, the Canada Research Chair in Book and Publishing History (Université de Sherbrooke) and the Fondation Desjardins.

Jennifer Mylander is Assistant Professor of English at the College of Humanities, San Francisco State University, where she teaches courses on Milton, Shakespeare and the British Atlantic World. Other work on the history of books and reading in England and its Atlantic World has appeared in the *Journal for Early Modern Cultural Studies* and the collection *Shakespearean Educations: Power, Citizenship, and Performance* (2010), edited by Coppélia Kahn, Heather S. Nathans, and Mimi Godfrey.

Michael O'Connor is Research Assistant in the School of History and Anthropology at Queen's University, Belfast. He completed his Ph.D. thesis on 'James Magee (1707–91) and the Belfast Print Trade, 1771–81' in 2007, and is currently completing further publications in relation to Belfast printing and print culture.

James Raven is Professor of Modern History at the University of Essex. Formerly Reader in Social and Cultural History at the University of Oxford, Fellow of Mansfield College, Oxford, Fellow of Magdalene College, Cambridge, and Munby Fellow in Bibliography and Fellow of Pembroke College, Cambridge, he is Director of the Cambridge Project for the Book Trust (www.cambridgebook.demon.co.uk) and Director of the Mapping the Print Culture of Eighteenth-Century London project. His most recent book *The Business of Books: Booksellers and the English*

Book Trade, 1450–1850 (2007) was awarded the SHARP DeLong Book History Prize for 2008. His 2010 Panizzi Lectures 'London Booksites: Places of Printing and Publication before 1800' will be published by the British Library in 2011.

Robert J. Scholnick is Professor of English and American Studies at William and Mary. Author of *Edmund Clarence Stedman* (1977) and editor of *American Literature and Science* (1992), his many articles on nineteenth-century literature have appeared in such journals as *American Literature, Journal of American Studies, New England Quarterly* and *American Periodicals.* Reflecting his interest in transatlantic patterns of cooperation and conflict in the antebellum period, he is completing a study, 'Evolution Comes to America', on Robert Chambers's *Vestiges of Creation* (1844) as an international publishing phenomenon.

Sandra Guardini T. Vasconcelos is Full Professor of English Literature at the University of São Paulo, and was Visiting Research Associate at the Centre for Brazilian Studies at the University of Oxford (2005). She is a specialist on the work of the Brazilian novelist João Guimarães Rosa. Over the past years, she has been researching the presence and circulation of the English novel in nineteenth-century Brazil. Among other publications, she is the author of *A Formação do Romance Inglês: ensaios teóricos* (2007), which was awarded the 2008 Jabuti Prize for Literary Theory and Criticism.

Eugenia Roldán Vera is Professor of the History of Education at the Department of Educational Research of the Centro de Investigacion y Estudios Avanzados, Mexico City, and is a former Research Fellow of the Comparative Education Centre of Humboldt University, Berlin. Her publications include *The British Book Trade and Spanish American Independence* (2003) and *Imported Modernity in Postcolonial State Formation* (co-edited, 2007). She is currently working on comparative and transnational projects on the history of education in nineteenth- and twentieth-century Latin America.

Nicholas Wrightson completed a D.Phil. in History at Jesus College, University of Oxford, in 2007. His doctoral thesis, 'Franklin's Networks: Aspects of British Atlantic Print Culture, Science and Communication, *c.* 1730–60', is available from the Bodleian Library, Oxford, the Library Company of Philadelphia and the American Antiquarian Society. He is now pursuing a career in law.

Abbreviations

AAS	American Antiquarian Society, Worcester, MA
APS	American Philosophical Society, Philadelphia, PA
adv.	advertisement
AWM	*American Weekly Mercury*
BAnQ-Q	Bibliothèque et Archives nationales du Québec, Centre d'archives de Québec
BEP	*Boston Evening Post*
BFA	*Benjamin Franklin's Autobiography: An Authoritative Text, Backgrounds, Criticism*, ed. J.A.L. Lemay and P.M. Zall (New York, NY, 1986)
BFBS	British and Foreign Bible Society
BFP	*Papers of Benjamin Franklin*, ed. Leonard W. Labaree et al., 37 vols (New Haven, CT, 1959–2003)
BFSS	British and Foreign School Society
BG	*Boston Gazette*
BNL	*Boston News-Letter*
BPB	*Boston Post Boy*
CCP	*Letters and Papers of Cadwallader Colden*, 9 vols (New York, NY, 1918–37)
CEJ	*Chambers's Edinburgh Journal* (Edinburgh, 1832–54 under that title)
DHP	David Hall Papers, American Philosophical Society, Philadelphia, PA
ERSNY	*Ecclesiastical Records of the State of New York*, ed. Edward T. Corwin, 7 vols (Albany, NY, 1901–16)
ESTC	*English Short-Title Catalogue 1473–1800*, British Library on-line database
HJF	P.F., *The History of the Damnable Life and Deserved Death of Dr. John Faustus. Newly Printed; and in Convenient Places Impertinent Matter Amended, According to the True Copy Printed at Frankford and Translated into English* (London, 1682)
HSP	Historical Society of Pennsylvania, Philadelphia
JBP	*Correspondence of John Bartram, 1734–77*, ed. E. Berkeley and D.S. Berkeley (Gainesville, FL, 1992)

LAC	Library and Archives of Canada/Bibliothèque et Archive, Wellington St, Ottawa, Ontario (and www.collectionscanada.gc.ca)
LCNY	*The Lutheran Church in New York 1649–1772. Records in the Lutheran Church Archives at Amsterdam, Holland*, trans. Arnold J.H. van Laer (New York, 1946)
LCP	Library Company of Philadelphia
LLA	*Littell's Living Age* (Eliakim Littell's *The Living Age* or simply *Littell's*, as it was familiarly known, published in Boston, 1844–1941)
NEWJ	*New England Weekly Journal*
NYSA	New York State Archives, Albany, NY
NYWJ	*New York Weekly Journal*
ODNB	*Oxford Dictionary of National Biography* (Oxford, 2004–)
PBLC	*Protocol Book of the Lutheran Church in New York 1702–1750*, trans. Simon Hart and Harry J. Kreider (New York, 1958)
PCP	*'Forget Not Mee & My Garden ...': Selected Letters, 1725–68 of Peter Collinson, F.R.S.*, ed. A.W. Armstrong (Philadelphia, PA, 2002)
SIE	Société pour l'Instruction Élémentaire
STC	A. W. Pollard and G. R. Redgrave (eds), *A Short-Title Catalogue of Books Printed in England, Scotland and Ireland, and of English books printed abroad 1475–1640*. 2nd edn, revised and enlarged, begun by W. A. Jackson and F. S. Ferguson, completed by K. F. Pantzer. 3 vols (London, 1976, 1986, 1991)
STCN	*The Short Title Catalogue Netherlands*
STCV	*The Short Title Catalogus Vlaanderen*
SPCK	Society for the Promotion of Christian Knowledge
SPG	Society for the Propagation of the Gospel in Foreign Parts
WRC	W. & R. Chambers Archive, National Library of Scotland

1
Introduction

Leslie Howsam and James Raven

As men and women have moved around the world, so have books. Books, periodicals and newspapers have served as ambassadors of thought, religion and nationhood, and they have connected peoples separated by land and sea and by political and sectarian borders. At the same time, books, in manuscript and in print, have created artificial boundaries and reinforced prejudices. Writers, publishers and readers have all used the trade in books – often in surprising ways – to promote political, literary and linguistic agendas. Written texts have ensured powerful bonds of shared identity between all those involved in their production, circulation and consumption.

Books between Europe and the Americas engages with a new history of trans-oceanic *livres sans frontières* which is beginning to overcome some of the cultural and linguistic limitations of older historical writing about the zone framed by the Atlantic ocean. This book of essays offers new insights into the development, over some 240 years, of long-distance networks of transatlantic cultural and literary exchange. The different chapters explore issues of cultural identity, the creation and circulation of knowledge, news and narratives, and the political and economic consequences of textual transmission between the Old and New Worlds.

Various studies of translation, reprinting and textual appropriation have already shown how certain authors and their texts have appeared, reappeared and been transformed outside their home countries.[1] Such mutations can be traced because each copy and each edition is a discrete physical object. Nevertheless, in the words of one historian of the transnational book, 'when books travel, they change shape. They are excised, summarized, abridged, and bowdlerized by the new intellectual formations into which they migrate.'[2] Books and periodicals become the media of cultural connection and difference between writers and their readers on both sides of an ocean.

The contributors to this book explore the travels and the transmutations of books and periodicals, across and within the Atlantic zone, by charting the histories of different transatlantic literary communities. To identify and trace a connection by books is to think about how peoples in Europe and the Americas made use not only of literature, but also of the trade in books as commodities. The processes of exchange were not passive or linear, and nor were the relationships they established and sustained. Transmission involved creation, protection and policing, and identities, not merely communities, often resulted. The research that underpins the essays gathered in this book does much to nuance, stretch and challenge the basic ideas of community and identity, by integrating the quantitative with the specific and by measuring in new ways the significance of transmission, receipt and exchange.

The study of migration has become a powerful mode of historical interpretation. Some of our ancestors emigrated and sought refuge, some immigrated only to move onward or return home, and others stayed at home while their neighbours went abroad. Some of this resettlement was enforced and much of it was painful. Among the most sorrowful chronicles of migration are those of slaves and native peoples. Attending to movement on a global scale transcends the narrow constraints of national histories and invites comparison rather than opposition.[3] It allows us to think about cultural relationships and the connections of identity that remain when physical proximity is broken. A transnational history can transcend the artificial boundaries of the nation-state by identifying networks and other patterns of relationship, but it also presents the historian with theoretical and methodological challenges. Patricia Clavin notes that

> It is better to think of a transnational community not as an enmeshed or bound network, but rather as a honeycomb, a structure which sustains and gives shapes to the identities of nation-states, institutions and particular social and geographic space. It contains hollowed-out spaces where institutions, individuals and ideas wither away to be replaced by new organizations, groups and innovations.[4]

Book writers and readers, collectors and collections, journalists and journalism, publishers and publishing are individuals and institutions that flourish (or decline) inside such an envisaged community. 'For a transnational community to survive,' Clavin continues, 'its boundaries must remain open, porous, revisable and interactive. If they are not, then gradually one honeycomb of national, regional and international relations is replaced with another. Charting the history of transnational communities...exposes hidden continuities and connections in time and space, as well as the gaps between them.'[5] In analogous ways, a transnational history of the book offers a robust methodology and intellectual approach to the history of communities and of cultural exchange.

Men and women sustained common identities by preserving and reproducing material objects, as well as by spoken and written communication. From paintings, portraits and ceramics to clothes and architecture, precious objects and familiar cultures travelled into the New World. But greater intimacy was established and extended by written correspondence between individuals. The exchange of letters offered personal interpretation of thought, ideology and news. Exchange might be familial, local, regional, national, international and sometimes several of these at the same time. The result of such exchange was often a community of shared interest and practice, one that flourished however large or small the scale, however long or short the distances between the participants.[6]

Books, pamphlets and magazines transmit knowledge by physical form (or the message by the medium). Books share some of the characteristics of other material goods. Tactility, design and ornamentation convey meaning even before a book is read. But books also carry texts whose reading conveys intellectual and ideological significance. The connections supplied by print fall short of the interactive exchanges possible between people not parted by distance, but in many ways print offers the same connectedness provided by letters and other received communication. Manuscripts and printed books and periodicals extended and widened the reach of such exchange into a transatlantic structure of communication – and one, as the following chapters demonstrate, that changed according to the mutations of colonialism, migration, exile, commerce, political independence and nationalism.

The Atlantic, as depicted centrally in global maps made in Europe as well as by Atlanticist historians, was a complex and competitive arena. Across the Atlantic moved ships, people and cargoes that together established, reinforced and modulated different communities of kinship and trade.[7] Transatlantic exchange and commerce in identities, goods and ideas have been investigated in different ways by many historians. Notable (and very different) Atlanticist histories of British America include influential studies by Bernard Bailyn and J.G.A. Pocock.[8] More recent but equally influential and comparative histories of transatlantic Spanish America include those by John Elliott and David Abulafia.[9] A long-standing conversation among French historians about *L'Amerique Française* and the French Atlantic world focuses upon the nature of colonialism.[10] Older Spanish and Portuguese histories that reflect the same concern have more recently been revised and challenged by very different approaches.[11]

This relationship between migration patterns and cultural products is fraught and complex, both historically and historiographically.[12] David Armitage has isolated three different but mutually reinforcing modalities in the writing of the history of the Atlantic: the fundamental 'transatlantic', international, comparative history that links otherwise distinct national histories; 'circum-Atlantic', the transnational and people-centred history of the Atlantic zone of exchange, interchange, circulation and transmission; and (arguably the most rewarding) 'cis-Atlantic', national or regional history within a broad Atlantic context (and potentially including landlocked countries). Each model, it is claimed, reveals great geographical and chronological fluidity and research potential.[13] However such studies are categorized, it is certainly the case that in the past 20 years advocates of 'New Atlantic History' have attempted to supplement national histories, with ambitious conceptual and comparative exercises in the oceanic-centred development of regions, states and empires. And to the fore in this writing is the exploration of national diasporas, personal connections and the economic development of transatlantic consumerism.[14]

A driving concern of most of those writing Atlantic history is to open up new perspectives, or, to put it another way, to expose weaknesses in existing accounts of national or imperial political, economic and social histories. Such accounts are compromised by the Eurocentric assumptions built into a centre/periphery model, which presupposes that books and ideas must always move out from Europe to its colonies and never from outpost to metropole. As Isabel Hofmeyr has argued, 'the space of empire' should be considered as 'intellectually integrated'. But her brilliant work *The Portable Bunyan* shows that this is a difficult task. Comparative studies of the different locales, peoples and initiatives linked by the Atlantic reveal the intimidating scale of the enterprise and highlight shortcomings and imbalances in historical coverage. Despite Hofmeyr's pioneering interpretation of a 'Protestant Atlantic', little comparative history, for example, has been written about religious transatlanticism beyond the initial immigrations and settlements.[15] Even more telling is the inability to break free of Anglo-Saxon perspectives (usually because of the absence of primary local research or because of the linguistic limitations of the historian).

Outstanding and pioneering comparative studies of migration, settlement and colonial encounter in North, Central and South America[16] have not yet been matched by comparative histories of the creation and maintenance of networks that linked different national and linguistic communities. Studies of French America such as those by Gilles Havard and Cécile Vidal that incorporate sections on 'échanges, transports et commerce',[17] are valuable yet relatively lonely relations to equivalent histories for British North America and the British Caribbean. Histories of Spanish, Portuguese, Dutch, German, Swedish and other transatlantic communities are little known beyond their country of publication.[18] In addition, they very rarely include studies of minority linguistic groups functioning within a majority culture (and where transatlantic connections and dependencies were even more significant). But a polyglot multiculturalism co-existed with the increasing dominance in speech and print of English in North America, of Spanish in Central America and of Spanish and Portuguese in South America. Not least of the opportunities afforded by a history of the book across the Atlantic is to understand more fully the operation of minority linguistic communities and to insist that numbers need not be all. Much is contained in the small, imperfect and discontinuous, in the minute but vital intermittent communities of importers and exporters of print, manuscripts, books and correspondence within ethnic and linguistic circuits.

This book begins 170 years after the introduction of movable type and the printing press in Europe. At this time, the number of manual printing presses was still relatively modest in all but a handful of cities stretching from Italy and Spain to France, the Low Countries and the states of Germany and the Holy Roman Empire. Although a printing press was carried to and operated (very intermittently) in Mexico City from 1539, in Lima from 1581 and in Boston, Massachusetts, from 1638, the vast majority of reading material for the colonists of the New World continued to be imported from the home countries. How many books were shipped across the ocean, and from which towns and cities did they originate? As the following chapters amply demonstrate (from a great diversity of archives), the most direct evidence of the shipments and of the origins of the books conveyed remains in booksellers' and customers' invoices, orders and memoranda, ships' dockets and customs records, sales advertisements and the correspondence, diaries and wills of book collectors. Many such sources, however, provide only sketchy titles of books and other print, and the detective work necessarily undertaken by this book's contributors crucially depends upon much larger bibliographical projects. The most notable of these larger resources are the various European catalogues of retrospective national bibliography.

It is a truism of modern bibliographical studies that the different retrospective national bibliographies exist in very different stages of completion, and, the more mischievous add, that their progress reflects different national histories and characteristics. Whatever the cause, it is certainly the case that the projects for English and for Dutch language retrospective short-title catalogues are far more advanced than for any other nation – and that, in turn, of course, compounds the national biases evident in the historical treatments of the Atlantic world. For study of British America, therefore, crude but very suggestive title counts can be constructed by use of the online *English Short Title Catalogue* (*ESTC*) which aims to record every surviving title, by edition, of letterpress items printed in England or any of its dependencies, in any language, 1473–1800, or printed in English anywhere else in the world during that period (about 450,000 separate titles).

Similar use can be made of *The Short Title Catalogue Netherlands* (*STCN*), the online but unfinished Dutch retrospective bibliography for 1540–1800 (currently 130,000 titles), designed to contain bibliographical descriptions of all surviving books published in the Netherlands and those in Dutch published abroad between those dates. The companion *Short Title Catalogus Vlaanderen* (*STCV*) describes surviving Dutch language materials printed between 1601 and 1700 within the present-day boundaries of Flanders (including Brussels) and, in the catalogue's second working phase, works printed in Flanders in other languages than Dutch (notably Latin, Spanish and French). Just as importantly, *ESTC*, *STCN* and *STCV* can be used to identify the often frustratingly short-title descriptions given in early dockets, invoices and the like. French and German *Short Title Catalogues* (*STCs*) are ongoing but so far limited by chronological range and by the collections consulted,[19] and nothing as accessible or comprehensive yet exists for those attempting to identify the scribbled titles of books and pamphlets originating from Spanish, Portuguese or Italian territories.[20]

Devotion to the new *STCs* should be curbed however, at least in using them to provide bibliometric profiles of comparative printing of different genres, items from different places and items by different types of author (among other variables). All *STC* title counts can be hugely problematic, disguising great variations in edition sizes, poorer survival rates for older items, and (as chapters in this book address) requiring further knowledge about importing from non-home country ports and publication centres. Nevertheless, simple use of *ESTC* title counts, for example, confirms the long-term dominance of London, the more so because there was no colonial printing to speak of before 1750. The *cumulative* ranking by place of publication of *ESTC*-recorded items by 1800 is therefore more remarkable given that the colonial challengers to London (and to Scottish and Irish publishing centres, also growing in importance in the eighteenth century) are the result of only about 50 or so years of more than occasional American publication. London's total number of titles remains more than twice the sum of all the imprints between 1473 and 1800, but (after Edinburgh and Dublin) Boston is ranked fourth, and Philadelphia fifth, both ahead of Oxford and Cambridge. New York and then several other North American towns appear among the rankings of English provincial towns.

The in-progress *STC*s can also suggest comparisons with other non-English printing in North America. *ESTC* (so far, the fullest *STC* in this respect) records 188 editions printed before 1801 in North America in French, all but two after 1700, an impressive 1,213 in German beginning in 1695, a few dozen in Dutch and a few in Spanish, and even fewer in Swedish and Italian. Well might Franklin have voiced his famous concern that the German language would overtake English in Pennsylvania by the middle of the eighteenth century. The earliest surviving American sales list of books in German dates from 1739, issued by Christoph Saur of Philadelphia, one of the leading German book traders who was in regular commerce with Wigand in Frankfurt. The English Navigation Acts supposedly restricted to English ships the shipment of German books to the English American colonies, but German publications also appear routinely in the cargo records of Dutch ships and other carriers to Pennsylvania and New York (among others).[21] The minority printings in French and Dutch (as well, of course, as printing in French North American territory itself) require, however, investigation beyond the limited pointers offered by *ESTC* – something which several of the chapters in this book seek to do.

Even allowing for the different languages and cultures that crossed the ocean, the most familiar transatlantic literary community (even to Hispanic audiences) is the one established and sustained by English literature and by the shared histories of Britain and the United States. Several contributors to this book address that relationship, and the ways in which not only literary texts but also Government documents, religious writings and political tracts sustained the different readerships in lively tension. But we enrich our understanding of the familiar routes of London, Glasgow and Edinburgh to New York and Boston by comparing and contrasting them with print and literary connections between Paris and São Paulo, Belfast and Philadelphia, Amsterdam and New Amsterdam, France and *La Nouvelle France*, London and Caracas, and Madrid, Seville and Mexico City. In such ways, the book's editors and contributors aim to extend understanding of a transnational and global history of the book. The attempt is not limited to international or centre-to-periphery relationships, but particularly includes ways in which readers abroad influenced publishers and writers at home, as much as the other way around.[22] The following chapters present a series of linked case studies and surveys in order to test the possibilities of writing such a history, and to suggest some methodological approaches for future research.

The first three chapters in this book, like several later chapters, use specific incidents in the creation and dissemination of news and knowledge to elucidate the means by which a sense of transatlantic community and identity was established and maintained. The opening essay examines early modern British America and its perception in Britain. Catherine Armstrong analyses the ways in which intelligence and rumour spread about the 1622 massacre by native Americans of over 300 English settlers on several plantations in the Virginia colony. It was an event that presaged the end of the founding Virginia Company itself. Armstrong argues that in the short term, news of the murders benefited the Virginia Company by keeping Company and colony in the public eye. But this was in spite of the Company's directives, which discouraged and then banned printed stories about the Virginia planters. The Company's American activities – and reversals – featured in a range of community matters from drama to penal policy, but at first the Company and then the Privy Council suppressed such accounts. Despite the wide circulation of manuscript accounts of the massacre, the Company feared public blame in the apparently authoritative medium of print.

The veracity of print, its comparison to manuscript and the question of which was the more believable and stable become recurrent themes in chapters in this book. Armstrong's examination of transported news of the Virginia Massacre raises the question of what history and accuracy mean. Numerous commentators, who appeared to suppress the sincere protests of American planters, rather believed themselves to be *historians* of the massacre. Reinterpreting and censoring the individual voices of their original transatlantic correspondents, English writers and publishers assembled information from far-flung sources and worked as self-conscious and self-appointed recorders for posterity. Their actions both responded to and further encouraged the development of corantos and then newspapers, where 'news' achieved new authority through the material form of the print that carried it. The newspapers conveyed events like that of the Virginia Massacre as authentic historical accounts, when they were, in fact, idealized narratives and didactic tragedies.

Jennifer Mylander's chapter offers a very different type of micro-history in which the *événement* is a static written document and the principal recovered history is of the reading and interpretation of a popular imported text. Mylander examines the 1683 inventory of an order for books made by Thomas Shepard, minister of Charlestown, Massachusetts. Shepard ordered London books from the importing bookseller of Boston, John Usher, who, in turn, bought them from the distinguished London bookseller Richard Chiswell. Shepard's inventory remains one of the very few surviving records that allow us to reconstruct not only the reading material of an early New England community, but also an early transatlantic network of communication and commerce. Mylander discusses the range of Shepard's want-list, encompassing both learned tomes and multiple copies of cheap books, but her focus is the order for 30 copies of the *History of Dr. Faustus*. She traces the links between the reading of 'popular wonders' literature like Faustus and their use as educational tools for a far-distant audience ranging widely in abilities and interests.

Mylander concludes that the readings of the Faustus *History* are consistent with pedagogies promoted by Frances Meres, Thomas Beard, John Milton and others. In a notable extension of Hofmeyr's construal of a Protestant Atlantic,[23] Mylander interprets the *History* as a damnation narrative that appealed to a wide range of early modern English and American readers by its emphasis on both civility and Reformed belief. Reading this text, she argues, was analogous to understanding the role of God's providence in the life of contemporary Englishmen and women on both sides of the Atlantic. Such advocacy of good manners in the late seventeenth century was therefore not simply a secularizing movement, but one based on an alignment between transplanted Protestantism and transplanted Englishness. In this respect, Mylander's exploration of the development and definition of a seventeenth-century American reading community through the popularity of a particular text complements Catherine Armstrong's recovery of English readings of printed versions of American events. It is a duality extended by the chapter that follows.

Phyllis Whitman Hunter broadens the perspective on transatlantic historicizing by considering early British American reports of occurrences in other parts of the world. She examines the long-disregarded foreign news that occupied the majority of space in colonial North American newspapers. Hunter focuses on the representation of three particular affairs – Admiral Anson's achievements and fame (notably conveyed by his *A Voyage Round the World*), the South Sea Bubble of 1720 and prominent events at the Ottoman Court. Her concern is with the role of print in relation to the circulation of goods, people, and ideas throughout the Atlantic world, and how this offers new perspectives on the social and political history of early eighteenth-century British North America.

As Hunter demonstrates, a variety of news items sustained the interconnection of colonial American ports with the larger project of European empire, but the localized interpretations also went beyond any simple acceptance of metropolitan culture. Her chapter takes us through the developments of the print world of the eighteenth century, from the advance of newspapers and periodicals to booksellers' commercial techniques and the establishment of circulating and social libraries. Publications concerning the scandalous and the heroic featured as part of the imperial and transatlantic experience, the reception of which revealed both the strengths and weaknesses of colonial transatlantic connections.

Hunter's reportage is global in reach but is created and disseminated in the British Atlantic world. François Melançon moves the spotlight to eighteenth-century French North America. He considers the familiarity of settlers in New France with the printed text and how they appreciated its versatility. As Armstrong's chapter acknowledges, and other recent studies have insisted, the world of manuscript was not suddenly or completely replaced by that of print.[24] The arrival of a printing press on the other side of the Atlantic, in this case in Quebec, and then in Montreal, was less of a divide than might be thought in the history of the availability of print in North America. The year 1764 and the establishment of the first printing press in the Laurentian valley has been a false reference point. In the French, as in the English and Spanish colonies, book circulation did not require local printing to be established. Rather, it was distance that brokered fundamental change. An understanding of the import trade in books is the key to unlocking the literary history of New France as it is of British and Spanish North and Central America.

Melançon's chapter demonstrates how historical and literary scholarship have been coloured by perceptions and assumptions about the civilizing power of the technology of printing. Here yet another example of transatlantic (mis)communication appears as evidence. A Swedish botanist visited New France in the 1760s and noted in his travel account the absence of a printing press. This narrative was published in German, translated into English and then into French. The French version, appearing in Montreal a century later, had the scientific traveller reporting the existence of a press, much to the satisfaction of nationalists who were not finally disabused until a new translation appeared in 1977. In this case, not only have books travelled and transmuted, but the very accounts of their production have also been subject to the vagaries of textual and political interpretation.

This theme is expanded in the next chapter, where Nicholas Wrightson reveals how the development of Atlantic history has transformed a historical debate that earlier turned on the difference between 'integrative' and 'fragmentary' interpretations of early modern and eighteenth-century society. Elements of both integration and diversity were said to co-exist in early modern European and early colonial society, but Wrightson's chapter advances questions already introduced by earlier contributors to the book and suggests ways in which the Atlantic offered opportunities for 'negotiated empire', united as much by the web of connections of private individuals as by larger political, institutional or ideological relationships.

Wrightson uses *Pennsylvania Gazette* advertisements, ledger accounts and diverse personal correspondence and business records to reconstruct two overlapping transatlantic connections. Benjamin Franklin appears here in his early incarnation as Philadelphia printer-bookseller. Franklin's wide circle of acquaintanceship intersects with that of the London Quaker, Peter Collinson, who established, in Wrightson's words, 'the period's first reliable, affordable, extensive and systematic network of transatlantic scientific exchanges'. In both cases, the need to oversee the quality and accuracy of correspondence and orders (and the profitability of business) confronted formidable obstacles of cost, risk and time. Collinson, the merchant-turned-naturalist, fostered transatlantic collaborations and, like Franklin, gained particular insight into how circuits of written information made and maintained transatlantic communities. Such social histories of communication amplify John Elliott's Atlantic history of 'people, commodities, cultural practices, and ideas'.[25]

This negotiated, cultural dominion can be demonstrated as much by minority groups as by larger and dominant societies. Joyce D. Goodfriend considers books and other print sent from Amsterdam ('the bookshop of the world') to New York. It was a comparatively small but highly selective trade. Overseas merchants importing Dutch books after 1750 concentrated almost exclusively on family Bibles, Testaments and psalm-books. These were the mainstays of the colonial Dutch transatlantic book trade. By use of wills and inventories, Goodfriend further reconstructs the ownership of imported literature and shows in particular how the descendants of emigrants sustained the Dutch Bible trade to New York.

The larger point is one of scale, where small is not just beautiful but vital. The Dutch book trade to New York City continued to be dwarfed by imports of English books. The city's major booksellers rarely sold a Dutch book. But in a region ruled by the English, and where English was already the *modus operandi*, the continuing importation and consumption of print in the Dutch language reinforced Dutch culture for generations of the descendants of New Netherlanders in the middle colonies. As in New France and the links to France described by Melançon, books provided a lifeline to the Netherlands' culture for the isolated but self-identified Dutch people of British North America.

Another minority language is the subject of James Raven's chapter, but this language aspired to serve elite, clerical and teaching communities in America, North and South. Latin, in Joseph de Maistre's mid-nineteenth-century phrase, constituted the 'European sign', but as that European lingua franca it offered very particular advantages and disservices when transported and transplanted to the New World. The influence of classical learning in the North American colonies and the early United States has long been acknowledged. Far less noted is the clerical, pedagogical and literary usage of Latin in Central America from the very first years of colonization. Moreover, just as Latin usage in Central America sharply declined, following the expulsion of the Jesuits from Hispanic lands in 1767, professional usage of Latin and Greek in North America became more adaptable and entrenched (if vigorously contested).

Raven examines what was left for the dead language to communicate and support, including when transmitted by translation into the vernacular. He explores the sustenance by the classics of a significant but neglected transatlantic community of producers and consumers, all contributing to a very real sense of shared belonging and purpose. How was passage from one continent to another envisaged in the sustaining notions of a classical heritage that contributed to the cultural authority of the colonists? Just as neo-Latin flourished in Mexico and then was physically removed and reprinted in Europe, North Americans first imported classical notions and then also later, in the national period, exported the same ideas back to Europe.

Philadelphia is prominent in this book as a centre of Latin learnedness and of the connections of Franklin and Collinson. The city features again in Michael O'Connor's study of another fragile but vital strand in the Atlantic book trade. By recovering the long-neglected career of James Magee (1707–97), chief Belfast printer, bookseller and publisher of the eighteenth century, O'Connor re-examines the connections between the Belfast and Philadelphia book trades in the eighteenth century. He assesses the reasons for their interaction and its impact on the status of Belfast printing. Recent histories observing the various connections between Irish booksellers and their counterparts in North America, primarily in Philadelphia and New York, have concentrated on the impact on the American book trade and the emergence of a local reprint tradition. O'Connor considers instead the implications of the development of Belfast American trade for Irish printing, especially in printing outside of Dublin.

This review of Magee's trade emphasizes the cultural as much as the economic value of Belfast and Dublin reprints. It challenges many parallel studies, but notably supports Richard Sher's account of Enlightenment publishing.[26] Irish printers and booksellers, by means of their reprinting activities, served as vital agents in disseminating Scottish Enlightenment culture to America. Just as great, however, was the impact of these reprints on the Irish market. O'Connor shows how transatlantic activity contributed to the growing confidence of Belfast business and its greater prominence as a town and a printing hub. It is an unexpected conclusion, in which trade to America can be assessed not just for the obvious impact made in the New World but for indirect effects on both sides of the Atlantic and for the subtle process of transatlantic mediation. It was a process, for example, in which Scottish ideas reached readers in the early United States via Irish printers and booksellers.

A similarly hidden influence is central to the next chapter, which also reminds us that by the end of the eighteenth century the increasing sophistication of trade and contact in North America was paralleled by developments in trade with the South. Sandra Guardini T. Vasconcelos reconstructs the literary history of early nineteenth-century Brazil by reassessing the precise mediation of Atlantic traffic. The suspension of censorship in Brazil in 1821 resulted in a freer and more regular circulation of books, magazines and newspapers in the bookshops, libraries and circulating libraries of Rio de Janeiro. Among the stock of the bookshops and libraries (the majority established in the 1820s and 1830s), novels and romances came mostly from Lisbon and Paris and were mainly in Portuguese or French. Little other literature appeared to arrive in Brazil from elsewhere. A more searching investigation of the imported books, however, reveals the critical influence of serial translation and, as mediated, very significant textual origination in Britain. As Vasconcelos is the first to demonstrate, English, Scottish and Irish novelists played a far more prominent role in the making of the Brazilian novel than has been recognized, and precisely because of 'secondary' translation based upon an initial translation from English into French.

Vasconcelos meticulously traces the course of the translations and importations from advertisements found in newspapers and the numerous British authors and novels available (in translation) in bookshop and circulating library catalogues. By such research, she not only reassesses the modes and consequences of transatlantic print traffic, but challenges the claimed primacy of French novels and novelists in the making and consolidation of the Brazilian novel as a literary form. From the infancy of Brazilian national fiction, to the works of the two most important nineteenth-century Brazilian novelists, José de Alencar and Machado de Assis, the development of Brazilian fiction crucially entailed an engagement with imported foreign literary models, among which translated British and French novels played a prominent role.

Continuing the exploration of this hybridity, the next chapter further examines the literary and intellectual connectedness of Britain and France with South and Central America in the early nineteenth century. South America supplied Europe with raw materials and received in return science, learning and books of instruction and entertainment. The continent became, in this period, a zone of both violent political revolution and social transformation. In her provocative essay on the importation of new educational methods, Eugenia Roldán Vera suggests how patterns of communication forged by print were not simply a means for the transmission of knowledge but also constitutive of that knowledge. She considers the intermediaries that conveyed the European theories, plans and models which were to provide guidance for Spanish American republics to break other transatlantic bonds and to declare and maintain political independence from Europe.

As Roldán Vera shows, the transatlantic flow of information created a particular kind of educational knowledge through the very process of the exchange. Her focus is the system of monitorial teaching established between the European and the Spanish American societies in which each party expected and received something by the exchange. And, in another parallel with the previous chapter, France remained the common intermediary in a communication network between Spanish America and Great Britain where the monitorial method (and so many early influential novels) originated. The obvious legacy of the exchange was the reputation of France as the great civilizing nation of Europe. Such communication between European and Spanish American societies also furthered the processes of internationalization in educational and other sorts of knowledge, as well as a better understanding of its relational dimensions.

The arrival of the steamship transformed the transatlantic communications between Europe and the Americas discussed in these essays. The final two chapters of the book consider the impact of steam and the resulting increase in the speed and reliability of communications – and in the new age of independence (political, at least) from the colonial powers. As Aileen Fyfe argues, the apparent imminence of an international copyright treaty advanced transatlantic book trade in the 1840s, but the traffic itself was extended as a result of more reliable and frequent steamship services. These conveyed people, goods, letters and bills of exchange between what were now separate nations. Focusing on the firm of W. & R. Chambers, Fyfe revisits an issue introduced earlier by Michael O'Connor, and examines the absence of copyright regulation across the Atlantic and the licence this gave to the activities of reprinters in the New World. She shows how from the late 1840s Chambers explored new possibilities in the United States market, experimented in distribution methods and investigated the marketability of different products.

British publishers became increasingly interested in the United States market in the 1850s. By the late 1850s, steamship freight costs had so diminished that use of steamers became almost routine. This greater ease of travel also enabled many more publishers and their representatives to cross the Atlantic. The first British publishers' branch offices in New York date from the mid-1850s. Chambers's many books and serials were successfully imported, suggesting that British and American publishers enjoyed mutually helpful business practises even without the legal protection of copyright. As Fyfe further demonstrates, the exception was *Chambers's Journal* where, although no American reprint proved successful in the long term, the ever present threat of a reprint severely limited the viability of the imported edition. Consideration of such constraints and limitations is recurrent in the contributions to this book. From the beginning of his long-term relationship with the Philadelphia publisher Joshua B. Lippincott, Chambers sent consignments to the English Book Depot in New York, but also directly supplied retail booksellers with stereotype plates for reprinting in the United States. The absence of a fully integrated banking and business community did prove a handicap, and tastes of readers diverged between each side of the Atlantic. Chambers scarcely altered the contents of their publications, but in order to attract American readers, the firm's Boston and Philadelphia partners changed the physical format of the reprinted books and magazines.

Concluding the book, Robert J. Scholnick continues the exploration of transatlantic nations and peoples brought together by the power of steam. Central to his study is Eliakim Littell's remarkable weekly *The Living Age*, and its extraction of material from British periodicals (including many published by Chambers) to confront the slave-holding opinions of the American South. Littell challenged the assumptions of many of his American readers by publishing opinionated pieces that conveyed a global perspective. The weekly became central to the anti-slavery movement. As Scholnick stresses, however, such inspiration for the cause of human equality and democracy came, paradoxically, from across the Atlantic. Monarchical England with its unwritten constitution and its aristocratic power nevertheless bred loud and successful advocates of abolition. This final chapter reveals that Littell understood that it was not possible to be true to the ideals of American citizenship without renewing citizenship in a larger global community. Such a community looked decidedly modern, founded on open, liberal and historic transatlantic dialogue. As Scholnick demonstrates, the mature system of transatlantic exchange incorporated and indeed nurtured new forms of literary communication. The medium of a new periodical embraced genuine Atlanticism, and, in this case, it proved an effective deliberation (if not swift deliverer) of liberal democracy.

Throughout these studies, the question of reception is as important as that of the composition, revision and circulation of news, literature and knowledge. This is the case whether we are thinking about national cultural traditions, personal correspondence or the reception of particular texts, ranging from chapbooks to Bibles to newspapers and magazines. In mass, majority and even partially literate societies, letters, print and books have contributed significantly to the aetiology of community, but how did different readers, many separated by great distance, conceptualize the connections that they established and re-established across the seas? Did they think of these as proactively transatlantic? One of our greatest challenges is to consider whether or not that is the case.

As all the following chapters disclose, the publications that made the fabric of literary communities came in many forms, both in textual genre and in material form. In terms of content, publications ranged from the official texts of government and of Church and social reform, and the literature of dissident or exile groups, to news reporting and imaginative writing and images designed for diversion, guidance or enlightenment. The pages that supported the written or pictorial content were equally varied, from private or public correspondence, to manuscript tract or book, single sheet or newsbook, newspaper or serial, chapbook or luxury folio. The words on the pages sometimes stood alone and at other times were accompanied (and sometimes led) by visual illustration. Together, the many types of text and their contrasting reception served to establish and extend the new as well as to reinforce and maintain the old.

But what of transatlanticism? In the first place, the many different transatlantic communities created and sustained by print were of themselves something new, built on a large scale. In addition, however, the temporal dimension crucially intervened – the distances extended the real time that it took for texts to be received, and in some cases, sent back. The sense of the transatlantic was, in often very precise ways, related to both the realities and the (often mediated) perceptions of the width of the Atlantic and the varying length of time taken for a ship to cross it, as it carried news, ideas, stories, letters, print or plates. Such variations remained seasonal as much as they changed in relation to different transport capacities, timetables, investment and technologies. To this extent, the technologies of transmission cannot be severed from the social and cultural histories of communities whose identities, practices and expectations were supported by print. Chapters in this book repeatedly return to the times and distances involved and to perceptions of how these changed between 1620 and 1860. Change was not always as great as we might imagine, or as great as the Victorians hoped from their vaunted technologies of steam and telegraph. The exchanges described by Fyfe and Scholnick were in many respects similar to the earlier frustrations of the seventeenth and eighteenth centuries – but they felt new. The overseas business of books required a close attention to detail and an energetic approach, which might be entrepreneurial, evangelical or diplomatic.[27] Yet in forging more modern arrangements, entirely new notions of competitiveness were introduced, while the accent remained on personal trust and individual relationships in order to secure successful exchange.

Much of this complexity can be explained by the endurance and preservation of something old within the processes that worked to create the new on the 'other' side of the Atlantic. Literature and knowledge were used to update and retain cultural authority. All the contributors to this book consider how material forms of authority have been transmitted across the ocean between diverse peoples. Sometimes, as with the Dutch trade to New York, this was to support minority voices in an alien larger community, and sometimes, as with imported texts to (very different) clerical and pedagogical communities in both North and South America it was to support pragmatic and practical agendas. But such transmission is also noticeable where functional needs – such as keeping up with events at home or acquiring social prestige – cannot entirely explain the course of specific textual importation. Examples of this are recurrent in the following chapters, from the importation of fiction and gossip to the nineteenth-century demand for classical literature publication in North America.

One other feature stands out. To examine and compare communities forged by print is also to recognize the signal importance of language in defining and delimiting authority. Translation was important not just in practical terms, but because certain languages carried social cachet as well as cultural power. At the same time, the attention to a diversity of languages across the Atlantic demonstrates how language was a cultural dimension of the colonial project. As Catherine Armstrong, Phyllis Whitman Hunter and other contributors suggest, on both sides of the Atlantic the manipulation of the reportage of events is a consequence of different and evolving understandings of the use of language. James Raven describes an 'empire' of the apparently dead language of Latin stretching across boundaries and oceans and offering a pervasive storehouse of social and intellectual power. Although this classical 'community' was not homogenous but divided according to national colonialisms, the importation and exchange of Latin continued to support genuinely transatlantic connections and communities with the extension of classical influence arguably greater in the North at the very time that its textual appreciation diminished in the South. And as Sandra Vasconcelos shows, translation mediated a relationship between two competing European powers in their contributions to the finished product. In a neighbouring part of the Continent, in the monitoring system and its manuals examined by Eugenia Roldán Vera, translated texts incorporated artificial identities and an internationalized knowledge. From English guides and textbooks, via mediating publications in French, the revolution in reading habits at the close of Spanish commercial and political monopoly linked directly to the mass production and overseas export of print by Britain and France. In the creation and promulgation of a new Brazilian literature, but also in aspirations to universal elementary instruction in northern South America, distinctiveness was in fact rooted in transatlantic imports and the authority of translated originals initially intended for very different communities.

At different rates in different places, empire and then revolution replaced colonial expansion and contestation. Greater independence and the reality of commercial and diplomatic alliances created various, sometimes contradictory, intents and practices within particular cultural and literary communities. From Catherine Armstrong's opening chapter to Robert Scholnick's closing one, we can review literature sent in both directions across the Atlantic as subject to manipulation and in need of different affirmations, in order not only to convey knowledge, but because such manipulations and affirmations were also needed to support distant social networks. Community links required reinforcement, sometimes in the voice of the major colonizing power, and at other times in the language of a small embattled group defined by its European nationality and also, or instead, by its religion or language. By such identifications, political ideas appeared the more focused and supported new aspirations and orientations. Connections made across the Atlantic by books and print ultimately encouraged and enabled an empowerment that ranged from the social and economic to the intellectual, scientific and political. The same connections, politically and culturally, demonstrate the tensions and expectations of reciprocity, obligation and exchange. The following chapters articulate that history.

Notes

1. Of diverse examples, Meredith L. McGill, *American Literature and the Culture of Reprinting 1834–1853* (Philadelphia, 2003); Isabel Hofmeyr, *The Portable Bunyan: A Transnational History of the Pilgrim's Progress* (Princeton, 2004); James Raven, 'An Antidote to the French? English Novels in German Translation and German Novels in English Translation' *Eighteenth-Century Fiction* 14 (2002): 715–34; Michael Winship, 'The Transatlantic Book Trade and Anglo-American Literary Culture in the Nineteenth Century', in Steven Fink and Susan S. Williams (eds), *Reciprocal Influences: Literary Production, Distribution, and Consumption in America* (Columbus, OH, 1999): 98–122.
2. Hofmeyr, *Portable Bunyan*, 2–3.
3. See for example, David Armitage and Michael J. Braddick (eds), *The British Atlantic World, 1500–1800* (Basingstoke, 2002); Carole Shammas and Elizabeth Mancke (eds), *The Creation of the British Atlantic World* (Baltimore, MD, 2005); and C. A. Bayly, *Imperial Meridian: The British Empire and the World, 1780–1830* (London, 1989).
4. Patricia Clavin, 'Defining Transnationalism,' *Contemporary European History* 14 (2005): 438.
5. Clavin, 'Defining Transnationalism,' 438–9.

6. For important, pioneering studies of oceanic networks, see Fernand Braudel, *The Mediterranean and the Mediterranean World in the Age of Philip II*, trans. Siân Reynolds, 2 vols (London, 1973); O. H. K. Spate, *The Pacific Since Magellan*, vol. 1, *The Spanish Lake* (London, 1979), and Ashin Das Gupta and M. N. Pearson (eds), *India and the Indian Ocean, 1500–1800* (Calcutta, 1987).

7. Introductions to the study of 'Atlantic History' are provided by Bernard Bailyn, 'The Idea of Atlantic History', *Itinerario*, 20 (1996): 19–44; Jack P. Greene, 'Beyond Power: Paradigm Subversion and Reformulation and the Re-Creation of the Early Modern Atlantic World', in Greene, *Interpreting Early America: Historiographical Essays* (Charlottesville, VA, 1996): 17–42, and Nicholas Canny, 'Writing Atlantic History, or, Reconfiguring the History of Colonial British America', *Journal of American History*, 86 (1999) 1093–1114; see also collections of journal articles in 'The Nature of Atlantic History', *Itinerario*, 23: 2 (1999); 'Forum: The New British History in Atlantic Perspective', *American Historical Review*, 104: 2 (1999): 426–500; and 'Oceans Connect', *Geographical Review*, 89: 2 (1999).

8. Bernard Bailyn, The *Ideological Origins of the American Revolution*, 2nd edn (Cambridge, MA, 1992); J. G. A. Pocock, The *Machiavellian Moment: Florentine Political Thought and the Atlantic Republican Tradition* (Princeton, NJ, 1975).

9. J. H. Elliott, *Empires of the Atlantic World: Britain and Spain in America 1492–1830* (New Haven and London, 2007); David Abulafia, *The Discovery of Mankind: Atlantic Encounters in the Age of Columbus* (New Haven and London, 2008).

10. Of more modern accounts, Robert and Marianne Cornevin, *La France et les Français outré-mer, de la première croisade à la fine du Second Empire* (Paris, 1990); Jean Meyer et al., *Histoire de la France coloniale, des origins à 1914* (Paris, 1991); Alain Saussol and Joseph Zitomersky (eds), *Colonies, teritoires, sociétés: l'enjeu français* (Paris, 1996); Philippe Haudrère, *Le grand commerce maritime au XVIIIe siècle* (Paris, 1997); and Gilles Havard and Cécile Vidal, *Histoire de l'Amérique française* (Paris, 2003 and new edn, 2008).

11. See, for example, Martha Patricia Irigoyen Troconis, *La Universidad Novohispana* (Mexico City, 2003); Jorge Cañizares-Esguerra, *How to Write the History of the New World: Histories, Epistemologies and Identities in the Eighteenth-Century Atlantic World* (Stanford, 2001); Edward G. Gray and Norman Fiering (eds), *The Language Encounter in the Americas* (New York and Oxford, 2000); and Tzvetan Todorov, trans. R. Howard, *The Conquest of America: The Question of the Other* (New York, 1984; French orig. 1982).

12. Introductions (for North and mostly British America) are given in T. H. Breen, 'Creative Adaptations: Peoples and Cultures', in Jack P. Greene and J. R. Pole (eds), *Colonial British America: Essays in the New History of the Early Modern Era* (Baltimore, 1984): 195–232; Colin G. Calloway, *New Worlds for All: Indians, Europeans, and the Remaking of Early America* (Baltimore, 1997); Alison Games, *Migration and the Origins of the English Atlantic World* (Cambridge, MA, 1999); James Horn, 'British Diaspora: migration from Britain, 1680–1815', in P. J. Marshall (ed.), The *Oxford History of the British Empire*, vol. 2, The *Eighteenth Century* (Oxford, 1998); and Sidney W. Mintz and Richard Price, *The Birth of African-American Culture: An Anthropological Perspective* (Boston, MA, 1992); see also Bernard Bailyn, *Voyagers to the West: A Passage in the Peopling of America on the Eve of the American*

Revolution (New York, 1987), and other contrasting studies are offered by Paul Butel, *The Atlantic,* trans. Iain Hamilton Grant (London, 1999); David Eltis, *The Rise of African Slavery in the Americas* (Cambridge, 2000); Paul Gilroy, *The Black Atlantic: Modernity and Double Consciousness* (Cambridge, MA, 1993); D. W. Meinig, *Atlantic America, 1492–1800* (New Haven, CT, 1986); John Thornton, *Africa and Africans in the Making of the Atlantic World, 1400–1800,* 2nd edn (Cambridge, 1999); and David Hancock, *Citizens of the World: London Merchants and the Integration of the British Atlantic Community, 1735–1785* (Cambridge, MA, 1995); David Eltis, *The Rise of African Slavery in the Americas* (Cambridge, 2000).

13. David Armitage, 'Three Concepts of Atlantic History', in Armitage and Braddick (eds), *British Atlantic World:* 11–27; Armitage's cis-Atlantic histories are led by Franklin W. Knight and Peggy Liss (eds), *Atlantic Port Cities: Economy, Culture, and Society in the Atlantic World, 1650–1850* (Knoxville, TN, 1991) and David Harris Sacks, *The Widening Gate: Bristol and the Atlantic Economy, 1450–1700* (Berkeley, CA, 1991); his circum-Atlantic histories by Alison Games, *Migration and the Origins of the English Atlantic World* (Cambridge, MA, 1999), and Ian K. Steele, *The English Atlantic: An Exploration of Communication and Community, 1675–1740* (New York, 1981).

14. Notably Kenneth R. Andrews, *Trade, Plunder and Settlement: Maritime Enterprise and the Genesis of the British Empire* (Cambridge, 1984); T. H. Breen, ' "Baubles of Britain": The American and Consumer Revolutions of the Eighteenth Century', *Past and Present,* 119 (1988): 73–104, Carole Shammas, *The Pre-Industrial Consumer in England and America* (Oxford, 1990); and Nuala Zahedieh, 'Overseas Expansion and Trade in the Seventeenth Century' in Nicholas Canny (ed.), *The Oxford History of the British Empire vol. 1 The Origins of Empire* (Oxford, 1998): 398–422.

15. Hofmeyr, *Portable Bunyan,* 231.

16. Notably by Nicholas Canny (ed.), *Europeans on the Move: Studies on European Migration, 1500–1800* (Oxford, 1994) J. Elliott, *Empires of the Atlantic World;* Abulafia, *Discovery of Mankind;* Aaron Spencer Fogleman, *Hopeful Journeys: German Immigration, Settlement, and Political Culture in Colonial America, 1717–1775* (Philadelphia, 1996); and Marianne S. Wokeck, *Trade in Strangers: The Beginning of Mass Migration to North America* (University Park, PA, 1999).

17. Gilles Havard and Cécile Vidal, *Histoire de l'Amérique française* new edn (Paris, 2008).

18. Claudia Schnurmann, *Kommunikation und soziale Netzwerke: Beziehungen zwischen Bewohnern englischer und niederländischer Kolonien in der amerikanisch-atlantischen Welt, 1648–1713* (unpublished Habilitationsschrift, Göttingen, 1995); Gregg Roeber, 'German and Dutch Books' in Amory and Hall (eds), *Colonial Book in the Atlantic World,* 298–313; Hendrik Edelman, *The Dutch Language Press in America* (Nieuwkoop, 1986).

19. The FB, now USTC (Universal Short-Title Catalogue), Project at the University of St Andrews, has published a 52,000-entry pre-1601 STC, Andrew Pettegree, Malcolm Walsby and Alexander Wilkinson (eds), *French Vernacular Books: Books Published in the French Language before 1601* 2 vols (Leiden, 2007), and is now mapping Latin publishing in France domains excluded by other projects (see Alexander S. Wilkinson, 'Lost Books Printed in French before 1601', *The Library* 7th ser. 10: 2 (June, 2009): 188–205), as well as

books published in Spain and Portugal and in Spanish abroad before 1601, books published in the Low Countries before 1601, and data on books published in Denmark, Sweden, Poland, Bohemia, Hungary, Croatia and Russia before 1601 (USTC plans to go on-line in 2011); CCFr (*Catalogue Collectif de France*) is accessible via the website of the Bibliothèque Nationale de France; more advanced, but limited to pre-1701 imprints, is the German *VD 16* and *VD 17* (*Verzeichnis der im deutschen Sprachaum erschienenen Drucke des 16./17. Jahrhunderts* – Bibliography of Books Printed in the German-Speaking Countries from 1501 to 1600 and from 1601 to 1700 respectively); VD 18 is in the planning stages. The VDs are largely limited to collections of German and Austrian libraries, and so far exclude single-leaf items.

20. For Spanish printing, the Biblioteca Nacional de España has commenced an online STC of fifteenth- and sixteenth-century imprints (see also USTC, note 19 above); in Italy, *EDIT 16 Censimento nazionale delle edizioni italiane del XVI secolo* (an initiative of the Laboratorio per la bibliografia retrospettiva of the Istituto Centrale per il Catalogo Unico [ICCU]) is also on-going; the Centre for the History of the Media at University College Dublin aims to publish a catalogue of all books printed in Spanish or Portuguese or printed in Spain, Portugal, Mexico or Peru before 1601 – see Wilkinson, 'Lost Books', 189.

21. See Robert E. Cazden, *A Social History of the German Book Trade in America to the Civil War* (Columbia, SC, 1984), esp, 8–31 'The Import Trade in German Books'.

22. Approaches to a transnational history of the book are suggested in *Books without Borders* (2 vols.), ed. by Robert Fraser and Mary Hammond (London, 2008) and particularly in 'Books without Borders: The Transnational Turn in Book History', Sydney Shep's chapter in volume 1, *The Cross-National Dimension in Print Culture* (13–37). See also two articles by I. R. Willison, 'Centre and Creative Periphery in the Histories of the Book in the English-Speaking World and Global English Studies', *Publishing History* 59 (2006): 5–60, and 'Towards an Agenda for Imperial and Post-Imperial Book History in India and Anglophone Sub-Saharan Africa', *Publishing History* 60:2006, 21–29.

23. See above, n. 15.

24. Harold Love, *Scribal Publication in Seventeenth-Century England* (Oxford, 1993); McKitterick, *Print, Manuscript and the Search for Order*, ch. 2; see also Arthur F. Marotti, *Manuscript, Print and the English Renaissance Lyric* (Ithaca, NY, 1995); Henry Woudhuysen, *Sir Philip Sidney and the Circulation of Manuscripts, 1558–1640* (Oxford, 1996); Peter Beal, *In Praise of Scribes: Manuscripts and Their Makers in Seventeenth-Century England* (Oxford, 1998); and Margaret J. M. Ezell, *Social Authorship and the Advent of Print* (Baltimore, 1999).

25. J. H. Elliott, 'Afterword: Atlantic History: a Circumnavigation', in Armitage and Braddick (eds), *British Atlantic World*, 230.

26. Richard B. Sher, *The Enlightenment and the Book: Scottish Authors and Their Publishers in Britain, Ireland, and America* (Chicago, 2007).

27. James Raven, *The Business of Books: Booksellers and the English Book Trade, 1450–1850* (London and New Haven, 2007): 143–53.

2
Reaction to the 1622 Virginia Massacre: An Early History of Transatlantic Print

Catherine Armstrong

In 1607, when they arrived in Virginia, the English encountered a powerful native American empire, a loose confederation of Algonquin-speaking tribes under the leadership of Powhatan.[1] Many settlers and commentators in England believed, wrongly, that they would easily subdue the native people and bring them under European control, just as a few hundred Spanish had gained control of a powerful and wealthy Native Central American empire nearly a century before. However, the English considered that they were going to behave with more civility than the Spanish, by providing the natives with knowledge that they might become civilized human beings, while educating them in Christian ways to save their souls.[2]

Linguistic and cultural confusion increased the tension between European and native, leading to an ambivalent relationship between the two. The natives perceived that the Englishmen's power came from their technological advantage – their ability to kill with sophisticated weapons – but they were vulnerable too.[3] Englishmen were concerned by the military strength of the natives and described living in constant fear of the warlike 'Indians' (as they were described), although in fact, the native people's assistance helped the settlers get through several harsh winters and Powhatan famously gave his daughter Pocahontas to an Englishman in a marriage alliance. The English respected Powhatan, believing him to be a leader in the European mould, and the Virginian Native Americans he governed to be living in groups comparable to English shires.[4] However, they underestimated the power of Powhatan, believing that he could be easily mastered and manipulated. The English took revenge on entire native populations for the misdemeanours of one or two members of that group and this led the natives to become increasingly hostile. The natives felt that the English were not repaying their hospitality, and their expansionist tendencies were greatly feared. It was this expansion that finally provoked the natives to defend their land, but it also left the English vulnerable. There were no regional centres of settlement in which the English could gather for protection. Tobacco-growing had encouraged the settlers to spread out along the James and York Rivers and left them exposed to the Native Americans' wrath. The deaths of Powhatan and Pocahontas, in 1618 and 1617 respectively, left Powhatan's brother Opecancanough in overall control of the confederacy and he, wanting to move quickly against the English, had the backing not only of his own forces but those of the Chickahominy tribe, 30 of whom had been massacred by the English in 1614. Eight years later, it was English settlers who were the victims of a massacre by Native Americans.

The murder by Native Americans on 22 March 1622 of over 300 English settlers on several plantations in the Virginia colony, most notably Martin's Hundred and Charles City, not only profoundly affected the policy of the English towards the original inhabitants of the region, but also sounded the death knell for the Virginia Company itself. Two weeks earlier, a tribal leader known by the English as 'Jack of the Feather' had been summarily executed for the supposed murder of an Englishman, Morgan, and this had been the trigger for various tribal groups, under the general leadership of Opecancanough, to turn on the English, massacring or taking captive men, women and children, and destroying homes and crops. The English allowed native warriors to move openly around their settlements, and some victims even breakfasted with their murderers before the massacre and were killed with their own weapons. The dead and dying were also mutilated, outraging the English survivors and provoking horrific reprisals. The outlying plantations with weaker defences and less manpower were the most severely affected, though Jamestown was spared a similar fate by a Native American servant, a convert to Christianity, who forewarned the residents of the proposed slaughter.[5] Even though the colony was saved from total destruction, the massacre did break down the pattern of subsistence living that Virginians had only just achieved for the first time, and several hundred more settlers probably died from famine later in the winter of 1622/23.

During the late sixteenth and early seventeenth centuries, print was essential in defining America for an English audience. Having watched Spain gain riches and reputation through her colonial activities in Central and South America, the English elite hoped their country would

surpass its example. The English, however, failed to establish a permanent colony, despite several attempts in Elizabeth I's reign, until April
1607, when three small ships carrying 105 Virginia Company employees arrived in Chesapeake Bay and established Jamestown. The Virginia
Company, one of two joint stock companies created by James I comprising many of the leading businessmen and noblemen of London,
had been awarded a charter the previous year and was responsible for
the political leadership, financial support and provision of manpower
for the settlement of Virginia. Its ambition was to create a 'staple'
settlement, one intended to provide a monopoly market sending commodities to England. Settlers were encouraged to gain control of field,
forest and minerals in an area reaching up to 100 miles from the
coast.[6]

The joint control exercised by the Virginia Company in London and
the Council, which ran affairs from within the colony itself, complicated
the governance of the colony. On a practical level though, the early settlers came to rely as much on the support of the local Native Americans
as on their distant paymasters in England. The Native Americans provided food and shelter for the English settlers, without which the
Jamestown colony would have failed just as the Roanoke ventures had
done in the 1580s. As it was, a large number of the English settlers died
in the first few years, both of famine and disease, problems that were
exacerbated by the positioning of Jamestown near stagnant and salty
water.[7]

Despite these early tragedies the Virginia colony did survive, although
how far it had achieved a measure of stability by the time of the massacre is still a matter for debate. The development of tobacco as a staple
crop coincided with the relocation of Jamestown to a more sanitary site
and it brought prosperity if not security to the settlers. As the acquisition of wealth influenced many of the decisions taken for the future of
the colony, a locally based elite began to form, leading to the first meeting of representatives from the colony's four boroughs at the Virginia
Assembly in Jamestown in 1619. Although most of these early leaders had greater interest in growing more tobacco than in establishing
a stable society, it has been argued that enough gains had been made
in the field of education by 1622 that the massacre could be regarded
as a real cultural as well as human tragedy for the colony.[8] However,
the existence of the Virginia colony was still a fragile one; in order
for it to succeed, the Company had to generate interest among English
investors and migrants to participate in the venture. It was also important that young women move to America to bring a calming influence

to the notoriously dissolute colony. All of the migrants in the early years were young men, and so, in 1620, the Company advertised for women to be their companions, to marry and produce another generation of Virginian settlers and to bring stability and gentleness to the rough life on the American frontier. 'Adventurers' (investors) in England contributed large sums of money towards this project and the first shipment of 57 women arrived late in the summer of 1621. These women, intended to be planters' wives, made the Atlantic crossing, bearing character references describing their virtues and their housekeeping skills.[9]

The colony's leaders in Virginia faced daunting challenges in overcoming the environmental problems as well as pulling together the fractious community. In the first decade of settlement, governors such as Thomas Gates and Thomas Dale demonstrated their control by ruling with martial law, although by the time of the massacre, the governor, Francis Wyatt, was ruling alongside the Council and burgesses in the Assembly. The rule of the soldier-governors of Virginia mirrored a pattern that unfolded in the other colonies and in England itself. Soldiers gained experience of leadership overseas, and then in local garrisons such as Berwick-upon-Tweed and the Isle of Wight. In Tudor England soldiers learned domestic policy and felt the first hint of American ambition, while in the seventeenth century, a stint in Ireland taught many of them the qualities needed to supervise new agrarian settlements in potentially hostile environments.[10]

As tobacco-growing expanded, more labourers were needed to do the hard work on the plantations, but this had to be balanced with provision of skilled craftsmen and members of the upper classes prepared to lead the colony through its troubled youth. By the time of the massacre, barely a quarter of the settlers migrating to Virginia survived.[11] Members of the Company in England and America were, however, aware of the importance of providing English readers with positive reports from Jamestown of present successes and future potential, as well as quashing any negative reports being spread by returning sailors or disaffected former settlers. There were varied and diverse networks of communication that linked the colony of Virginia with her supporters and detractors in England, especially in the period immediately after the Virginia Massacre of 1622. These years present particular difficulties to historians of the book; the activities of both printmaker and consumer are shrouded by the lack of the sorts of evidence that illuminate the topic in later periods. Printers and booksellers did not keep accurate records as to the production and sale of books during this early period, and so, often, the only literature available about a particular printed artefact is its entry in the Stationers' Company Register.

It was not until 1638 that a printing press was established in the English American colonies, in Boston.[12] But throughout the first half of the seventeenth century the vast majority of American authors had their work printed and distributed in London. Authors aimed their texts at a specifically English readership. Most settlers who ventured into print chose to publish in England not only because the information was most pertinent to English readers, but also because the prestige of the London trade was considerably higher than that of Boston. They also reaffirmed their English identity by sending texts to England, despite the many difficulties such as problems corresponding with proofreaders.[13] Although the colonial book trades were not as dependent on London as the trades in the English provinces, they still operated within an information and economic network with London at its heart.[14]

A bewildering array of printed literature was available about America during this period, including translations of the exploits of European explorers as well as those written specifically for an English readership. Explorers formed the first wave in the colonial experiment, travelling to America for a few weeks or months, cataloguing the coastline, ·the flora and fauna, and the climate they found. Writers used a confusing mixture of classical and biblical symbolism, in one sentence describing the landscape as a vacant wilderness awaiting the English plough, and in the next a plentiful Garden of Eden that provided food without labour.[15] Often these sorts of narratives provided the interested reader with his or her first exposure to the ways of the Native Americans, including physical descriptions of their bodies and clothes as well as information about their day-to-day lives and cultures. Readers of these early narratives were encouraged to judge the Native Americans as passive and naive towards the white man, but with a capacity for cruelty towards each other. Authors saw them as the key to unlocking the great storehouse of commodities provided by the rich landscape.

These authors were certainly not representative of the majority of migrants to the New World. Very few servants in Virginia put pen to paper; the culture from which these texts emerged was that of the leaders: the ministers, military men, adventurers and investors, most of whom came from the educated classes in England and who formed the political elite in North America. Some wanted to promote investment by wealthy landowners and merchants of England, or to encourage poorer people to advance themselves. Others were worried about Virginia's shortage of labourers, skilled or otherwise, and wanted poor people to migrate as indentured servants if they did not have a skill useful to the settlers.

During the early decades of the seventeenth century the newspaper developed and soon became one of the most popular and enduring forms of print culture. This, too, became a medium through which information about Virginia reached an English readership. These early news sheets and newspapers were probably distributed at the same shops and stalls as smaller pamphlets and books, via the printers and book-shops of the St Paul's Churchyard area of London.[16] While it is widely acknowledged that the newspaper proper came to prominence during the English Civil War, there were scattered examples of regular printed news sheets emerging much earlier than that, dating from around the time of the Virginia Massacre, and these assisted in the spread of the unfortunate news. These news sheets were closely related to other gen-res of print such as the pamphlets that described in lurid detail the latest criminal trials for notorious crimes such as murder, infanticide and witchcraft, or the executions themselves, or such apocalyptic events as monstrous births. However, the true forerunner of the English news sheet was the European example that appeared on the continent around the turn of the century. One of the earliest weekly summaries of polit-ical and military bulletins emerged from Amsterdam in 1607, but only survived for a short time.[17] These continental news sheets printed offi-cial news and offered no personal opinion or 'human interest' stories. English news sheets began around 1622, the year of the massacre, by copying this European format, and rarely carried any other news than descriptions of the European armies' activities in the Thirty Years' War. This makes it all the more surprising that a story, albeit a brief sentence or two, was printed about the distant North American colonies, showing the impact of the news of the massacre. Compared to the usual infor-mation about the New World, this news must have been thought to be very unusual and shocking.

It was not only individuals who used print to describe events in Virginia during these early years of settlement. The Virginia Company, whose most powerful officials, such as Sir Thomas Smith, were drawn from members of the elite, close to the king and court, initially used the medium of printed broadsides to convey information. Later it used small promotional tracts printed in quarto or octavo format, often with less than 40 pages, in the form of a sermon preached by a supporter of the colonial cause, or a positive report from a settler in America. The Virginia Company was always careful in its choice of preacher. In 1609, for example, it used Daniel Price, who had gained the approval of London's merchants by praising them in an earlier sermon.[18] Another of the sermons, by Robert Gray, was published in 1609 and intended by the Company to encourage investment and to counter negative reports from Virginia of shortages of food and lack of order. Gray symbolically compared the Virginian migrants to Joshua and the Israelites, arguing that the two purposes of this American migration were to assist the multitudes of England by putting them to work abroad, and to 'reduce this people [Native Americans] from brutishness to civilitie'.[19] The Company also used the experienced preacher Patrick Copland, a passionate and well-travelled supporter of English expansion across the globe, who was at that time involved in raising money for a school in Virginia.

Print was not the only medium chosen by those wishing to convey information from Virginia to England. Many migrants from all social classes, apart from the very lowest, used manuscript letters to carry news, to reassure family and friends that they were safe and prospering, or to persuade the authorities not to abandon them.[20] The leaders of the colony communicated privately by letter with the Company or the Government in England. These texts often included sensitive information they did not want revealed to the general public. After the Virginia Massacre, as during other sensitive times, many in the Company feared that migrants and investors would withdraw support, so it was essential that the release of news was perfectly stage-managed. Other manuscript materials, sometimes not intended for printing, such as an informative letter to an acquaintance, also became the staple material of the great collections of printed travel narratives assembled by Samuel Purchas.

Audiences reacted variously to what they had read, perhaps influenced by the spread of news with negative connotations, such as the threat of forced migrations or the corruption of the colony's leaders. Some readers became authors themselves, incorporating information they had read into their own work. Other authors reflected public interest in the New World by bringing American references into their ballads, plays or poems, sometimes laudatory, though more often satirical. Published works, operating alongside oral networks of information transmission, reached a wide audience from diverse social backgrounds, even negative references helping to raise public awareness of English activity in North America.

Historians have few contemporary accounts with which to reconstruct and verify the chain of events during the massacre and to follow the network of communication from Jamestown to London. However, the few extant documents speak with a variety of 'voices' because of authorial or editorial intention. The massacre of 22 March was mentioned in an early news sheet, dated 11 July and presumably distributed in the days imme-diately following, entitled *A True Relation of the Proceedings*. The short item on the massacre appeared alongside a much larger concentration of European news.[21] It is clear from the State Papers Domestic that news of the massacre first reached Virginia Company officials in London on 13 July when John Chamberlain wrote to Sir Dudley Carleton inform-ing him, again among the reports of other domestic and European matters, that a ship had just arrived bringing news that about 350 of the English settlers in Virginia had been massacred 'through their own supine negligence.'[22] This was confirmed the following day by a let-ter from Sir Thomas Wilson written from his home in the Strand to the Earl of Salisbury, who also mentioned the blessing of the Native American informant's warning to Jamestown without which, Wilson believed, every settler in the entire colony would have been lost.[23]

Ironically, the news of the massacre had taken so long to reach England that, as late as May 1622, Patrick Copland was preaching of the bounty and wonder of Virginia. Copland's sermon was structured around Psalm 107, in which the dangers of crossing the oceans are dis-cussed, clearly relevant to the gathered audience of Virginia Company members. Copland's upbeat address included assertions that the dan-gers of pirates or enemies at sea had abated, and that the success of the colony after such hesitant beginnings should encourage the audience to praise God.[24] He motivated investors to contribute funds towards the establishing of a school for the natives when the massacre had already claimed the life of George Thorpe, the only planter truly com-mitted to the Indian college. Copland raised £70 towards the project and was duly appointed rector of the school, but he was never called upon to use his missionary skills: the college assisted a few English labourers and then corrupt Company officials squandered the rest of the money.[25]

It is possible to speculate that news of the massacre filtered through to London a few days prior to the official records. The Stationers' Company Register records an entry for 10 July of three ballads, one mysteriously entitled 'Morninge Virginia'. This title is very ambiguous, it could refer to the colony or an individual woman, and no copies of the ballad have survived to reveal its topic. Elizabeth I was remembered with great fond-ness during the early seventeenth century, so it is plausible that the title recalls the Virgin Queen. If it does however refer to the tragedy in North America, as is assumed by H.E. Rollins in his *Analytical Index to Ballad Entries*, then this means that certain individuals in London had prior knowledge of the massacre, before the planters' letters to the Virginia

Company had reached their destination. The only explanation of this is that word of mouth travelled from the port faster than the manuscripts.

Such speculations aside, Francis Wyatt, governor of Virginia 1621–26, continuously kept his political masters in London informed of the progress of rebuilding the colony after the massacre. Wyatt, inexperienced in leadership, was the eldest son of George Wyatt, a gentleman of Kent, who sent his son a letter of advice on how to govern Virginia in the aftermath of the massacre.[26] He was also related to the Sandys family, who held key positions in the Virginia Company in both Jamestown and London. The constant criticism of Virginia upset Wyatt and he tried his best to quash the rumours of hunger and violence that seem to have spread with renewed vigour in the period following the massacre, just as they had done in the first few difficult years of the colony's existence.[27]

Wyatt's job was a difficult one. Not only did he have to defend a weakened Virginia from further Native American attack, but he also had to handle the requirements of an increasingly factionalized Company in London. The tolerant approach of Wyatt and his friend George Sandys towards the natives was increasingly, and some say unfairly, blamed for causing the massacre.[28] Wyatt senior recommended his son wage a war of attrition, destroying natives' crops and homes, but George Wyatt did not make the fatal mistake of underestimating the foe. He thought Native Americans capable of great courage and advocated a policy of moderation towards innocent natives.[29] George Wyatt also acknowledged that it was the murder of 'Jack of the Feather' that finally triggered the massacre, something that pamphleteers employed by the Virginia Company did not do for propaganda reasons. The Virginia Company did not release for printing Wyatt senior's pragmatic and at times machiavellian letter to his son, perhaps as much because of his honest assertions as to the true culpability for the massacre as his controversial tactical advice.

Francis Wyatt's letter, written immediately after the massacre and carried by the *Seahorse* from Virginia, is found in the records of the Virginia Company and was the source of information mined by Edward Waterhouse who wrote the first account of the massacre to go into print, entitled *A Declaration of the State of the Colony and Affaires in Virginia with a Relation of the Barbarous Massacre in the Time of Peace and League, treacherously executed by the Native Infidels upon the English, the 22 of March last*. The Stationers' Company records show that Robert Mylbourne registered the Waterhouse tract on 21 August, only five weeks after news of the massacre first reached England. Waterhouse's pamphlet was intended to defend the behaviour of Company members who felt the spotlight of blame unfairly fell upon them. Waterhouse's history is not clear, though he is named as a 'colonist' in the *Oxford Dictionary of National Biography* (*ODNB*).[30] But he did not refer to his own experiences in Virginia to validate the claims made in his tract, which is unusual as many narratives about America during this period used eyewitness testimony to support their arguments.

Waterhouse took the opportunity of rehearsing the old arguments about the wealth of flora and fauna, the excellent climate and landscape to be found in Virginia, as well as using a letter written by Wyatt before the massacre to show how unexpected the attack had been. Much of the early part of his work is a direct copy of a tract published by the Virginia Company in the summer of 1620 (and printed again in 1626) to encourage investment in and migration to the colony. Waterhouse spared no venom when describing the behaviour of the natives who were, he said, like 'bryers' overrunning a beautiful country, and worse than 'lyons and dragons' because they showed no mercy to those (the English) who fed and clothed them.[31] By mid-August when Waterhouse's tract was published, he was able to write in his epistle dedicatory to the Company that 'the fame of our late unhappy accident in Virginia ... is talked of of all men', and that letters bearing the sad news had already been read in the public court.[32]

In November 1622 the Company chose John Donne, poet and dean of St Paul's and long-time supporter of the Virginia enterprise, to give a sermon to their members. He did not refer to the events of the massacre in any great depth, but rather looked to the future. He exhorted the gathered crowd not to give up on Virginia, saying that 'a land never inhabited or utterly derelicted and immemorially abandoned by the former inhabitants becomes theirs that will possess it', but he warned that 'neither does a man become lord of a maine continent because he hath two or three cottages in the skirts thereof'.[33] His sermon was printed only days after he preached it, at the request of the Virginia Company.

Christopher Brooke, a poet close to the Stuart court, in his work *A Poem on the Late Massacre in Virginia*, also published in 1622, acknowledged that the story of the massacre had already been published (referring to Waterhouse's work), and chose the genre of tragic poetry as the most fitting means to eulogize those who died. Brooke extolled the virtues of the members of the governing Council killed in the massacre, such as Captains Powell and Thorpe, and also praised those who survived, urging them to exterminate the natives: 'the very dregs, garbage and spawne of earth'. Prior to the massacre, the English residents who commentated on America had been noticeably less hostile towards the natives than the American settlers. Brooke's poem seems to represent a change in direction as his hostile view displaced Copland's desire to educate and reform the Native American.[34]

A flurry of transatlantic manuscript communication contested the influence of the printed word. Especially in times of crisis, representations of Virginia in manuscript format seem to have been more critical than those in print, thus revealing a subversive alternative to the story that Virginia's Government hoped to tell. Most notably, a letter from Captain Butler, the former governor of the Summer Isles, heavily criticized the way the colony was governed. He claimed that it had been situated wrongly, 'upon salt marishes full of infectious boggs', and that the houses built by the settlers were 'the worst I ever sawe the meanest cottages in England beinge in every way equall if not superior with most of the beste'. His most strident criticism was reserved for the governors of Virginia: 'I found in the Government there not onely ignorant and enforced strayings in divers particulars, but willfull and intended ones.'[35] The following year, a group of planters composed a manuscript answer to Captain Butler defending the governing of the colony, arguing that the disarray in Virginia, and especially its outlying areas, was entirely due to the massacre. John Smith insinuated that Butler had abandoned his post in the Summer Isles, and that his report 'did more hurt then the massacre'.[36] Butler probably intended his report to be widely distributed, perhaps in printed format, but the Virginia Company managed to protect its reputation by suppressing it. It is clear that the decision by the author, patron or publisher to use scribal or printed media is significant and complex.

During the first half of the seventeenth century, print culture in England underwent a radical development. Printed material became available to more people, of the lower social orders as well as the elite, because of more comprehensive distribution and a greater public demand for cheap, popular print.[37] News about Virginia appeared in both small books and pamphlets, affordable to most readers, and also large volumes whose price restricted their sale to all but the most dedicated collector.[38] However, an increase in the use of print did not cause the immediate decline of what Harold Love has called 'scribal publication'. Love demonstrates that texts of great political and intellectual weight were often disseminated in manuscript form.[39] Some of the manuscript material that this chapter is concerned with, such as the Wyatt letters, was not 'published' at all, as they remained in the hands of an individual or family, and no further copies were made for distribution to other readers.[40] The exceptions are the multitude of letters and reports, such as Butler's, sent to and produced for the English leadership of the Virginia Company. These reports were distributed among members of the Company or the Government and occasionally other interested parties. It seems obvious that, with the Company choosing to print reports from Virginia on a regular basis, not to do so reflected a deliberate attempt to manipulate the distribution of the news in England.

By the time John Smith's epic *The Generall Historie of Virginia, New England and the Summer Isles* was published in 1624, the massacre had become old news, but Smith still thought the event significant enough to offer a detailed synopsis of the tragedy, much of it almost identical to the account written by Waterhouse two years earlier. Smith also claimed to make use of the letters of 'Master George Sands and many others'. Smith's interpretations of events differed slightly from those of Waterhouse. He made a pointed remark about the misguided authors who thought that the massacre might be good for the plantation, because the settlers now had an excuse to exterminate the natives, a view that Waterhouse expounded in his pamphlet. Smith argued that 'it had beene much better it had never happened for they have given us an hundred times as just occasions long agoe to subject them', and Smith used his own few difficult years living in the colony, between 1607 and 1609, as an example.[41] Interestingly, following the massacre, both Smith and Waterhouse offered the Spanish example of bringing the natives to total subjection with only a small force as one to be emulated by the English; the Spanish way of doing things was no longer the 'Black Legend' of Elizabeth I's reign, reflecting a change in European politics and in relations between Englishman and Native American.[42]

A tract from Captain John Jeffries registered with the Stationers' Company in July 1624 purporting to contain the latest news from Virginia is now lost. A new manuscript report did arrive in England in February 1624, but this appeared too late for Smith to use in his narrative, which was registered with the Stationers' Company in the July of that year. Based on his observations in Virginia and discussions with local planters, John Harvey's report for the Privy Council on the state of the colony after the massacre argued that the threat from the natives was growing ever more dangerous, thus perhaps explaining why the report was not published, or taken up by Smith or later by Samuel Purchas.[43] This report sealed the fate of the Virginia Company, which had been bankrupted following the king's removal of their right to raise money by holding a lottery in 1621. The leaders of the Company had managed to annoy James I, who called it 'a seminary for a seditious Parliament', and then proceeded to distribute as many other patents for American settlement as he could to weaken the Virginia Company's position. The charter was dissolved in the early summer of 1624 by the Court of the King's Bench, leading to the creation of England's first royal colony.

The taking of Virginia under the Crown's wing does not reflect an absolutist desire of James I, who really did not have any plans for the future of the colony. It was a move forced on him by the Company's inability to manage its own affairs. Francis Wyatt said that the Company tended to ignore the advice of the Council of Virginia (the governing body within the colony itself) and heeded the contrary opinions of some of the more aristocratic gentlemen planters, a divisive action which caused the formation of hostile factions.[44] On James's death, Charles I took official control of the colony, ruling by a royal governor and royal council, although, significantly for future debates over sovereignty, he did not did not dismember the Virginia Assembly, allowing it to remain in place and to assist with the administration of the colony.

Samuel Purchas used the layout and content of the published versions of Waterhouse and Smith in his comprehensive edited collection of letters and other documents relating to the history of Virginia, but supplemented these with his own editorial entitled 'Virginia's Verger', a passionate plea to his readers not to abandon the enterprise. As well as emphasizing the treacherous nature of the natives who murdered those who had welcomed them to the English tables, Purchas, like Smith, also examined the immediate aftermath of the massacre in which many plantations were closed so that all might live closer together for safety. Like Waterhouse and Smith, Purchas commented on the generous and welcome donation by King James of 'divers armes' from the Tower of London to the colonists. The corresponding order of the Privy Council tells a different story, however. On 29 July 'certain old cast arms in the Tower, altogether unfit for modern use' were offered.[45]

The massacre, and the haphazard way the English authorities reacted to it, caused some writers to turn their adventuring intentions away from Virginia and towards New England. News of the successful landing at Plymouth Rock by the famous separatist pilgrims had filtered back to London in the summer of 1622, and the reportedly plentiful supply of fish and timber and the friendly natives intrigued readers. Christopher Levett's voyage of exploration began in 1623 and the printed report of that voyage was very influential in this change of colonial direction. John Hagthorpe's *England's Exchequer*, published in 1625, recommended for the greater good of the English nation, investment in navigation and planting overseas by mirroring the Spanish example. He thought

Virginia had 'corrupted ayre' and New England and Newfoundland would make more promising settlements as a massacre was unlikely because the 'savages were few and far off'.[46] Hagthorpe's mistrust of Virginia is revealed in his entry in the *Oxford Dictionary of National Biography*, which states that he was so fearful of becoming destitute and thus being compelled to migrate to Virginia that he begged James I for a place for his son at Charterhouse School.[47] By 1622 the great champion of Virginia's cause, John Smith, was also dissatisfied with the Virginia enterprise, and he too began to focus on New England in his promotional writing.

Reports of the massacre caused those who did keep faith with the Virginia colony to change drastically their policy with regard to the Native Americans. No more did English commentators suggest that in time white man and converted Native American might live side by side in North America. From 1622 onwards, the English pursued a relentless campaign of enmity against the neighbouring tribes, whether they had been complicit in the massacre or not. A letter from Robert Bennett to relatives in England showed how commonplace aggression towards the natives had become by June 1623: 'We purpose God willing after we have weeded our tobacco and corne...to goe upon the Waresquokes and Nansemones to cute down the corne and put them to the sorde.'[48] Englishman and native were at war for ten years before an uneasy truce was declared, but fighting broke out again in 1644–46. This time, however, the settlers were too strong and they defeated the natives and captured and killed Opecancanough, the warmonger who had ordered and led the 1622 massacre. The Powhatan confederacy was broken up and their lands taken, a pattern that was followed across the American continent in the subsequent centuries.[49]

Did, then, the voices of the American settlers become lost as the desperate Virginia Company tried to maintain its authority over them? On the one hand, the transatlantic networks of communication seemed to have worked well in transmitting news of the massacre, albeit with a delay of three-and-a-half months. The printed reports of Waterhouse, Smith and Purchas were based on the accounts that arrived in London on that fateful July day. However, each author for his own reasons chose to employ the medium of print to distort the story, to put his own slant on the tale, to make it his own. In Waterhouse's case, he wanted to protect his paymasters in the Virginia Company, while both Smith and Purchas believed that England's future lay in her exploitation of overseas colonies. Brooke openly admitted his motivation to write a tragic poem eulogizing the dead and exhorting his readers to revenge upon the perfidious natives. These authors wanted to encourage migration and investment, to protect the colony of Virginia, but theirs was a particularly English version of the story, despite the fact that Smith had lived in Virginia. However, he had not been in Virginia for over ten years and was unable to do more than relate the massacre to his own encounters with natives during the first three years of settlement. While Purchas did print a few letters from the planters in full, such as one from Samuel Argall describing the aftermath of the massacre, most were heavily edited and paraphrased by him.[50]

In some ways the spread of news about the massacre benefited the Virginia Company, as it kept the colony in the forefront of the public imagination at a time when news from New England, the Caribbean and, of course, Europe took centre stage. Following the massacre, all levels of London society were once again discussing Virginia.[51] Its topicality is shown by the play licensed by the Master of the Revels in August 1623 to be played at the Curtain Theatre, entitled *A Tragedy of the Plantation in Virginia*.[52] The City of London once again acceded to the Company's demand for pauper orphans to be sent to the colony, transporting 100 children in the autumn of 1622 for the first time in two-and-a-half years. Prior to that the City had not backed out of providing labour because the vagrancy problem had disappeared, or because it had a prick of humanitarian conscience, but, rather, simply that there was a lack of interest in Virginia until the massacre brought it back to the public's attention.[53] Why then, did the Virginia Company and later the Privy Council not encourage or permit the stories direct from the mouths of the Virginia planters to be transmitted in print, especially as they were circulating widely in manuscript and their contents had been divulged in the public court? The letter that brought the news of the massacre to England reflected the fears of the men on the ground in Virginia in no uncertain terms. They wrote that the Native Americans tried to 'cutt us of all and to have swept us away at once through owte the whole lande'.[54]

The description of the horrors of the massacre does not seem to justify the Company's suppression of these letters. Rather, the planters' search for someone to blame for the incident probably caused the Company's reticence. The letter went on 'our first and princypall care should have beene for our safetie', and requested that 'the generall assemblie here may have the full power and awthoritie to remove to such a place'. The planters hinted that the greedy company in London, granting patents without thought for the security of the plantation, had caused their difficulties.[55] The authors of the letter also raised the spectre of famine, as the massacre had interrupted their planting season. Many felt that it was too dangerous to be outdoors tending one's fields, so they begged their masters in London to send them a 'sufficient portion of corne'. In fact, the only plea that the Company heeded was for more arms, although, as previously mentioned, the quality of the arms they sent to Virginia left a lot to be desired. The attitude of the Company towards its servants is revealed in its reply to that letter on 1 August, promising to send more men to fortify the settlement, but patronizingly suggesting that the massacre was a warning from God 'for the punishment of yours and our transgressions'. They told the planters we 'earnestly require the speedie redresse of those two enormous excesses of apparel and drinkeing, the crie whereof cannot but have gon up to heaven'.[56]

Nonetheless, the work of Waterhouse, Brooke, Smith and Purchas can also be understood very differently. Rather than trying to smother the honest voices of the planters of Virginia with their own sweetened propaganda, these authors probably saw their role as *historians* of the massacre. In choosing to gather together information from diverse and disparate sources and distil them into one continuous, chronological narrative, these men were recording, for posterity, the lives and deaths of Virginians whose voices, if not in print, would fade as the years went by. The manuscript letters written in a time of crisis by frightened and lonely men provided the initial burst of news and pleas to those in authority to send assistance, but it was by using print that other authors turned the massacre into history.[57] Within the next few years, print increasingly became a medium for the transmission of news of more immediate and temporary interest, with the development of corantos, and, later, newspapers, describing domestic and continental events and the increase in distribution of cheap print products, telling tabloid-like stories of crime and passion. The printed portrayals of the Virginia massacre reveal a more conventional use of print, an attempt to describe a rather classical ideal, recording the tragic lives of a few good men. The way this single event was reported and understood created a new link in the transatlantic network of communications between colony and mother country.

Notes

1. James Axtell, *Natives and Newcomers: The Cultural Origins of North America* (Oxford, 2001): 233.
2. Thomas Scanlon, *Colonial Writing and the New World: Allegories of Desire* (Cambridge, 1999): 113–14.
3. James Axtell, *The Invasion Within: The Contest of Cultures in Colonial North America* (Oxford, 1985): 11.

4. Karen Kupperman, *Settling with the Indians* (New York, 1980): 49.

5. The most significant interpretation of the impact of the massacre on English policy towards the natives is Alden Vaughan, 'Expulsion of the Savages: English Policy and the Virginia Massacre of 1622', *William and Mary Quarterly*, 35 (1978): 57–84.

6. James O'Mara, 'Town Founding in Seventeenth-Century North America', *Journal of Historical Geography* 8 (1982): 1–11, 3.

7. Carville Earle, 'Disease and Mortality in Early Virginia', in Thad Tate and David Ammerman (eds), *The Chesapeake in the Seventeenth Century* (Chapel Hill, NC, 1979): 96–125, 97.

8. L. B. Wright, *The First Gentlemen of Virginia* (San Marino, CA, 1940): 100. See also T. H. Breen, *Tobacco Culture: The Mentality of the Great Tidewater Planters on the Eve of the Revolution* (Princeton, NJ, 1985) and T. H. Breen, *'Myne Own Ground': Race and Freedom on Virginia's Eastern Shore 1640–76*, 25th anniversary edn (Oxford, 2005).

9. For a comprehensive study of the origins and experiences of the 57 women who went to Virginia in 1621, see David Ransome, 'Wives for Virginia 1621', *William and Mary Quarterly*, 48 (1991): 3–18.

10. S. Saunders Webb, *The Governors-General* (Chapel Hill, NC, 1979): 7, 15, 436.

11. Richard Middleton, *Colonial America: A History* (Oxford, 1992): 58.

12. A summary of the beginnings of book production in America can be found in Hugh Amory, 'Reinventing the Colonial Book', in Hugh Amory and David Hall (eds), *A History of the Book in America*, vol. 1 (Cambridge, 2000): 26–54.

13. Samuel Eliot Morison, *The Intellectual Life of Colonial New England* (New York, 1956): 118.

14. Amory, 'Reinventing the Colonial Book', 34. His main focus is on the movement of print and materials from England to America, whereas my interest is in the flow of knowledge eastwards towards Europe.

15. James Horn, *Adapting to a New World* (Chapel Hill, NC, 1994): 127.

16. James Raven, *The Business of Books: Booksellers and the English Book Trade 1450–1850* (London and New Haven, 2007): chapters 2 and 3.

17. Joseph Frank, *The Beginnings of the English Newspaper* (Cambridge, MA, 1961): 2; Joad Raymond, *The Invention of the Newspaper: English News Books 1641–49* (Oxford, 1996).

18. L. B. Wright, *Religion and Empire: The Alliance Between Piety and Commerce in English Expansion 1558–1625* (New York, 1943): 94.

19. Robert Gray, *A Good Speed to Virginia* (London, 1609): 18.

20. Karen Kupperman, *Indians and English* (New York, 2000): 3.

21. Frank, *The Beginnings of the English Newspaper*, 18.

22. PRO, *Domestic Correspondence, Jac I., CXXXII:.* 38, Cal., 424. This contradicts Alden Vaughan's statement that the *Seaflower* arrived in London in mid-June, for which I could find no evidence. See Vaughan, 'Expulsion of the Savages', 76.

23. PRO, *Domestic Correspondence, Jac I., Vol. CXXXII*, no. 41, Cal., 425.

24. Patrick Copland, *Virginias God be Thanked* (London, 1622): 9, 11.

25. Patrick Copland, *A Declaration of How the Monies ...* (London, 1622); Francis Jennings, *The Invasion of America* (Chapel Hill, NC, 1975): 55. Jennings is typically harsh in his judgement of the Company as a whole, claiming that their missionary attempts were merely a moneymaking sham. However, he does

imply that Copland behaved in good faith, and that many of the ministers working for the Company truly believed in the potential of the Virginians to do good works.

26. J. F. Fausz and J. Kukla, 'A Letter of Advice to the Governor of Virginia 1624', *William and Mary Quarterly*, 34 (1977): 104–29, 114.

27. Francis Wyatt, 'Letter of Sir Francis Wyatt, Governor of Virginia 1621–1626', *William and Mary Quarterly*, 2nd series, 6 (1926): x–xi.

28. James Ellison, *George Sandys: Travel, Colonialism and Tolerance in the Seventeenth Century* (Cambridge, 2002): 127.

29. Fausz and Kukla, 'A Letter of Advice to the Governor of Virginia', 108.

30. Andrew Lyall, 'Waterhouse, Edward', *ODNB*.

31. Edward Waterhouse, *A Declaration of the State of the Colony and Affaires in Virginia* (London, 1622): 11, 15.

32. Ibid., sig. A3.

33. J. Donne, *A Sermon upon the VIII verse of the I chapter of the Acts of the Apostles preached ... to the Virginia Company* (1622): 26. It was in this sermon that Donne famously declared 'now I am an adventurer, if not to Virginia then for Virginia, for everyman that prints, adventures', sig. A3.

34. C. Brooke, *A Poem on the Late Massacre in Virginia* (London, 1622), sig. C. See Vaughan, 'Expulsion of the Savages', 60.

35. Anon, 'The Virginia Planters' Answer to Captain Butler, 1623', in L. G. Tyler (ed.) *Narratives of Early Virginia 1606–1625* (New York, 1907): electronic version at http://etext.lib.virginia.edu/etcbin/jamestown-browse?id=J1042.

36. John Smith, *The Generall Historie of Virginia, New England and the Summer Islands* (London, 1624): 313.

37. For a general discussion of the changes in the distribution and consumption of printed material at the lower ends of the social scale, see Tessa Watt, *Cheap Print and Popular Piety 1550–1640* (Cambridge, 1991); Bernard Capp, *Astrology and the Popular Press* (London, 1979); R. C. Simmons, 'ABCs, Almanacs, Ballads, Chap Books, Popular Piety, Textbooks', in John Barnard, D. F. McKenzie and Maureen Bell (eds), *Cambridge History of the Book in Britain*, vol. IV (Cambridge, 2002): 504–13.

38. For more on this, see Catherine Armstrong, 'The Bookseller and the Peddler: The Spread of Knowledge of the New World in Early Modern England', in John Hinks and Catherine Armstrong (eds), *Printing Places: Locations of Book Production and Distribution Since 1500* (London and New Castle, DE, 2005): 15–30.

39. Harold Love, *Scribal Publication in Seventeenth Century England* (Oxford, 1993): vi.

40. Love states that a manuscript can be called 'published' if it has been disseminated and distributed. I am following his definition. Love, *Scribal Publication*, 36.

41. Smith, *The Generall Historie*, 284, 286.

42. For a comparative study of the political impact of colonisation in Spain and England, see Ralph Bauer, *The Cultural Geography of Colonial American Literatures* (Cambridge, 2003).

43. John Harvey, 'A Brief Declaration of the State of Virginia ...', *Massachusetts Historical Society Collections*, series 4, 9 (1871): 60–73.

44. Sir Francis Wyatt, 'Governor of Virginia to the Privy Council, 1626', *Virginia Historical Magazine*, II (1894–5): 51.
45. Samuel Purchas, *Purchas, His Pilgrims*, XIX (Glasgow, 1957): 170; *Colonial Correspondence, 1622 July 29, Calendar*, p. 32.
46. John Hagthorpe, *Englands Exchequer* (London, 1625): 29, 33.
47. Gordon Goodwin, 'Hagthorpe, John', rev. Joanna Moody, *ODNB*.
48. J. B. Boddie, 'Edward Bennett of London and Virginia', *William and Mary Quarterly*, 13 (Apr, 1933): 117–30, 118.
49. Middleton, *Colonial America*, 62.
50. Purchas, *Purchas, His Pilgrims*, 210.
51. Warren Billings, *Jamestown and the Founding of a Nation* (Gettysburg, PA, 1990): 50.
52. Wright, *Religion and Empire*, 102.
53. Robert Johnson, 'The Transportation of Vagrant Children from London to Virginia 1618–1622', in H. S. Reinmuth, Jr. (ed.), *Early Stuart Studies* (Minneapolis, MN, 1970): 145–6.
54. 'Council in Virginia to the Virginia Company in London, April (after 20) 1622', in S. M. Kingsbury (ed.), *The Records of the Virginia Company*, vol. III (Washington, 1908): 612.
55. Ibid., 613.
56. 'Treasurer and Council for Virginia, Letter to Governor and Council in Virginia: August 1, 1622', *Records of the Virginia Company*, vol. III: 666.
57. For more on the understanding of the past in early modern England, see Daniel Woolf, *The Idea of History in Early Stuart England* (Toronto, 1990) and *Reading History in Early Modern England* (Cambridge, 2000).

3
Fiction and Civility Across the Seventeenth-Century English Atlantic: Teaching the *History of Faustus*

Jennifer Mylander

In 1683, Massachusetts minister Thomas Shepard placed a special order with Boston bookseller John Usher for books from London. The surviving inventory of Shepard's purchase allows us a rare glimpse into the reading lives of the minister and his Charlestown, Massachusetts parish.[1] This simple list formed an official record for Shepard, Usher and the London bookseller Richard Chiswell of an agreed exchange. The exchange was similar to countless other, everyday book purchases. And yet, as an accidental survival, this inventory is one of the few material records of an early modern network of communication and trade that connected the 3,000 miles between English merchants and North American readers. The inventory offers a provocative trace of what Bernard Bailyn has called the 'pan-oceanic commercial webs' that spanned the Atlantic world.[2] Shepard, Usher and Chiswell, together with unrecorded printers, packers, shippers and sailors, participated in a transatlantic English book culture.

Shepard's order was at once conventional and, at first sight, unexpected. The order included learned works of theology and geography, but also requests for multiple copies of inexpensive books with widespread circulation and popular appeal. Shepard asked for seven copies of 'Academy [of] Compliments', ten copies of 'Burtons Wonderful Prodigies' and 30 copies of the 'History of Dr. Faustus'. Given the clerical practice of distributing books in early New England, we can assume that Shepard dispersed these books in his own parish.[3] While works of romance, magic and fiction (as we understand them today) seem a poor fit for an orthodox New England minister and his community,

Shepard's request for Christopher Marlowe's source text *The History of the Damnable Life and Deserved Death of Dr John Faustus* (hereafter, *Faustus*) suggests that he understood the book as an educational tool useful for a wide range of readers. After all, the only book that Shepard ordered in more copies than the Faust tale was the *Bay Psalm Book*.[4] Popular culture was no 'separate sphere' when readers like Thomas Shepard read such a wide variety of printed books, and his order reinforces Tessa Watt's conclusion that for most readers 'there was no clear line between "religious" belief and a fascination with the magical and miraculous' in seventeenth-century English culture.[5]

As a steady seller in England, *Faustus* was one of a core collection of titles familiar to readers throughout the Atlantic world. Significantly, Shepard and his parish were not alone in colonial English America in reading it. Surviving records indicate that between 1682 and 1686 Usher imported at least 66 copies of *Faustus*, more than ten times the number of other fiction titles during the same years. Usher was only one of several full-time book dealers in 1680s Boston, and thus his dealings represent only a *minimum* estimate of the book's transatlantic circulation in the late seventeenth century.[6] But why *was* it so popular? If, as David Hall argues, most godly tales were successful because they told of the overthrow of the devil, how do we account for the demand for *Faustus* in America?[7] Shepard's book order may provide some clues. It reflects an interest both in tales of fantasy and the miraculous (or 'wonders literature') and in courtesy books. These genres are found *within* the English Faust book as well as in other titles in the list. Early modern readers of popular wonders literature like *Faustus*, it has been argued,[8] accepted that they needed to glean 'truths' from narratives littered with embellishments, rumour or sinful episodes.

Faustus embodied English educational models. Faustus is catechized, given a grand tour of Europe, and ultimately educated about the afterlife. While the protracted tale of the part-turns by Faustus towards God (and his returns to sin) resembles prominent conversion narratives, it is a story of the failed education and damnation of a stiff-necked pupil. Although his pact with the Mephistopheles makes Faustus guilty of the damnable art of witchcraft, the text encourages readers to empathize with his spiritual struggles in scenes where he becomes a representative of Protestantism when confronted with stereotypical Roman Catholic and Islamic characters. Furthermore, Faustus uses his infernal powers to discipline not just alien religious figures, but also uncivilized clowns and poorly educated elites in a series of jests whose humour relies on an identification by readers with Faustus's condescension towards those he shames. The popularity of *Faustus* throughout England and New England suggests the increasing – and transatlantic – importance of Protestantism and 'civility' as integral components of Englishness.[9]

Given the popularity of this tale of contracting with the devil in Boston in the 1680s, how might *Faustus* have influenced the 1692 witch trials in Salem, Massachusetts? In terms of percentage of total output, there was no significant increase in books about witchcraft issued from London presses in the 1680s (although the decade saw a small increase in the appearance of 'witch' on title pages owing to the use of 1 Samuel 15:23 'For rebellion is as the sin of witchcraft' during the Exclusion Crisis and Monmouth's Rebellion).[10] Although the Salem witch trials are justly notorious – 200 citizens were accused of witchcraft, of whom 19 were executed – placing *Faustus* as a necessary catalyst in the hunt for New England witches may obscure rather than illuminate this complex social crisis.

The events in Salem need to be contextualized in larger patterns of English witch-hunts. Before 1692 at least 100 people had been accused of witchcraft in New England, with 15 executions. The existence of these witch trials prior to the popularity of *Faustus* weakens any argument that the book contributed to the crisis. More significantly, the Faust tale does not resemble trial accounts of early modern witchcraft as closely as we might expect. While Faustus's blood contract (or bond) with the devil is understood as a key component in a legal conviction of the crime in the period, it does not seem to be the central defining characteristic for the laity. As David Hall notes, 'for most people, witchcraft was doing someone harm by occult means.'[11] Faustus, of course, does use magic against others in *Faustus*, but his pranks (including selling imaginary horses and making a love charm) hardly constitute the kinds of black magic that dominated English accusations of witchcraft. The most common complaints of self-identified victims of witchcraft were illness or the death of children, cattle or crops. Faustus commits none of these crimes in *Faustus* – and they were considered crimes rather than heresies in New England. Those executed for witchcraft were hanged not burned.[12] In reading the Faust tale, readers found support for belief in the possibility of compacting with the devil. Rather than resembling court records from witch trials, *Faustus* resembles popular print genres, notably catechisms, courtesy books, jest books and gallows literature. A comparison of *Faustus* with other available popular print suggests how Shepard might have used (or at least hoped to have used) the Faust narrative to encourage active reading and the correct interpretation of special providence in the lives of his parishioners.

For more than two centuries following the first printing of *Faustus*, the Faust tale prospered in the English book market. Based on the German text first printed in 1587, the English history 'far outliv[ed]' its source and became deeply entrenched in early modern English culture, maintaining popularity while inspiring a variety of dramatic and cheap print adaptations. In addition to innumerable inventive changes in phrasing, the English translator P. F. showed his education when he added vivid, up-to-date descriptions of world travel, scientific discourse on cosmology and legal details about Faustus's contracts. The distinctly English tenor of the translation also came through in the book's condescending jokes about German drunkenness and in its anti-Catholicism. While the German Faustus blew in the Pope's face, the English Faustus hit him. Although it was derived from the German Faust tale, *Faustus* quickly became an integral part of English print culture.[13]

The first extant edition of the prose *Faustus* was printed in London in 1592 (STC 10711), but the book may have been printed in London as early as 1588, only one year after its appearance in Germany. By 1600, *Faustus* had already been printed at least twice; it had also inspired Marlowe's *Tragedy of Dr Faustus*, an early ballad and a prose sequel about Faustus's servant Wagner. Omissions in the Stationers' Company Register make it difficult to trace the early publications of Faust tales in England, but surviving records point to the sustained popularity of *Faustus*. The full-length English tale survives in 15 editions between 1592 and 1700, and notwithstanding its longer length (and, therefore, greater expense), *Faustus* was reprinted more often than Marlowe's tragedy. Despite the wide variety of cheap print inspired by *Faustus*, it continued to be available in its full-length form throughout the seventeenth century. Although publisher Edward White and the printers he worked with reduced the production costs from 11 sheets of paper to 10 sheets by the early seventeenth century, they did so by using contractions and reduced leading, rather than by editing the text.[14]

Evidence from seventeenth-century editions suggests that the Faust book was marketed to English readers as something akin to a brand. The name 'Faustus' appeared on various seventeenth-century title pages and was commonly recognized as a name for a mournful tune for ballads. The title page woodcut of Faustus conjuring Mephistopheles represented a significant marketing strategy for *Faustus* in the seventeenth century. Even as the rights to print the book changed hands, the same woodcut was used on successive title pages. The visible deterioration of the woodcut in the 1670s and 1680s confirms that publishers sold the woodcut with the text as an integral part of the rights to publish *Faustus*. Just as the name 'Faustus' had become proverbial for torture and tragedy, the woodcut portrayal acquired iconic status. The picture of Faustus with book and staff in hand and of Mephistopheles half-revealed in the floor fixed the image of Faustus for early modern readers on both sides of the Atlantic, just as it does for literary historians today.

Bibliographers have been able to map the genealogy of later seventeenth-century editions of *Faustus* and have recognized successive series of small changes as letters were turned and errors were reproduced. Early modern stationers imitated previous editions to present a consistent and reliable book to potential buyers. Although there are slight variations in the text of *Faustus* from which we might better understand the methods of the book's *production,* these minor differences were unlikely to have detained contemporary readers. Despite changes of publisher and printer, the Faust text remained remarkably consistent. Throughout the seventeenth century, *Faustus* began on A2r and ended on K3v or K4r, and cost between 4d. and 6d.[15] Many of the seventeenth-century editions, including the 1682 printing that is the focus of this chapter, were copied and set page-for-page from previous printed editions. This consistency suggests that stationers found this length the most marketable, even though there were shorter and cheaper adaptations also available.

Widely read in England throughout the seventeenth century, *Faustus* probably travelled to the New World with an English reader before the end of the 1630s. Certainly, by the 1680s, we can glimpse the acquisition of early fiction or 'histories' in seventeenth-century English America in the records of bookseller John Usher. Usher had taken over book dealing from his father Hezekiah by 1669, and became one of the most successful colonial book merchants of the 1670s and 1680s. This was exactly when the Boston trade expanded rapidly. The town supported as many as 15 booksellers in the 30 years, 1669–99, a total that excludes about a dozen merchants who participated (probably as investors) in the publication of one or more Massachusetts imprints. Even allowing for a rapid turnover in personnel, the Boston book market seems to have sustained eight to ten book specialists at a time in the last quarter of the seventeenth century.[16]

Surviving records from John Usher's business in the 1680s show that a colonial book dealer's business was by no means small, even in comparison with London traders. When the London bookseller John Dunton arrived in Boston in the 1680s to sell excess stock, he described Usher as 'very Rich, adventures much to sea; but has got his Estate by Bookselling'. After Usher offered to buy Dunton's entire stock, Dunton describes him with the respect he might offer a colleague, on par with London book dealers.[17] Invoices in Usher's letter book give us a detailed look at the range of English imprints imported regularly during 1682–85. In March 1683/84, Usher imported approximately 750 copies of 71 English titles. Usher paid London stationer Richard Chiswell £61 5s. 6d. for these volumes and spent an additional £50 17s. 0d. on stationery in the same shipment. Only two and a half months later, Usher purchased more books and stationery totalling £40 3s. 7d. This inventory records 48 English imprints in just over 300 copies, a remarkable volume for less than three months later; moreover, this total does not include the books ordered for individual customers such as Shepard.[18] Looking at these records Hugh Amory concludes, 'between 3,500 and 4,000 volumes were annually exported to Boston in the 1680s, and... they sold out, since orders would not otherwise have continued'.[19]

Generic analysis of the surviving inventories shows that the largest segments of Usher's stock are devoted to works of divinity, devotional manuals and textbooks. Divinity books for the clergy make up around 25 per cent of imported titles; if these books are grouped together with devotional guides for laypersons, they make up approximately 42 per cent of imported titles. Textbooks – ranging from copybooks to Latin grammars – make up an additional 18 per cent, with practical manuals such as recipe books and husbandry manuals making up the next largest segment when taken as a group. But Usher also imported a surprising range of literary and topical texts in small quantities. In these lists Usher imported nearly as many 'Oxford Jests' as he did 'Oxford Grammars', and he saved space in his shipments for works like 'Erle of Rochesters Poems' and 'Wonders of the Femall world'. Most of England's steady-selling early fiction – books thought of in the period as romances, histories and jest-books – are listed in surviving records of the 1680s. Other works of early fiction such as *Guy of Warwick*, *The Pilgrim's Progress* and *Argalus and Parthenia* appeared in modest numbers, usually between four and ten copies in total, in the surviving invoices.[20] But the work of early fiction imported more than any other was the story of Dr Faustus, with at least 66 copies imported in only six years.

Although surviving records do not provide full bibliographical information, at least 48 (if not all) of the 66 copies referenced are to *Faustus* rather than to abbreviated, repackaged versions of the Faust tale. In Usher's invoices 36 of the total 66 listed are given the abbreviated title 'History of Dr. Faustus', which surely refers to the 1682 *History of Faustus*. The inventory entry that lists only '12 dr Faustus' might refer to any version of the Faust tale then available in the English book market, but the price of the copies offers a further clue. The 12 copies are listed at 4s. 6d. or a per book price of 4½d., representing an appropriate price for a ten-sheet history (and too high a price for a chapbook). Another, more ambiguous record comes from a 3 March 1683/84 invoice: '18 Dr. Faustus. 1st and 2d pt. 4° sh. 00-12-0'. Of the extant Faust books, only *Faustus*, the prose sequel entitled *The Second Report of Doctor John Faustus*, and Marlowe's tragedy were printed in quarto. Given that the quarto format (4°) is specified, the phrase '1st and 2d pt' probably refers to the *History of Faustus* (1682) and the *Second Report* (1680) bound together with inexpensive sheepskin and priced to sell at 8d.

When, in the autumn of 1683, the minister of Charlestown, Massachusetts, Thomas Shepard (1658–85), received a special order of London books and stationery, he represented the final link in a transatlantic exchange that connected ordinary New England planters with the discourse, information and goods circulating in London markets. At 26, Shepard was young to be a New England minister, but he was a third-generation minister with a name respected throughout the English Atlantic. His grandfather Thomas Shepard (1605–49) fled the regime of Archbishop Laud but remained influential in both England and New England with steady-selling publications such as *The Sincere Convert* and *The Sound Believer*. His son Thomas Shepard (1635–77) was minister at Charlestown parish before *his* son Thomas Shepard III, and he too sought to encourage active intellectual communities. He participated in the beginnings of a New England movement that Richard Gildrie has termed the 'reformation of manners', a clergy-driven programme of reform and accommodation that led to eighteenth-century conceptions of 'civility'.[21] Like his Harvard classmate Cotton Mather, this third Thomas Shepard was a youthful prodigy from an established family. Unlike Cotton Mather, the young Shepard did not survive even to his thirtieth birthday, and his clerical career can be captured only through minimal surviving records such as his book order from Usher. The books listed had all been printed within a few years of Shepard's order, which suggests that he was aware of the newest products of the London presses and that he ordered books regularly. The *Term Catalogue* included free with his shipment was probably not the first that Shepard had seen.

Shepard's order is clearly not designated for his sole use. In addition to the five books ordered in single copies, Shepard ordered a number of comparatively inexpensive titles in large quantities. Of the 13 titles listed in the document, Shepard requested 100 and 91 copies in total. The largest order for a title was for 100 copies of the *Bay Psalm Book*, '50 New England psalms 12° qs/50 Idem 12° sh' (50 copies in quires and

another 50 bound in sheepskin), which suggests that Shepard is buying a copy for each family in Charlestown, with copies in quires ready
to be bound as the church grew. In *Magnalia Christi Americana* Cotton
Mather eulogizes the third Shepard's love of books and notes that his
church grew under his brief leadership.[22] In addition to psalters and the
learned works of divinity, Shepard ordered ten copies of *Wonderful Prodigies of Judgment and Mercy* (1682; hereafter *Prodigies*), seven copies of *The
Academy of Compliments* (1670; hereafter *Academy*) and thirty copies of
the 1682 *History of Faustus*.[23] These books – with their vivid descriptions
of lavish feasting, witty conversation, classic jests and violent deaths –
seem incompatible with our expectations of the reading of an orthodox
Puritan minister, let alone of the books that such a minister might rec-
ommend to lay readers. And yet, even in New England, the godly clergy
did not control the community's culture. Ministers did not eliminate all
connection to what were vibrant and inclusive English popular cultures.
Shepard sought to influence local readers by providing books of his own
selection, but his choice of books also suggests *their* influence on *him*,
and how he accommodated the interests of the unlearned by choosing
steady sellers.[24]

The steady sellers of fiction, unlike the Lord's Prayer horn-book or the
traditional catechism, required not memorization, but an active interpretation of the sort Shepard surely intended his parishioners to apply
to their own spiritual journeys. Both *Prodigies* and the *Academy* antholo-
gize materials culled from a wide range of manuscript and print sources.
Such volumes presented English culture as multi-vocal and heteroge-
neous. Rather than displaying unitary, orthodox Massachusetts values,
the books Shepard chose encouraged readers to evaluate and select
among excerpts, as if Shepard were promoting active reading and interpretation of texts. Although all reading is always mediated, Shepard's
attempts to shape the reading of his parishioners highlight both the
extent and the limits of his influence in the community. As Matthew
Brown has shown, the laity in early New England did not simply read
passively (as is sometimes imagined from the oft-cited practice of reading through the Bible in the space of a year) but also employed radically
discontinuous and non-linear strategies for active reading.[25] Significantly, Shepard's attempts to reform his flock also extended beyond
the solely spiritual to cultivating aspects of English civility, appropriate social behaviour being deeply implicated in godly living. The books
ordered by Shepard reflected an emergent English discourse of the late
seventeenth century that articulated the importance of refinement and
civility.[26]

Prodigies is a collection of brief narratives examining wonders and special providences compiled from other printed and manuscript books. The anthology was modelled upon (and took material from) Thomas Beard's *Theatre of Gods Judgments*. The main contribution of the *Prodigies* to the English book market was not its content, but its availability. Its smaller size, woodcuts and lower price made the volume an accessible commodity for a wide audience. Like one of today's lurid tabloids, the title page of the *Prodigies* promises hundreds of cautionary tales about the 'Miserable Ends' of sinners and the 'Admirable Deliverances' of saints. Some stories are focused on historical persons, such as the tale of Christopher Marlowe, stabbed to death by 'his own Dagger into his own head' during a struggle, so that the 'hand which had written those Blasphemies, was made an instrument' to kill him.[27] Others narrate classic legends of anonymous sinners where, like many jokes told today, the tellers might change details at will. One such story tells of a drunken man declaring at a tavern that 'Heaven and Hell were mere Fables' and offering his soul to anyone who would buy it. After the man trades his soul to a friend in exchange for another drink, a third man buys the mortgaged soul at the same price from the friend. This third man turns out to be the 'Devil himself' who carries the drunkard away in order to teach him that 'Hell was no Fable'.[28]

This tale is a Faust legend in miniature, and the legend is repeated, with different emphases, over hundreds of stories. Stories like these expressed 'a mentality that united the learned and unlearned'; Alexandra Walsham explains that the concepts of providence these tales are founded on were 'not a marginal feature of the religious culture of early modern England, but . . . a cluster of presuppositions which enjoyed near universal acceptance'. If Shepard bought ten copies of *Prodigies* for the same readers for whom he bought the psalters, he likely took wonder tales seriously. To assert that Shepard took wonder tales seriously is not to say that he was an uncritical reader of the books that contained them. Despite publishers' title page claims to authenticity and 'undoubted Authority', many readers surely felt that they would need to reject any 'unwitnessed fictions' or false interpretations that remained in the printed book. To be fully fluent in what David Hall calls the transatlantic 'language' of wonders, especially after the discourse became increasingly politicized in the English Civil War, is to be an active interpreter of such stories, rather than a passive receiver of others' interpretations.[29]

Whether one interprets the providential frame of *Prodigies* as a superficial guise or not, the book was understood in the period as didactic (no matter how entertaining for readers); *The Academy of Compliments*, by contrast, does not have an explicitly Protestant frame, although it, too, asserts its utility. A printed miscellany of verse, prose letters, and witticisms, the *Academy* announces its use: Ladies, Gentlewomen, Schollers, and Strangers, may accommodate their Courtly practice with gentile Ceremonies, Complementall amorous high expressions, and Formes of speaking or writing of Letters most in fashion.

Printed in 12 editions between 1640 and 1685, the miscellany was fashionable and successful, even at a price of 1s. before binding. The book is arranged for quick reference, with tables and charts. Like a 'portable tutor' in polite conversation, the *Academy* offers a list of polite sayings and compliments appropriate for a range of circumstances, conveniently titled for reference, such as the quatrain honouring the beauty of '*a Gentlewoman disfigured by the small pox*' that compares her scars to constellations of stars. The book anticipates both male and female readers, suggesting appropriate responses for sophisticated, sometimes flirtatious conversation, with poems like Jonson's 'Still to be Neat' and charts of couplets suitable for engraving on a ring for a friend or lover. The *Academy*'s most recognizably educational feature is its brief dictionary of fashionable words – described as 'A Table for the understanding of the hard *English* words contained in this book'.[30] Although it may be difficult for us to imagine the 'use' of a book like the *Academy*, studies of seventeenth-century readership substantiate this interpretation. Randall Ingram's study of a handwritten index inserted into a volume of Donne's poetry shows that at least one seventeenth-century reader wanted efficient access to Donne's verse organized topically, to facilitate frequent quoting. Another of the most prominent uses of the *Academy* was as a source for model letters, because, by the second half of the seventeenth century, 'facility in letter writing was aligned with good manners and civility'.[31] The *Academy* was designed for comprehensive reference so that a reader could extract what he or she found appropriate, and sample letters are included in full. In his study of printed miscellanies in the late seventeenth century, Adam Smyth examines patterns in surviving marginalia to show that books like the *Academy* supported 'active, interventionist readers.... [because] readers *thought* in terms of selection, dissection, alteration, and use'. This readiness to adapt and edit printed texts for everyday use suggests that readers conceived of the miscellany's contents as 'positioned within a wider genre of instructional or exemplary writing'.[32] Based on our current generic conceptions, *Prodigies* and the *Academy* do not seem educational, yet compelling evidence from the seventeenth century suggests that they were read in this way. This historically minded conception of the use of books like *Prodigies* and the *Academy* may explain Shepard's choice to order these books, educating his American parish in reading and social skills. Like his father's advocacy of the 'reformation of manners', Shepard seems to have understood spiritual guidance as including the cultivation of civility.[33]

Like the tales of sinners in wonders literature, *Faustus* delivers the miserable and 'deserved' death of its protagonist. And yet, contrary to what we might expect, most early modern tales of learned magicians end happily (both Friar Bacon and Prospero successfully give up their magic books). For some readers, then, *Faustus* may have shocked when it delivered its promised ending and Faustus is damned. Readers were used to conversion narratives in which humans' dullness, stupidity and sinfulness were emphasized until the conversion had begun (and then, often, continued well after the first signs of grace); as a result, readers may have felt a kind of suspense as they waited for Faustus finally to recognize special providence and begin a spiritual new birth. Contextualizing *Faustus* within the tradition of providence interpretation is instructive, because narratives of divine justice were, in the words of Thomas Beard, 'an easie and profitable apprentiship or schoole for every man to learne to get wisdome at another mans cost'. Milton famously advocated such reading in *Areopagitica*, proclaiming Spenser a skilled 'teacher' in the *Faerie Queene*, and Donne makes a similar point in his *Devotions* about the wisdom of applying another man's affliction to oneself. Louis Wright traced the idea to sixteenth-century English culture: 'As Bees out of the bitterest flowers ... so out of obscene and wicked fables some profit may be extracted.' These idealized readers are active, selecting and retaining that which is 'profit[able]' from its dangerous surroundings. More recently, Matthew Brown has identified this idea of the reader-as-bee as one of the 'two central tropes' for reading in the seventeenth century.[34] Such perceptions surely influenced Shepard when ordering *Faustus* for colonial readers.

The advice about extracting wisdom from reading was also given directly by a late seventeenth-century English bookseller marketing histories and early fiction like the Faust tale. Francis Kirkman's preface to *The Honour of Chivalry* (1671) describes a method of reading pleasant histories that promises to educate his readers. Kirkman proposes a history 'curriculum' designed by experienced readers to make the novice seem knowledgeable at bookstalls. Kirkman recommends that the beginner starts with an anthology of short narratives called *The Seven Wise Masters*. Like *Prodigies*, this book uses images to convey the narrative to those not fully literate, and includes brief selections accessible for those who may read slowly, have limited vocabulary or have limited attention spans. Kirkman identifies the book as an educational tool 'next to the *Horn-Book'* for teaching reading. Once readers have mastered the history anthology, Kirkman concludes that they are prepared for a book that is 'one entire Story, both Pleasant and Profitable'. Looking at Shepard's book order of two anthologies and the extended *Faustus*, we see a pattern from New England not unlike Kirkman's suggested pedagogy from London.[35]

This reading of *Faustus* as 'Pleasant and Profitable' challenges the conclusion commonly arrived at by Marlowe scholars that the prose work is a simple text that offers the humour but neither the theological and intellectual significance nor the catharsis available in Marlowe's tragedy. Most Marlowe critics still agree with Louis Wright's conclusion that the text wears a 'coat of moral varnish' that barely conceals its celebration of Faustus's hedonistic lifestyle. *Faustus*, as expressed by Roma Gill, 'easily degenerates into a jest-book with a few moralizing tracts'. While *Faustus* presents a range of tones as Faustus moves between despair and pleasure, these readings attempt to assert that the text is really only about pleasure. Instead, the repeated shifts as Faustus turns to God, but then returns to sin, must have been themselves appealing since it is in this pattern that *Faustus* resembles the powerful genre of conversion narrative.[36] This damnation narrative operates very similarly to a conversion narrative. Each details the inadequate repentance of a repeat sinner, but *Faustus* inverted the traditional pattern when Faustus fails to learn from his experiences. Faustus is, of course, headed for damnation and not conversion, and so fails to recognize the importance of special providence in his life. When Faustus pricks his skin to prepare to write the bond in his own blood 'for certainty thereupon were seen on his hand these words written as if they had been written in his own blood, *O homo fuge*...but Faustus continued in his damnable mind.' Here, a significant moment of special providence, which appears 'for certainty', is ignored by Faustus, who 'continued' unconverted as he was before.[37] By choosing a text that required readers to recognize moments of special providence even when the protagonist does not, Shepard encouraged his parishioners to read actively, learning the skills necessary for interpreting similar moments in their own lives. Of course, the Faust tale also warned of the consequences for those who do not recognize God's providence in their lives.

It may seem that *Faustus* did not encourage active engagement given that Faustus is always already damned. Readers were told in the first chapter that 'there is no hope of his Redemption'.[38] But the representation of Faustus was a complex one, alternately asking readers to identify with Faustus's earthly desires and encouraging them to judge him for his poor decisions. Like the narratives of modern horror films, *Faustus* told a protracted tale in which Faustus makes mistake after mistake leading to his overdetermined damnation. And just as horror film audiences have been known to shout at characters on screen, expressing sympathy for the characters' dilemmas as well as their confidence in their own evaluation, *Faustus* encouraged a similar relationship with Faustus. Readers shared in the reactions of Faustus as he experiences delight, fear and despair, but their sympathy did not preclude judgment of his sinfulness, especially for readers who believed in sinfulness as a shared human condition. When, for example, Faustus insists that Mephistopheles must give him a wife, the devil's response terrifies Faustus and, potentially, readers: '[Faustus] was not able to stir [because]...then round about him ran a monstrous circle of fire, never standing still, that Faustus cryed as he lay.'[39] Readers may respond to Faustus's understandable human fear and sympathize with him, especially because the narrative only describes Faustus and the visions that torture him. In Marlowe's theatrical version, by contrast, the actor playing Mephistopheles in this scene probably remained visible to the audience, perhaps gesturing to mime control of the terrifying visions or visibly enjoying Faustus's pain, mocking it as absurd. The elimination in *Faustus* of everything except the description of Faustus and the tortures encourages readers to sympathize with him rather than simply laugh with Mephistopheles. And yet, most readers would simultaneously dissociate themselves from Faustus as a way to feel less vulnerable to the devil's wrath themselves, critiquing Faustus since his blasphemous contract put him into this dangerous position.

Just as Beard described stories of divine justice as a 'schoole' and Milton praised Spenser as a 'teacher', *Faustus* offered English educational models within its larger cautionary tale. Although Faustus is introduced as one who has completed formal education, the reader recognizes immediately that Faustus needs instruction in the application of scripture to his own life; although he was 'excellent perfect' in memorization of scripture, he does not comprehend the relevance of biblical passages like 'no man can serve two Masters' as he plans to serve Lucifer. Faustus's contract with Mephistopheles begins a new stage in his education. Once catechized anew by Mephistopheles, Faustus learns about the world through travel and exploration, but he only comes to *true* knowledge – knowledge of himself and of God – as his time on earth expires. Furthermore, the dialogue between questioning Faustus and knowledgeable Mephistopheles follows patterns consistent in English catechisms of the period. Catechisms were usually the first book children were taught after the ABC and horn-book, and *Faustus* narrates the standard education of a beginner.[40] The similarity between these chapters and early modern catechisms is increased because Mephistopheles answers in accordance with standard Protestant English doctrine. The German source has the devil spirit answer with recognizable heresies. The German Mephistopheles defends Lucifer using classical texts, much like Marlowe's Faustus citing Pythagoras in his final soliloquy. By contrast, the English translator P. F. changed Mephistopheles' answers so that he critiqued Lucifer. P. F. thus narrowed the gap between *Faustus* and printed English catechisms.

By Chapter 21, *Faustus* resembles another early modern educational print genre: the courtesy book. In this section the narrative structure falls away, as readers are given direct access to the carefully composed letter Faustus writes to an old classmate. Faustus, as an exemplary letter writer, emphasizes his superior education and lifestyle and, for the moment, ignores the state of his soul.[41] The chapter is immediately followed by a description of Faustus's travels throughout the world, written like a contemporary travelogue of a genteel grand tour of Europe. Here we find another genre represented from Shepard's book order: the kind of travelogue included that the minister sought in 'Mordens Geography'. While the German Faust book appropriated the text of a century-old travelogue, P. F.'s English translation doubles the length of the chapter, updating and adding accurate details throughout. P. F., it might be ventured, had recently travelled extensively on the continent. In this section, Faustus advances from beginner's catechetical instruction to the finishing school of European travel. Here, as in the epistolary chapter, the despairing and foolish Faustus vanishes, and the reader – on whichever side of the Atlantic – is encouraged to identify with the protagonist as an experienced and knowledgeable traveller with occasional xenophobic wit.

Faustus's primary identity throughout these chapters is not as a German but as a Protestant fighting idolatry through attacks on the Roman Catholic Pope, the Islamic Turkish prince and a Jewish moneylender. P. F.'s translation downplays Faustus's German nationality throughout *Faustus*, with the designation of 'German' invoked only for minor characters who display what is to be understood as fairly typical German ignorance or drunkenness.[42] Faustus's pan-Protestant identity, based not in specifics of doctrine but in xenophobic rhetoric, would appeal to a wide range of English readers. The text of Faustus's prank on the Jewish moneylender comes directly from the German Faust book, but P. F. extends and elaborates Faustus's attacks on the Pope and Turkish prince, furthering the humiliation of the alien religions and expressing deeply resonant chauvinistic English attitudes that, through this steady-selling *Faustus* if not before, circulated widely in early modern English culture. When Faustus steals the Pope's rich food, the Pope at first calls for his cardinals to help what he believes is a desperate soul in purgatory, but P. F.'s Faustus escalates the prank and aggressively 'smote the Pope on the face'. The confused Pope then calls for the futile ceremony of 'bell, book, & candle' to attempt to damn the soul in punishment. This challenge to the Pope's ritual as a list of mundane material objects suggests a Protestant critique of the perceived carnal nature of the Roman Catholic Church.[43] More significantly, the Pope is associated with poor interpretative skills: just as Faustus earlier misreads special providence in his life, the Pope completely misinterprets the meaning of what is happening to him.

In the episode with the Turkish prince, the German source and P. F.'s additions associate Islam with other heretical 'heathen' practices, especially with the sin of idolatry, unaware of Muslim prohibition against representations of Mohammed. Faustus disguises himself as Mohammed by making himself appear 'as they used to paint Mahomet' and Muslim worship is described as the people 'calling on their God Mahomet, and worshipping of the Image'. This degradation of perceived image worship further underscores the identification of Faustus with Protestantism, which constructs itself as uniquely free from idolatry. After observing the kingdom of the Turkish prince, Faustus conjures a stinking fog to surround the Turk's harem and presents himself as Mohammed to the Turk's wives and 'delighted himself sufficiently' with the fairest women for six days. When Faustus departs, the Turk asks his wives about their interactions with this supposed Mohammed and P. F. adds a punch line: one wife tells her husband that the sex could not have been better 'if you had been there your self'. The cuckolding of the Islamic prince emasculates him, as the Turk has been passively waiting throughout the fog, and the Islamic world is feminized compared to the vigour of masculine Protestantism. The Turk applies his own interpretive skills foolishly and incorrectly, 'perswading himself (and so did all the whole people who knew of it) that out of [the wives who slept with Faustus]...Mahomet should be raised a mighty Generation'.[44] Here, as with Faustus previously and the Pope, the narrative foregrounds characters misinterpreting the events in their lives, fully expecting that readers have come to the 'correct' interpretations. This persistent pattern of the readers supplying the active interpretation Protestant practice encouraged them to apply in their own lives shows the potential educational use (by Shepard and others) of *Faustus*.

In later chapters, Faustus's pranks are directed at Europeans who are coarse characters lacking refinement, whether these are uncultivated rustic clowns or poorly educated elites; as in the xenophobic pranks on religious leaders, here the reader is encouraged to mock the uncultivated victims of Faustus's pranks from a comfortable sense of superiority. The focus of these attacks is not only on the uneducated, but also on the educated who betray their superior knowledge. The knight, for example, sleeps 'to no little disgrace of the Gentleman' in a window at the Emperor's court. The passage here emphasizes the shame that this high status man should feel at his bodily indulgence of napping, a shame that is reinforced in the jest that he is a beast through the conjuring of animal antlers on his head. Unlike Marlowe's theatrical version, this knight does not mock or ignore Faustus, so the doctor has no personal motivation to humiliate him. Instead, the knight's simple lack of bodily control, signified in his sleeping, is worthy of Faustus's correctional punishment. Another of Faustus's jests punishes the behaviour of uneducated rural workers at an Inn: 'wherein were many Tables full of Clowns...they were all drunken: and as they sat, they so sang and bellowed, that one could not hear a man speak for them: this angered Doctor Faustus.'[45] Faustus, punishes the clowns for their unruly, overpowering noise and conjures their mouths wide open, and makes them unable to close them. Not harmed permanently, the clowns regain control of their mouths after they leave the inn. Their temporary lack of control over their mouths implies that the clowns had already lost reason and control over their bodies, due to their drunkenness. Faustus's jests function as social discipline: these and other jests attack uncultivated persons who are characterized by a connection with their bodies, rather than with any effective use of their reason or soul. Significantly, Mephostophiles is seldom mentioned in these travelogue and jest chapters. Faustus is even portrayed as performing illusions and jests without his satanic assistance. Mephostophiles is a central character in early chapters focused on Faustus's bond with the devil and re-emerges as important as Faustus despairs near the end of his allotted time, but because he is seldom mentioned in this middle section, readers are allowed temporarily to disassociate Faustus with demonic interests and, instead, identify with him as he makes fools of poorly educated and uncivilized characters.

In the final chapters of the book, *Faustus* returns to the tragic narrative of the doomed sinner, but even here the text encourages a more complex relationship to its protagonist than we might expect. Immediately before his death, Faustus is transformed from a terrified sinner seeking further sin to a model criminal walking knowingly towards his 'deserved death'. Suddenly wise in his knowledge of God and damnation, Faustus stops crying and delivers his rhetorically polished 'oration' calmly, clearly blaming his 'stiff-necked and rebellious will'. Unlike Marlowe's tragic figure, this Faustus does not bargain, plead or dabble in new heresies. Like the exemplary speaker in gallows literature, which was popular in both England and its colonies, Faustus performs the role of repentant prisoner, offering recently acquired wisdom to those who take his message seriously.

From the beginning of the seventeenth century, the printing of New England execution sermons began in the 1670s, 'modelled on a series of contemporary British publications regularly prepared in conjunction with executions by the chaplain (or Ordinary) of Newgate Prison in London'.[46] In Massachusetts, printed pamphlets with a confession, sermon and account of the execution were sometimes available within a few weeks of the event, spread throughout the colonies by hawkers. Faustus's calm delivery signals a humble submission to his doom that was an expected part of the ritual of English executions. As Daniel Williams explains, 'This was the final scene in the ritual drama.... they were expected to edify the saintly and terrify the sinful.'[47] By resembling gallows literature these chapters underscore their use for readers who choose to learn from the school of others' experience, as Faustus pleads that the students in his company will take his life story as a 'sufficient warning'. Faustus's concern with the effects of 'evil fellowship of wicked companions' occurs repeatedly in gallows literature, such as the words of John Steers who, in England in 1686, blamed 'bad Company'. Alice Millikin, executed the same year, sounds like Faustus in her concern for the souls of her audience; she is described as recommending that they do not 'distrust God's Providence ... [so that] the like fatal end will not attend them'.[48] Because readers do not directly witness Faustus's fate later that night when he is torn apart, this final chapter of *Faustus* more directly resembles gallows literature, rather than the in-person experience of standing before English gallows on execution day.

Even as *Faustus* appropriates the modes of death-day speeches, it continues the theme of Faustus's failed education. When the students have listened to Faustus's account, they advise Faustus about repentance, '*teaching* him this form of prayer'. But, despite his oration with its calm acceptance of his doom, Faustus fails as a pupil, just as he has earlier failed as a reader of special providence: 'This [prayer] they repeated to him, yet he could take no hold.'[49] Rather than suggesting that the damnation of Faustus has been long since determined by his pact with the devil, this scene implies his ongoing failure to recognize the role of God's grace in human lives. Rather than, as in the ending to Marlowe's tragedy, placing the audience as a voyeur gazing on Faustus's miserable end, readers are now asked to identify with the students who have been told to take his death as 'warning'. While the narrative has, until this point, consistently followed its protagonist, in the final chapter Faustus's experiences are left a mystery, as the narrative focuses on the fearful experience of the students in the next room. While the narration ignores what happens in Faustus's chamber as the clock approaches midnight, 'The Students... wept... none of them could sleep.' After midnight when the house begins to shake with violent wind, *Faustus* focuses on the students' 'fear' and their attempts to 'comfort[ ] one another' despite the horrible sounds of snakes and the cries of Faustus.[50] Readers then follow the students the next morning as they collect the remaining pieces of Faustus's body scattered around the property. In this final chapter, as throughout the book, readers of *Faustus* are placed in the position of students, and *Faustus* enacts the sort of English educational models already available in print. While the educational or moral 'use' of the English Faust book is usually disregarded by literary critics as an implausible marketing ploy, *Faustus* might also be read to suggest the significance of issues of interpretation and learning.

A book order like Thomas Shepard's, unaccompanied by other manuscript traces of Shepard's use for 30 copies of a popular *Faustus*, cannot tell us conclusively how Shepard evaluated the text, let alone confirm absolutely how it was read by other readers of English in Massachusetts or elsewhere in the Atlantic world. There is much about the surviving record that is frustratingly silent. And yet, the suggested conclusions here about *Faustus* and its active reading are consistent with contemporary pedagogies promoted by Frances Meres, Thomas Beard and John Milton.[51] This was a damnation narrative that appealed to a wide range of early modern English and North American readers by its focus on the conjoined significance of civility and Protestant values. With its combination of books of Protestant doctrine and books of social graces, Shepard's transatlantic book order reminds us that the late seventeenth-century movement towards the cultivation of manners is not a secularizing movement. The wide circulation of *Faustus* in seventeenth-century England and English America reveals the broad popular base for an alignment between Protestantism and Englishness that, within a few short years, was to be politically formalized in the Glorious Revolution – and in New England, in the re-establishment of colonial self-rule.[52] From this, according to at least one interpreter, colonists developed a new politics that insisted upon equality with Englishmen at home.[53]

Notes

1. Hugh Amory, 'Reinventing the Colonial Book', in Hugh Amory and David D. Hall (eds), *The Colonial Book in the Atlantic World vol. 1; A History of the Book in America* (Cambridge, 2000): 26–54, 31; Worthington Chauncey Ford, *The Boston Book Market 1679–1700* (New York, 1972): 116–9; Thomas Goddard Wright, *Literary Culture in Early New England 1620–1730*, 2nd edn (New York, 1966): 230; I do not follow Ford's suggestions for the manuscript's abbreviations.

2. Bernard Bailyn, *Atlantic History: Concept and Contours* (Cambridge, MA, 2005): 84.

3. David D. Hall, *Worlds of Wonder, Days of Judgment: Popular Religious Belief in Early New England* (New York, 1989): 45; Daniel A. Cohen, *Pillars of Salt, Monuments of Grace: New England Crime Literature and the Origins of American Popular Culture, 1674–1860* (Oxford, 1993): 5; see below for identification of 'Mr. Shepard' with Thomas Shepard (1658–85).

4. P. F., *The History of the Damnable Life and Deserved Death of Dr. John Faustus. Newly Printed; and in Convenient Places Impertinent Matter Amended, According to the True Copy Printed at Frankford and Translated into English* (London, 1682), hereafter *HJF*.

5. Tessa Watt, *Cheap Print and Popular Piety 1550–1640* (Cambridge, 1991): 126; Martin Ingram, 'From Reformation to Toleration: Popular Religious Cultures in England, 1540–1690', in Tim Harris (ed.), *Popular Culture in England, c1500–1850* (New York, 1995): 95–109, 106; Alexandra Walsham, *Providence in Early Modern England* (Oxford, 1999): 1–6.

6. Hugh Amory, 'Printing and Bookselling in New England, 1638–1713', in Amory and Hall (eds), *Colonial Book in the Atlantic World*, 83–116 (96–7).

7. Hall, *Worlds of Wonder*, 57, 85–93.

8. Walsham, *Providence*, 2; Matthew P. Brown, *The Pilgrim and the Bee: Reading Rituals and Book Culture in Early New England* (Philadelphia, PA, 2007): 106.

9. Michael J. Braddick, 'Civility and Authority', in David Armitage and Michael J. Braddick (eds), *The British Atlantic World, 1500–1800* (New York, 2002): 93–112; Anna Bryson, *From Courtesy to Civility: Changing Codes of Conduct in Early Modern England* (Oxford, 1998); Richard L. Bushman, *The Refinement of America: Persons, Houses, Cities* (New York, 1992); Richard P. Gildrie, *The Profane, the Civil, and the Godly: The Reformation of Manners in Orthodox New England, 1679–1749* (University Park, PA, 1994).

10. Stuart Clark, 'Witchcraft and Magic in Early Modern Culture', in Bengt Ankarloo and Stuart Clark (eds), *Witchcraft and Magic in Europe: The Period of the Witch Trials* (Philadelphia, PA, 2002): 97–169, 142.

11. David D. Hall (ed.), 'Introduction', in *Witch-Hunting in Seventeenth-Century New England: A Documentary History, 1638–1693*, 2nd edn (Boston, MA, 1999): 4, 5–16, 9, 10; John Demos, *Entertaining Satan: Witchcraft and the Culture of Early New England* (Oxford, 2004): 12, 402–9.

12. Carol F. Karlsen, *The Devil in the Shape of a Woman: Witchcraft in Colonial New England* (New York, 1987): 4–7; Jim Sharpe, 'The Devil in East Anglia: The Matthew Hopkins Trials Reconsidered', in Jonathan Barry, Marianne Hester and Gareth Roberts (eds), *Witchcraft in Early Modern Europe: Studies in Culture and Belief* (Cambridge, 1996): 237–54, 242; Keith Thomas, *Religion and the Decline of Magic* (Oxford, 1971): 436–7; Hall, *Witch-Hunting*, 11.

13. John Henry Jones (ed.), *The English Faust Book: A Critical Edition Based on the Text of 1592* (Cambridge, 1994): 1, 10–13, 21–6.

14. Ibid., 34–8, David Bevington and Eric Rasmussen (eds), 'Introduction', in *Doctor Faustus and Other Plays* (Oxford, 1995): vii–xxxv, xvi, xxvi–xxvii.

15. Philip Gaskell, *A New Introduction to Bibliography* (Oxford, 1972): 178; W. W. Greg, *Some Aspects and Problems of London Publishing Between 1550 and 1650* (Oxford, 1956): 17; Margaret Spufford, *Small Books and Pleasant Histories: Popular Fiction and Its Readership in Seventeenth-Century England* (London, 1981): 97–8; see below for the *History* sold unbound, for 4d or 4½d.

16. Amory, 'Printing and Bookselling in New England,' 96–100; Benjamin Franklin (ed.), *Boston Printers, Publishers, and Booksellers: 1640–1800* (Boston, MA, 1980): 473–8; George Emery Littlefield, *Early Boston Booksellers 1642–1711* (New York, 1900): 67–8; Hellmut Lehmann-Haupt, *The Book in America* (New York, 1939): 44–5.

17. Amory, 'Printing and Bookselling in New England', 90; Lehmann-Haupt, *Book in America*, 45.

18. Ford, *Boston Book Market*, 121–39; Wright, *Literary Culture*, 231–4.

19. Amory, 'Printing and Bookselling in New England', 105.

20. Ford, *Boston Book Market*, 83–150.

21. Francis J. Bremer, *Shaping New England: Puritan Clergymen in Seventeenth-Century England and New England* (New York, 1994): 114–15; David D. Hall, 'Readers and Writers in Early New England', in Amory and Hall (eds), *Colonial Book in the Atlantic World*: 117–51, 137, 142; James Savage, *A Genealogical Dictionary of the First Settlers of New England*, 4 vols (Boston, MA, 1862), 4: 76; Gildrie, *The Profane, the Civil, and the Godly*, 13–15, 21.

22. Cotton Mather, *Magnalia Christi Americana: Or, the Ecclesiastical History of New-England, from Its First Planting in the Year 1620* (London, 1702): 179.

23. *The Academy of Complements Wherein Ladies, Gentlewomen, Schollerrs, and Strangers, May Accommodate Their Courtly Practice with Gentile Ceremonies, Complemental Amorous High Expressions, and Forms of Speaking or Writing Letters Most in Fashion* (London, 1650).

24. Ingram, 'From Reformation to Toleration', 95–100; Gildrie, *The Profane, the Civil, and the Godly*, 7–9; Hall, *Worlds of Wonder*, 3, 7, 70.

25. Brown, *Pilgrim and the Bee*, 14–20, 106; Hall, *Worlds of Wonder*, 43, 70, 72; David D. Hall and Elizabeth Carroll Reilly, 'Practices of Reading: Introduction', in Amory and Hall (eds), *Colonial Book in the Atlantic World*, 377–9, 379; Ingram, 'From Reformation to Toleration', 107.

26. Bryson, *From Courtesy to Civility*, 3, 277–8; Gildrie, *The Profane, the Civil, and the Godly*, 2–3, 15; Bushman, *Refinement*, xii–xv.

27. Marlowe's 'Blasphemies' were his alleged anti-Trinitarian tracts (not his dramas).
28. R. Burton, *Wonderful Prodigies of Judgment and Mercy: Discovered in above Three Hundred Memorable Histories* (London, 1682), t.p.: A3v–A4r.
29. Walsham, *Providence*, 2; Burton, *Wonderful Prodigies*, t.p; Hall, *Worlds of Wonder*, 94.
30. *Academy*, t.p., I4r, P1r, K3r, A9r, M1v; Bryson, *From Courtesy to Civility*, 155–6; Adam Smyth, *Profit and Delight: Printed Miscellanies in England 1640–1682* (Detroit, MI, 2004): 1, 38.
31. Randall Ingram, 'Seventeenth-Century Didactic Readers, Their Literature, and Ours', in Natasha Glaisyer and Sara Pennell (eds), *Didactic Literature in England 1500–1800: Expertise Constructed* (Burlington, VT, 2003): 63–78; Bryson, *From Courtesy to Civility*, 157–8; Gary Schneider, *The Culture of Epistolarity: Vernacular Letters and Letter Writing in Early Modern England, 1500–1700* (Newark, DE, 2005): 44–5.
32. Smyth, *Profit and Delight*, 53–4, 44.
33. Gildrie, *The Profane, the Civil, and the Godly*, 21, 13–15.
34. Walsham, *Providence*, 69; John Milton, 'Areopagitica', in Merritt Y. Hughes (ed.), *Complete Poems and Major Prose* (New York, 1957): 728–9; Louis B. Wright, *Middle-Class Culture in Elizabethan England*, 3rd edn (New York, 1980): 394; Brown, *Pilgrim and the Bee*, xii.
35. Jeronimo Fernandez, *The Honour of Chivalry, or, the Famous and Delectable History of Don Bellianes of Greece*, trans. Francis Kirkman (London: 1671): A4r; Lori Humphrey Newcomb, *Reading Popular Romance in Early Modern England* (New York, 2002): 152, 247–60; Spufford, *Small Books*, 73–4.
36. Wright, *Middle-Class Culture*, 377; Roma Gill (ed.), *Doctor Faustus vol. 2 The Complete Works of Christopher Marlowe* (Oxford, 1990): xviii; Charles C. Mish (ed.), *Short Fiction of the Seventeenth Century* (New York, 1963): xii; Patricia Caldwell, *The Puritan Conversion Narrative: The Beginnings of American Expression* (Cambridge, 1983): 1–3.
37. *HJF*, B1r, Walsham, *Providence*, 20.
38. *HJF*, A2v.
39. *HJF*, B2v; cf. scene 5 of Marlowe's A-text and Act 1, scene 5 of the B-text.
40. *HJF*, A2v; Ian Green, *The Christian's Abc: Catechisms and Catechizing in England C. 1530–1740* (Oxford, 1996): 172–5; R. C. Simmons, 'ABCs, Almanacs, Ballads, Chapbooks, Popular Piety and Textbooks', in John Barnard, D. F. McKenzie and Maureen Bell (eds), *The Cambridge History of the Book in Britain* (Cambridge, 2002): 504–13.
41. *HJF*, E1r; Schneider, *Culture*, 22–8; Bryson, *From Courtesy to Civility*, 157–8.
42. *HJF*, D4v, H2r.
43. *HJF*, E2v–E3r; Achsah Guibbory, *Ceremony and Community from Herbert to Milton* (Cambridge, 1998): 4–9.
44. *HJF*, F2v.
45. *HJF*, G2r, H1r; cf. scene 10 of Marlowe's A-text and Act 4, scene 1 of the B-text.
46. *HJF*, K2v; Cohen, *Pillars of Salt*, 3; Hall, *Worlds of Wonder*, 178–82; Lincoln B. Faller, *Turned to Account: The Forms and Functions of Criminal Biography in Late Seventeenth- and Early Eighteenth-Century England* (Cambridge, 1987); Michael Harris, 'Murder in Print: Representations of Crime and the

Law c. 1600–1760', in Rosamaria Loretelli and Roberto De Romanis (eds), *Narrating Transgression: Representations of the Criminal in Early Modern England* (Frankfurt am Main, 1999): 13–26.

47. Cohen, *Pillars of Salt*, 14, 3–4; Daniel E. Williams, 'Behold a Tragic Scene Strangely Changed into a Theater of Mercy': The Structure and Significance of Criminal Conversion Narratives in Early New England', *American Quarterly* 38: 5 (1986): 827–47, 843.

48. *HJF*, K3r; John Steers, *The Account of the Behaviour and Confession of the Criminals* (London, 1686): 3; *The True Account of the Behaviour and Confession of Alice Millikin, Who Was Burnt in Smithfield on Wednesday the 2d of Junes, 1686. For High-Treason, in Clipping of the Kings Coin* (London, 1686): 4.

49. *HJF*, K3v, my emphasis; Jones, *English Faust Book*, 179. The earliest surviving edition (1592), by contrast, states, 'yet *it* could take no hold' (my emphasis). At some point the text was changed, probably simply by error; however, this small change from 'it' to 'he' further emphasizes Faustus's failure to learn by this late seventeenth-century edn.

50. *HJF*, K3v; cf. scene 14 of Marlowe's A-text and Act 5, scene 2 of the B-text.

51. This reading of the *History* as a text encouraging active interpretation, analogous to the work of 'reading' the role of God's providence in an English Protestant's life, aims to contribute to similar work on seventeenth-century reading by Matthew Brown, Randall Ingram, Lori Humphrey Newcomb, Adam Smyth, and others.

52. See Gildrie, *The Profane, the Civil, and the Godly*; Bushman, *Refinement*; Robert E. Moody and Richard C. Simmons (eds), *The Glorious Revolution in Massachusetts: Selected Documents, 1689–1692* (Boston, MA, 1988); and Richard R. Johnson, 'The Revolution of 1688–9 in the American Colonies', in Jonathan I. Israel (ed.), *The Anglo-Dutch Moment: Essays on the Glorious Revolution and its World Impact*, ch. 6 (Cambridge, 2003).

53. David S. Lovejoy, *The Glorious Revolution in America* (New York, 1972).

4
Transatlantic News: American Interpretations of the Scandalous and Heroic

Phyllis Whitman Hunter

> There's not an ear that is not deaf
> But listens to the News.[1]

Andrew Bradford (1735)

Until recently, historians studying colonial America often disregarded the foreign news that took up the majority of space in colonial newspapers. Now that an Atlantic history paradigm is reshaping our perspective, 'foreign news' appears to be of greater importance in understanding early America and its place in a broader circulation of goods, people and ideas throughout the Atlantic world.[2]

Early newspapers serving the 13 colonies reported spectacles of empire that ranged from the celebratory entry of the European Ambassador at the Court of the Ottoman Empire to the implausible projects of joint-stock companies founded just prior to the crash of the South Sea Company in 1720. The newspapers also printed news about 'unruly' crowds of London cloth-workers protesting the fashion for imported calicoes, or pirates and hurricanes that menaced European and American fleets in the Atlantic, Caribbean and Mediterranean.[3] Filling the pages of early American newspapers, these stories pictured spectacles of great riches and sudden losses alternating in unsettling rapidity. As they were read aloud and discussed in coffeehouses and taverns, printed accounts of stock speculation, diplomatic processions, imported goods and sea disasters found in Boston, New York, Philadelphia and Charleston newspapers connected colonial Americans not only to metropolitan London but to the broader Atlantic world.[4] In doing so, newspapers raised persistent concerns of how to negotiate in a transatlantic marketplace based on slave labour, consumer goods, distant markets and imperial rivalry and they also portrayed heroic ideals shared by fellow Britons on both sides of the ocean.

While the American colonies certainly did not compare with metropolitan London in terms of population, sophistication or print output, the leading American ports, especially Boston, did keep pace with English provincial cities in terms of printing newspapers and forming circulating and social libraries.[5] After an abortive single-issue news sheet issued by the proprietor of Boston's London Coffeehouse and immediately quashed by the Massachusetts authorities in 1690, the first local American newspaper appeared in 1704. Emerging only two to three years after the *Bristol Post Boy* and the *Norwich Post*, the *Boston News-Letter (BNL)* published by printer and postmaster John Campbell followed the model of the *London Gazette* as did the papers in Norwich and Bristol. Campbell's paper – designed to be a paper of record – reigned as the sole American newspaper until 1719 when a competitor brought out the *Boston Gazette (BG)* designed for 'the trading part of the town' and Andrew Bradford in Philadelphia started the *American Weekly Mercury (AWM)* to reach a regional mid-Atlantic audience. The early publications consisted mainly of foreign news from various sources: accounts reprinted, often word for word, from London newspapers, summaries of letters received from gentlemen and ship's captains in foreign ports, personal reports from newly arrived ship's captains and visitors, correspondence to local elites, official royal or parliamentary proclamations and notices acquired from the colonial governors.[6] By the early 1730s, Philadelphia had two newspapers as did New York, while Maryland, South Carolina and Rhode Island each had one. For a time, Boston had as many as five newspapers including two with literary aspirations.[7]

News of European commercial, diplomatic and military forays into neighbouring countries or into the Middle East and Asia filled the columns of colonial newspapers, where pages of foreign dispatches far exceeded local news until the 1760s. In fact, a desire for information on foreign affairs called forth the early American newspapers, first in the major port cities of Boston and Philadelphia in the 1720s and 1730s and by mid-century in smaller ports such as New Bern and Edenton, North Carolina, as well as inland towns. John Campbell, the printer-publisher of the *Boston News-Letter*, Boston's first newspaper, explained the purpose of his venture. He began the paper 'to give a true Account of all the Publick Affairs of Europe, with those of this and the Neighbouring Provinces', thus providing 'for the Interest and Advantage of the Post-Office, Gentlemen, Merchants and Others, both of Town and Country'.

This accurate information would, he assured his readers, 'prevent a great many false Reports'. Andrew Bradford initiated Philadelphia's first newspaper to 'Promote Trade' hoping that his venture would be 'encouraged by the merchants of this City'. His title, *American Weekly Mercury*, signalled his ambition to reach beyond Philadelphia to a regional audience and eventually he drew advertisements from New York, Rhode Island, Massachusetts and Virginia, partly through the efforts of his father William, a leading printer in New York.[8]

Colonial newspapers reported diplomatic, military and mercantile developments as soon as the news arrived – usually two months or more after the events. Campbell made weekly, sometimes daily visits to merchants, travellers and seamen just arriving at the docks in an effort to acquire the latest information from distant countries.[9] Bradford encouraged 'Gentlemen that receive an Authentick Account of News from Europe, or other places, which may be proper for this paper, that they will please to favour Us with a Copy.' But at times, especially during the winter as shipping declined, early papers had to fall back on reprinting older items from London periodicals because, as Bradford explained, they had 'but few remarkable Occurrences to fill up this our Paper with at present'.[10]

Continuing the history presented above by Catherine Armstrong in chapter 2, foreign news served a number of purposes for colonial American readers. Certainly, as Campbell alluded to in his opening issue, newspapers provided vital commercial knowledge – almost all contained a section called 'Entrances and Clearances' listing the seagoing vessels arriving and leaving home port and, when available, listings from other Atlantic ports as well. Advertisements often beginning with 'Just imported from London' also reinforced transatlantic links. News of wars and skirmishes among the European powers also played a crucial role in the planning of merchants and their crewmen shipping overseas. But coverage of European events and celebrities also provided an imperial linkage that both integrated the British Atlantic and simultaneously constituted local and colonial difference through appropriating and refashioning representations of empire.[11] In this respect, the transatlantic transmission and reinterpretation of news by print gained much greater depth and complexity than the early corantos described in Armstrong's chapter with their often sensationalized accounts of domestic and continental events.[12]

Colonial newspapers, like many current publications, provided a mix of pragmatic information and sensational accounts. In the 1720s, the *Boston Gazette* portrayed an extensive involvement in the Atlantic world and demonstrated a pervasive atmosphere of speculation – as if all the world were a market (or a casino) and everything in it for sale or purchase. The news from foreign cities – London, Paris, the Hague, Hamburg, Vienna – was replete with a variety of get-rich-quick schemes. News ranged from lists of lottery prizes awarded in London and accounts of an English gentleman marrying a wealthy heiress worth £30,000 to the Duke of Chandos who gained an equal amount in South Sea stock.[13]

The financial crisis that came to be known as 'the South Sea Bubble' provided one example where newspapers played a critical role in linking colonials with the metropolitan environments of London and Paris and, yet, simultaneously emphasized the distance in prevailing attitudes. Through personal and business letters and in the pages of Boston and Philadelphia newspapers, numerous Americans followed the rise and sudden crash of speculative investment during the South Sea Bubble in 1720. The British South Sea Company, formed in 1711 on the anticipation of extensive trading privileges to be granted by Spain at the conclusion of Queen Anne's War, attracted a wide range of shareholders from dukes and viscounts to brewers and timber merchants. The South Sea Company acquired 'the Assiento', a 30-year contract to provide 4,800 slaves per year to the Spanish dominions in America. In practice, the slave trade reaped only minimal returns for the company, but belief in future profits continued to appeal to investors. Few gave any thought to the reprehensible nature of a trade in human beings.

In France, Scots financier John Law, advisor to Louis XIV, established a new investment 'system' (some would later say *scheme*), known as the Mississippi Company. The Company of the West, as it was called in early American newspapers, held a monopoly on profits from the French lands in North America that stretched from the mouth of the St Lawrence River through the Great Lakes and down the Mississippi to New Orleans. The company planned to establish settlements in the area and take control of the fur trade.[14]

The funding and fortunes of both John Law's Mississippi Company and the British South Sea Company were followed in detail in the pages of Boston's newspapers. They reported the founding of the Company of the West 'with the sole Privilege of the Trade for Beavers and other Furs in Canada.... exclusive of all others for 29 years' as well as 'the sole Trade in the Province or Government of the Louisiana'. The following week, the paper quoted an 'Extract of the Registers of the [French] Council of State' describing the arrangements for setting up the Company of the West. One Company proposal aimed to export 'a great Quantity of Silk... as Mulberry Trees grow in the country'. In July, the *Boston News-Letter* reported the discovery of a mine in Louisiana. The French

Mint office – controlled by John Law – claimed that the ore 'proves very rich' but apparently scepticism was already abroad in France because the report continued, 'People will not give Credit to it, because they have had of late several Stories of the like nature, that have proved altogether groundless.'[15]

Law was a master of public relations. He became a celebrity in Paris, and newspapers in Europe and America chronicled not only the activities of his company but also his own investments and advancements. The *Boston Gazette* reported on the construction of Law's new house in Paris, noting that he pulled 'down 2 old ones' to create the new edifice. During the same month, Boston's other paper reported that 'Mr. Law has now given the finishing Stroke to his own Greatness. On the 6th . . . he was declar'd Comptroller of the Finances, which, in a Word, is no less than Lord High Treasurer of France.' The account noted that Law's position was 'perhaps the greatest Post that any Subject enjoys in the World, except the Grand Vizier at Constantinople'. And, 'not only does no man envy Mr. Law this Preferment; they call him the Good Genius of France' and 'expect still greater things from his Conduct than have yet been seen.' According to John Carswell, 'the secret of Law's success' lay in making the Mississippi fashionable among a French aristocracy that had lacked a focus of interest since the death of the king yet remained with little purpose 'in ostentatious leisure at the capital'. Law tantalized the aristocracy not only with the hope of new profits but also with the opportunity to do good via a missionary effort in Louisiana; to reinforce the message, his ships returned with 'specimen Indians' he then displayed in the salons of Paris.[16]

English investors sent substantial sums to France to be a part of this frenetic exchange of money and fantasy. Worried about the loss of its capital, the South Sea Company borrowed some of Law's methods, including selling on the margin. In 1719, the directors of the South Sea Company proposed to take over the entire national debt. To do this they would convince investors to exchange their bonds and annuities for South Sea stock. As the market waited to hear Parliament's response, South Sea shares increased in price. After Parliament accepted, a flood of other new companies appeared, each offering future riches based on ever more flimsy schemes. The excitement spread; over 100 new English companies appeared in May and 87 more in June, many with improbable plans for 'trading in hair', importing broomsticks, gathering salt peter from human waste and, most implausible of all, a company 'for carrying on an undertaking of great advantage but no one to know what it is'. Banished from the Royal Exchange itself, shares in these fanciful companies were traded by 'stock jobbers' in nearby Exchange Alley.[17]

Meanwhile, the South Sea Company continued to issue new shares. The stock price, chronicled in the Boston papers at a two to three month delay, rose rapidly from £128 in January. An issue of 2 million shares at £300 in mid-April vanished within an hour. In the first two days of June, the price soared from £610 to £870, even as Law's Mississippi Company was showing signs of trouble; its share value had fallen from 9,000 to 6,000 livres in about a month. When Law devalued French currency by 50 per cent, disturbances broke out in Paris and the French were forced 'to pose Guards in the Market-Places of this City, to prevent Tumults'. In spite of the spectre of French disaster, the price of South Sea stock had risen to near £1,000 by mid-June. A new issue on 15 June for 50 million at £1,000 per share required only a 10 per cent deposit and sold out within a few hours. More than half of the members of Parliament had purchased shares.[18] Ironically, as the financial frenzy continued, trade itself dwindled and during that Bubble summer more than 100 vessels sat at anchor along the Thames, for sale or virtually abandoned.[19]

Through the summer, as the Company became unable to meet its promised returns of 30–50 per cent, the speculative bubble began to deflate. By the end of September, the price of South Sea Company stock had fallen to under £200 per share.[20] Bankruptcies listed in the *London Gazette* reached an all-time high. The mounting concern prompted Daniel Defoe to coin the term 'South Sea Face' worn by those mourning the loss of short-lived gains. A modern author described the 'economic confusion of the last three months of 1720 . . . as a tangle of ruined credit sprawled over the country like a vast, overgrown beanstalk, withering.'[21]

Most Americans escaped direct involvement in the South Sea Bubble; for them it was a spectator sport to be enjoyed in the pages of a newspaper or in conversation at coffee houses and taverns. For some, the Bubble provided an explanation for a depression in Philadelphia that most historians now attribute to a glutted market for grain in the West Indies. However, the scandal of rampant self-interest and the uncertainty associated with financial speculation readily spilled over into the colonial discussions about paper money.[22] Underlying these debates lay the unsettling question of how to negotiate value in the financial marketplace.

The South Sea Bubble became an icon of danger for Americans who mistrusted the unpredictable nature of the future and doubted the benefits of change. Pamphleteers caught up in currency debates in Boston used references to the Bubble as a symbol of all that was wrong with paper credit and as evidence for the disaster that would ensue if paper credit replaced tangible metal coin. In *The Second Part of South-Sea Stock*, printed in Boston in 1721 – just a few months after the Bubble, an anonymous author recounts the dizzying effects of stock speculation. 'When I heard of Men of low Degree, being advanced to their Coaches; What could I think but the World is turning upside down.' He deplored the diversion of capital from commerce to investments, noting 'The Trade of the city of London, one of the finest in the World, hath been very much shortened, few Ships have been built, or fitted to Sea, during the Reign of the South-Sea company.' The purported author, John Higginson, may have recognized the value of trade, in part through knowledge of his elder kinsman Nathaniel Higginson who had amassed a fortune through private trade in India.[23]

To the pamphleteer, it was not only England that had turned upside down. Higginson asked 'why do I talk of South-Sea stock only, is not Mississippi Stock as bad, or worse, Are not Holland, and Spain, and others contriving to be at the same Sport?' In fact, Higginson would have it that all of the Western World was caught up in this treasure hunt: 'Truly, as far as I can learn, the Greatest part of Europe, is infatuated with the same spirit.' He also echoed the swiftness of disaster, when he noted, 'all of a sudden the Scale is turned; the next News is that abundance are broke by the fall of Stocks.' In Paris and the French ports, 'they tell you, all things are so exceeding dear, that the People are brought into great want, they cant get food to Eat, nor Fewel for the Fire.' And certainly paper bills were no help, because, 'The People who have such things [food and fuel] hoard them up, rather than take Paper-Money for them.' Drawing on accounts from the newspapers, the author used the South Sea and Mississippi Bubbles as a means of illustrating the danger of paper money, not only abroad but also in provincial Massachusetts. The scare tactics did not work and Massachusetts issued a flood of paper currency that was often not accepted by the leading merchants and only contributed to the economic problems. The distressed state of the economy reinforced people's fears of rapid change and the deceptive promise of bills and stocks.[24]

The Bubble dramatically confirmed that fortunes could disappear as quickly as they arrived. During the same year as the financial collapse of the South Sea Bubble (1720), the *Boston Gazette* reported on a company of London merchants 'in pain' at the loss of a commercial vessel 'richly laden from Turkey'. Just a few weeks later a storm destroyed the 'homeward bound London Fleet' from Jamaica, driving several of the ships ashore on the western end of Cuba; 150 lucky seamen survived but between 200 and 300 perished along with an inestimable value of goods. The same issue of the *Gazette* informed readers that a Spanish privateer captured a Boston ship loaded with lumber, fish and oil.[25]

Later that summer, news arrived that pirates had ruined most of the fishing vessels in Newfoundland. The story as described in Philadelphia's *American Weekly Mercury* seems scarcely credible. After reportedly destroying 30 French and British vessels on the Grand Banks, a pirate sloop carrying 160 men and 12 guns terrorized an entire harbour for days on end – a harbour filled with 22 large sailing vessels and 250 small runabouts. The unnamed villain imprisoned ships' masters and cut the shrouds and stays so none could sail out of his reach. In spite of advanced knowledge of the pirate's movements and intentions, the residents and ships of Trepassey on the south-eastern tip of Newfoundland were 'so Confounded that they could not put themselves in a posture of Defence' even though there were 1,200 men and 40 guns among the ships in port. The sailors who gave witness to the events from offshore decamped when they saw a 'great smoak' rising from the harbour indicating the pirate had carried out his threat to burn all vessels but his own. The *Boston Gazette*'s much shorter account of the Newfoundland disaster was also accompanied by reports of a ship headed from London to Boston limping into port after being attacked by pirates who ignominiously hoisted a black banner with a white death's head, the traditional pirate flag, over the wounded vessel. Via London came an account of a British slave ship taken by pirates off the coast of 'Guiney' where 'pirates have done great Damage and . . . ruin commerce, to the great Detriment of our Merchants'.[26] In these reports, British and American merchants shared a common risk at the hands of scandalous predators.

Storms, disease, privateers and pirates took a significant toll on commercial profits and continually reminded dwellers of busy Atlantic seaports that trade was a risky business; riches quickly gained could just as easily be lost. The term 'adventure', used to denote investment in a ship's cargo and passage, like the word bubble, signified the risks associated with commercial and financial speculation and scandal in distant places – risks that were brought home in the pages of local newspapers, in the tallies of lost cargoes and in the memorials to missing sailors enacted and re-enacted in ports throughout the Atlantic world.

Colonial newspapers also attempted to represent events beyond the Atlantic world. Information from Asia appeared less frequently in American newspapers. In the *Boston News-Letter*, Campbell noted, 'We have very seldom any Advices from the Indies, for their being no

Intercourse of Communication by Post with those Countries.' In the view of Campbell and his compatriots, it was not for want of enterprise that little Asian intelligence appeared. Rather, it was 'by reason of the Tyrannical Governments in the East' which not only controlled their own people but also kept a tight rein on news about the uprisings and rebellions against what many British American readers viewed as 'Eastern despotism'. As a result, Campbell explained, knowledge of 'several remarkable Events, that happen in those Countries, does very seldom come to us'. The Boston printer went on to recount both a 'Revolution' in Ispahan, 'the Capital City of Persia' and a 'Conspiracy against the Great Mogul' in his capital of Agra.[27]

Campbell frequently complained that 'our Advices from Turkey are very barred... all that we have to observe from thence is' that the Plague 'has swept across Constantinople and that Turkish Forces are on the move in Transylvania.' In spite of his difficulties, Campbell was able to provide detailed descriptions of the diplomatic embassies of Britain and the Holy Roman Empire to the Turkish Court. In March of 1720, he filled a whole column with a detailed list of the gifts given by the Austrian envoy to the Sultan, Sultana and their entourage featuring many clocks and watches, silver and gilt beakers and several large mirrors. Gathered together, these items seemed to be a sumptuous collection but none of these objects would have been completely unfamiliar to the paper's readers. On the other hand, when a later issue described the gifts offered from the Sultan's 'Prime Vizier' to Austria's Prince Eugene, many Boston readers might have puzzled over the 'Tuffet of Hern Feathers... adorned with 71 Diamonds' and been dazzled (or horrified) by the extravagance of a harness and horse collar 'enriched with 494 Diamonds of the largest and middling size' all set in gold or a rosette for the horse's forehead 'set with 155 diamonds and 14 rubies'. From the printed information, Bostonians could form a mental picture of the 'large and sumptuous tent' of white and yellow satin trimmed in green and covered with a top of red and white striped fabric. The tent had latticed windows made of silver wire and sported tent poles 'covered with Mother [of] Pearl and Tortoiseshell' topped with silver knobs all held together with ropes of red and blue silk. Exactly how they might have responded to the final item listed – a gift of 'Two Lyons' – we do not know. However, the myriad of gifts encrusted with jewels and covered with sumptuous gold-embroidered fabrics portrayed a kind of orientalist fantasy that seemed radically different from the bustling port of Boston. Even the grandeur visible in wealthy merchant Andrew Faneuil's stone mansion and garden surmounted by a fashionable summer-house seemed simple and modest in comparison to the display of (foreign) Turkish opulence recorded in the *Boston News-Letter*. Yet the very act of reading allied Bostonians with their transatlantic cousins as imperial spectators.[28]

In her study of the development of an imperial consciousness in Britain, Kathleen Wilson argues that by the 1740s and 1750s newspapers created 'an "imagined community" of producers, distributors, and consumers on both sides of the Atlantic who shared an avid interest in the fate of the "empire of goods" that linked them together'. She sees a 'cartographic mania' in the proliferation of maps, gazetteers and trade directories and in the attention to foreign and imperial affairs in print culture.[29] But in the 1720s, the sole American newspapers in Boston and Philadelphia, while clearly constructing an international community of English-language readers, also reinforced the difference between the heady atmosphere of Georgian London and cosmopolitan Paris and the provincial culture of colonial ports. In London and Paris, intangible 'credit', often portrayed with a female identity as the goddess Fortuna or 'Lady Credit', promised infinite possibilities. In the seaports of America, possibilities took on a more concrete form of ships' cargoes piled on the wharfs of prosperous merchants or sailors and goods foundered in the depths of the ocean.[30]

Foreign news did not centre exclusively on financial and commercial matters, nor was John Law the only celebrity to be created by the press. The movements of British aristocrats were followed like those of present-day Hollywood celebrities. News of the Duke of Chandos, who profited notoriously from the South Sea Bubble, appeared numerous times in the colonial papers. In one issue of the *American Weekly Mercury* from 1727 for example, Americans learned that the Earl of Berkeley was 'dangerously indisposed' at his country seat at Cranford, that the Marquis Carnarvon, son and heir apparent to the Duke of Chandos, had arrived from Hanover, that one of the 'Royal Yachts' will carry the Earl of Sunderland to Scotland and that Windsor Castle is readying to receive 'their Majesty's, who design to go thither for a short Time'. From that same issue readers also learned that the infamous South Sea Company had captured an exceptionally large 'Sea-Horse' (they meant sea lion) that rendered into 50 gallons of oil with preserved tusks 'near a Yard long'; the Company also saved 'a Bone taken out of its Penis' that was at least 2 feet long.[31] Few aristocrats could compete with that.

Aristocrats (and natural oddities) were not the only kind of celebrities to crowd the pages of American newspapers. As might be expected in provincial ports of the Atlantic world, the colonial press revered British naval heroes. The exploits of Admiral Edward Vernon spread across the columns of early American newspapers, especially during the years 1739–41 – a crucial time in Britain's ongoing struggle with Spain and France. In September 1739, the *Boston Post Boy (BPB)* printed a dispatch declaring that Captain Vernon was spotted off the coast of Portugal with orders to 'Take, Sink, and Destroy all Spanish Vessels', which signalled to local readers that war with Spain was near. A month later, another Boston paper trumpeted Vernon's promotion to Rear Admiral of the Blue. In December, a report from Spain observed that Vernon and his fleet had not been seen for several days, causing some to assume he had sailed for the West Indies.[32]

Vernon-watching continued in the Boston and New York newspapers, with constant speculation on just where he would mount an attack against either the French or Spanish and detailing his preparations for such an event. In early January of 1740 the papers reported that Vernon was spotted in Jamaica preparing for an attack on the Spanish colonial empire. The *New York Weekly Journal (NYWJ)* and several other papers published a list of the ships in the Admiral's fleet with his own flagship the *Burford* with 70 guns heading the roster. Speculation continued in the public prints about which Spanish locations he would target, with Porto Bello (the Panamanian port where vessels with Peruvian silver embarked for Spain) and Cartagena, Colombia, the most frequent candidates. In mid-February, the *Boston News-Letter* reprinted a portion of a letter from an officer in Vernon's fleet at Jamaica detailing extensive preparations, but even the officer did not know the intended destination. The unnamed officer did portray the heightened intensity of those under the Admiral's leadership, saying, 'Revenge is the general Cry among us.' He also reinforced the heroic image of Vernon, writing, 'we are headed by a Gentleman who knows well how to lay a Scheme, and as well to Execute it.'[33]

A month later, the *New York Weekly Journal* published a long, two-column account of preparations, conditions and speculations about the fleet which had just left its port in Jamaica. The article was based on the descriptions of a Captain Fowles who had just arrived in New York from Jamaica. Fowles described the British land forces that had joined the naval vessels and lamented the 2,000 sick and dying men that had had to be left behind. He added further confusion to the conjectures about the fleet's destination by noting that some thought Vernon was out to destroy the French fleet. About the same time, in what may have been an unrecognized journalist coup, the *Boston Evening Post (BEP)* reported from masters of two ships that had just arrived in Massachusetts an account of the 'brave action' of Admiral Vernon in the taking of Porto

Bello. After destroying the fort and munitions, Vernon generously preserved the town from 'Pillage and burning' in return for a ransom of 3 million pieces of eight. The same article, reprinted almost word for word, appeared the following day in the *New England Weekly Journal* and two weeks later surfaced in the New York papers. Immediately following his victory, the Admiral had dispatched a ship to England with the news but, in this case, the information no doubt reached New England first. This extended by-play of reportage demonstrated not only the brave action of the heroic Vernon but also the complex circulation of news among printer-publishers in provincial and metropolitan cities.[34]

The following year, after many more columns of speculation about his next action, Vernon lay siege to Cartagena on the coast of Colombia. He was unsuccessful but that barely dimmed his lustre among his British and colonial admirers. In 1741, the *Boston Evening Post* reported London's 'extraordinary Rejoicings...in Honour of Admiral Vernon's birthday'. Bonfires blazed throughout the city and its suburbs to the extent that 'the High Streets...seem'd all in a Flame...whilst Bells were ringing, and Guns firing without'. Within, the taverns 'had their various Companies carousing over their Bottles and Bowls, with Healths to his Majesty, the Royal family, Admiral Vernon, and all true Patriots'. Since colonists also loved to raise a glass, it is likely that huzzahs to Vernon could be heard in North American ports as well.[35]

The Admiral's fame reached beyond the newspapers and the taverns; in 1741 a periodical entitled *The General Magazine and Historical Chronicle for all the British Plantations in America* published a collection of 'Poetical Essays' that included 'A Ballad to Admiral Vernon' originally from the *London Gazette*. The ballad was followed by a poem taken from the *Boston Post Boy* entitled 'On the Taking of Porto-Bello by Admiral Vernon' that portrayed the hero as 'Britannia's Genius'.[36] More than 100 years after the reporting of the Virginia Massacre, as described by Catherine Armstrong,[37] the same news derivatives – ballads, chapbooks, verse and hastily penned catch-pieces – bolstered the fame of a foreign episode – and of a patriotic hero – but now on an entirely new scale.

To this day, Vernon's name remains closely linked with American historical memory. George Washington's elder brother served under Vernon during the siege against Cartagena, and when he inherited the family estate, he honoured 'his admiral, from whom he had received many civilities' by naming his new mansion Mount Vernon.[38] Thus, a landmark named in honour of a celebrated British military hero is visited daily by American schoolchildren as the home of a founding father.

In spite of Vernon's fame, Admiral George Anson most fully captured the Anglo-American image of a heroic figure. Anson published his exploits in *A Voyage Round the World in the Years MDCCXL, I, II, III, IV*. *A Voyage Round the World* offered a traveller's account – of peoples in the New World and Asia – combined with a sea adventure. Anson's chronicle of his four-year voyage quickly became a bestseller after it was published in 1748. Five editions appeared in London during the first year. It was soon translated into French and published in Paris here in 1749.[39]

A Voyage Round the World was a bestseller in America as well.[40] In the 1750s and 1760s, a reader could have found Anson's *A Voyage Round the World* in Philadelphia at the Union Library and in the stock of the two leading purveyors of books – David Hall and William Bradford, who advertised it extensively in local newspapers.[41] Bradford even offered the account in the form of an inexpensive chapbook. In New York, readers could have located the volume in Garrett Noel's offerings of 'polite literature' or in the New York Society Library. The collection of the Charleston Library Society included a copy; the sea captains and merchants of Newport Rhode Island read about Anson's disastrous passage around Cape Horn at the Redwood Library Company; while the scientifically inclined might have found Anson among the collection of books and 'Philosophical Instruments' belonging to the Juliana Library-Company in Lancaster. In nearby Philadelphia, Thomas Mathias offered 'a curious collection of perspective views, done in the highest taste...on the principles of Sir Isaac Newton's' Opticks', including 'the form of Chinese shipping' and the 'watering places' Commodore Anson came to anchor during 'his voyage into the great south sea'. After the American Revolution, libraries and booksellers in Philadelphia, New York, Boston and Salem, Massachusetts, continued to stock Anson's account; Thomas Jefferson had a copy at Monticello which, after 1815, resided with Jefferson's other books donated to the Library of Congress.[42]

Even before publication of his book, Anglo-Americans had followed Anson's adventures in the pages of their local newspapers. Printer-publishers grabbed the opportunity to recount Anson's vaunted exploits. Reports of his fortunes or misfortunes appeared in colonial newspapers throughout his four-year passage. In 1742, the *Pennsylvania Gazette* published an account of 'Commodore Anson's Misfortunes, in his voyage to the South Seas' describing the difficult passage around Cape Horn accompanied by 'hard Winds, Snow and Sleet with a great Sea' and 'so many Sails slit and blown away,...and their Rigging and Shrouds all broke' that two of the six ships were forced to turn back.

The description, published under a Boston byline, was based on a letter from a British naval officer in Brazil 'by the Way of Lisbon'.[43] The *South Carolina Gazette* printed an 'abridgment' of Anson's *Voyage*, parcelled out in a series of issues in 1750.[44]

Much of Anson's story focused on harrowing experiences with violent storms in the desolate territories around Cape Horn at the southern tip of South America where they encountered 'a continual succession of such tempestuous weather, as surprized the oldest and most experienced Mariners'. The 'violence of the winds' brought with them a great quantity of snow and sleet that 'cased our rigging and froze our sails'. Not only did the winds shred the sails but it put 'the men in perpetual danger of being dashed to pieces against the decks, or sides of the ship'. The storms 'raised such short, and ... mountainous waves, as greatly surpassed in danger all seas known in any other part of the globe' and 'filled us with continual terror'.[45] After surviving the passage around Cape Horn, the commander and his seamen sacked a Peruvian city called Paita. The Spanish were so impressed by Anson's refusal to kill all the inhabitants that he 'acquired a distinguished reputation ... which is not confined merely to the coast of the South-Seas'. Apparently his reputation endured for generations; in 1821, a British naval officer reported 'that the kindness with which that officer [Anson] invariably treated his Spanish prisoners' was still 'dwelt upon by the inhabitants of Payta.'[46]

Capturing the Acapulco–Manila galleon proved to be Anson's most important achievement in the eyes of Anglo-Americans and the British state as well. The 'Manila galleon' made an annual voyage from Mexico to Manila and back. Loaded with silver and pieces of eight in Mexico, the vessel traversed the Pacific (the South Sea) to Manila where merchants used the money to pay for luxury items such as Chinese silks and Indian cottons gathered from the inter-Asian or 'country trade'. A large Chinese expatriate community in Manila, estimated at 20,000 by Anson, played a key role in supplying the Spanish with their return goods. The annual galleon carried Asian goods back to the New World where they supplied the Spanish colonists in Mexico and Peru and, after 1760, consumers in Europe as well.[47]

In 1744, off Cape Espirito Santo south-east of Manila, Anson in his *Centurion* succeeded in capturing the much larger galleon *Nostra Signora de Cabadonga*, with over £1 million of silver and gold on board.[48] The treasure was purchased at the cost of over 1,300 seamen, most of whom died from scurvy and other diseases during Anson's voyage. Anson was forced to seek food supplies and repairs in China before returning to England with his prize in tow. On his return to England Anson received acclaim and promotions; he was later knighted and placed on the Board of Admiralty – the highest post a British naval officer could hope to achieve.[49]

American readers gained a rare glimpse of China through newspaper accounts of Anson's experiences. In *A Voyage Round the World*, Anson limned a rather negative portrayal of the Chinese that received wide attention. At base, Anson's account was shaped by commercial interests. When the Chinese bureaucracy stymied his efforts to resupply his vessel, he condemned their character and culture. Chinese mistreatment of Anson, combined with his descriptions of 'the perfidy of their Mandarines, the venality of their courts of justice, and the fraud of their traders' presented a very negative representation of the Chinese that contrasted with earlier positive depictions influenced by admiration for Chinese craftsmanship and by sympathetic Jesuit writings from China. A shortened version of Anson's visit to China appeared in the *South Carolina Gazette*. The paper noted that Chinese locals regarded 'the English Commodore as no better than a powerful pirate'.[50] The *Boston Evening Post* included an extract from one of Anson's letters printed in the *London Gazette* about his experiences in China; this letter emphasized Anson's successes rather than the failures and frustrations expressed in *A Voyage Round the World*. In the letter Anson claimed that the Chinese 'Vice-King received me with great Civility and Politeness, having 10,000 soldiers drawn up, and his Council of Mandarines attending the Audience, and granted me everything I desired.'[51] However, the popularity of Anson's *A Voyage Round the World* and its serialized reviews and abridgments combined to disseminate a critical portrayal of the Chinese people, while leaving Anson's reputation unblemished. In 1763, the occasion of Anson's death offered another opportunity to salute the naval hero. The *Boston Evening Post* published 'An Account of the Life of the late Lord Anson' that included a short section on his relations with the Chinese authorities – a somewhat more benign account than the book had portrayed.[52]

American admiration for Anson extended beyond the written page. In Charleston, South Carolina, as the city expanded, a neighbourhood called Ansonborough was laid out in honour of the Admiral with streets bearing the names of each of his vessels. Anson had worked as a young naval officer commanding a British ship in Charleston's harbour from 1724–35, defending shipping against pirates and potential Spanish incursions. At that time he acquired a tract of land north of town. It was on this property, in 1746, as Anson's fame spread throughout the British Empire, that Ansonborough arose. Streets named George and Anson honoured the Admiral while Scarborough, Squirrel, and Centurion memorialized the ships he had commanded.[53] An American real estate development mapped the Admiral's fame onto the suburbs of Charleston, thus reinforcing heroic bonds of empire through local signs.

Although most Americans did not participate directly in the South Sea Bubble nor have any immediate connection to events at the Ottoman Court, they followed foreign events closely through the pages of newspapers and conversations in coffee houses. Imported calicoes and disasters at sea often had more immediate consequences however. Combined in the pages of weekly gazettes, accounts of scandalous speculation, advertisements of 'East-India goods just imported from London' and encomiums to British admirals made clear the interconnection of colonial American ports with the larger project of European empire. Nevertheless, local interpretations also disclosed a negotiation with, rather than a simple acceptance of, metropolitan culture. The circulation of print, particularly visible in the history of Anson's *A Voyage Round the World*, from newspaper accounts, to printed volumes available to a somewhat smaller circle via circulating and social libraries, and back to the newspapers in booksellers' advertisements, indicates both the extent of transatlantic connections and their limitations as well. The provinces were still dependent on the metropole to generate the majority of the content. Colonial newspapers continued, until mid-century, to privilege foreign news even as they interpreted it in relation to their own provincial concerns. As they translated foreign scandals into local contests over paper money or adopted British heroes by mapping them onto the colonial landscape, Americans also confronted the changing nature of the scandalous and heroic that accompanied their membership in an expanding British Empire.

Notes

1. Carrier's address, Broadside, Philadelphia: Printed by Andrew Bradford (1734).
2. See for example, Bernard Bailyn, *Atlantic History: Concepts and Contours* (Cambridge, MA, 2005).
3. On riots of London cloth-workers, see Beverly Lemire, *Fashion's Favourite: The Cotton Trade and the Consumer In Britain, 1660–1800* (Oxford, 1991) On reports in colonial American newspapers, see Phyllis Whitman Hunter, *Purchasing Identity in the Atlantic World: Massachusetts Merchants, 1670–1780* (Ithaca, NY, 2001): 100–1.
4. Charles Clark in his important work on early American newspapers argues that the readership reached well beyond the target audience. Not only were newspapers discussed and read aloud but were also saved, bound

and sometimes annotated. Charles E. Clark, *The Public Prints: The News-paper in Anglo-American Culture, 1665–1740* (New York, 1994): 245–8; for a British provincial comparison, see the list of newspapers available along with 'Coffee, Tea, [and] Chocolate' as advertised by Child's coffeehouse in Salisbury, C. Y. Ferdinand, 'Selling It to the Provinces: News and Commerce Round Eighteenth-Century Salisbury', in John Brewer and Roy Porter (eds), *Consumption and the World of Good* (London, 1993): 393–411, 401.

5. See Hunter, *Purchasing Identity*, 142, 145; On growth of social and circulating libraries in England, see James Raven, *Judging New Wealth: Popular Publishing and Responses to Commerce in England, 1750–1800* (Oxford, 1992); and James Raven, 'Libraries for Sociability: The Advance of the Subscription Library, c. 1700–1850', in Giles Mandelbrote and Keith Manley (eds), *The History of Libraries in Britain and Ireland*, vol. 2 (Cambridge, 2006): 241–63.

6. *Boston Gazette*, 29 Feb–7 Mar 1726 (all dates given are new style).

7. On the early newspapers, see Ian K. Steele, *The English Atlantic 1675–1740: An Exploration of Communication and Community*, ch. 8 (Oxford, 1986); on comparisons with early British provincial newspapers, see Clark, *Public Prints*, 57–64.

8. *Boston News-Letter*, 7 May 1705; on Bradford's regional goal, see *American Weekly Mercury*, 16 Feb, 23 Feb and 1 Mar 1720.

9. *BNL*, 4 Jan 1720. Of Boston's first and until 1719, its only newspaper, Clark says 'by far the greatest amount of space...was taken up by for-eign news' often 'copied straight out of the London newspapers'. However, in developing his argument about early American newspapers as 'a ritual expression of community', Clark downplays the importance of information and correspondence from commercial sources. Clark, *Public Prints*, 79, 96, 82–3.

10. *AWM*, 16 Feb 1720 and 23 Mar 1720.

11. See for example, 'Just imported from London, in the Ship Speedwell...A NEAT Assortment of European and India goods'. *Pennsylvania Gazette*, 19 Jul 1750; '*Just* Imported in the Ship Mary, Capt. Martin, from **LONDON**. A Choice Parcel of Copper Stills', *Pennsylvania Gazette*, 22 Jan 1745.

12. See above, pp. 28–9.

13. *BG*, 29 Feb–7 Mar 1720; 16–23 May 1720.

14. John Carswell, *The South Sea Bubble* (Stanford, CA, 1960): 68, 65–6, 84–5; Immanuel Wallerstein, *Mercantilism and the Consolidation of the European World-Economy, 1600–1750* (New York, 1980): 255; *BNL*, 15–22 Jun 1720; Edward Chancellor, *Devil Take the Hindmost: A History of Financial Speculation* (New York, 1999): 60–1; Peter Garber, *Famous First Bubbles: The Fundamentals of Early Manias* (Cambridge, MA, 2000): 89–113; see also, Richard Dale, *The First Crash: Lessons from the South Sea Bubble* (Princeton, NJ, 2004).

15. *BNL*, 15–22 Jun 1720; *BNL*, 8–11 Jul 1720; *BNL*, 8–11 Jul 1720.

16. *BG*, 25 Jul–1 Aug; *BNL*, 1–8 Aug 1720; Carswell, *South Sea Bubble*, 86.

17. Carswell, *South Sea Bubble*, 156; *BG*, 11–18 Jul 1720; Chancellor, *Devil Take the Hindmost*, 71–2. Chancellor's figures disagree with the May number but do support the figure of 87 new proposals for June.

18. Garber, *Famous First Bubbles*, 96–103; *BNL*, 8–15 Aug 1720; Carswell, *South Sea Bubble*, 156–7; in some instances one paper could trump the competition as did the *BG* when it reported 'We have private Letters in Town that say the

South Sea Stock was Nine Hundred.' *BG*, 15–22 Aug 1720; Chancellor, *Devil Take the Hindmost*, 67, 73.

19. Carswell, *South Sea Bubble*, 156–7, 191, 195; Chancellor, *Devil Take the Hindmost*, 67, 73, 76–7; Max Weber quoted in Wallerstein, *Mercantilism and the Consolidation*, 2: 282.

20. Various accounts give values that range from £135 to £185 and £200.

21. Carswell, *South Sea Bubble*, 156–7, 191, 195; Chancellor, *Devil Take the Hindmost*, 67, 73, 76–7; some who sold out early did well: The Duke of Chandos reportedly gained £30,000 'as he formerly did by Mississippi'. *BG*, 16–23 May, 1720.

22. Gary B. Nash, *The Urban Crucible: Social Change, Political Consciousness, and the Origins of the American Revolution* (Cambridge, MA, 1979): 119.

23. [John Higginson] *The Second Part of South-Sea Stock. Being an Inquiry into the Original of Province Bills or Bills of Credit* (Boston, MA: for D. Henchman, 1721). Reprinted in Andrew McFarland Davis, *Colonial Currency Reprints, 1682–1751*, 4 vols (Boston, 1910–11), 2: 304–05.

24. [Higginson], *Second Part of South-Sea Stock*; Davis, *Currency Reprints*, 2: 305, 317.

25. *BG*, 20–27 Jun 1720; 25 Jul–1 Aug 1720; 15–22 Aug 1720.

26. *AWM*, 22 Sept 1720; *BNL*, 11–18 Jul 1720.

27. *BNL*, 9–13 Jun 1720.

28. *BNL*, 9–13 Jun 1720; *BNL*, 7 Mar 1720; *BNL*, 9 May 1720.

29. Kathleen Wilson, 'The Good, the Bad, and the Impotent: Imperialism and the Politics of Identity in Georgian England', in Ann Bermingham and John Brewer (eds), *The Consumption of Culture 1600–1800: Image, Object, Text* (London, 1995): 237–62, 240–2. Here Wilson is drawing on Benedict Anderson's concept of nationalism as an imagined community. Benedict Anderson, *Imagined Communities: Reflections on the Origin and Spread of Nationalism*, rev. edn (New York, 1991). For a somewhat different viewpoint, see T. H. Breen, *The Marketplace of Revolution: How Consumer Politics Shaped American Independence* (Oxford, 2004).

30. On the portrayal of credit as feminine, see Catherine Ingrassia, *Authorship, Commerce, and Gender in Early Eighteenth-Century England: A Culture of Paper Credit* (Cambridge, 1998): 20–28; Laura Brown, *Ends of Empire: Women and Ideology in Early Eighteenth-Century English Literature* (Ithaca, NY, 1993): 44–5; On credit and Fortuna, see Ruth H. Bloch, 'The Gendered Meanings of Virtue in Revolutionary America', *Signs* 13 (1987): 37–58.

31. *AWM*, 16–23 Nov 1727.

32. *BPB*, 9 Sept 1741; *BNL*, 4–11 Oct 1739; *BG*, 29 Nov–3 Dec 1739.

33. *BPB*, 7 Jan 1740; *NYWJ*, 14 Jan 1740; *BNL*, 17–24 Jan 1740; *NEWJ*, 8 Jan 1740; *BNL*, 7–14 Feb 1740.

34. *NYWJ*, 16 Mar 1740; *BEP*, 17 Mar 1740; *NEWJ*, 18 Mar 1740; *NYWJ*, 31 Mar 1740; *NEWJ*, 18 Mar 1740.

35. *BEP*, 2 Feb 1741.

36. 'A Ballad to Admiral Vernon' (from the London *Daily Gazetteer*), 'On the taking [*sic*] Porto-Bello by Admiral Vernon', (from *BPB*), in 'Poetical Essays, &c.', *The General Magazine and Historical Chronicle for all the British Plantations in America*, Mar 1741.

37. See above, ch. 2.

38. 'Memoirs of George Washington, Esq.' *The Philadelphia Monthly Magazine; or, Universal Repository of Knowledge and* . . . Jan 1798, 3.

39. Paul Mapp, 'French Reactions to the British Search for a Northwest Passage from Hudson Bay and the Origins of the Seven Years War', *Terrae Incognitae* 33 (2001): 13–32, 18, 21. Mapp argues that Anson's voyage and British efforts to find a Northwest passage to the Pacific convinced the French of a British conspiracy to take control of the Pacific.

40. In my study in progress of 38 book catalogues published between 1717 and 1829, from booksellers, social, circulating and private libraries in colonial and early national America, Anson's *Voyage* showed up in 24 of the 31 catalogues published after 1748. It appeared in more catalogues than any of the other works that included substantive information about Asia (information derived from a database of library catalogues and booksellers' advertisements compiled by the author).

41. See for example, 'Just imported in the Two Last Ships from London, and to be Sold by DAVID HALL, at the Post Office, the Following Books, viz.' *Pennsylvania Gazette*, 10 Dec 1751; [William Bradford], *Catalogue of books Just Imported from London and to be Sold by W. Bradford, at the London-Coffee-House* (Philadelphia, PA, n.d. [1760]).

42. *The South Carolina Gazette*, 16–23 Apr 1750; *Pennsylvania Gazette*, 23 Jan 1750.

43. George Anson, *A Voyage Round the World in the Years MDCCXL, I, II, III, IV,* Glyndwr Williams (ed.) (London, 1974); *Pennsylvania Gazette*, 27 Jan 1742.

44. *The South Carolina Gazette*, 16–23 Apr 1750.

45. Anson, *Voyage Round the World*, 85–6.

46. Ibid., 192; and Captain Basil Hall, *Extracts from a Journal Written on the Coasts of Chili, Peru, and Mexico in the Years 1820, 1821, 1822*, 2 vols (London, 1824), 2: 99 quoted in Anson, *Voyage Round the World*, 383.

47. On the Spanish galleon and the world-wide circulation of goods and money, see Andre Gunder Frank, *Reorient: Global Economy in the Asian Age* (Berkeley, CA, c. 1998) and Kenneth Pomeranz, *The Great Divergence: Europe, China, and the Making of the Modern World Economy* (Princeton, NJ, 2000).

48. Anson, *Voyage Round the World*, 338–40. Williams estimated the value aboard the Spanish galleon at about £3,000,000 in 1974. 'Introduction', xvi.

49. Williams, 'Introduction', *Voyage Round the World*, xv–xvi.

50. *The South Carolina Gazette*, 16–23 Apr 1750.

51. *BEP*, 29 Oct 1744 from the *Gentleman's Magazine* (London) June 1744.

52. 'An Account of the Life of the late Lord Anson', *BEP*, 3 Jan 1763.

53. George C. Rogers, *Charleston in the Age of the Pinckneys* (Norman, OK, 1969): 57.

5

Print and Manuscript in French Canada under the Ancien Régime

François Melançon

No printing press was set up in the Laurentian valley of North America, the colony known as New France, until the late date of 1764.[1] That date has become important in the historiography of the book and of printing in Canada, a reference point signifying a cultural break between a French past, little affected by print culture, and a very different English future. In fact, the history of the book in Canada under the French colonial regime is still relatively unknown and evidence is scarce (as in other French colonies of the seventeenth and eighteenth centuries). The commonplace, and oversimplified, explanation of what was actually a remarkable but complex phenomenon is well illustrated by a passage from the work of a pioneer of research on the book in Canada: 'Before 1764, there was neither a printing press nor a bookstore in New France, though books were being imported by institutions and individuals. Only after the Conquest did printing presses, the book trade and libraries develop.'[2] In the same vein, it is worth quoting a 1976 review of the history of New France that discusses colonial relationships with books:

> Cultural objects, whether for decoration or instruction, were profoundly marked by French traditions. Often they were imported directly from the mother country. The Jesuit missionaries ordered paintings and images from Europe that they used in evangelizing the 'savages' and propagating the Catholic faith. The few paintings decorating the churches came from France or had been executed by Frenchmen.... The same was true of literature. The books gracing the libraries of the few people of substance had all been published in Europe.... Common folk made do with oral literature. There was little circulation of chapbooks.[3]

But 1764 did not bring about such a revolutionary transformation, because the printed word had long been circulating in New France, and its means of production was already accessible, albeit with difficulty.

To advance beyond the commonplace, we must first place the study of the book in New France in the social and political context that gives it meaning, that of the kingdom of France. The colony, we must remember, was a modest spot on the vast map of America. The book in Canada was an integral part of the much larger book market of France and of the centralized administration of the French book trade. But the geographical remoteness of the colony from the rest of the kingdom, and the specificity of its social development, represented a rather different cultural space. Together, the unusual nature of colonial settlement, the absence of secular customs, the new exploitation of natural resources that laid the groundwork for economic relations and the necessary amalgamation of cultural traditions introduced new types of engagement with writing and with books.

An economic and cultural framework allows historians of the book to re-appraise early studies of the book in New France and to open up new areas of investigation that offer insights into the social and intellectual life of settlers in French America and their cultural and material universe.[4] In part, the book conveyed knowledge formerly carried by word and gesture. In the colonial context, the book contributed to reinforcing cultural ties to the Old World. While the colonial space allowed and encouraged new experience, the intellectual referents of both State and Church were Old World. Access to the book as cultural object therefore remained crucial. In an emergent colonial society, what place was given to the consumption of what were, in effect, luxury cultural goods? This chapter returns to the problem of the material factors conditioning the circulation of printed books in the colony. It begins with the absence of local means of production, followed by a corollary, the import trade, particularly in the capital, Quebec, which was the hub of commercial activity in the colony.

With few exceptions, all print circulating in New France came from Europe. No full study yet exists of the penetration by newspapers and gazettes from the neighbouring British colonies. It appears however that the administrative authorities of New France were on the lookout for information from these areas, particularly during times of military conflict.[5] As with most manufactured goods, the metropolis enjoyed a monopoly on the production of books and other printed matter. Until the second third of the eighteenth century, no printing press existed in the North American territory of the kingdom of France. Or at least, there remains no direct or indirect trace of one. It therefore seems certain that the first printing house in the Laurentian valley was established shortly after the colony came under British authority in 1764. At the other extremity of the territory, in the Mississippi delta, the printing press also arrived only with the advent of a new political regime. For it was under the Spanish flag that the first printing house opened in New Orleans. Even in the French Caribbean Islands, where early attempts at printing were made in the 1720s, royal authorities waited until the end of the Seven Years War before seriously considering the soundness of such an enterprise in colonial territory. There are few works of historiography on printing in the French colonies of the Americas in the eighteenth century. Most are old and painfully lacking in a comprehensive view of the phenomenon.[6] According to an informant cited in a Detroit newspaper in 1890, there was at the time in East Jordan (Charlevoix County, Michigan) an old printing press that had been discovered in Cross Village (L'Arbre Croche). The printing press had apparently been brought by the Jesuit Pierre Du Jaunay (1704–80) to print religious texts in the Outaouais language. Du Jaunay worked among the Outaouais in the Fort Michillimakinac area (now Mackinaw City, Michigan) from 1735 to 1765. No other document has been found to confirm this.[7]

It has taken time for a historical consensus to emerge in Quebec that the first local printing press was founded under the British regime. Those who viewed the technology of print as 'an integral part of civilization' – indeed an instrument of its hegemony – found it hard to 'conceive that there was a time when it did not exist' in the country.[8] This is why the slightest evidence supporting the notion of printing in Canada *during* the French regime was eagerly welcomed – and reluctantly abandoned.

The history of this refinement of ideas about early printing in Canada has yet to be written. At first glance it seems to have developed in counterpoint to the formalization of literary institutions and to the emergence of a historiography focused on national identity. Interest in the historical roots of the publishing infrastructure of Quebec appeared around the middle of the nineteenth century, in contrast to earlier ignorance and indifference. Witness the absence of any allusion to the subject in the first retrospective bibliography, by Georges-Barthélemi Faribault, published in 1837.[9] Subsequently, the politicization of the dominant historiographical discourse led to a polarization of the two founding events of the world of Quebec publishing: on the one hand, in 1764, the Anglophone establishment of William Brown and Thomas Gilmore in Quebec; and on the other, in 1777, the Francophone establishment of Fleury Mesplet in Montreal. The two events seem stripped of organic connection, as if belonging to completely different time-lines. The various works published by Maximilien Bibaud are revealing. In 1853, in his *Catéchisme de l'histoire du Canada à l'usage des écoles*, the author makes no reference to the printing house of Brown and Gilmore for 1764, while in answer to the question 'What was happening in 1778?', he notes among other events that 'printing was established in Canada by M. Fleury Mesplet, who had exercised his art in Philadelphia, and was on the side of England.'[10] Similarly, in 1857, in his *Dictionnaire historique des hommes illustres du Canada et de l'Amérique*, he makes no mention of Brown or Gilmore, but calls Fleury Mesplet the 'father of printing in Montreal' and refers to John Neilson as the founder of the *Gazette de Québec*. The following year however, in his *Bibliothèque canadienne ou Annales bibliographiques*, he gives the following entry for the year 1764: 'Printing shop established in Quebec – Gazette of Quebec in English and in French';[11] for the years 1766–67: 'P. Labrosse, of the Company of Jesus, had books of prayers, catechisms and alphabets printed up'; and then for 1777: 'French printing shop established in Montreal'; and for 1778: 'Gazette Littéraire de Fleury Mesplet'.

From the 1880s onward, there was increasing interest in the question of the appearance of printing in the Laurentian valley and publication of the colony's incunabula. The flawed translation of a travel account, combined with the discovery of two episcopal works dated 1759, caused much discussion in the small Canadian republic of letters. Louis-Wilfrid Marchand created the initial confusion. In his adaptation and translation[12] of a travel account by the Swedish botanist Pehr Kalm, which appeared in 1880, he ascribed to the traveller a statement destined for a long and active life: 'there are no printing shops in Canada now, though at one time there were'.[13] For generations of scholars, this affirmation would nourish the dream of finding, in an invented New France, the traces of this cultural technology.[14]

The new chronicle of Philéas Gagnon in the July 1888 *Union libérale*, 'Antiquités canadiennes', joined in this symbolic quest for the proofs of cultural maturity. Repeated nearly in whole by the *Toronto Mail* a few days later, it reported the existence of two printed copies of pastorals by Mgr de Pontbriand dating from the final days of the French regime. Though the learned collector reserved judgement as to whether a small private press had been provided to Mgr de Pontbriand by Louis XV, that did not stop him from presenting, in his chronicle of the following December, arguments in favour of the thesis by the archivist of the Quebec archdiocese, Charles-Octave Gagnon. Finally, in 1895 Philéas Gagnon rallied believers by publishing the first volume of his

Essai de bibliographie canadienne. From then on, the idea of the existence of a small printing press for the exclusive needs of the head of the Church in New France haunted Canadian scholars for years. Not until the bibliographical study by Marie Tremaine, in 1952, followed by those by Jean Gagnon and the John Hare/Jean-Pierre Wallot collaboration, was the notion definitively shelved in the closet of historical misinterpretations.[15]

Contemporary evidence in letters by individuals, travel accounts or administrative documents tends to corroborate the absence of a printing press. In a letter addressed to his sister in Limoges, in the autumn of 1737, Reverend Joseph Navières, himself originally from Limoges and at the time the parish priest of St Anne de Beaupré, expressed regret at not having with him certain books that he had left in France, because 'books are as common in France as they are rare in this country, where there is neither a printing shop nor a bookstore'.[16] A little over ten years later, the Swedish botanist Pehr Kalm, sent to North America by Linnaeus, made a similar observation. A good friend of Governor Barrin de La Galissonière, who shared his curiosity for natural science, Kalm noted in his journal, during a stay in the colonial capital, that 'no printing shop exists in Canada, and no one has ever founded one, rather all the books come from France, and all the ordinances published here are written out by hand, including paper money.'[17] Similarly, in 1757 aide-de-camp Louis-Antoine de Bougainville made a point of underscoring, in one of his memoirs on the colonial situation, that 'paper money [...] is printed on the royal presses in Paris', but was silent about the presence or absence in the colony of any establishment for the production and distribution of printed matter. He does mention the existence in Quebec of a 'literary society' and the presence of a professor of hydrography, and lists the colony's various educational establishments. The attention given to these beacons of learned culture makes all the more eloquent his silence about printing presses or merchants who specialized in the sale of books.[18]

Notarial records report the same. The inventories of the imposing collections of books assembled by François-Etienne Cugnet, an administrator, businessman and man of law, and by Attorney General Guillaume Verrier, illustrate the absence of book professionals in the colony.[19] First, in 1751, following the death of Cugnet, the bailiff was assigned another person (apparently a merchant) to help him estimate the value of the books. Then, in 1759, after the death of Verrier, the notary made a point of noting that, after the removal of seals from the door of the cabinet that had served as a library, the inventory and appraisal of the works were simply performed by the bailiff on duty, 'since in this country there are neither bookstores nor experts to do such an appraisal'.[20]

For some members of colonial society, the absence of printing shops was a hindrance to their work. So great, in fact, was the absence felt that some colonists attempted to establish a local press, beginning, in the seventeenth century, with the missionaries. Perhaps the new offensive to evangelize and teach French to the indigenous peoples of North America, led by royal authorities wanting to strengthen the social and religious organization of New France, had something to do with this interest in acquiring the tools of print. The Jesuits of Quebec, who had already published a version in Huron of the Ledesma catechism (printed in Rouen in 1630 and reprinted in the 1632 edition of the travel account of Champlain published by Louis Sevestre in Paris) were by 1665 studying the question seriously. Gathered in council in the fall of that year, they decided 'to write to ask for a printing press here for languages'.[21] The Sulpicians of Montreal apparently did the same some 15 years later, as revealed in a letter by the superior of the mother house in Paris.[22]

And then there is silence. Are the archives hiding something, or did the players lose interest? Impossible to say for the moment. Political and economic instability may have led to a certain *modus vivendi* in the colony. The missionaries resorted to manuscript publication. Both religious and secular administrations opted, depending on need, either for local manuscript publication, which was often more ephemeral and certainly faster (edicts, ordinances, notices), or for printed publication by tradesmen in the metropolis when the authority, credibility and longevity of a document warranted it (various administrative forms). Not until the middle of the eighteenth century does another request to establish a printing shop in the colony appear in the archival record. A sign of the times, on this occasion the request is from the offices of the senior commandant of the period, the Marquis Rolland-Michel Barrin de La Galissonière. As the colony's temporary head of Government, due to the captivity of the official incumbent, he addresses the President of the Council of Marine. Once again, the original request has disappeared from the archives; only the answer remains, and it illustrates the changing nature of the needs expressed by the authorities of the colony. In his letter to the Marquis Taffanel de La Jonquière, who has finally taken up his post as Governor in Quebec, the President reveals the administrative justification for the project proposed by Barrin de La Galissonière: 'M. de La Galissonière has [...] proposed to establish a printing shop in the colony, which he argues would be an asset of great utility for the publication of ordinances and police regulations, for *congés* to give to soldiers [...], and many other purposes.'[23]

All of these attempts resulted in failure. In the case of the Jesuit missionaries in Quebec, we have no evidence as to how their request was received, nor of the reasons invoked to justify the refusal. In fact, we do not even know if the superior of their mission followed up on the decision taken in council. In the case of the Sulpicians, it was the complexity of the printing craft that officially led the Paris administration to reject the request of the Montreal establishment. In a letter of 1683, Louis Tronson explained to François Vachon de Belmont that 'it was decided that it would be useless to send the printing characters you asked for because, we had been told, you would not be able to use them, nor could you learn enough from books to be capable of succeeding.'[24]

For its part, the royal administration justified its decision in more nuanced fashion at the end of the 1740s. This time, economic arguments held sway. The feasibility of the project did not depend on mastery of the technology, but on the availability of capital and the interest of a tradesman. Most significant was the response by the President of the Council of Marine to Barrin de La Galissonière's request: 'the King considering that this is not the time for the expense of such an establishment, you must wait until a printer comes forward; and in that case, I will examine the conditions under which it would be suitable to grant a privilege.'[25] The needs were considered, but the politics required prudence. The royal authorities deferred any direct involvement, while leaving the door open to private initiative. In the meantime they preferred to meet the sporadic needs of the colonial administration by sending printed matter expected to become necessary – playing-card and other monetary notes, forms, and so on. The circulation of print increased rapidly in the final decade of New France, and, above all, the circulation of paper money. The object of repeated requests for over 20 years by local officials responsible for colonial finances, printed money was supposed to replace the traditional playingcard money, which, because it was handwritten, was susceptible to falsification and labour-intensive. There also appeared greater numbers of printed forms for use in general administration, such as bills of lading, soldiers' *congés*, tax receipts and so on. In April 1757, a printer known as Boyssoun was authorized to travel to New France. Should this be seen as a major turnaround by the royal authorities? In the absence of further evidence we cannot be sure, but the conjuncture is suggestive.[26]

Some historians view this absence of a local press as the manifestation of a concerted will on the part of royal and religious authorities to muzzle written communication in New France.[27] Others, and they are many, seek an explanation in the economic and demographic contingencies of colonial life: the sheer labour of clearing the land left little time or energy for activities of the mind, and the small numbers of settlers made that sort of investment hard to justify; there was a need to stick to essentials, vital needs, and printing presses were not among them.[28] The archives do not help us. No document has yet been found to explain the local absence of the printing press.

The observant botanist Pehr Kalm, in his travel notes of 1749, undertook his own interpretation. Kalm was fed by both his Calvinist, antipapist view of the Catholic society of New France and by his exchanges with the colony's lettered elite. In many respects Kalm's interpretation was in harmony with that of the Old World, and his reflections expressed both his own prejudices and the Enlightenment attitudes of that elite. First, Kalm noted what he presented as allegations gleaned from the local community: 'the fact that no printing shop has yet been established in Canada is because, it is said, by this means no book or other printed matter injurious to religion, royalty or good morals may be printed and circulated among the people. For nothing of the sort could occur with manuscript texts.' Continuing with his own analysis, Kalm added: 'the principal reason must be that, in a country whose inhabitants are still poor, the level has not yet been reached where a printer can find sufficient buyers for his production and thereby earn his living; the second reason is probably that France benefits from this, by letting Canada depend on her.'[29] Kalm therefore advanced a political reason: the desire for censorship. But he also suggested an economic reason: the absence of a viable market and the colony's structural dependence on the metropolis. These are the two poles around which the Swedish scientist constructed an explanation to justify the absence of a printing press in New France.

Because it is contemporary with Barrin de La Galissonière's request for a press, the reading Kalm proposed has much to tell us. Of its kind, it is the only one known. What is lacking, however, is a clearly expressed general explanation by royal authorities of the period, or by other players. In the absence of this, a new interpretation might be advanced by combining scholarship on colonial New France and the professional organization of book crafts in the kingdom of France (and its governing politics) with the double status of the press – at once a vehicle for ideas and a manufactured product. Official French policy did not favour the installation of a printing press in New France. At the same time as royal authorities took charge of direct administration of the colony, in the early 1660s, they tightened controls over the book industry throughout the kingdom. This took the form of a strengthening of the monopoly of the Paris presses, a ban against setting up new printing houses, severe restrictions on access to the printing craft and close surveillance of commerce in professional equipment (presses, types, etc.). Presses in the provinces were increasingly restricted to job printing (posters, notices, factums, funeral invitations) and the printing of primers or religious booklets, while the industry as a whole lost nearly 30 per cent of its presses in the first two-thirds of the eighteenth century. Moreover, convents, colleges and individuals were not allowed to own presses. The very process of publishing, formalized in 1701 by letters patent, was prejudicial to outlying regions because it required that written permission be obtained from the chancellor, 'sealed with the Great Seal', before going to press.[30]

The fear of trade in illicit books was also a significant factor. Discussions around the nomination of the printer Devaux to Fort Royal (Martinique) illustrate the state of mind of colonial administrators in Versailles: the printer's nomination included a clause prohibiting him from selling books. This irritated local administrators, who argued that because no control was exercised over the entry of books into the colonies, therefore it made no sense to prohibit Devaux from selling books. On the contrary, if he were allowed to sell books, at least the authorities could exercise a minimum of control.[31]

The economic system preferred by royal authorities was anything but favourable to the opening of a printing shop in New France. The mercantile system operative in the kingdom imposed a hierarchy between the metropolis and its colonies, the latter being viewed essentially as providers of raw materials and as markets for products manufactured in the metropolis. Many local promoters of economic development in other areas of activity were stymied by this implacable rule.[32] At the same time, as the principal driver of the colonial economy – and for some printers a regular customer – the State was no longer able, after the military conflicts of the seventeenth century, to support the development of New France. Furthermore, for printers themselves, the colonial market offered little attraction. The costs of setting up and operating a business were enormous, and because the colony's need for their services was slight, production costs would be high. At the beginning of the eighteenth century, New France numbered just 16,000 inhabitants, and when the colony was ceded to Great Britain in 1760, barely more than 70,000 inhabitants. That population was scattered over a vast territory in which the principal settlement, crucial for the dynamics of written culture, had in 1744 only 1,000 households. Yet in order to be efficient, a printing shop required at least two working presses providing work for four or five people (though it is true that numerous exceptions appear in the metropolitan censuses of 1701 and 1771.) The supply of paper, 50–75 per cent of the production cost of any printed document, also played an important role.[33]

Alongside these economic questions, it is worth noting that local authorities in the colony took the liberty of issuing paper money to counter the chronic lack of hard cash. This bold initiative, roundly condemned by Versailles, did nothing to reassure a royal administration with a tendency for economic and political centralism. The cultural dynamics of the colony may also have curbed local development of a book industry. More extensive research needs to be done in this area. At first glance it appears that the principal agents of print in New France, the lettered elite composed of civilian and military officers along with merchants and traders, identified more with the European metropolis than the North American colony. Versailles, for the first group, and La Rochelle and Bordeaux, for the second, exerted a decisive cultural attraction. An investigation of the desire to preserve and nourish ties to European culture, instead of vesting the colonial territory with new meaning by redirecting the royal project into the literary creation of local representations, would be a stimulating avenue for further research. The whole body of manuscript and printed material that was circulated or produced in New France during the seventeenth and eighteenth centuries is in this sense revealing. Books and print were received much as they were in the French kingdom; print culture, indeed, was almost exclusively European. Expectations were defined by European models for an implicitly European reader. This avenue of analysis is worth extending beyond the chronological confines of the French ancien régime to understand better the first manifestations of literature in Canada.

Broader cultural factors may also have intervened. For one thing, the heterodoxy creeping into the Roman Catholic Church in the seventeenth century, through the quarrels over the Chinese rites, Jansenism and Quietism, did nothing to help Church initiatives in New France. Some congregations responded to this delicate situation with a pronounced centralism in editorial matters, a sort of self-censorship. Among the Sulpicians, for example, only Paris could approve publication of any text whatsoever by a member of the congregation, regardless of the establishment to which he belonged. Regarding the project to print the *Catéchisme de la Foy et des mœurs chrétiennes* of

M. de Lantages, who was at the du Puy seminary, Louis Tronson, superior of the mother community of Paris, pointed out to the author:

> If there were time to return them here after they are corrected, before printing them, we would think this important so as to follow the general rule, to print nothing in the provinces that one of the Doctors named by the King for the examination of books has not seen beforehand. For, although one may be able to get by without doing so on many occasions, and in certain matters there is nothing to fear, it would be difficult to remedy things in other more delicate matters, without making it a general rule. [...] For the future, we hope you will take care to arrange things in such a way that what is to be printed is ready soon enough to be able to send it to us before printing [...][34]

Perhaps the unspoken assumption behind the technical justifications presented by the Paris administration in 1683 had been something like this: allowing the Montreal Sulpicians to establish a printing press would be to risk losing control over the publications of the North American congregation, thereby weakening its adherence to doctrine.

At the same time, the drift in intellectual interest from the western missions to those of the East, starting in the 1660s, created a further unfavourable circumstance. For it seems that in the last third of the seventeenth century, works about the East Indies multiplied rapidly, whereas those about western colonists declined. That attrition crystallized in the suspension of annual publication of the relations of the Jesuits of New France.[35] This situation, combined with power struggles in the Catholic Church engendered by the rise of the Jansenists, may explain the initiative of Pierre Le Petit in south-east Asia. A printer and bookseller in Paris, well considered at court and an avowed Jansenist, in 1677 he offered the missionaries of Thailand a fully equipped printing shop.[36]

Finally, the conflict over the first printing house on the island of Saint-Domingue, in 1724–25, certainly did nothing to encourage other such attempts in the colonies. It was in fact a short-lived experiment. Named in letters patent as King's Printer and Bookseller to the colony, with exclusive privileges, Joseph Payen came into conflict with the local governor. Forced to leave the island, he abandoned the project. In 1742 the new local administrators requested the establishment of a similar enterprise, only to receive the same response as the Governor of New France in 1750: find yourselves a printer and we will provide the permits. The discussions that followed (at the speed of transatlantic communication), the death of the intendant, and of course the war, delayed fulfillment of the project until 1763[37] – that is, just under a year before the opening of Brown and Gilmore's printing house in Quebec under the British regime. Similarly, Quebec's geographic remoteness from the vital centre of French publishing, and the fact that ice on the St Lawrence kept the colony in isolation for nearly six months out of the year, inspired little confidence among Government authorities anxious to monitor and control the production and circulation of books.

The absence of printing presses in the colony had a variety of consequences, which multiplied as the colony matured and demographic growth put manuscript production under pressure. Missionary activities, the circulation of legal and Government information, and the organization and conservation of Government records, all suffered from this state of affairs. The absence of presses directly affected trade in books and other printed matter, limiting that trade to a market of imports. This market was based on three principal networks: the merchant network, the institutional network and the private network.

There were no designated bookshops in Canada under the French ancien régime. Rather, it seems from nearly 50 surviving probate inventories drawn up for the settlement of estates in the colonial capital, that the principal agents of the commercial circulation of books in Quebec were for the most part merchants, whether wholesalers or retailers. To these may be added a few general traders. The great majority were of French origin, but well integrated into the local community through marital ties. The dozen or so born in New France were not necessarily the least among them.[38] Among the book dealers identified by the probate inventories there were, strictly speaking, no book professionals, no booksellers or bookbinders. They were all business people and specialized in the trade in imported products. Among these, books were simply one product among many other objects of daily life, such as lengths of cloth, household goods and accessories of clothing. For some colonists, commerce was a part-time activity, conducted in parallel with the exercise of a profession or the practice of a trade. Prominent examples include the notary Chambalon, the ship's captain Dehogue and the blacksmith Morin. There were no peddlers in the capital, at least not officially.

The impression of a general trade in books is reinforced by the fact that most of these traders were located in Quebec's Lower Town, near the docks and the principal market. Only four of those listed in probate inventories operated stores in the Upper Town near to the Jesuit college, the diocesan seminary and the convent of the Ursulines. Here, books were not put in an exclusive ghetto, as in those European cities where specialized bookstores were located alongside luxury boutiques.[39] Books in these general shops were generally stocked in small numbers. Of the 49 inventories found, nearly half listed fewer than 30 volumes, while 11 recorded more than 100 volumes. Among the latter, one estate worth noting is that of the grandson of a Norman hatter, established in the colony in the middle of the seventeenth century: this inventory listed nearly 600 volumes.

Books generally enjoyed good sales. They did not seem to suffer like other products from the difficulties of a small, unprofitable local market. Competition was fierce.[40] In large part the choice of titles that were offered explains this commercial success. The merchants of Quebec took no risks. Like the book dealers of early New England, discussed in Chapters 2 and 3 of this volume, the merchants of Quebec offered their customers almost exclusively what was of interest to the majority: the little books required for basic schooling and devotional practice. Spelling books, often found by the hundreds, were offered by some 20 or so vendors, while books of hours, less numerous, were more widespread; they were found in 35 stores.

Alongside these steady sellers were occasionally found a few books intended for more advanced students, including the *Rudiments, Particules* and Latin grammars. Latin authors and dictionaries notably vied with the classics of religious literature from the Counter-Reformation or the old tradition: *Vie des saints, Offices de la semaine sainte, Imitation de Jésus,* the *Pensez-y bien,* Abelly's *Pensées chrétiennes,* Jean Busée's *Méditations,* the works of St François de Sales and a few copies of the New Testament, in whole or in part. The absence of novels, plays, poetry or other works of fiction suggests the influence of ecclesiastical authority, indeed one so obvious and uniform as to suggest a certain selection of the books before the arrival of notary and bailiff, or else the omission of offending books from the lists.[41] In this respect, surviving probate inventories might not tell the whole story. In addition to this, however, the absence of the kind of books that were popular with the kingdom's humbler readership – catechisms, almanacs and canards (facetious broadsides) – may in part be explained in other ways. With respect to catechisms, the one composed by Mgr de Saint-Vallier for the needs of his diocese of Quebec virtually disappeared. It is not clear whether the first shipment of this 1702 text, published in Paris in wartime by Urbain Coustelier, ever reached its destination; few copies are to be found in colonial probate inventories. More broadly, the lack of consensus among the clergy on adopting a single diocesan catechism was presumably damaging for trade in this type of work. Uncertainty is always bad for business: when in doubt, do not stock up.

Further research into those involved in the transmission of catechistic knowledge, such as educational or parish authorities, may eventually add to this explanation. As for almanacs and canards, the seasonal pace of communications with the metropolis had a discouraging effect. Transportation delays meant that any almanac or calendar was out of date before it had even arrived, causing a disconnect between day-to-day experience on either side of the Atlantic. But aside from these missing pieces and the limitations of transatlantic exchanges, the colonial book situation differed little from that in many French cities of the period. There, too, non-specialized vendors dominated the book trade. Professional booksellers catered largely for the most dedicated readers, people whose interests went beyond the required reading of ecclesiastical and pedagogical discourse and who wanted to enjoy the latest literature or to acquire works of learning or natural science.[42]

Little is known about the workings of the book trade in the colony. There has yet to be written for New France a study like Jane McLeod's on the trade in books conducted by the merchants of Bordeaux with the 'French islands' towards the end of the ancien régime.[43] Between the geographical hierarchy in the kingdom (with a book market centred around Paris and supported in the provinces by presses of varying importance) and the hierarchy of cities involved in the colonial trade (with the port cities of Rouen, Bordeaux and La Rochelle leading the way) every conceivable intersection was possible. McLeod argues that apart from the distance between Bordeaux and the industry's centre of power, the trade in books with Saint-Domingue, Martinique and Guadeloupe played a determining role in the prosperity of Bordeaux booksellers. One undeniable attraction contributing to the prosperity of these merchants was the opportunity to sell, on return from the West Indies, sugar, coffee, cotton and indigo. In fact, most of the booksellers in the provincial capital of Guyenne participated in one way or another in such transatlantic activities, especially from the 1740s onwards, although the low level of publishing activity there also obliged them to seek book supplies in Paris.[44]

In Quebec, all of the evidence suggests that the organization of the transatlantic book trade depended on that of other imported goods. In trade, as on the shelves of shops, a book was simply merchandise, one consumer good among others. Wholesalers and traders, whether established in Quebec or in the ports of the metropolis (La Rochelle,

Bordeaux, Rouen), supplied the market with all sorts of products, either on their own initiative or to fill the orders of correspondents. Traders then sold their goods directly to the public or else distributed them to retailers, their travelling salesmen or their correspondents.

Given that books were not an absolutely necessary product – especially perhaps in the colonial context – they were particularly vulnerable to the economic and political fluctuations affecting trade and communications with the metropolis. The colonial economy was largely dependent on capital from the metropolis and on the financial involvement of the state. A chronological analysis of the 4,000 volumes listed in Quebec shops between 1690 and 1759 reveals three grand phases in the book trade in New France. In the first phase, from 1690 to 1704, the 16 merchants of the capital boasted a remarkable number of books. On average, they stocked 94 volumes each (a total of 1,509 volumes recorded in probate inventories). In the second phase, from 1705 to 1750, there was in contrast a comparative dearth of books. Although the number of merchants was the same as in the first period, the average number of volumes on their shelves was only 29 (for a total of 471 volumes inventoried). The third phase, consisting of the last two decades of the French regime, marked a massive return of books in the market of the colonial capital. The 17 merchants inventoried offered an average of 112 volumes (from a total of 1,900), initially to their customers in the capital and ultimately to their associates in Montreal and the countryside. But these numbers alone do not tell the whole story. Although the proportion in the third phase is greater than that in the first, it does not indicate any improvement in meeting the demands of the Quebec market. The offer of books did not keep in step with growth in the capital's potential market. While the population of the city had quadrupled during this period, the number of books offered by merchants had increased only slightly.

Institutions rarely purchased books on the local market. Generally, they bought directly from the metropolis. In religious communities, this task usually fell to their procurator in Paris or a sister institution there. This direct access to the source of production allowed them to avoid the sometimes substantial fees of intermediaries. Institutional book-buying was a complement, not a threat, to the merchant trade, ensuring the circulation of small-market books that were proper to the needs and functions of the institutions it fed. To give one example, the Séminaire des Missions-Étrangères (at once a society of lay priests, collegial boarding school, residence for candidates for the priesthood and residence of the parish priest for Quebec) supplied classical literature to boarders attending the Jesuit college, and theological literature to those in charge of sacerdotal training. The seminary used the same solution, at the end of the French regime, to correct the chronic lack of catechisms in the parish of Quebec.

The Church enjoyed privileged access to the nerve centre of French publishing, Paris. Together with its extensive network of both metropolitan and colonial religious institutions, the Church also provided a solid foundation for the promotion and distribution of new devotions. Devotion to the Virgin and the Holy Angels, popularized in the metropolis by Reverend Henri-Marie Boudon, benefited significantly from the support of the administrators of the Quebec seminary. A long-time friend of the diocesan and missionary institution,[45] Boudon regularly sent them his books to distribute to other religious institutions in the colony or to individuals. In the same manner, the Augustinians of the Hôtel-Dieu de Québec offered their network of alliances to facilitate distribution of the devotion to the Arras Calvary, of which the brother of the superior of the establishment was the spearhead in Europe.[46]

In a way, the Government also took part in book distribution in the colony. Its interventions were more sporadic than those of merchants and clerics, however, generally focusing on the internal needs of administrative and legal institutions. It handled the supplying of books for the teaching of law by the attorney general of the Conseil Supérieur and ensured that new printed legislative statutes (such as compilations of royal ordinances) were provided to the colony's various administrative and legal centres.[47] Occasionally the government intervened directly in the colonial book market, as in 1750. That year, at the request of the Bishop of Quebec, Mgr de Pontbriand, Versailles, agreed to send nearly 2,000 religious books of all kinds to New France. This royal donation, whose effect on the colony's regular book trade is essentially unknown, seems, however, to have been an exception.[48]

For book-lovers whose needs could be satisfied neither by the local market nor by the institutions where they worked, private distribution was often the only solution. Sometimes this was done through networks of relatives, but more often through social networks related to a profession or scientific interest. Frequently, purchasing was delegated. Remoteness from the large publishing centres, combined with lack of information about recent publications, favoured this mode of acquiring books. New literary releases proved an undeniable attraction for many of the colony's lettered folk. Such books represented a 'social sign' that was visible to one's peers and kept alive the sense of cultural community with the centre of the kingdom. In this respect, French Canada differed little from the various British colonies in North America. As Benjamin Franklin emphasized in his autobiography, 'those who lov'd reading were obliged to send for their books from England'.[49]

Although the absence of a printing press in the Laurentian valley under the French regime was regretted by certain 'enlightened' minds, as well as by Church and Government, there was no absence of printed matter. Whether in complex form like books, or in simple jobbing form like administrative blanks or paper money, print was very much present and interwoven into the social fabric of the colony, especially in the towns. Though this chapter has not tackled the question directly, it is worthwhile to emphasize that the difficulty of accessing the tools of print did not prevent some colonists from using it. Thus the Jesuit *Relations* used print to promote the colony, as with Boucher's *Histoire véritable et naturelle*. Others used print for personal promotion, as did Bacqueville de La Potherie and Nicolas Denys. Print also entered into parish life, notably the catechism for the Quebec diocese and for the Confrérie de la Sainte Famille [Confraternity of the Holy Family]; and it was print that maintained ecclesiastical regulations and diocesan rituals.

In varying degrees, therefore, the settlers of New France were very much in contact with print. Though they did not always possess print themselves, all settlers were aware of its presence and knew its many and varied uses. This observation calls for a change in scholarly perspective. The book history of the old Canada of the seventeenth and eighteenth centuries is far from being a straightforward historical indicator, cutting off a past that was poor in printed resources, and making the first printing house (whether in Montreal or Quebec) a truly revolutionary establishment. On the contrary, the complex history of the book during the French ancien régime further challenges the technological determinism that, from the beginning, has tinged both literary studies and historical studies of the book and printing in Canada.

The book trade operated long before local printing shops had been established. With this in mind, a new question emerges: how did the book market respond to the change of political allegiance, the social reconfiguration that went with it and the new proximity of the means of production? The time has come to abandon the symbolic value applied by scholars at the turn of the twentieth century to the initiatives of Brown, Gilmore and Mesplet. The arrival of the printing press in Quebec, and later in Montreal, did not provoke in colonial culture the kind of transformations suggested by Elizabeth Eisenstein in her influential study of the printing press in Renaissance Europe.[50] In New France, neither a cultural nor even a technological revolution occurred. Books were already circulating in the colony under the French ancien régime, and even the tools of print production were already available, albeit at a distance. A fundamental change did take place, however, when the distance between producers and consumers was reduced. It was not the advent of technological resources, but rather their proximity, that little by little would transform the world of the book in Canada, and in so doing favour the construction of a local literature.

Notes

1. This chapter is a modified translation of an article which appeared in the *Papers of the Bibliographical Society of Canada* 37: 2 (Fall 1999): 35–58. The author and editors are grateful to the Bibliographical Society of Canada for permission to publish the translation, and to the Université de Sherbrooke for funding the original translation made by Rod Wilmott.
2. Claude Galarneau, 'Livre et société à Québec (1764–1859). État de la recherche', in Yvan Lamonde (ed.), *L'imprimé au Québec. Aspects historiques (18ᵉ–20ᵉ siecle)* (Quebec, 1983): 131.
3. The extract is a translation from French. Jacques Mathieu, 'Province de France', in Jean Hamelin (ed.), *Histoire du Québec* (Toulouse and Saint-Hyacinthe, 1976): 168.
4. Patricia L. Fleming and Yvan Lamonde (eds), *History of the Book in Canada/Histoire du livre et de l'imprimé au Canada*, 3 vols (Toronto, 2004–07).
5. See the numerous references to these gazettes by Mme Bégon in her correspondence; Claude de Bonnault (ed.), *La correspondance de Madame Bégon, 1748–1753* ([no pl., no pub.], [1935]): 58, 59, 64 for example.
6. Nevertheless, see Louis-Élie Moreau de Saint-Méry, *Description topographique, physique, civile, politique et historique de la partie française de l'île de Saint-Domingue*, Blanche Maurel and Étienne Taillemite (eds), 3 vols (Paris, 1984): 1; Lenis Blanche, 'Petite histoire de l'imprimerie et de la presse à la Guadeloupe', in *Histoire de la Guadeloupe* (Paris, 1938): 163ff.; Roger Philip McCutcheon, *Early Printing in New Orleans* (New Orleans, LA, 1929).
7. The *Detroit Free Press* of 31 Jul 1890 reports the existence of a printing press in the 'back country' in the second third of the eighteenth century, a claim repeated by Douglas C. McMurtrie, *Early Printing in Michigan* (Chicago, 1931): 17–24, and by George Paré, *The Catholic Church in Detroit, 1701–1888* (Detroit, 1951): 677, n. 3.
8. Ægidius Fauteux, *L' Introduction de l'imprimerie au Canada. Une brève histoire*, ch. 3 (Montreal, 1957): 9 (trans. of *The Introduction of Printing into Canada: a Brief History* (Montreal, 1930)).
9. Georges-Barthélemi Faribault, *Catalogue d'ouvrages sur l'histoire de l'Amérique et en particulier sur le Canada, de la Louisiane, de l'Acadie et autres lieux* [...] (Quebec: William Cowan, 1837): 207.
10. Maximilien Bibaud, *Catéchisme de l'histoire du Canada à l'usage des écoles* (Montreal: P. Gendron, 1853): 65.
11. The quoted text is a translation from French.

12. Louis-Wilfrid Marchand, *Voyages de Kalm en Amérique* (Montreal: T. Berthiaume, 1880), 2 vols (trans. from the English trans. by John Reinhold Forster, published in London in 1770 and 1771, itself a trans. of the German version of the Swedish original).

13. Ibid., vol. 2, p. 137. Marchand's trans. remained the standard until a new trans. by Jacques Rousseau and Guy Béthune (eds), *Voyage de Pehr Kalm au Canada en 1749* (Montreal, 1977). See also Peter Kalm, *Travels in North America [1753–61]* Adolph B. Berson (ed.) (New York, 1966).

14. Returning to the original manuscript version initiated by Jacques Rousseau restores the meaning of the text. The passage reads as follows [translation from French]: 'No printing shop exists in Canada and no one has ever founded one, rather all the books come from France [...]'; Rousseau and Bethune, *Voyage de Pehr Kalm*, fol. 758.

15. Biblo [Phileas Gagnon], 'Antiquités canadiennes', *Union Libérale* (20 Jul 1888); C.O.G. [Charles-Olivier Gagnon], 'Antiquités canadiennes ou les petites choses de notre histoire: L'imprimerie au Canada: Le premier imprimé canadien', *Union Libérale* (28 Dec 1888); Phileas Gagnon, *Essai de bibliographie canadienne*, 2 vols (Quebec, 1895); Marie Tremaine, *A Bibliography of Canadian Imprints, 1751–1800* (Toronto, 1952); Jean Gagnon, 'Notes sur un mandement de Monseigneur de Pontbriand daté du 28 octobre 1759', *Cahiers de bibliologie* 1 (1980): 25–8; John Hare and Jean-Pierre Wallot, 'Les imprimés au Québec (1760–1820)', in Yvan Lamonde (ed.), *L'imprimé au Québec. Aspects historiques (18ᵉ-20ᵉ siecle)* (Quebec, 1983): 79–125.

16. Joseph Navières to Mlle Navières de Deschamps, Oct 1737, in Ludovic Drapeyron (ed.), *Lettres inédites du missionnaire J. Navières sur le Canada (1735–1737)* (Paris, 1895): 13.

17. Rousseau and Béthune, *Voyage de Pehr Kalm*, fol. 758.

18. Louis-Antoine de Bougainville, 'Mémoire sur l'état de la Nouvelle-France (1757)', in Roland Lamontagne (ed.), *Louis-Antoine de Bougainville. Écrits sur le Canada* (Sillery and Paris, 1993): 99ff.

19. In the larger cities of the kingdom, the appraisal of major collections of books was left in the hands of masters of the corporation of bookseller printers, as one of their privileges.

20. Probate inventory of Guillaume Verrier, Quebec, 10 Jan 1759, Bibliothèque et Archives nationales du Québec, Centre d'archives de Québec (BAnQ-Q), *Greffe de Claude Barolet*; Probate inventory of Francois-Étienne Cugnet, Québec, 31 Aug 1751, BAnQ-Q, *Greffe de Jean-Baptiste Decharnay*.

21. Charles-Honoré Laverdière and Henri-Raymond Casgrain (eds), *Journal des jésuites* (Montreal, 1973): 335.

22. Louis Tronson to Francois Vachon de Belmont, [1683]; quoted in Fauteux, op. cit. (1957): ch. 3, p. 4.

23. President of the council of Marine to the Marquis de La Jonquière, 4 May 1749, Library and Archives of Canada (LAC), *Series B*, 89: 68v. There is no trace of the letter sent by Barrin de La Galissonière apparently in late Sept or Oct 1748.

24. Fauteux, op. cit. (1957): ch. 3, p. 4.

25. LAC, *Series B*, vol. 89, 68v.

26. 'J'ai procuré M.r au no.é Boyssoun Imprimeur son passage pour Canada. Vous aurez agréable de l'ordonner par la p.re occasion qu'il y aura pour cette

Colonie', letter from François-Marie Peyrenc de Moras to Charles-Claude de Ruis-Embito de La Chesnardière, 16 Apr 1757, LAC, *Series B*, 106, 9.

27. Jean-Paul de La Grave, *La liberté d'expression en Nouvelle-France (1608–1760)* (Montreal, 1975): 81–2.

28. See among others Lionel Groulx, *L'enseignement français au Canada*, vol. 1: *Dans le Québec* (Montreal, 1931); Antoine Roy, *Les lettres, les sciences et les arts au Canada sous le Régime français* (Paris, 1930).

29. Rousseau and Béthune, *Voyage de Pehr Kalm*, fol. 758.

30. For an overview of the period in the French metropolis, see Henri-Jean Martin, *Livres, pouvoir et societé à Paris au xviiᵉ siecle* (Geneva, 1969): 695–6; 'La prééminence de la librairie parisienne', in Henri-Jean Martin and Roger Chartier (eds), *Histoire de l'édition française vol. 2 Le livre triomphant, 1660–1830* (Paris, 1990): 331–56; Jean Quéniart, 'L'anémie provinciale', in Martin and Chartier (eds), *Le livre triomphant*, 358–72.

31. Jane McLeod, 'The Bordeaux Book Trade to the West Indies at the End of the *Ancien Régime*', in Lawrence J. McCrank (ed.), *Bibliographical Foundations of French Historical Studies* (New York and London, 1992): 201–15, 203–04.

32. Joseph-Noël Fauteux, *Essai sur l'industrie au Canada sous le Régime français* 2 vols (Quebec, 1927); Maurice Filion, *La pensée et l'action coloniale de Maurepas vis-à-vis du Canada (1723–1749)* (Montreal, 1972).

33. Robert Darnton (ed.), 'Entre l'auteur et le lecteur', *Gens de lettres, gens du livre* (Paris, 1992): 224; Jean Quéniart, *L'imprimerie et la librairie à Rouen an xviiiᵉ siècle* (Paris, 1969).

34. The extract is a translation from French. Louis Tronson to M. de Lantages, 25 Nov 1676, in Louis Bertrand (ed.), *Correspondance de monsieur Louis Tronson* (Paris, 1904): 4–6.

35. Martin, *Livres, pouvoir et societé*, vol. 2, 852ff.

36. Martin, 'La prééminence de la librairie parisienne', 337.

37. Maurel and Taillemite, *Description topographique*, pp. 1, 350–2.

38. This exploration of old inventories is in large part thanks to the intellectual generosity of Gilles Proulx, who, accompanied by Yvon Desloges, directed a team of the Canadian Parks Service (Quebec region) charged with retracing and examining all probate inventories in the capital of New France. The team included: Louise Déry, Adrienne Labbé, Johanne Lacasse, Rénald Lessard and Gérald Sirois.

39. See James Raven, *The Business of Books: Booksellers and the English Book Trade, 1450–1850* (London, 2007): ch. 6.

40. According to certain administrators, there were twice as many merchants as were needed by the city; Memoir by Desauniers to Beauharnois, 1741, LAC, *Series C¹¹A*, 75: 9v.

41. See also François Melançon, 'Façonner et surveiller 1'intime: lire en Nouvelle-France', in Manon Brunet and Serge Gagnon (eds), *Discours et pratiques de l'intime* (Quebec, 1993): 17–45; and François Melançon, 'Émergence d'une tradition catholique de lecture au Canada', *Cahiers de la recherche en éducation*, 3 (1996): 343–62.

42. See the now classic example of western France analysed by Jean Quéniart, *Culture et societé urbaine dans la France de l'Ouest au xviiiᵉ siècle* (Paris, 1978).

43. McLeod, 'Bordeaux Book Trade to the West Indies'.

44. Ibid., pp. 202–11.

45. He succeeded Rev. Montmorency de Laval, named Bishop *in partibus* of Samos and then titular Bishop of Quebec, as the Archbishop of Évreux, on the latter's recommendation, and with the principal founders of the Quebec seminary frequented the Caen hermitage led by Jean de Bernières. On connections between the founding members of the Quebec seminary and devout circles linked with the Compagnie du Saint-Sacrement in Paris, see Louis Chatellier, *L'Europe des dévots* (Paris,1987); Raoul Allier, *La cabale des dévots, 1627–1666* (Geneva, 1970, a reprint of the Paris edn, 1902); Alphonse Auguste, *Les sociétés secrètes catholiques du xviie siècle et H.-M. Boudon, grand archidiacre d'Évreux* (Paris, 1913); Maurice Souriau, *Le mysticisme en Normandie au xviie siecle* (Paris, 1923).

46. François-Xavier Régnard Duplessis to his sisters: 11 Nov 1738; 25 Apr 1740; 28 Mar 1742; 22 Apr 1744; 14 Mar 1746; 25 Jun 1748; 9 Feb 1749; 4 Jun 1750; 11 Mar 1751; in Joseph-Edmond Roy (ed.), *Lettres du P.F.-X. Duplessis de la Compagnie de Jésus* (Levis: Mercier & Cie, 1892).

47. André Vachon, 'Louis-Guillaume Verrier', in Frances G. Halpenny (ed.), *Dictionnaire biographique du Canada* (Quebec and Toronto, 1974), 3: 701; André Morel, 'Mathieu-Benoît Collet', in David M. Hayne and André Vachon (eds), *Dictionnaire biographique du Canada*, 15 vols (Quebec and Toronto, 1969), 2: 157–8.

48. See Nelson-Martin Dawson, *Le paradoxal destin d'un catéchisme à double nationalité: l'histoire du manuel de Monseigneur Languet à Sens et à Québec*, 2 vols (unpublished Ph.D. dissertation, Université Laval, 1989).

49. Benjamin Franklin, *Autobiography*, quoted by James Gilreath, 'American Book Distribution', in William L. Joyce David D. Hall, Richard D. Brown and John B. Hench (eds), *Printing and Society in Early America* (Worcester, MA, 1983): 116.

50. Elizabeth Eisenstein, *The Printing Revolution in Early Modern Europe* (Cambridge, 1983).

6
Bookmen, Naturalists and British Atlantic Communication, c. 1730–60

Nicholas Wrightson

Systems of information exchange were the sinews of British Atlantic society. Every transatlantic transaction depended upon access to them. A detailed anatomy of their operation between 1730–60 is beyond the scope of this chapter, but the systems can be briefly illustrated through two transatlantic networks: the Anglo-American book trade serving the mid-Atlantic and southern colonies, and the international scientific community enmeshing America in the European 'Republic of Letters'. The former demonstrates how a public and commercial information network developed and adapted to serve the demands of participants and customers. The latter identifies how one important group harnessed existing infrastructure to meet its private members' needs.[1]

Both communities relied heavily upon the exchange of printed information: they were undoubtedly 'connected by books'. During the early eighteenth century American book trade customers became increasingly hungry to enjoy the fruits of intensified British publishing and the London-centred 'public sphere'. Metropolitan curiosity about the colonies, meanwhile, made American authors and audiences a focus of British commercial speculation. At once, scientific print provided the textbooks and treatises on which commonly held transatlantic conceptual and methodological frameworks developed between natural historians and philosophers. As scholarly institutions like London's Royal Society, and journals like its *Philosophical Transactions*, began to arbitrate between naturalists' claims to respectability, moreover, print became crucial in maintaining regional, national and inter-continental scientific reputations.

Nevertheless, the flow of print in both spheres relied upon other types of conversation: those conducted through script and speech. In the book trade, it was transatlantic exchanges of handwritten correspondence and direct meetings between printers, booksellers and customers that refined methods for negotiating credit, balancing supply and demand, and overcoming a hostile ocean. In transatlantic philosophical discussions, too, the contribution of print was determined by older traditions of genteel sociability, active manuscript circulation and handwritten letters. The negotiated relationships between scientific Europeans and Americans dictated research agendas and publication criteria. The interactions between naturalists and their agents in the book and instrument trades determined whether experimenters were equipped with the information and apparatus they needed.

With so much of his business resting on London suppliers, the Philadelphia printer-bookseller Benjamin Franklin badly needed to control the quality, accuracy and profitability of his transatlantic orders and overcome 'formidable obstacles of cost, risk and time'.[2] During his stay in London as a teenager, Franklin probably had little opportunity to make contact with the powerful metropolitan businessmen capable of investing in the Atlantic trade. Consequently, throughout the 1730s he depended upon irregular ventures, taking his chances when merchants 'propos'd supplying me with Books' and stationery.[3] *Pennsylvania Gazette* advertisements and ledger accounts suggest that in the 1730s Franklin received imports in only 1734 and 1738, compared to almost annually from 1744 onwards: especially striking since during the peaceful 1730s, 'Ships were constantly dropping in at some Port on this Continent', while in the war that followed 'by their waiting for Convoy, and other Hindrances and Delays, we [were] sometimes Months without having a Syllable'.[4] Irregular shipments made it difficult 'to build up the needs and expectations of the customers'.[5]

Because Franklin's London suppliers had no incentive to prioritize his shipments, he was left exposed to costly errors and the kind of exploitative practices ('larding...shipments with old, unsaleable books') used by unscrupulous dealers like James Rivington as the infamous reverse side of their 'unheard of' bulk discounts.[6] The mailboats offered at best monthly correspondence, and transatlantic transactions entailed a round trip averaging nine months: rendering mistakes intolerable and disputes interminable.[7] As James Raven and John Bidwell have emphasized, no successful printer simply accepted this situation. Instead, men like Franklin resolved to 'secure a resident agent to manage the affair on the other side of the Atlantic': 'locating specific booksellers, [and] securing credit, finance and transit arrangements'.[8]

In 1743, William Strahan was looking for an American position with prospects for his friend David Hall. Almost as soon as Franklin learned that the London printer was open to correspondence, he wrote offering a post with exceptionally favourable terms – to 'set up a fourth' printing house under Hall's management, and that 'If we should not agree, I promise him however a Twelve months Good Work, and to defray his Passage back' to England.[9] In the very letter announcing Hall's arrival, Franklin informed Strahan that he had 'long wanted a Friend in London, whose Judgement [he] could depend on' – and suggested a tentative business association whereby Strahan would send pamphlets 'worth Reading on any Subject... for there is no depending on Titles and Advertisements'.[10] By his fourth and fifth surviving letters (February and April 1745 respectively) Franklin pushed to broaden the relationship to include 'Books that I shall want for Sale in my Shop' and made a trial book order – 180 copies of a dozen staple imports like 'Esop's Fables'. Once these arrived 'in good Order' he systematically shifted his overseas dealings to Strahan, and the connection underpinned the business until Hall's death in 1772.[11] In less than five years, before 1748, Strahan supplied £363 5s. 6d. worth of books and newspapers.[12]

It is clear from Franklin's impetuosity that he understood the importance of the relationship he was pursuing for his future; and his reasoning is evident from his letters. Based in London, Strahan was at the hub of the English book and stationery trades and had first-hand access to Britain's most diversified markets. His standing also 'insured prompt and efficient attention' to orders and when he could not supply Franklin and Hall himself, he was 'an invaluable negotiator... with other merchants in London and Edinburgh'.[13] Franklin used Hall for books (common and rare); movable type for Philadelphia and his fledgling partnerships in Antigua and Connecticut; map scrolls for the Philadelphia Assembly house; specialist binding and a multitude of stationery orders.[14] In meeting these demands Strahan offered relative reliability and precision, advantageous credit terms, a chance to negotiate face to face with suppliers and (above all) trustworthiness as Hall's lifelong friend.[15]

Franklin frequently expressed his gratitude that Strahan 'never charg'd me commissions and [has] frequently been in Advance for me'.[16] Typical book trade credit terms did not adapt easily to the needs of the American market, as the standard six months often led to debts being collected before goods had even arrived, let alone been sold. Likewise, bills of exchange drawn on London contacts were seldom readily available – further complicating repayment. Franklin apologized in 1746 for sending six bills of exchange on different London firms totalling only £32 19s. 7d., complaining that 'Bills have been scarce lately, and we were glad to get any.'[17] John Smail has emphasized that liberal credit terms became increasingly common towards 1760, as most colonial merchants came to 'expect, even require, a relatively generous credit from their English suppliers' to accommodate their own need to extend 6–12 months of credit to their customers, and allow for frequent short-term remittance crises.[18] But as a book trader Strahan was operating outside an established network of returns, and was unusual for the time in allowing Franklin to finally settle his pre-1748 accounts as late as 1757 'when I was in London'. The contrast between this treatment and the merchant 'who grew impatient and su'd us all' for repayment of a two-year-old debt in 1730 demonstrates why Strahan was so highly valued as an agent. He enabled Franklin to develop a strong imported stock before investment in the Atlantic book trade had proved its profitability in London, granting him a substantial competitive advantage.[19]

Yet Strahan truly proved his worth as a reliable decision-maker. To remain profitable Franklin needed cutting-edge stock despite distance. Because of the time lag, this required his agent to sense 'the sort of books that could be sent...without orders'.[20] Franklin repeatedly relied on Strahan's judgement on pamphlets and '[his] newest and most saleable books' as well as on typefaces, requesting that 'As Mr. Caslon has different Longprimmers, Pica's &c. I beg the Favour of your Judgement to chuse and order the best.' He also found invaluable Strahan's capacity to interpret his instructions appropriately: 'We are very pleas'd that you omitted Catesby's [unexpectedly expensive] Carolina, and we shall, as you judg'd, chuse rather to have Savery entire, than in Numbers.'[21] Franklin probably received occasional advice on book imports from Pennsylvania's principal bibliophile James Logan, just as he and Logan exchanged ideas about his proposed edition of the *Universal History* in 1747. Moreover, it is likely that Franklin kept in touch with literary developments in Britain and 'knew exactly what to order from his [London] bookseller' through learned periodicals like the *Present State of the Republic of Letters* just as we know Logan did.[22] Nevertheless, 'Given the difficulty of specifying, in words, and at a distance of several thousand miles and several months, exactly what was wanted' (especially when it came to new releases not yet reviewed), American printer-booksellers 'wanted to be able to trust their [British] correspondents to supply [the] vitally important assortment' they needed to profit and preserve their cultural gateway status.[23] Strahan's intuition made this possible for Franklin.

Although it was partly the 'presence of his close friend Hall in Philadelphia, that led Strahan into the American trade' (Hall became Franklin's business partner there), Strahan's main incentive for involvement was not his existing friendship with Hall and its guarantee of one 'best and most punctual customer', but rather Franklin's ability to act as his agent, facilitating Strahan's international entrepreneurship as Strahan did Franklin's own.[24] In his first letter to Strahan, Franklin presented himself as owner of 'already three Printing-Houses in three different Colonies', representing an inter-colonial network of clients.[25] Franklin's wide circles of correspondence also offered opportunities for Strahan, who won contracts with the Library Companies at Philadelphia and Trenton on Franklin's recommendation. Although Strahan undoubtedly benefited less from his relationship with Franklin than he had hoped – finding Franklin's other partners James Parker, Thomas Smith and Benjamin Mecom to be uniformly untrustworthy debtors – he repeatedly expressed his satisfaction at the profits he had made through his American connection, declaring as early as 1749 that in return for these he had 'the greatest Inclination for friendship and Gratitude to do everything in my Power that may Promote and enlarge your Business'.[26] The 'consensus of norms' Franklin and Strahan negotiated in their dealings underpinned their mutual commercial success.

It is true that tension and suspicion was a constant undertone, exacerbated over the years by Strahan's careless mistakes, his sporadically uncompetitive prices, and Hall's unreasonable expectations. Indeed, the strain culminated in Hall's 1759 ultimatum: 'I don't want Books of you, or any other Bookseller, without paying the Current price for them...I [must] have my Goods on an equal Footing with others here, else it will not answer.'[27] But while a transatlantic 'culture of credit' emerged neither quickly nor painlessly in the colonial period – and British Atlantic commercial communities were often defined less by confidence than the limits of distrust – Anglo-American book-men understood the impossibility of traversing the Atlantic without maintaining their equilibrium. Strahan recognized the competitive necessity of granting the Atlantic market the focus it deserved, while Franklin and Hall renewed their confidence in Strahan's steady good intentions. 'Believe me with the greatest truth and affection Dear Davie', Strahan exclaimed in 1764:

I will venture to assert (and this I do upon the Information of several Gentlemen who have lately come from North America) that for one

Book [your competitor] sells cheaper than you he sells, or endeavours to sell, six Dearer; and as he *pays here* it must be so.– Believe me, therefore, all [claims to the contrary] which he for obvious Reasons, will ever endeavour to propagate, are wholly groundless.[28]

In the next decade Franklin and Hall reminded their London friend of his obligations with the occasional further protest, but they accepted that, all things considered, Strahan was probably right.[29]

As a hands-on cloth merchant as well as a naturalist, the London Quaker Peter Collinson was better positioned to cultivate transatlantic collaborations and comprehend the infrastructure they depended upon than most British botanists or, indeed, most financiers of and entrepreneurial investors in science.[30] Just as in Franklin and Strahan's case, trade sensitized Collinson to the risks (and the tricks) of transporting goods across the Atlantic in ways unavailable to his scientific colleagues. His close relationships with the custom house and the docks enhanced his ability to ship delicate scientific cargoes safely.[31] He adapted existing merchant networks for scientific purposes, relying upon his close colleague and co-religionist John Hanbury's company of captains to manage his transatlantic scientific exchanges, just as they did his cloth shipments.

These advantages set the stage for Collinson's establishment of the period's first reliable, affordable, extensive and systematic network of transatlantic scientific exchanges. As Collinson informed his American correspondents when recommending Hanbury's company to them, 'There are two Captains, Richmond & Wright, whom I Love & esteem & will take Care of Anything for Mee...[and] Little Matters they are So kind to bring Free.'[32] This reliable arrangement cut Collinson's losses and reduced his expenses, increasing his capacity to invest in his network. It strengthened his appeal among potential American collaborators because he could offer them a neat bundle of services: supporting colonial scientific activity with the right resources, enriching it with the necessary correspondences, publicizing its output in Europe and, above all, managing the infrastructure required for all this to proceed stably. These advantages amply compensated for Collinson's otherwise less appealing personal circumstances, enabling him to solicit transatlantic botanical connections unencumbered by his fixed location, contestable status and modest means.

The strength and utility of eighteenth-century naturalist relationships depended heavily on access to a common framework of scientific knowledge, principally provided by print. Collinson took time to realize this, as his relationship with John Bartram shows. Before 1736, Bartram cut a marginal figure in Collinson's transatlantic scientific network. A Pennsylvanian farmer with little formal education, he appeared destined, at best, to become one of what Steven Shapin has called 'invisible technicians'.[33] By the 1750s, however, his acute observations of America's underexploited and freely available natural resources had won him extensive Old and New World connections and an unexpected respectability.

At first, Bartram's role was strictly limited. Collinson sent him instructions from London that consistently prioritized the collection of physical samples (and their dispatch to the metropolis for analysis there) over Bartram's own interpretations of nature *in situ*. Collinson tersely dismissed Bartram's thoughts and observations with 'pray send us a Specimen of the plant', and frequently discouraged him explicitly from speculating further:[34]

> The Box of seeds came very safe & in Good Order. thy Remarks on them are very Curious but I think take up to much of thy Time & Thought...only number the papers & give the Country Name or any name thee may know [the enclosed seed] by [for ease of identification.][35]

Even where collecting was impossible and interpretation necessary – for example, when Collinson requested observations on the hunting techniques of rattlesnakes – Bartram was encouraged less to think for himself than to answer specific factual questions formulated by his London benefactors. Understandably, therefore, after five years of Collinson's pressure, Bartram had little confidence in his own interpretive ability. When attempting the more ambitious task of classifying plants he apologetically confided to a friend that he had exerted himself 'with what judgment & ingenuity I was capable of...but if thee sees mistakes I hope thee will consider that I am at ye best but A learning'.[36] Simply put, Bartram was a servant: employed to follow instructions without deviation, or risk the loss of his patrons' support.

This subservience sprang, above all, from Bartram's lack of access to scientific literature. Bartram realized this early on, when Collinson dismissed his first seed shipments for containing species already widespread in England. Printed reference works would have prevented this by providing Bartram with the foundation of shared knowledge necessary to participate in a common transatlantic enterprise – including guidance on which American plants British botanists would label curious rather than commonplace. With only his correspondents' vague requests and minimal accompanying description as his guide, however, Bartram was seriously hampered in attributing meaning to his shipments and in winning the respect of his peers. Of course, this realization made him eager to acquire books at every opportunity, saying that 'I love reading [them] dearly and I believe if Solomon had loved women less & books more he would have been a wiser & happier man then he was.'[37] Yet, while Collinson was willing to assist his American agent's 'Improvement in the knowledge of plants' in small ways – suggesting in 1734, for example, that 'I will gett [your specimens] nam'd by our most knowing Botanists & then Returne them again' – he consistently rejected Bartram's appeals for books, sending him clothes instead. Keen to keep Bartram from approaching London naturalists without his help, and perhaps ignorant of the virtual absence of even basic botanical reference works in the colonies, Collinson steadfastly asserted that the act of collection itself 'will Improve thee more than Books for it is impossible for any one Author to give a General History of plants'.[38]

Fortunately for Bartram (and ultimately also for Collinson), science was as much an arena for social negotiation as was the book trade.[39] In 1736, the powerful Pennsylvanian naturalist and administrator James Logan offered Bartram the tools to redefine his position.[40] Logan knew Collinson through the Quaker religious network and wrote to rebuke him for abusing Bartram's delicate circumstances:

[He] has a genious perfectly well turned for botany and the production of nature: but he has a family that depend wholly on his daily labours, spent on a poor narrow spot of ground that will scarce keep them above the want of the necessaries of life. You therefore are robbing them while you take up one hour of his time without a proper compensation for it.[41]

Logan intervened further by introducing Bartram to his own extensive scientific library, beginning with Carolus Linnaeus' *Systema Naturae*. He expressed confidence in Bartram's potential as more than a mere collector, saying that while the book would require explanation ('being in Latin'), yet once 'I have given thee [the tools], thou wilt, I believe, be fully able to deal with it thyself.' He underscored this faith, and his criticism of Collinson, by ordering more books for Bartram from London, instructing Collinson himself to manage the affair.[42]

Whatever the reason for Logan's patronage, Bartram was now doubly connected to London, and his newfound access to print helped him contest metropolitan evaluations of his scientific status. Chastened by Logan's censure and impressed by Bartram's engagement with the Linnaean system, Collinson was quickly convinced that his technician's interpretive talent indeed exceeded initial expectations. Sensing Bartram's potential, he treated him increasingly as colleague rather than contractor: nurturing his speculations with letters and specimens, and (at last) advancing his thinking with gifts of print. As Bartram informed a new correspondent in 1742: 'I have had ever since I was 12 years of age A great inclination to botany & natural history but could not make much improvement therein for want of bookes or other instruction' until Collinson and some noble patrons finally provided funds, specimens and 'several books' for that purpose.[43] These changes laid the foundations for Bartram's future prominence, enabling him to graduate from collecting to interpreting natural phenomena. Bartram, in turn, passed on the information print provided to instruct and assist other Americans collecting on his behalf. Ultimately, these outcomes also supported European objectives. As Collinson later explained, one of the greatest frustrations of English botanists was that Americans constantly encountered 'Such wonders...to Which Wee are great Strangers, Butt because you see them Every Day they are thought Common & not worth Notice.'[44] Unless Bartram's patrons passed on all the information he needed in their letters, only books could help him serve them better by allowing him to see America afresh with European eyes.

Nor was Bartram's an isolated example. The New York naturalist Cadwallader Colden communicated a comparable account of his development as a naturalist to Swedish master botanist Linnaeus in early 1749. 'When I came into this part of the world near forty years since' Colden explained:

I understood only the Rudiments of Botany & found so much difficulty in applying it to the many unknown plants that I met with every where that I was quite discouraged & laid aside all attempts in that way near 30 years till I casually met with your Books which gave me such new lights that I resolv'd again to try what could be don with your assistance If then I have been able to do any thing worth your notice it is intirely owing to the excellency of your method.[45]

While Colden, unlike Bartram, had the wherewithal to acquire books for himself (and the Latin to read them), assimilating their meaning underpinned both men's scientific maturation equally.

Print performed an essential long-term role in the maintenance of scientific relationships and the conduct of experiments. As much as correspondence, print exchanges and reading recommendations reciprocally bound natural historians and philosophers together. One might argue that because colonial naturalists were physically isolated from one another (and from the mother country), books were even more vital to their activities than to those of scientific Europeans. But the frequency with which Collinson, John Fothergill and others in London similarly exchanged books and referred to their reading suggests the indispensability of print even in the metropolis, amid constant opportunities for verbal instruction and dialogue.[46] The exchange and discussion of print reinforced all naturalists' mutuality by allowing their initiation into shared frameworks of knowledge and familiar concepts.[47]

After 1736 almost all of Collinson's myriad correspondences were alive with print transactions, while his colleagues unfailingly employed them in support of their own connections. Just as in the case of Franklin, Strahan and Hall, print helped these dispersed correspondents to negotiate their own transatlantic 'consensus of norms' and provided ways of enforcing common standards. As naturalists digested books and pamphlets, they referred to letters and conversations, and subscribed to social expectations and exchanges. They therefore imagined (and regulated) their community through the composite lens of these complementary modes of communication, combined in proportion to their circumstances.

Here too, tension could easily flare: Bartram's frustration at the limits imposed on him by poor access to books remained with him his whole life, while his status-anxiety became plain whenever he felt that his contributions were unjustly overlooked. When his early patron Lord Petre sent him a copy of the second part of Miller's popular *Gardener's Dictionary* in late 1739, Bartram complained bitterly to Collinson:

> pray return my hearty thanks for his good will in sending it to me ye reading of which afords me A pretty deal of satisfaction but in reading millers account of ye Colinsonia I think he has neither done me nor my province Justice, for this plant hath been observed by mee this 20 years...I was ye first that ever sent it into Europe & I think he ought to have taken care to mention ye word ye true place where it was sent from & who sent it seeing he hath so very often mentioned ye names of [other collectors].[48]

Bartram feared that Miller's public snub (deliberate or not) jeopardized his attempts to expand, and threatened even to diminish, his small stock of social capital. To shore up the core of his support, therefore, he had to resensitize his friends to his contribution. So great was Bartram's sense that he would slide into obscurity without books and public recognition that his ire at Miller's mistake was still smouldering five years later. Writing to Cadwallader Colden in January 1745, he was still rifling through his letters and (now pretty decent) working library to criticize Miller's attribution of *Collinsonia* to Maryland and reassert his own indispensability.[49] '[T]his is a shamefull error' he seethed, 'for I sent ye seed of it first to Peter Collinson ... & If I had not sent it out of Pensilvania I suppose Miller would not have known that there had been such a plant upon ye earth'.[50] Yet, as in the book trade, the need to preserve mutually beneficial relationships led naturalists on both sides of the Atlantic to respond decisively to signs of strain. Following Collinson's intervention, Miller admitted his mistake and sent Bartram seed samples and gifts by way of apology.[51]

In 1986, Ian Steele's study of improvements in transatlantic communication between 1675 and 1740 argued that community 'can be defined better as an experience than as a place'. As the eighteenth century progressed, he believed, those on both shores of the North Atlantic increasingly shared the same 'experiences'. Over time the ocean 'united [the British] empire more than it divided'.[52] Sketching this process, the above examples have stressed the turbulence of British Atlantic society throughout the period 1730–60, and how informal negotiation made possible its cultural, commercial and scientific integration in the face of persistent parochialism and fragmentedness. Through them, we have briefly explored the relationship between print, script and speech in the way information, commodities and social norms were agreed and communicated through particular networks. Finally, these examples have indicated how transatlantic book trade and scientific communities both fuelled and responded to the gradual but cumulatively transformative increase in transatlantic connectedness.

The mutualities and obligations that were forged through these transactions reflected slightly different conventions. Printer-booksellers were part of the wider economy: bargaining over the exchange of goods for cash and bills of exchange (or their equivalents). Intellectual relationships, by contrast, were more rooted in a culture of patronage and gift giving: bartering favours, information, samples, equipment, and frequently also books or manuscripts, in transactions where precise value and fairness were much harder to quantify. Nevertheless, participants in both networks were wrestling with the problem of communicating not only material objects, but also cultural systems of expectations, values and social distinctions across an ocean. The dynamics of this process tell us a great deal about the nature of eighteenth-century society and identity.

Paper communication, both printed and handwritten, made dispersed communities of this kind a possibility. To be sure, face-to-face contact, when it was possible, could deepen relationships and make them vivid in ways that letters could not match.[53] But the reality of separation could never be wholly overcome. Indeed, the frustration of knowing that distance interfered with the implicit sympathy between friends, and produced misunderstandings, actually compounded the tension between correspondents once their suspicions had been aroused. Maybe it was for this reason that members of scientific and book trade networks used every means at their disposal (when they were apart) to call to mind the closeness they had experienced in person, or to conjure up a vicarious intimacy if they had never met. In 1752 Peter Collinson wrote to thank Christopher Jacob Trew for 'the Lively Portrait of my Dear Friend, which will perpetually Smile on Mee, and remind Mee of our Friendship, as well as reproach Mee, If I am [or] can be guilty of Ingratitude to so Generous a Benefactor'.[54] In 1755 he wrote again, telling the German: 'Your Dear Picture smiles on mee Dayly & reproaches Mee Why don't you write. This I can bear no longer but I immediately putt Penn to paper to Inquire after your Welfare.'[55] The Atlantic world and the wider world in which it was entangled were patchworks of 'intersecting local contexts'. As this chapter, and these letters in particular, suggest, these contexts were as often mental as physical. They consisted of common experiences, shared frameworks of knowledge, or reminders of extra-local bonds and obligations, all deeply bound up with access to print. These intimate personal intersections were the coordinates by which book-men and naturalists mapped the contours of a new cultural landscape.

We have seen that anxiety and instability were chronic characteristics of the novel relationships these people of middling status negotiated to bridge the British Atlantic between 1730 and 1760. Yet the apparent threat that these emerging transatlantic communities of readers, writers and booksellers might easily dissolve did not prevent them from contributing indispensably to the affairs of their participants. If anything, the constant perceived risk of their collapse increased the sensitivity with which the members of these networks negotiated the terms of their involvement, stiffened their efforts to comprehend their differing circumstances and enhanced the creativity with which they maintained their ties by sustained correspondence. Refined as they were by constant tension, transatlantic relationships thrived.

At mid-century, this developing transatlantic culture was at once increasingly interconnected and persistently parochial. For some, the 'British Atlantic world' was a living reality manifested in mercantile commerce and material consumption, shared allegiances and common cultural resources. From the perspective of others, on the frontiers or off the beaten track, the influences of imperial governance and the shipping lanes were muted by their relative remoteness from everyday life.

This mixed historical experience is reflected in the historiography of the period, in which scholars generally divide behind two alternative stances: favouring either what I will call a progressively 'integrative', or a stubbornly 'fragmentary' reading of life in Britain's infant empire. Since the 1990s this bifurcation has intensified with the rise of the 'New Atlantic History' and its eastern imperial equivalents. This new approach embodies a manifesto for the reconfiguration of historical space. It proposes to 'supplement and even replace' existing national histories (the dominant organizing categories of traditional historiography) by broadening historians' analytical horizons to encompass a wider sphere of transnational interaction. Stressing the interplay between dispersed actors, it underscores 'the continuities between processes usually kept apart, such as state-formation within Europe, and empire-building beyond it'.[56] The utility of such a 'comparative' approach has long been recognized by historians of all contexts and periods. 'If you analyse any given society (or polity, or culture, or economy), in any aspect of its practices', the medievalist Chris Wickham explains:

> you have to be aware of how it compares with other societies, and which alternatives are the most useful comparators. Historians who study one society alone, never looking at others, lack an essential control mechanism, and not only risk misunderstanding, of what are real causal elements or turning-points and [of] what are not, but also are in danger of falling into the metanarratives of national identity, the teleologies of what makes Us special, which bedevil the historical enterprise.[57]

Yet in deliberately connecting as much as comparing the once distinct histories of Britain and her colonies, proponents of the 'Atlantic' approach naturally privilege a narrative of progressively intensifying connectedness over any countervailing trends within the imperial (even global) systems that are their concern. In other words, while they undoubtedly recognize the presence of diversity, they concentrate their energy on analysing the forces driving integration.

While promising to explain the interaction between 'local particularity' on the one hand, and 'a wider web of connections' on the other, 'Atlantic history' has (to date) been successful in exploring mainly the latter.[58] Bernard Bailyn has forcefully advocated the methodological advance inherent in this form of history, which, by merging 'national histories and their extensions overseas', achieves 'more than the sum of its parts'.[59] Deployed in the intrinsically transnational spheres of imperial governance, ideology, political economy, trade and migration (both free and coerced), it has indeed enriched our understanding.[60] Yet the transatlantic and global dimensions of social and cultural change – how the great majority of British imperial subjects interacted with these superstructures in their daily lives – have been less systematically investigated.[61] As a result, some of the ambivalent consequences of the emergence of the Atlantic world have been neglected. Despite their pretensions of abolishing 'the nation-state' as a unit of analysis, and the parallels they draw with the '*New* Social History' called for in Laslett's *The World We Have Lost*, Atlantic historians apparently remain content to leave 'history from below' largely to exponents of traditionally conceived national historiographies. This is an especially ironic twist in relation to British America, considering the self-evident debt Atlantic history owes to the 'Anglicization' theory that strongly influences early American social history, which argues both that Anglo-America became increasingly socio-culturally unified in this period and that *this* was the greatest consequence of transatlantic integration (and, ultimately – by raising expectations of equality, bringing differences into sharper relief, and encouraging State intervention in the colonies – a prime cause of American Independence).[62] Before the inception of Atlantic history as a coherent movement around 1995, we understood the process of British Atlantic integration to be profoundly ambivalent: involving the complex interrelationship of conflicting trends. Today, the significance of this turbulence appears powerfully challenged.

One of the aims of this chapter has been to restore a sense of turbulence and of the difficulties of establishing and maintaining an integrated world across such distances and in the face of differences in both context and circumstances. Writing before the 'Atlantic turn', historians already recognized that the structures of religion, commerce, government and social order that provided the scaffolding for Britain's expansion in America relied 'nearly absolute[ly]' upon the written transmission of information and ideas.[63] Colonial vice-regal and denominational networks were interrelated with governmental and religious organizations in Britain and beyond. Entrepreneurs and financiers on both shores relied on extra-local connections to service the market. Dispersed families and communities remained coherent only in so far as they enjoyed regular correspondence. All these groups made 'impressive use of the written word' to remain connected. These links were therefore reinforced by the transformative improvements in communications infrastructure that occurred between 1675 and 1740: as the colonial population quadrupled, inter-colonial shipping tripled and the monthly Atlantic packet boats were finally regularized. These developments 'shrunk' the ocean. They enabled colonial society to respond rapidly to cultural developments in Britain and initiated such a thickening of social bonds that, by 1760, British migrants to the New World could believe they were merely moving 'from one of London's provinces to another'.[64] With this 'convergence toward the centre' came a greater recognition of 'common interests and strong ties' that spurred imperial subjects everywhere to modify 'the meaning of the word "empire" to include themselves and their localities in an organic [transatlantic] union'.[65]

In the 1980s, Ian Steele and T. H. Breen emphasized the developmental consequences of this intensifying transatlantic traffic. They argued that by the 1740s, since the Atlantic was no longer seen to be significantly wider than the Irish Sea, people 'behaved rationally in sailing to seek offices, collect debts, settle estates, sell cargoes, or even to recover their health'.[66] New consumer behaviour, moreover, trickled down the Anglo-American social order, reaching 'even the lowest [and most isolated] levels of society'. In Breen's example, Indian cotton and nails from England crept 'slowly round the coast and up the waterways, over packhorse trails, past the furthest villages, and so at last into the hands of frontiersmen'.[67] To some degree, therefore, British subjects of all stripes – from the metropolis to Scottish highland hamlets and the American backcountry – participated in a recognizably common 'empire of goods' and expressed their mutuality through 'a shared language of consumption'.[68]

These Americanists, however, wrote alongside colleagues whose work exposed the enduring *limits* of integration well beyond the Revolution. Richard Bushman accepted a converging transatlantic elite culture, identifying a dramatic importation of status symbols, manners and social practices into America in the half-century after 1720. This increased awareness of (and access to) the accoutrements of British polite society, however, remained the preserve of a privileged minority. Beyond the urban elite of the burgeoning port-cities, he concluded, 'Gentility flecked [colonial] lives without colouring them.'[69] Even at the top, transatlantic cultural linkages generally did little more than emphasize the impossibility of adequately replicating Britain in America: where assemblies had to be held in taverns rather than ballrooms, and African slaves frequently replaced white servants.[70] Likewise, Richard Brown starkly contrasted the privileged social position and ability to communicate of well-lettered clergymen and lawyers with the rural world they daily served. Out there, they alone 'possessed an extensive network of extra-local connections' to support their social and cultural aspirations.[71] Indeed, even in print-saturated Massachusetts only those living 'along the trade routes bought books'. This was generally not from want of interest, but because beyond these 'lines of cultural demarcation' the underdeveloped infrastructure serving the sparsely populated frontiers kept them insulated from the flow of information and, consequently, the diffusion of European culture.[72] Improvized local norms grew up to fill the vacuum.

In short, the evolving structures that controlled the transmission of information and ideas across the ocean and within America (and there are obvious parallels in provincial Britain itself) interacted differently with each of the empire's constituent communities and social groups. A large literature exists on the convergence, or resistance to it, of metropolis and provinces in the British Isles. It stresses the role of infrastructural improvement in integrating society, and the negotiation between locally generated socio-cultural norms and those diffusing from the capital. It provides a somewhat earlier (and faster) timetable for change than that of America.[73] The result was what now seems a baffling diversity of experience. It was moulded chiefly by geographies (local, national and imperial), as both Britain and America exhibited considerable regional variegation. Yet wealth, status, occupation and gender also produced significant variety, while the separate but related issue of integration between diverse peoples further complicated the process of integration over space. Welsh, Scottish, Irish, German, Swedish, Finnish, Dutch, Italian and French Huguenot settlers arrived in America (and, to a lesser extent, in Britain) in 'unprecedented...unexpected and kaleidoscopic combinations' during the early eighteenth century. The growing challenges of racial and immigrant mixing raised questions about the priorities of communication. Which transatlantic and transnational connections mattered most and needed stabilizing? Who was best served by them and, indeed, which culture was to be transmitted?[74] Despite the growing integrative influence of advances in commercial and communications infrastructure, from the many stand-points of its diverse citizenry the British Atlantic world clearly remained disorderly and ambivalent: retaining a wild propensity to fragment. As Robert Harms has recently asserted, 'a [slaving] voyage that spanned three continents was largely shaped by local events and local rivalries originating in widely scattered parts of the Atlantic world.' This empire was not a unified leviathan but a patchwork of 'intersecting local con-texts' connected (often only momentarily) by the coming and going of seafaring vessels. The influence of these fleeting connections lived on and developed in local ways even after the 'various worlds' had slid apart. But without constant, dependable connections, for many, decentralized and myopic parochialism remained the rule.[75]

This complex composite model survives within Britain and America's national historiographies, but the mainstream emergence of Atlantic history has changed the terms of the debate. Previously, the bifurcation between 'integrative' and 'fragmentary' interpretations was a matter of emphasis on a sliding scale – conflicting currents in the same stream. Over a decade of concertedly Atlantic history, however, has so promoted integration, and engaged separately with countervailing social and cultural trends (as impediments to that process), that it risks dividing up the discussion. This threatens to undermine past work, because British and American historians typically analysed the interactions between different individuals, communities, structures and geographies precisely to illuminate how integration and diversity were able to co-exist in their respective societies. This objective remains vital to recovering the intricate social reality of the early modern period. The utility of Atlantic history would further increase, therefore, if its practitioners pursued the same goal more concertedly across its larger canvas. Rather than obscuring the compatibility of the integrative and fragmentary tendencies of the British Atlantic world, their field would indeed be 'greater than the sum of its parts' if it reasserted the need to explore these propensities' complex relationship.

This chapter has been a gesture towards that goal, and a simple demonstration that (in terms of social and cultural life as well as governance) the British Atlantic was a 'negotiated empire'.[76] This sprawling system was held together as much by the networks of connections that private individuals bargained to build in their varying local contexts (while attending to their particular needs) as by overarching political, institutional or ideological relationships. Such 'circuits of information' made transatlantic communities possible.[77] In turn, transatlantic society emerged from the overlap and intersection of many such mutualities. When contemporaries tried to visualize transatlanticism, therefore, they drew upon their idea of their own social networks. This was, as T.H. Breen understood in 1986 more clearly than many subsequent scholars, 'an empire not of formal institutions [and grand designs] but of common men and women making decisions about the quality of their lives, of thousands of people on the move, a human network'.[78]

Negotiations over distance like these were often, given existing levels of literacy and systems of communication, necessarily conducted in writing. To a significant degree, then, the British Atlantic was indeed 'a literate empire, a paper empire', relying on the infrastructure of regional and long-distance communication to maintain relationships.[79] Yet, the myriad uses to which this paper was put and the afterlife of the information it contained as it percolated into conversation and influenced local social activity can never be adequately expressed in the abstract. Case studies of the kind offered above, however, by providing a close analysis of how 'human beings continually construct, manipulate and even recast [their] social worlds', offer a basis for appraising this intricate tapestry of experience and how different forms of communication (print, script and speech) were woven into it. Like microhistories, detailed case analyses can 'test and refine standing generalizations' or refine syntheses by demonstrating that they are 'based more on prescriptive literature and slightly-informed assumptions than empirical, archival evidence'. They can lend precision to our understanding of broad geographical arenas like the Atlantic world, and begin to distil intelligibly what we might regard as this world's *essence*: its irreducible social complexity. Formulated to observe small groups of 'individuals making choices and developing strategies within the constraints of their time and place', this approach can also untangle the same negotiations between the more dispersed participants in well-documented transatlantic communities.[80] By concentrating in this way on specific groups of individuals and how they maintained their relationships, we can begin to give the vast British Atlantic arena a human face: identifying how a variety of particular perspectives combined with, and complicated, whatever collective affinities were uniting its myriad subjects. Only by more concertedly incorporating this approach – what could be called a 'social history of communication' – can Atlantic history fulfil what John Elliott saw as its ultimate purpose: the explanation of those *interdependent* 'movement[s] across and around the Atlantic basin, of people, commodities, cultural practices, and ideas'.[81]

Notes

1. I am grateful to the Library Company of Philadelphia; the American Antiquarian Society (AAS); Jesus College, Oxford; and the Arts and Humanities Research Council for their generous support of this project. I also wish to thank the staff at the American Philosophical Society (APS) and Yale Franklin Papers for their kind assistance. For a fuller discussion of the themes raised in this chapter, see N. M. Wrightson, 'Franklin's Networks: Aspects of British Atlantic Print Culture, Science, and Communication c.1730–60' (Oxford University, D.Phil. thesis 2007) and N. M. Wrightson, ' "[Those with] Great Abilities Have Not Always the Best Information": How Franklin's Transatlantic Book-Trade and Scientific Networks Interacted, ca. 1730–1757', *Early American Studies* (Philadephia, PA, volume 8, number 1, 2010).

2. James Raven, *London Booksellers and American Customers: Transatlantic Literary Community and the Charleston Library Society, 1748–1811* (Columbia, SC, 2002): 6.

3. J. A. L. Lemay and P. M. Zall (eds) *Benjamin Franklin's Autobiography: An Authoritative Text, Backgrounds, Criticism* (New York, NY, 1986): 54 (hereafter *BFA*).

4. *Gazette*, 4 Jul 1734, in *Papers of Benjamin Franklin*, 37 vols, vol. 1 (New Haven, CT, 1959–2003): 379 (hereafter *BFP*). See also, *Pennsylvania Gazette* 493, 25 May 1738 (hereafter *Gazette*), *BFP*, 2: 211–12; *Gazette* 807, 31 May 1744, *BFP*, 2: 451; *Gazette* 841, 22 Jan 1745, *BFP*, 3: 53; *Gazette* 929, 2 Oct 1746, *BFP*, 3: 98–9; *Gazette* 956, 9 Apr 1747, *BFP*, 3: 232; Yale Franklin Collection, MS. 24434, Ledger 'D' 1739–47, 117–20 (hereafter *Ledger 'D' 1739–47*).

5. John Smail, *Merchants, Markets and Manufacture: The English Wool Textile Industry in the Eighteenth Century* (Basingstoke, 1999): 77.

6. J. N. Green, 'English Books and Printing in the Age of Franklin', in Hugh Amory and David D. Hall (eds), *The Cambridge History of the Book in America: The Colonial Book in the Atlantic World* (Cambridge, 2000): 280–1.

7. Ian K. Steele, *The English Atlantic 1675–1740: An Exploration of Communication and Community* (Oxford, 1986): 11; Raven, *London Booksellers*, 11.

8. Raven, *London Booksellers*, 9; John Bidwell, 'Printers' Supplies and Capitalization', in Amory and Hall (eds), *The Colonial Book in the Atlantic World* (Cambridge, 2000): 181–2.

9. Franklin to Strahan, 10 Jul 1743, *BFP*, 2: 384.

10. Ibid., 4 Jul 1744, *BFP*, 2: 410–11.

11. Ibid., 12 Feb 1745, *BFP*, 3: 14; Franklin to Strahan, 16 Nov 1745, *BFP*, 3: 46; J. A. Cochrane, *Dr. Johnson's Printer: The Life of William Strahan* (London, 1964): 90–1.

12. Ledger 'D' 1739–47, 117–19.

13. R. D. Harlan, 'A Colonial Printer as Bookseller in Eighteenth-Century Philadelphia: The Case of David Hall', *Studies in Eighteenth-Century Culture*, 5 (1976): 357–61.

14. *BFP*, 3: 77; 4: 339, 487; 5: 81.

15. This relationship and its limitations are discussed more fully in Wrightson, 'Franklin's Networks'.

16. Franklin to Strahan, 18 Apr 1754, *BFP*, 5: 263.

17. Ibid., 25 Sept 1746, *BFP*, 3: 81.

18. Smail, *Merchants, Markets and Manufacture*, 82.
19. Ledger 'D' 1739–47, 119, *BFA*, 52.
20. Harlan, 'A Colonial Printer as Bookseller', 355–70, 361.
21. Franklin to Strahan, 27 Oct 1753, *BFP*, v: 82; Franklin to Strahan, 16 Nov 1752, *BFP*, iv: 380.
22. Logan to Franklin, 13 Jul 1747, *BFP*, iii: 146–7; N. S. Fiering, 'The Transatlantic Republic of Letters: A Note on the Circulation of Learned Periodicals to Early Eighteenth-Century America', *William and Mary Quarterly* 33 (1976): 654–7.
23. Smail, *Merchants, Markets and Manufacture*, 83.
24. Cochrane, *Dr. Johnson's Printer*, 62; R. D. Harlan, 'William Strahan's American Book Trade, 1744–76', *The Library Quarterly*, 31 (1961): 235–44.
25. Franklin to Strahan, 10 Jul 1743, *BFP*, ii: 384.
26. Strahan to Hall, 16 Jul 1763, American Philosophical Society (hereafter APS), MS. 638: William Strahan, 1715–85. Letters 1751–76 (hereafter *Strahan Letters*); Strahan to Hall, 6 Feb 1749, *Strahan Letters*.
27. Hall to Strahan, 9 Aug 1759, in *Letterbook II, Commencing Anno 1759* (1759–64), APS, MS. 1768, B H142.1.3: David Hall Papers (5).
28. Strahan to Hall, 30 Jan 1764, Historical Society of Pennsylvania (hereafter HSP), Society Miscellaneous Collection.
29. Rivington had forced Strahan to lower 'his prices to Hall (sometimes below cost)' and otherwise improve his terms. These tactics started a trend that 'made the book business more profitable to Americans': Green, 'English Books', 281.
30. This assessment of Collinson's scientific network differs markedly from the approach of Susan Scott Parrish, whose *American Curiosity: Cultures of Natural History in the Colonial British Atlantic World* (Chapel Hill, NC, 2006) presents the dynamics of Collinson's network as distinctively American. For a fuller analysis of Collinson's community and Parrish's work, see Wrightson 'Franklin's Networks'.
31. G. W. Edwards, 'Peter Collinson, F.R.S., F.A.S., 1694–1768', *Journal of the Royal Horticultural Society*, 93 (1968): 331.
32. Collinson was saving postage. Hanbury was a prominent Quaker merchant and ship-master: A. W. Armstrong (ed.), *'Forget Not Mee & My Garden...'*: *Selected Letters, 1725–68 of Peter Collinson, F.R.S.* (Philadelphia, PA, 2002) (hereafter *PCP*): 85 (n. 2); Collinson to Bartram, 16 Aug 1735, *PCP*, 35; J. M. Price, 'Hanbury, John (1700–58)', *ODNB*; J. M. Price, 'The Great Quaker Business Families of Eighteenth Century London', in R. S. Dunn and M. M. Dunn (eds), *The World of William Penn* (Philadephia, PA, 1986): 363–9.
33. E. Berkeley and D. S. Berkeley (eds), *Correspondence of John Bartram, 1734–77* (Gainesville, FL, 1992) (hereafter *JBP*): xii; Parrish, *American Curiosity*, 157, suggests Bartram inherited 650 acres of land at age 24, a relatively substantial holding. Even so, he had to continually work the land to earn his living and was unable to travel without sponsorship. Logan certainly did not regard him as wealthy.
34. Collinson to Bartram, 20 Mar 1736, *JBP*, 26.
35. Ibid., 24 Jan 1735, *JBP*, 6.
36. Collinson to Logan, 19 Aug 1737, *JBP*, 61.

37. Bartram to Collinson, May 1738, *JBP*, 89.
38. Collinson to Bartram, 24 Jan 1735, *JBP*, 4.
39. B. Latour, *Science in Action: How to Follow Scientists and Engineers Through Society* (Milton Keynes, 1987): 129–30. This had been true since at least the time of Galileo: M. Biagioli, *Galileo, Courtier: The Practice of Science in the Culture of Absolutism* (Chicago, IL, 1993).
40. For Logan's status as Pennsylvania's pre-eminent intellectual: F. B. Tolles, 'Philadelphia's First Scientist, James Logan', *Isis*, 47 (1956): 20–30.
41. Extract from Logan to Collinson, 3 Jun 1736, HSP MS. 83 (Carlotta Herring Brown Collection), Mss.Sec.B, Case 3: 'Peter Collinson' (2 vols).
42. Logan to Bartram, 19 Jun 1736, *JBP*, 31–2; Collinson to Bartram, 20 Sept 1736, *JBP*, 34.
43. Bartram to Alexander Catcott, 26 May 1742, *JBP*, 193–4.
44. Collinson to Colden, 26 Apr 1745, *PCP*, 126.
45. Colden to Linnaeus, 9 Feb 1749, *Letters and Papers of Cadwallader Colden*, 9 vols, vol. iv (New York, NY, 1918–37): 95–6 (hereafter *CCP*).
46. John Fothergill told a colonial correspondent that in London 'Not a day, not an hour [was] exempt from calls': Fothergill to Israel Pemberton, 12 Jun 1758, *JBP*, 194.
47. L. R. Stewart, *The Rise of Public Science: Rhetoric, Technology, and Natural Philosophy in Newtonian Britain, 1660–1750* (Cambridge, 1992): xxi, xxix–xxxi, argues that naturalists increasingly used public displays, experiments, and accessible publications like the *Philosophical Transactions*, in 'an effort to establish an epistemology of common experience' and legitimize their work as having public utility both within their own community and outside it: thus removing the threat of censorship and encouraging investment. I agree, but do not believe this resulted in a significant 'democratization of natural philosophy' breaking down the role of specialist knowledge as a barrier to participation before 1750 – especially outside the major European cities. In America, and other contexts where few public experiments took place and conversations between naturalists were infrequent because of distance, print and correspondence remained the primary sources of such an epistemology at least until Kinnersley's lectures in the 1750s, for which: J. Delbourgo, *A Most Amazing Scene of Wonders: Electricity and Enlightenment in Early America*, ch 3 (Cambridge, MA, 2006): 72–5.
48. Bartram to Collinson (late Dec 1739), *JBP*, 130.
49. Bartram and Collinson's requests persuaded most of Bartram's correspondents to repay his services with print. By 1743 he summarized his (fairly respectable) library/reading: Bartram to Sir Hans Sloane, 23 Sept 1743, *JBP*, 224. Bartram could not rely on friends to send what he wanted: Bartram to Alexander Catcott, 24 Nov 1743, *JBP*, 225.
50. Bartram to Colden, 10 Jan 1745, *JBP*, 248–9. The ubiquity of Miller's works in American scientific libraries must have added to Bartram's sense of injustice. Kalm tried to correct the public record in his *Travels*, which pointed out Miller's mistake (see A. B. Benson (ed.), *Peter Kalm's Travels in North America: the English version of 1770* (New York, NY, 1987): 105).
51. Bartram to Collinson, 27 Apr 1755, *JBP*, 382; Miller to Bartram, 2 Feb 1756, *JBP*, 396.
52. Steele, *English Atlantic*, 273.

53. Strahan to Hall, 10 Aug 1762, *BFP*, x, 141. The two men had been correspondents since 1743.
54. Collinson to Trew, 18 Jan 1752, *PCP*, 162.
55. Ibid., 5 Apr 1752, *PCP*, 182.
56. D. Armitage, 'Three Concepts of Atlantic History', in D. Armitage and M. J. Braddick (eds), *The British Atlantic World, 1500–1800* (Basingstoke, 2002): 11, 23.
57. C. Wickham, *Framing the Early Middle Ages: Europe and the Mediterranean, 400–800* (Oxford, 2005): 825; John Elliott argues that 'Atlantic history is always likely to remain a history framed more in terms of connections than of comparisons': J. H. Elliott, 'Afterword: Atlantic History: A Circumnavigation', in Armitage and Braddick (eds), *The British Atlantic World, 1500–1800*: 237; Similar to my interpretation: T. Bender (ed.), *Rethinking American History in a Global Age* (Berkeley, CA, 2002): 9, 109.
58. Armitage, 'Three Concepts', 21.
59. B. Bailyn, *Atlantic History: Concept and Contours* (Cambridge, MA, 2005): 60.
60. For imperial governance: C. A. Bayly, *The Birth of the Modern World, 1780–1914* (Oxford, 2004); S. Conway, *The British Isles and the War of American Independence* (Oxford, 2002); E. H. Gould and P. S. Onuf (eds), *Empire and Nation: The American Revolution in the Atlantic World* (Baltimore, MD, 2005); P. J. Marshall, *The Making and Unmaking of Empires: Britain, India, and America c. 1750–83* (Oxford, 2005). For political economy and ideology: David Armitage, *The Ideological Origins of the British Empire* (Cambridge, 2000); Bernard Bailyn, *The Ideological Origins of the American Revolution* (Cambridge, MA, 1967); Linda Colley, *Britons: Forging the Nation, 1707–1837* (London, 2003). For trade: David Hancock, *Citizens of the World: London Merchants and the Integration of the British Atlantic Community, 1735–85* (Cambridge, 1995); J. J. McCusker and K. Morgan, *The Early Modern Atlantic Economy* (Cambridge, 2001); N. Zahediah, 'London and the Colonial Customer in the late Seventeenth Century', *Economic History Review*, 47 (1994): 239–61. For slavery and migration: A. Games, *Migration and the Origins of the English Atlantic World* (Cambridge, MA, 1999); A. G. Roeber, *Palatines, Liberty, and Property: German Lutherans in Colonial British America* (Baltimore, MD, 1993); Kenneth Morgan, *Slavery, Atlantic Trade and the British Economy, 1660–1800* (Cambridge, 2000).
61. Atlantic culture: Linda Colley, *Captives: Britain, Empire and the World, 1600–1850* (London, 2003); T. L. Ditz, 'Formative Ventures: Eighteenth Century Commercial Letters and the Articulation of Experience', in R. Earle (ed.), *Epistolary Selves: Letters and Letter-Writers, 1600–1945* (Aldershot, 1999): 59–78; Sarah Knott, 'A Cultural History of Sensibility in the Era of the American Revolution' (Oxford University D.Phil. thesis, 1999); Ned C. Landsman, *From Colonials to Provincials: American thought and Culture, 1680–1760* (New York, NY, 1997). Important works not engaging with the historiography of early-modern Britain: J. E. Chaplin, *The First Scientific American: Benjamin Franklin and the Pursuit of Genius* (New York, NY, 2006); G. S. Wood, *The Radicalism of the American Revolution* (New York, NY, 1992). Unlike race and gender 'Class is very little discussed in the historiography of early America' and little Atlantic social history exists: K. E. Wrightson, 'Class', in Armitage and Braddick (eds), *The British Atlantic*

World, 1500–1800, 304–5. Further examples: T. M. Devine, *Scotland's Empire, 1600–1815* (London, 2004); Patrick Griffin, *The People with No Name: Ireland's Ulster Scots, America's Scots Irish, and the Creation of a British Atlantic World, 1689–1764* (Princeton, NJ, 2001); Raven, *London Booksellers*.

62. J. P. Greene, *Pursuits of Happiness: The Social Development of Early Modern British Colonies and the Formation of American Culture* (Chapel Hill, NC, 1988); Peter Laslett, *The World We Have Lost* (New York, NY, 1965); John M. Murrin, *Anglicizing an American Colony: The Transformation of Provincial Massachusetts* (Yale University PhD thesis, 1966); Colley, *Britons*, 134–6; Steele, *English Atlantic*, 229–31.

63. D. S. Shields, 'Eighteenth-Century Literary Culture', in Amory and Hall (eds), *The Colonial Book in the Atlantic World*, 444.

64. Steele, *English Atlantic*, 5, 213, 264.

65. Ibid., 278; Greene, *Pursuits of Happiness*, 168–71; N. Kilian, 'New Wine in Old Skins? American Definitions of Empire and the Emergence of a New Concept', in David Armitage (ed.), *Theories of Empire, 1450–1800* (Aldershot, 1998): 307–8; Peter Linebaugh, *The London Hanged: Crime and Civil Society in the Eighteenth Century* (London, 2003): 116–17.

66. Steele, *English Atlantic*, 6, 274.

67. T. H. Breen, 'An Empire of Goods: The Anglicization of Colonial America, 1690–1776', *Journal of British Studies*, 25 (1986): 467–99, 487, 490.

68. T. H. Breen, ' "Baubles of Britain": The American and Consumer Revolutions of the Eighteenth Century', *Past and Present*, 119 (1988): 73–104 (76).

69. R. L. Bushman, *The Refinement of America: Persons, Houses, Cities* (New York, NY, 1992): xii.

70. R. D. Brown, *Knowledge is Power: The Diffusion of Information in Early America, 1700–1865*, ch. 2 (Oxford, 1989); Peter Thompson, *Rum Punch & Revolution: Taverngoing & Public Life in Eighteenth-Century Philadelphia* (Philadelphia, PA, 1998): 19. For the anatomy of 'unfree labour': D. Waldstreicher, *Runaway America: Benjamin Franklin, Slavery, and the American Revolution* (New York, NY, 2004).

71. Brown, *Knowledge is Power*, 67.

72. E. C. Reilly, 'The Wages of Piety: The Boston Book Trade of Jeremy Condy', in W. L Joyce (ed.), *Printing and Society in Early America* (Worcester, MA, 1983): 111.

73. For integration: Peter Borsay, 'The English Urban Renaissance: the development of provincial urban culture c.1680–c.1760', in *The Eighteenth-Century Town: A Reader in English Urban History 1688–1820* (London, 1990); J. Brewer, *The Sinews of Power: War, Money and the English State, 1688–1783* (London, 1989); C. Y. Ferdinand, *Benjamin Collins and the Provincial Newspaper Trade in the Eighteenth Century* (Oxford, 1997); D. R. Hainsworth, *Stewards, Lords and People: The Estate Steward and His World in Later Stuart England* (Cambridge, 1992); L. E. Klein, 'Politeness and the Interpretation of the British Eighteenth Century', *Historical Journal*, 45 (2002): 869–98; Neil McKendrick, John Brewer, and J. H. Plumb (eds), *The Birth of a Consumer Society: The Commercialization of Eighteenth-Century England* (London, 1982); S. Pincus and P. Lake, 'Rethinking the Public Sphere in Early Modern England', *The Journal of British Studies*, 45 (2006); D. Wahrman, 'National Society, Communal Culture: An Argument About the Recent Historiography of Eighteenth-Century

Britain', *Social History*, 17 (1992): 43–72. For fragmentedness: J. Barry, 'Civility and Civic Culture in Early Modern England: The Meaning of Urban Freedom', in Peter Burke, B. H. Harrison and Paul Slack (eds), *Civil Histories: Essays Presented to Sir Keith Thomas* (Oxford, 2000); J. Barry, 'Provincial Town Culture, 1640–1780: Urbane or Civic?', in J. H. Pittock and A. Wear (eds), *Interpretation and Cultural History* (Basingstoke, 1991); A. R. Ekirch, 'The Transportation of Scottish Criminals to America During the Eighteenth Century', *Journal of British Studies*, 24 (1985): 366–74; H. R. French, 'Social Status, Localism and the "Middle Sort of People" in England 1620–1750', *Past and Present*, 166 (2000): 66–99; Harold Love, *Scribal Publication in Seventeenth-Century England* (Oxford, 1993); R. Paley, ' "An Imperfect, Inadequate and Wretched System"? Policing Long Before Peel', *Criminal Justice History*, 10 (1989): 95–130.

74. Alan Taylor, *American Colonies: The Settling of North America* (London, 2002): xi–ii; Steele, *English Atlantic*: 260, 270. Native Americans also contributed to creolisation: Nancy Shoemaker, *A Strange Likeness: Becoming Red and White in Eighteenth-Century North America* (Oxford, 2004).

75. R. W. Harms, *The Diligent: A Voyage Through the Worlds of the Slave Trade* (Reading, MA, 2002): xix–xx.

76. C. Daniels and M. V. Kennedy (eds), *Negotiated Empires: Centres and Peripheries in the Americas, 1500–1820* (London, 2002).

77. Miles Ogborn, *Spaces of Modernity: London's Geographies, 1680–1780* (New York, NY, 1998): 209.

78. Breen, 'Empire of Goods', 472.

79. Steele, *English Atlantic*, 265.

80. E. Muir, 'Introduction: Observing Trifles', in E. Muir and G. Ruggiero (eds), *Microhistory and the Lost Peoples of Europe* (Baltimore, MD, 1991): viii. I agree with Richard Brown's distinguishing of case-studies from microhistories on the basis that the former are less focused on studying exceptional individuals, exploring a particular (narrowly defined) locality over time, or analysing a specific event. Like microhistories, however, the best case-studies still seek 'to pose wholly new questions or to assert original interpretations': Richard D. Brown, 'Microhistory and the Post-Modern Challenge', *Journal of the Early Republic*, 23 (2003): 13, 18; see also Carlo Ginzburg, *The Cheese and the Worms: The Cosmos of a Sixteenth-Century Miller* (London, 1980).

81. T. H. Breen first described my work as attempting a 'social history of transatlantic communication' (North American Conference of British Studies, 2006). Elliott, 'Afterword', 239.

7

The Dutch Book Trade in Colonial New York City: The Transatlantic Connection

Joyce D. Goodfriend

On 23 January 1764, Peter T. Curtenius, a New York City merchant at the Sign of the Golden Anvil and Hammer, placed a lengthy advertisement in the *New York Gazette* offering a wide array of goods that he had just imported from Bristol, London and Amsterdam. Known primarily as an ironmonger, Curtenius inserted a separate section at the end of his notice under the heading '*Likewise the undermentioned* DUTCH BOOKS: Titles in Dutch as follows, viz.' Here followed an enumeration of more than 60 books and types of books, all presumably published in the Netherlands.[1]

Curtenius had every expectation of selling these books to men and women who were capable of reading works in the Dutch language. As the son of a Dutch Reformed minister who had preached in New Jersey and in present-day Brooklyn, he was well aware that Dutch remained the everyday language of thousands of people whose ancestors had lived in the Dutch colony of New Netherland. Though the transfer of sovereignty to the English had occurred a century earlier, in 1664, the great majority of the residents of the largely Dutch towns of New York's Hudson Valley (including Albany), western Long Island (Brooklyn) and northern and central New Jersey, as well as a small but vocal segment of New York City's population, spoke and, in all likelihood, could read Dutch.

The market for Dutch-language books in New York City and its hinterland in the second half of the eighteenth century may have been well known to Curtenius, but scholars have paid little attention to colonial New York's Dutch book trade.[2] The most important work related to the subject of Dutch-language books in New York is Hendrik Edelman's *Dutch-American Bibliography 1693–1794*, which catalogues the

92 Dutch-language books and broadsides printed in America between 1693 and 1775 (and 100 more from 1775 to 1794).[3] In a subsequent study of the Dutch-language press in America, Edelman provides a brief narrative of Dutch printing in the colonial era.[4] Local Dutch imprints are also mentioned in a dissertation on printing in colonial New York.[5]

The emphasis on Dutch-language books produced in New York found in existing scholarship distorts our picture of colonial New York's Dutch book trade. Local imprints could not entirely satisfy the demand of the region's Dutch readers for works in their native language and therefore Dutch books had to be imported from the Netherlands. The aim of this chapter is to explore this overlooked dimension of New York's Dutch book trade and to place it in historical context. I will proceed by proposing answers to four interrelated questions: Why did the market for Dutch-language books in New York City and the surrounding area persist into the eighteenth century? Why was it necessary to import Dutch books from the Netherlands to New York City? What evidence do we have of imported Dutch books in colonial New York? What sorts of Dutch books were imported into colonial New York City? The following concludes with brief comments on the historical significance of this enterprise in the light of the history of colonial New York and of its book trade.

The territory that subsequently became New York and New Jersey was colonized by the Dutch West India Company. Dutch books routinely circulated in New Netherland during the 40 years of its existence (1624–64), having been brought from Europe by the settlers or shipped into the colony.[6] The seizure of the Dutch colony by the English in 1664 (the colony reverted to Dutch jurisdiction briefly in 1673–74) did not immediately change the cultural demography of the region, since the great majority of New Netherlanders took advantage of the lenient terms of surrender and chose to remain in their homes.[7] Even as English settlers and a sizeable group of French Protestant refugees filtered into the formerly Dutch province and began to alter the composition of the population, most Dutch or culturally Dutch people continued in their old ways and indeed established new zones of cultural influence in northern and central New Jersey. Throughout the seventeenth century and well into the eighteenth century, most Dutch in the rural areas of the Hudson Valley, western Long Island and New Jersey, as well as in the city of Albany, kept Dutch as their primary language. In New York City, the English language had made substantial inroads among the descendants of New Netherlanders by the second quarter of the eighteenth century, but not until the 1760s, and after a long and bitter battle,

English-language preaching was introduced into the Dutch Reformed Church. Even then, a hard core of Dutch-language advocates remained in the city.[8]

Historians have remarked on the staying power of the Dutch language in New York and New Jersey, but few have paused to ponder its causes. The Dutch adhered to their native tongue in part because of an aversion to English. 'Now it seems that it has pleased the Lord [to ordain] that we must learn English', Jeremias van Rensselaer confided to his mother in Amsterdam in 1668. 'The worst of it all is that we have already for nearly four years been under this jurisdiction and that as yet I have learned so little. The reason is that one has no liking for it.'[9] But more important was their affinity for Dutch, a partiality that was enhanced by their sustained exposure to Dutch speech and texts. Since the great majority of those living in heavily Dutch precincts could read in Dutch, their continuing access to Dutch print culture arguably played a critical role in reinforcing their allegiance to the language of their forbears. Poring over printed Dutch texts and immersing themselves in the rhythms of a language rooted in a distant place and time, far from being an exercise in nostalgia, was a vital means of rejuvenation in a world that was becoming increasingly alien. In this sense, the Dutch language became a proxy for the version of Dutch culture that imbued their life with meaning.

It has been insufficiently recognized that the many descendants of New Netherlanders who kept Dutch as their primary language for generations after their colony came under English rule (and even into the nineteenth century in the new American nation) had a high rate of literacy and yearned to read in their native language.[10] These were the people who purchased Dutch books.

For most of the seventeenth century, under both Dutch and English rule, all books, of whatever language, were imported into New York because no printing press existed on Manhattan. Books were either brought in by colonists or shipped from England, Europe and, in some cases, Boston. After William Bradford established a printing press in New York City in 1693, the opportunity arose to produce Dutch-language books. Although a number of Dutch titles were issued by Bradford and other New York printers in subsequent years, these publications did not meet the needs of the mid-Atlantic colonies' Dutch audience for several reasons.

For the educated men who produced most local Dutch texts, the main problem was the deficient knowledge of local printers. Familiar with the quality of printing in the Netherlands, they felt that working with New York's non-Dutch printers forced them to compromise their standards. In 1696, shortly after Bradford commenced work, the city's learned Dutch Reformed minister, Henricus Selyns, lamented the lack of printing outlets for Dutch authors: 'One has no occasion here to publish and to make anything known in print as our printer understands nothing but the English language.'[11] Other Dutch New Yorkers agreed with the sentiments expressed by Selyns. Dissatisfied with William Bradford's 1706 and 1712 editions of a catechism written by Domine Gualtherus Du Bois, Jacobus Goelet, Jnr., went so far as to send the book to be reprinted in the Netherlands in 1725.[12] Tobias Boel, the principal author of the *Klagte Van Eenige Leeden der Nederduytse Hervormde Kerk...*, a work jointly printed by Bradford and John Peter Zenger in 1725, entered this caveat in the text. 'All errors in punctuation, spelling and the use of capital letters, the indulgent reader will be pleased to excuse, for the reason that the printers are not familiar with the Dutch language.'[13]

A low estimate of the ability of printer William Bradford to produce a work in Dutch probably played a part in the decision of Domine Bernardus Freeman of Midwoud to send two of his manuscripts to the Netherlands for printing: *De Spiegel der selfkennis...* (Amsterdam, Gedrukt by J. Roman, 1720) and *De Weegschale der genade Gods....* (Amsterdam, Gedrukt by J. Roman, 1721). Freeman may have hoped for better results when Bradford's apprentice, German-born John Peter Zenger, set up his own press. Among Zenger's earliest imprints were a series of works by Dutch ministers and laymen published between 1725 and 1729. Yet Zenger's imperfect command of the Dutch language also became an issue. In the *Verdeediging Van D. Bernardus Freeman*, printed by Zenger in 1726, the author states: 'If here or there the sentence, spelling or great or small letters are not seen as art requires, the good reader please forgive it while the printer is still young and inexperienced in the Dutch language. The printer's errors which may obstruct the sentence he may please correct.'[14] There follows a list of errors.

A quarter of a century later, in 1752, Domine Lambertus De Ronde was a bit more generous in his remarks on the imperfect work of the local printer who published his sermons. After reminding the reader of 'how little Dutch is printed here [in New York]' he advises 'forgiving the printer's errors...when he does not see the basic terms of the text printed in the original language'. After all, 'this printing press is not in the same state of readiness as those in other countries', meaning that New York printers lack all the type and equipment that printers have in the Netherlands.[15] In another sermon issued the same year, De Ronde counseled tolerance on the part of the reader: 'Since seldom something comes off the press both here and in Holland without printing errors, with which even the greatest lovers of languages have to be patient, it may behoove the reader to ignore the printing errors found here and there in this booklet.'[16] The implication of all these comments, however phrased, is clear. To obtain high-quality Dutch books, one needed to import them from the Netherlands.

For the general reader, a more important reason for importing Dutch books was the limited range of titles produced in New York. The output of New York's printers consisted mainly of almanacs and theological works written by Dutch ministers in America. Yet the most essential books for Dutch families were the Great Dutch Bibles that were the repository of family births, marriages and deaths, and the psalters containing the New Testament and the Psalms which women, in particular, carried to church.[17] Unless these works were acquired through inheritance, they had to be procured from the Netherlands, where they were published. Although there were a few locally produced catechisms and one schoolbook, these commonly used books were in short supply and also had to be obtained from abroad.[18] Schoolteacher Abraham De La Noy, who doubled as a trader, had a vast collection of Dutch schoolbooks, including multiple copies of catechism books, song books, 'Books of Cortimus', and 'the Golden trumpet' in stock when he died in 1702. The 1702 inventory of Samuel Mynderts, who immigrated to New York City from Utrecht around 1686 with his wife and daughter, and who had two brothers in Utrecht, included four dozen ABC books, seven dozen catechisms, and 22 copies of 'France Tyranny' and 'Speigle of Youth'. Among the items appraisers found in Gertye Splinter's shop in 1722 were '52 small Dutch Childrens School Books'.[19] In short, there was a pressing need to supplement local Dutch imprints with imported Dutch books.

The demand for publications in the Dutch language in New York was satisfied in a variety of ways. Often acquiring a Dutch book depended on individual initiative. As they had done in New Netherland, colonists could request relatives in the home country to send them books. In 1660, Jeremias van Rensselaer wrote to his mother in Amsterdam to ask her 'to have Cornelis De Key...make me a psalter to fit these golden clasps, one of the thinnest and most oblong kind, to carry in the pocket'.[20] At another time, he requested a rhymed psalter. More commonly, residents had to make do with Dutch books already in the colony, acquiring some through inheritance and borrowing others. In 1674, Gerardus Beekman, in the course of studying to be a doctor, resorted to making a manuscript copy of 'the original Dutch edition of the great medical textbook by Sylvanus of Leiden which was published in 1672'.[21] Others may have taken old texts to a former apprentice of a well-known printer of Middelburg in Zeeland who 'sometimes bound old books, and was the only bookbinder in the country'.[22]

One merchant, Margaret Hardenbroeck, who was married to seventeenth-century New York City's wealthiest man, Frederick Philipse, but who was a trader in her own right, realized the potential market for Dutch books in a colony that still had a majority Dutch population. Aiming to supply New York's Dutch residents with books in their native tongue, her ship, the *Charles*, sailed from Amsterdam to New York via Plymouth, England, in 1679 with a cargo that included 'A pcell of Dutch Printd Books valld L29 subs'.[23] Two years later, the cargo of the *Charles* included Dutch Bibles.[24]

Alternatively, one could ask visitors who were returning to the homeland to ship books to New York. In 1680, on the eve of his departure for the Netherlands, Labadist missionary Jasper Danckaerts, who had arrived on the *Charles* in 1679, recorded that his new friend Ephraim Hermans had asked him 'to send him from Amsterdam a good new Bible.'[25] Once in Amsterdam, Danckaerts went Bible-shopping for Hermans. He proceeded to buy him a 'large Bible,' noting that 'It cost ... twenty-eight guilders, because it was the last one of Ravestyn's edition.' Danckaerts also kept the needs of Arnoldus de La Grange, a New York City resident who stocked books in his shop, in mind. 'There was a new edition [of the Bible] in press at the Fish Market, at the place where we bought this one, upon the point of the gate as you go to the Post Office.' This volume was put on board a ship to New York, addressed to the shopkeeper.[26]

Over the years, individuals learned of books published in the Netherlands and at times were sent specific volumes. Merchant George Brinkerhoff was informed by a commercial correspondent in Amsterdam of certain pamphlets criticizing the Moravians and, in 1741, Domine Gualtherus Du Bois noted that he had received an anti-Moravian tract sent to him by a minister in Amsterdam.[27] In 1764, Domine Lambertus De Ronde requested a member of the Amsterdam Classis to send him a copy of a controversial theological work, Marshall (on Sanctification). 'Although I understand the sentiments expressed in that book, in the English language,' De Ronde wrote, 'yet since ... informs me that it is also extant in Dutch, I would feel greatly obliged to you, if you would send a Dutch copy to me. I will gladly pay the charges.'[28] On 4 February 1765, the Classis of Amsterdam informed De Ronde 'This book [Marshall (on Sanctification)] with one in the Dutch language, we send you as a brotherly present, though a small one.'[29] On 9 September 1765, De Ronde acknowledged that he had received 'that book of Marshall'.[30]

Instances of individuals acquiring Dutch books from abroad could no doubt be multiplied, but far more significant in ensuring the presence of Dutch books in New York were the concerted efforts of ministers and religious institutions on both sides of the Atlantic. At the turn of the eighteenth century, Britons were well aware that large segments of New York's population could read only Dutch and that most of these people were affiliated with the Dutch Reformed Church. Anglican leaders wanted nothing more than to win these men and women over to the Church of England through their missionary organizations, the Society for the Propagation of the Gospel in Foreign Parts (SPG) and the Society for the Promotion of Christian Knowledge (SPCK). Furnishing religious texts in the colonists' native language was a step in this direction. In New York, they reached out to the Dutch colonists mainly by supplying Anglican printed material in the Dutch language. They sponsored translations of the *Book of Common Prayer* and shipped it along with Bibles and other religious works to New York, mainly to areas outside New York City.[31] In 1711, a bilingual English and Dutch edition of the *Book of Common Prayer* was printed by John Crellius in Amsterdam for the SPCK.[32] Crellius also printed 'a 750 copy edition of the Church Liturgy in English and Low Dutch prepared by Vandereyken, reader at the Royal Dutch Chapel at St. James' for the SPG.[33]

The translation and printing of Dutch-language versions of Anglican religious volumes were undertaken in England, but it was SPG missionaries in New York who were entrusted with the distribution of these books. After Thomas Barclay, Albany's Anglican minister, requested books in 1710, he was sent 'Dutch Bibles and Prayer Books, sermons, New Testaments, psalters and other printed materials'.[34] Although some Dutch New Yorkers may have been grateful for the reading material in their native tongue, more than a few likely harboured reservations about Anglican emissaries deciding what they should read. Those who belonged to either of the colony's Dutch Churches – the Reformed and the Lutheran – preferred religious texts that supported their own doctrines and beliefs.

The Amsterdam Classis of the Dutch Reformed Church had made clear in 1656 that it wished only the instructional works it had sanctioned to be used in New Netherland. After New Netherland Domine Johannes Megapolensis attempted to have a catechetical book that he had written printed in the Netherlands and circulated in New Netherland, they enunciated their policy in no uncertain terms. 'In [our] churches no other catechisms beside the Heidelberg and the Compendium of the same, called the Short Inquiry, is in use in the catechetical sermons, catechism classes and schools.'[35] Although Amsterdam ministers advised that 'it would be more edifying to send thither...a goodly number of the Netherland catechisms, and the Compendiums of the same', no record of such volumes being shipped to the colony has been found.[36] Religious books, no doubt, were included in the cargoes West India Company ships carried to New Netherland, but such items are difficult to trace. In a 1657 letter to an Amsterdam minister, schoolmaster Evert Pietersen, stationed on the South River in Delaware, posted an urgent request for teaching materials. 'I am engaged in keeping school, with twenty five children in it; but I have no paper nor pens for the use of the children, nor slates and pencils....The books mentioned on the enclosed memorandum, please to take care that they be sent by the first ship, for I am especially in need of them.'[37] Available sources contain only scant mention of the West India Company or the Amsterdam Classis supplying religious books to Dutch colonists in either New Netherland or New York. In the late seventeenth and early eighteenth centuries, however, the deacons of the Dutch Reformed Church in Flatbush, New York, ordered numerous copies of Dutch religious books – Bibles, various catechisms and other theological works, some of them controversial – for their communicants.[38]

Far more complete documentation of the importation of Dutch religious books exists for the small congregation of Dutch Lutherans. Almost immediately after English authorities recognized the Lutheran Church in New York City, ministers began to write to the Consistory of the Lutheran church in Amsterdam for the religious books they required for their pastoral work. In 1669, Jacobus Fabricius articulated his need for 'a hundred hymnals and small Lutheran catechisms'. Then the new minister began to think more expansively: 'Should there be a printer who could supply us with a small collection of type to print ABC books and catechisms, together with some samples of reading and writing, he could earn his living to his ample satisfaction.'[39] Bernhard Arensius, the next Lutheran minister, underscored the high prices of books in New York in his plea to Amsterdam Church leaders in 1671 to 'send to these poor churches in this heathen country at the first opportunity a quantity of Lutheran psalm books, either in cloth or in linen (which on account of the high cost cannot be bought here by us)'.[40]

In 1705, Justus Falckner explained why his small dispersed congregation required books: 'The majority of them are poor and many, especially the young people, ignorant on account of the lack of Bibles, Catechisms, Psalm and Hymn books.' In light of the Dutch Reformed majority in the area, he made a very specific request: 'It would be of great service here to have a booklet in which, by means of short questions and answers, the difference between the Lutheran and the so-called Reformed opinions were exposed, every point thus concluding, "Therefore the Lutheran opinion is the better one."'[41]

A subsequent request for books from Falckner was answered in 1712 by the Elders of the Lutheran Church at Amsterdam, who decided to send him 'One folio Bible, 50 Psalters, 50 *Paradijshofkens*, and 50 Haverman's prayer books and to offer the same to [his] congregation'.[42] Falckner exulted over the receipt of these books: 'There has until now been a spiritual hunger among many of this small congregation here for this food of their soul which they, each in his measure, draw from such holy and spiritual books.'[43] In his eyes, the impact of the books was profound. They were 'a blessed present' since 'many members of the small scattered congregation, who were as good as asleep, yes dead, have through these books become awake and alive and found renewed zeal and courage to remain within the obedience of our Holy Church and to exercise themselves in the true faith and in godliness.' Prior to this, 'they hardly dared openly to confess their faith, as almost no books thereof are seen here and none can be obtained here.' He added that 'especially the psalters, so far as the 50 have been able to go, are a potent means of arousing the young people, of attracting them to practice true Christianity and of teaching them what is needed thereto'.[44] Heartened by the willingness of his co-religionists overseas to provide books for him and his congregation, Falckner wrote that he would be obliged if he was sent 'a church agenda, containing all the formularies, not only of confession, the sacraments, marriage, burial, etc., but those of ordination in octavo, with good, large print'.[45]

When Wilhelmus C. Berckenmeyer arrived on the scene in 1725, he summed up the local situation regarding books:

> I have found here a folio Bible, also a church liturgy.... there is a universal complaint about the scarcity of hymn-books, catechisms and Bibles. Nearly all the [Bibles] that we have here are those sent by the...Consistory of Amsterdam and contain the name of the Rt. Rev. J Wesling. They know little of catechisms; Bibles are found with the older families, but the new families have to borrow one from another.[46]

Lutheran records offer particulars on the mechanics of transporting Dutch books to New York. The Consistory of Amsterdam's Lutheran

Church wrote that it had sent the New York Lutheran congregation 'a small case of books, wherein are packed a large folio Bible, 50 Psalters, 50 *Paradijshofkens*, and 50 Haverman's prayer books, which case marked L.G.N. 1, was loaded at London by Messrs. Luttman & Remmers, on November 7, 1712, in the ship "Succer", Charles Stow, master, bound for New York.'[47] By 1724, the Amsterdam firm of Laasbye and Nieuwgaard, whose partners were active in Lutheran affairs, served as the channel through which communications and goods were sent to New York. These men performed more than mercantile services for their overseas coreligionists. 'I am glad that Mr. Nieugaard is back again in his church position', pastor Berckenmeyer wrote in 1730. 'One result of this is doubtless the reason why the honorable reverend Consistory listens to us again.'[48]

Books were seen by New York Lutherans not only as cherished texts but as commodities with value. In 1715, Church leaders decided that 'the 24 books which the Consistory in Amsterdam presented to the Lutheran Church in New York' were to be sold and 'the receipts...are to be used to pay for [Pastor Justus Falckner's] expense and trouble in having a catechism printed at his own cost for the benefit of the congregation.'[49] In 1708, Falckner had enlisted New York printer William Bradford to publish his *Grondlycke Onderricht van Sekere Voorname Hoofd-Stucken, der Waren, Loutern, Saligmakendam, Christelycken Leere*.[50] In 1730, local Lutherans wanted to return unsold books to Amsterdam, presumably for credit. 'I had thought that the books sent back by us could be sold through a bookseller in Holland where there are more book lovers, which is better than to let them lie around here unwanted.'[51] This remark offers clues to the reading tastes of New York's Lutherans, most of whom likely had only a minimal education.

What is striking about the Lutheran book trade to New York is the specificity of the requests submitted by the local ministers and their apparent knowledge of which titles would appeal to their congregants. In letters to Laasbye and Nieuwgaard, his suppliers in Amsterdam, pastor Wilhelm Berckenmeyer furnished precise details regarding the volumes he wanted. 'We note that the books by Masius on the doctrine of the Lutherans and the Reformed have met with great approval', he wrote in 1728.

And since we had in time past received some books for which there are no buyers in our land, and therefore they are of no use to us, we request that your Honors please take the trouble to exchange them for as many books by Masius as can be gotten for them.[52]

He continued 'Also there are still a dozen psalters in quarto with clasps, and 30 small Catechisms of the kind from Konijnberg [?]. And when Muller's postil by Dezius is published, we are expecting a half a dozen.'[53] Obtaining particular books took time, since in 1730 he wrote, 'The Postils by Muller for use in the home remain on order with you, whenever they can be gotten, so that in the first shipment I shall expect three copies. Meanwhile I am ordering the following:

3 Postils by Velten on the Gospels
1 Manne's Postil on all the texts of the Epistles
3 Lutheran Hymnals, translated
3 Arnd's Paradise Gardens
3 Masius
6 small, long duodecimo Psalters
6 New Testaments
6 large Psalters
2 Bibles'[54]

Correspondents in Europe presumably kept Berckenmeyer informed on the latest Lutheran literature and guided his choices.

The reprinting of a Dutch book of religious controversy in New York suggests that ordinary Dutch New Yorkers were eager for news of religious affairs in the Netherlands and would buy and read examples of these wars of words. Having somehow acquired a copy of a book written by the ministers of Groningen to refute a book published by Jacob Ten Cate in 1718, John Peter Zenger was confident that an audience for this type of literature existed in New York. In 1736, he issued a reprint of *WAARSCHOUWING tegens zeker Boekje, genaamt VADERLIKGESCHENK, & c. DOOR JACOB TEN CATE Waarin de Dweperyen en Vrygeestery van Ten Cate en de befaamde Antoinette de Bourignon Duidelyk ontdekt worden, ten dienste der klein-weetendee misleide Zielen, en Bestierenge der Regtzinnigen. OPGESTELT DOOR De Predikanten van Groningen voor heen te Groningen by Jurjen Spandaw, nu gedrukt TE NEW-YORK door J. Peter Zenger, 1736.*[55]

Directly ordering books through mercantile firms in Amsterdam was the best way of obtaining specific titles, but for most Dutch New Yorkers, this was not feasible. Those whose needs could not be stated precisely or who lacked the requisite connections in the Netherlands had to rely on city merchants to supply them with Dutch-language books. In the early years of English rule, Dutch books were available in the local marketplace. Upon entering the 'little shop' of Arnoldus de La Grange in 1678, Jasper Danckaerts observed that 'there were plenty of books around'. When asked what books he liked most, shopkeeper La Grange 'brought forward two of the elder Brakel, one of which was, *De Trappen des Geestelycken Levens* ... [and] another written by a Scotchman ... and translated by Domine Koelman'.[56]

The most likely successor to La Grange as a purveyor of Dutch books in New York City was Jacobus Goelet, a former schoolmaster who ran a stationery shop in the early eighteenth century.[57] In 1706, he had arranged for the catechism written by Domine Gualtherus Du Bois to be printed by William Bradford.[58] By 1730, his son, Jacobus Goelet, Jnr., had become a bookseller and stationer and was working in conjunction with printer John Peter Zenger to bring Dutch books to the market. On the title pages of several of the Dutch books printed by Zenger, the phrase '*Te Koop*' by Jacobus Goelet appears, indicating that Goelet was the primary distributor for Zenger's output of Dutch books. Though we have no inventory of the imported Dutch books that Goelet carried, it is fair to assume that he engaged in a small book trade with Amsterdam. His earlier career as a mariner and ship captain had brought him to Amsterdam in 1710 and again in 1720. With family members in the mercantile business in the Netherlands, Goelet no doubt had trading connections there.[59]

Goelet and perhaps other local merchants saw a need for the importation of Dutch Bibles and other religious works from the Netherlands. By the early eighteenth century, New Netherland families were into the third and fourth generation. In light of this expanding Dutch population, the need for editions of the Great Dutch Bible (*Statenbybel*) printed only in cities in the Netherlands grew exponentially among the Dutch-descended families of New York and New Jersey. Inheritance was the primary means by which Dutch families conveyed Bibles and religious works to their progeny. The wills and inventories of Dutch New Yorkers contain numerous references to Great Dutch Bibles and occasionally psalters or other religious books. In their wills, and perhaps more commonly through tacit understandings, Dutch New Yorkers left Dutch Bibles and Testaments as well as other books to their children. In 1711, for example, cordwainer Evert Van Hook bequeathed his Great Dutch Bible to his eldest son, his Great Book of Emanuel de Meter to another son, and his Great Marturas [Martyrs?] Book to his daughter in his will.[60] Years later, Mary Gouverneur, the widow of Abraham Gouverneur, bequeathed to her grandson 'my Large Book of Martyrs, with silver hooks, and all other printed books that did belong to my deceased husband'.[61]

But since the family Bible, originally brought or imported by the immigrant settler, normally passed to the eldest son, all the other adult sons would need to purchase a copy after they married. We can infer, then, that virtually all the Great Dutch Bibles with a publication date after 1674 that have come down over the generations in Dutch American families were imported. Numerous examples of such Bibles can be found in archives, museums and presumably in private collections. A Dutch Bible belonging to Samuel Kip and containing family records in Dutch was published in Dordrecht and Amsterdam in 1702.[62] On display in the Brooklyn Museum is a large leather-bound Dutch Bible with brass fastening clasps, published in Dordrecht in 1741, and originally belonging to the Ditmars family of Kings County, New York.[63] *De Cl. Psalmen des Propheten Davids*, a Dutch psalter published in Amsterdam in 1671 and inscribed with the date 1679 and the words 'Johannes Schenck/Zyn Bock' and a Dutch New Testament published in Amsterdam in 1728 and inscribed for Abraham Schenck are also owned by this museum.[64]

Over the course of their lives in New York and New Jersey, individuals purchased Dutch books printed abroad, but tracing these acquisitions is very difficult. The best evidence of book ownership comes from references to the book collections of ministers. Anglican Henry Barclay of New York City's Trinity Church had previously been stationed in Albany, where Dutch was the common language. Barclay, who had married Mary Rutgers, a member of a prominent Dutch family, not surprisingly became fluent in Dutch and owned Dutch reading material. When he made his will in 1764, he specified that his wife was to inherit 'all my printed books in the Low Dutch language'. Though she might have brought a few of these volumes into the marriage, it is probable that Barclay had purchased at least some imported Dutch books.[65]

Books were prized by Dutch Reformed domines, since they served as resources for writing sermons and theological treatises. The books in a minister's library were assembled with care over many years, starting with a nucleus of books brought from overseas and supplemented by later purchases.[66] New Amsterdam minister Samuel Drisius, whose career extended into the English period, specifically referred to his library when he wrote his will in 1669. After stipulating that his wife was to receive 'all his goods, movable and immovable (excepting his books)', he went on to leave 'to Isaac Steenwyck, son of Cornelis Steenwyck, mayor, whereof he is God father, his whole Bibliotheque of books'.[67] Two of

New York City's best-known domines possessed impressive libraries. In May 1751, Gualtherus Du Bois showed Lutheran minister Henry Melchior Muhlenberg 'his whole library and the manuscripts [of the sermons he had composed] throughout all the years of his ministry on practically every book and portion of the Holy Scriptures'.[68] Domine Johannes Ritzema also put together a notable library. In 1786, New England minister Ezra Stiles visited the 'venerable Dutch Divine' in retirement at Kinderhook and noted that he had 'viewed his learned Library of I judge 1000 or 1200 volumes'.[69] Albany minister Eilardus Westerlo kept a meticulous record of the items in his library, preparing a 'Register of Books and Their Prices in the Library of Domine E. Westerlo A.D. 1771 May 2nd. Most Books are Written in Latin, Dutch and English Covering Religion, The Bible, Poets, Ancient and Recent Arts and History.'[70] It is improbable that these and other ministers did not add to their libraries with Dutch books imported from the Netherlands.

As educated men, Dutch Reformed ministers acquired books in many languages, but Dutch books were a staple in their libraries. The 1695 estate of Margarita Van Varick, the widow of Domine Rudolphus Van Varick of Flatbush, included 'Seven and thirty dutch Bookes, printed, in quarto, forty six ditto in octavy and four ditto in folio' as well as 'a parcell of printed books...most of them High German and forring [foreign] Languages'. Most of these books likely had been the property of the late minister.[71] Schenectady's Dutch Reformed minister Cornelius van Santvoord noted in his 1746/47 will: 'As to my books, I have set the names of the children in some of the Dutch books, the rest to be sold at most profit, except them in which I have set Gedachtenise ['In memory'].'[72] Flatbush Minister Vincentius Antonides had 'a large collection of Latin Books, with some Greek & Hebrew' as well as books in Dutch.[73] In his 1743 will, Antonides left instructions that his eldest son receive 'all the books in which I have written this in Dutch, "Dit book behoort tot myn zoon Johannes Antonides"' and directed that his 'writing library, both in Latin and Dutch' go to his heirs.[74] When Domine Du Bois drew up his will in 1750, he bequeathed to his son Gualtherus and his daughter Elizabeth 'all my Dutch books and manuscripts belonging to my library' and specified that his Latin books were to be divided among his three grandsons.[75] Some of these ministers' Dutch-language volumes likely circulated in the community, serving local Dutch speakers in search of reading material in their native language.[76]

A rare reference to Dutch Reformed ministers ordering books from the Netherlands is found in a 1696 letter of Domine Henricus Selyns.

Selyns noted that his correspondent 'had sent us [Revd Van Zuuren and Selyns] a package containing published books. This was undoubtedly done in Frederick Philipszen's little barkentine, which was captured by the French. I suffered a private loss in this in that I had sent for goods and books.'[77] In 1727, Lutheran minister Wilhelm Berckenmeyer noted that 'any merchant [in New York City] could order Lutheran Bibles if these were wanted, the same as I myself had bought from Mr. de Lancey.'[78]

City merchants must have welcomed individual orders for books from the Netherlands, whether from ministers or other persons, but they doubtless hoped to anticipate the needs of the region's Dutch readers by importing popular Dutch titles in bulk. At least eight city merchants active after 1750, men largely but not exclusively of Dutch ancestry, sold Dutch-language volumes during the quarter-century before the American Revolution – Philip Livingston, Robert Crommelin, Cornelius C. Wynkoop, Lodewick Bamper, Peter Low, Cornelius Clopper, Nicholas Bogert and Peter T. Curtenius.[79] While eighteenth-century New York's book trade with England was concentrated in the hands of a few booksellers, the limited market for Dutch-language books in the city precluded this degree of specialization. In the newspaper advertisements of the merchants and shopkeepers who sold imported Dutch books, these volumes were included among a variety of unrelated items. The occasional exception was a notice that a locally printed Dutch volume was available for purchase.

Insight into the sale and distribution of imported Dutch books in the New York region comes from the account books of Cornelius Clopper, Jnr., who traded regularly with London, Amsterdam and Curaçao and 'imported many Dutch books, Bibles, and Psalmbooks'.[80] Between 1753 and 1775, Clopper recorded sales of Dutch books to 11 individuals as well as to the 'Dutch Church', which he supplied with '4 quarto Bibels' in October 1754.[81] The majority of his customers seem to have been shopkeepers, most of them in rural areas of the Hudson Valley and New Jersey, whom he supplied with multiple copies of Dutch books. In November 1760, he sold 'Dirk Weynkoop of Soopes [Esopus] ten Books of W[illia]m Brakel in two folm', and in October 1763, John Schenck of the Rareton received '3 Dutch folio Bibels'. The previous year, he had sold three Dutch Testaments to Abraham Schenck. In October 1760, Clopper noted that he had given William Elting of Soopes '3 dutch folio Bibels to sell for me at 73/[.] If cannot sell them to be returned.'

Clopper also dealt with merchants in New York City. He sold David Abeel folio Dutch Bibles on 11 August and 14 August 1758 and on

12 May 1766. In September 1765, he sold Nicholas Bogert '6 Dutch folio Bibels'. A decade later, in February 1775, he apparently transferred his entire stock of basic Dutch religious books to Bogert – '100 Dutch Testaments and 12 Bibels'. Clopper, who eventually became a Loyalist, probably feared for his livelihood as the political crisis in the city deepened.

The fact that Clopper conducted business on the wholesale level did not prevent him from selling at retail. Among the individuals who bought books from him were Cornelis Seebring, miller of Long Island, who purchased '2 Dutch folio Bibels' in August 1767, Alexander Furbush, who bought one Dutch Testament in November 1753, and Mary Van Dyke, who obtained 3 Dutch Testaments in November 1771. Clopper's specialty was Dutch Bibles and Testaments, but he did carry other Dutch-language books including the works of William Brakel sold to Dirk Weynkoop, one book of 'drillinkoert' purchased by 'William Elsworth of this city gunsmith', and a book titled 'verscheure bevindelyke god geleerthyt' bought by Abraham Schenck. Clopper also included English Bibles in his stock, selling one to Abraham Schenck and his son Henry and another to 'James Seca of this city masoner'.

Cornelius Clopper, Jnr., never advertised the Dutch books that he imported from Europe, but other city merchants did. On 12 August 1765, Peter Low listed a range of goods 'Just imported from Amsterdam, and to be sold cheap', including Delftware, superfine Holland linen, and more than a score of Dutch books listed by title and type.[82] But New York's largest importer of Dutch books from the Netherlands in the 1760s and 1770s was almost certainly Peter T. Curtenius, who catered to this niche market. His numerous newspaper advertisements, which at times state that he had Dutch books for sale 'as usual', coupled with his family connection to Jacobus Goelet, Jnr., Dutch New York's publishing entrepreneur, reinforce this conclusion.

Jacobus Goelet's publishing ventures ceased with Zenger's death in 1746, but he likely continued to make Dutch-language books available to New Yorkers through the 1750s.[83] In 1756, when he was in his late 60s, Goelet was the vendor of what was advertised as a 'A Dutch Elogium, on the Death of the Reverend Mr. Antonius Curtenius, late Pastor of the Dutch Reformed Churches in King's County on Long Island.'[84] Domine Curtenius had become a part of Goelet's family circle after marrying the widow of Goelet's brother Philip in 1751. The bonds between the Goelets and the Curteniuses were reinforced in 1754, when Peter T. Curtenius, the minister's son, formed a mercantile partnership with his stepbrother Isaac Goelet, taking over the business run by John Dies,

the husband of Jannetie, Jacobus Goelet Jnr.'s daughter.[85] In 1755, Peter
T. Curtenius married Catherine Goelet, his stepsister and the goddaugh-
ter of Jacobus Goelet. Antonius Curtenius's death the following year
thrust Jacobus into the role of paterfamilias, since he was the sole surviving Goelet brother of his generation. Peter likely became a surrogate son
for Jacobus, whose only surviving child was his daughter Jannetie. This
was significant for the history of New York's Dutch book trade, since
Jacobus Goelet, Jnr., probably influenced Peter T. Curtenius, best known
as an ironmonger, to add a sideline in imported Dutch-language books
after he went into business on his own at the Sign of the Golden Anvil
and Hammer in 1760.[86]

Peter T. Curtenius, who no doubt inherited a love of books from
his minister father, succeeded his wife's uncle, Jacobus Goelet, Jnr., as
prime supplier of Dutch-language books in New York City. In December
1761, he advertised 'Dutch Bibles, testaments and sundry sorts of small
school books'.[87] Three times during the month of January and once
in March 1764, he appended a lengthy inventory of 'DUTCH BOOKS:
Titles in Dutch' to the basic commodities that he advertised. Curtenius
must have had well over 60 imported Dutch books in stock, since
he noted at the end of the list 'behalven nog verscheyden soorten
meer die hier niet genoemt zyn [besides still various sorts more which
are not named here]'.[88] In September 1765, he advertised a variety of
goods that had arrived in 'the Brig Catherine, Capt; Lawrence, from
Amsterdam'[89] including 'Dutch Folio and Quarto Bibles, Testaments,
and Psalm Books, in coarse and fine Print; a few Lutheran Bibles and
Testaments, in Quarto and Octavo; and a great variety of Hymns,
Catechise, Prayer, School, and other Books, by the most approved
authors.'[90] In 1771, he listed 'Dutch folio and pocket bibles, testaments and psalm books, Lutheren bibles and testaments, translated
from Luther's German bible into low dutch, hymns and prayer books,
school and other Dutch books as usual'.[91] In 1773, at the end of a
lengthy list of commodities 'lately imported from Europe', he noted
'ALSO Dutch Bibles, testaments and psalm books and sundry other
Dutch books, some of them second hand, which last will be sold at half
price'.[92]

Amsterdam enjoyed a reputation as 'the bookshop of the world.'[93]
Reading was a fixture of daily life among urban dwellers in the early
modern Netherlands, which boasted a high rate of literacy. One scholar
has noted that 'there was a huge demand for the flood of printing from
the many cheap presses.'[94] Daniel Elzevier's 1675 stock catalogue alone
had contained 20,000 titles.[95] New York's slice of this trade was not

only tiny, but highly selective. Most of the overseas merchants who imported Dutch books in the years after 1750 confined themselves to family Bibles, Testaments and psalm-books (psalters), the mainstays of the colonial Dutch book trade and, by far, the Dutch books most commonly mentioned in wills and inventories. Since only one child could inherit the Great Dutch Bible, the supply of Dutch Bibles in New York had to be continually replenished to meet the needs of successive generations. Cornelius C. Wynkoop offered 'large Dutch Bibles with plates', Lodewick Bamper advertised 'large Dutch Bibles with copper plates', Peter Low listed 'Kinder bybel' among the titles he merchandised, and Peter T. Curtenius specified 'Gerformeerde en Lutherse Bybles ... in Quarto and Octavo, fyn and gros Druck'.[96]

Testaments and psalm-books, smaller volumes that worshippers carried with them to church, were also in continuous demand and were advertised by most of these merchants. Music historian Robin Leaver, who has made a study of eighteenth-century Dutch psalm-books, states that virtually everyone owned one.[97] Catechisms and schoolbooks, the volumes that children kept at hand, were regularly imported as well.[98] A Dutch schoolbook entitled *Trap der Jeugd (Stairway for Youth)* inscribed by Catharina Haring in 1742 is extant as are several other catechisms, complete with the scrawls of their youthful owners.[99] In the 1760s, Peter Low advertised 'Cathechismus, and andere Schoolboeken' and Peter T. Curtenius listed 'Schrifteurlijke Schoolboekjes, A.B. Boekjes, [and] Catechismus' among books for sale.[100]

Not everyone who dealt in imported Dutch books in eighteenth-century New York City was content to sell only these core religious volumes.[101] Lodewick Bamper offered 'Testaments, Psalm-Books, and sundry Sorts of other Dutch books' (1762), Peter Low noted 'sundry other Dutch Books' (1765) and Nicholas Bogert sold 'Dutch Folio Bibles, and other Dutch Books' (1768).[102] Which books New York's Dutch readers sampled from the vast array of literary, philosophical, religious, medical, legal and geographical texts issuing from the presses of the Netherlands remains a matter of conjecture. Clues come from the titles of imported Dutch books listed in the newspaper advertisements of Peter T. Curtenius and Peter Low in 1764 and 1765.[103]

There can be little doubt that the writings of Dutch clergymen were the staple of the Dutch book trade to New York. A book buyer entering Curtenius's shop would have found an assemblage of theological and devotional volumes by prominent Dutch Reformed ministers. Some titles were originally published in the seventeenth century while others dated from the eighteenth century as, for example,

Wilhelmus Schortinghuis, *Het Innige Christendom* (1740) and Balthazar Van Gravenbigt, *Een Kristen beproevd en verzeekerd* (1714). Authors came from different positions in the Dutch religious spectrum. Campeius Vitringa, who wrote *Over de Grondstucken van de Christelyke leer,* was a follower of Cocceius.[104] Many, however, were aligned with Voetius, and more specifically were pietists associated with the Nadere Reformatie (Further Reformation) such as Jacobus Koelman, Theodorus à Brakel, Wilhem [William] à Brakel, Francis Ridderus and J. van Lodensteyn.[105] Many of their books were originally published in the seventeenth century and became classics. Jacobus Koelman's *De Pligten der ouders in kinderen voor Godt op te voeden,* for example, was published in Amsterdam in 1679. Remarkably, Theodorus à Brakel's *De Trappen des geestelyken levens,* a book advertised by both Peter Curtenius and Peter Low, was one of the volumes pointed out to Jasper Danckaerts in Arnoldus de La Grange's shop in 1678 (see above, p. 113). The continuing popularity of the writings of the Brakels among Dutch New Yorkers is confirmed by Cornelius Clopper, Jnr.'s marketing of William Brakel's books in 1760, as noted above, and the inclusion of two works by Brakel in the 69 or so books of Cornelius Clopper, Jnr., sold at vendue in 1777.[106] When artist John Wollaston painted a portrait of Catharina van Brugh Livingston, wife of Philip Livingston, in 1752, he depicted her holding the book *Het Geestelyke Leeven* (The Spiritual Life), which may well be the familiar work by Brakel.[107]

Since classic works such as these were reprinted frequently, there is virtually no way of knowing which editions were shipped to New York. A rare exception is a copy of a book by Francis Ridderus which is inscribed 'Anna Ten Eyck Haer Boeck Dn: 12th Octob 1765', found in the New York State Library. The title page of *Dagelyksche Huys-Catecisatie: Bestaande in Morgen-Oeffeningen, over de Articulen des Christelyke Geloofs, Middag-Oeffeningen over de Plichten van een Chriselyk Leven. Ende in Avond-Oeffeningen, over de Geschiedenissen der H. Schrifture* indicates that it is 'Den Elfden Druk [the eleventh edition]' and was published at Amsterdam by 'Gysbert De Groot Keur, Boekverkooper, op den Nieuwen-Dyk, in den grooten Bybel', in 1743.

The predominance of devotional and theological works among imported volumes strongly suggests the preference of Dutch New Yorkers for religious texts, yet the presence of books by Jacob Cats, the most popular Dutch author of the seventeenth century, such as 'Cats trowing' (*Trou-ringh* (Wedding ring)) and '[Cats] Spiegel van de uude en niewen Tydt' (*Spiegel van den ouden ende nieuwen tijdt* (Mirror of ancient and modern times)) reminds us of the broader interests of

Dutch-Americans. *Spiegel van den ouden ende nieuwen tijdt* was an emblem book that provided moral guidance for all stages of life.[108]

That New York's Dutch readers craved works that were not solely religious in nature is also evident from an advertisement in the 4 May 1747 issue of the *New York Gazette Revived in the Weekly Post-Boy*. Among the Dutch volumes listed in 'A Catalogue of a choice Parcel of French and Dutch Books' to be sold by 'Publick Vendue' at the house of James Aarding were travel, geography and history books, the principles of geometry, and dictionaries: *C. de Bruyns reizens, Groot algemeen Historis Wordenbook Eerste Deel, Halmas Woordenbook, Beschryvinge Van Suriname, Beginselen Van Euclides, Natuurkundige Verbandel Van Swangere Vromoe, J. Hubner's Oude & Nieuwe Geographie, Duytslandsr Oudbeeden, Werdadige Konst, Britannische ryk in America, and Algemeene Historie*.[109] This variety of books may alter our understanding of the range of Dutch reading materials that circulated in New York and New Jersey.

One book in this list, *Britannische ryk in America* (British Empire in America) hints at colonial Dutch readers' curiosity about English culture, a concern manifested in a few of the titles advertised in the 1760s. In 1765, Low offered 'Sewels Wegwyzer na de Engelsche Taal'. This was William Sewel's *Korte Wegwyzer der Engelsche Taale... A Compendious Guide to the English Language*, which had been published in Amsterdam in 1705.[110] A second-hand copy of this book, which spoke to a fundamental need of Dutch-speaking people in a British world, had been advertised by Isaac Goelet in 1763.[111]

Thomas Noble, a New York merchant who regularly imported English-language books from Boston bookseller Daniel Henchman, clearly assumed that large numbers of Dutch New Yorkers would be eager to read the work of seventeenth-century Massachusetts Puritan minister Thomas Shepard. Shepard's book orders for the *History of Faustus* and other publications and what these reveal about transatlantic connections have already featured in this volume.[112] Noble proposed a Dutch edition of Shepard's most popular work, *The Sincere Convert*, originally published in 1641. In May 1735, Noble wrote to Henchman: 'Please to let me know upon what terms you woud reprint Mr Shephards Sincere Convert in the low Dutch.'[113] Noble followed up in detail in August 1735:

> I wrote you some time agoe about reprinting Shephard in Low Dutch but you could not give any Acct of the cost not having seen it[.] However I can suppose you can let me know what you would have a sheet to print 5 or 6 hundred & what for ye binding and whether

you have any person to do it yt understands ye language & to correct ye press[.] pray don't omit answering pr first sloop for if would not do with you we could get it done here[.] you must also let me know how soon you coud compleat it after ye receipt of ye coppy [sic][.] I suppose it will not be many sheets more than the English one.[114]

In a letter the following week, Noble reminded Henchman, 'Be sure [to] answer me fully as to reprinting Shephard in Dutch',[115] but nothing seems to have come of the project.

The popularity of Dutch translations of English religious works such as *'Guthrys Christens groote Interest'* (*The Christian's Great Interest* by William Guthrie) and 'the late Rev. Mr. Hervey's Works translated in Dutch' – especially when placed alongside the locally produced translations of sermons by George Whitefield and Jonathan Edwards – confirm the attraction that the writings of English pietists had for devout Netherlanders on both sides of the ocean.[116] Large numbers of such works were translated and sold in the Netherlands.[117] The popularity of well-known English religious books in Dutch translation among eighteenth-century Dutch New Yorkers is best illustrated by the presence of John Bunyan's works in the colony. Curtenius advertised two volumes by Bunyan in 1764 – *Bunjans Heilegen Oorlog* (The Holy War) and *Pilgrims Straat, na den Berg Zion* (The Pilgrim's Progress) – and Peter Low included three Bunyan works in his 1765 advertisement – *J. Bunjan Komest en welkomst, tot Christus* (Come and Welcome to Jesus Christ), *Heylige Oorlog* (Holy War) and *Christens Reyse* (The Pilgrim's Progess).[118] Four decades earlier (in 1723), Benjamin Franklin had been on board a boat leaving New York when 'a drunken Dutchman' fell overboard. After being rescued, the man took a book out of his pocket and gave it to Franklin to dry for him. As recounted by Franklin 'It prov'd to be my old favourite Author Bunyan's Pilgrim's Progress in Dutch, finely printed on good Paper with copper Cuts, a Dress better than I had ever seen it wear in its own Language.'[119] Much still remains to be learned about the assortment of Dutch books available in New York City's shops, but it is safe to conclude that the demand of local Dutch readers for works in their native language did not abate in the 1750s, 1760s and 1770s.

No one can dispute the small scale of the Amsterdam–New York Dutch book trade. Shipments of Dutch books to New York City constituted a very tiny portion of the Amsterdam Dutch book trade. In New York City itself, imports of English books dwarfed those in Dutch. Virtually every book in the New York Society Library collection was in English.[120] The city's major booksellers rarely sold a Dutch book. Clearly the economic and cultural impact of imported Dutch books on New York and the surrounding region was negligible. But focusing solely on these larger contexts obscures the significance of the continuing importation and consumption of Dutch-language titles in a region ruled by the English. For the many descendants of New Netherlanders living in the mid-Atlantic region, the trade in Dutch books reinforced Dutch culture at a time when it might have evaporated. Maintaining the transatlantic connection to the ancestral homeland was vitally important. It served as a lifeline to Dutch culture for the many self-identified Dutch people stranded in an English colony.

Notes

1. *New York Gazette*, 23 Jan 1764.
2. On the early New York book trade, see Linda M. Kruger, 'The New York City Book Trade, 1725–1750' (unpublished D.L.S. dissertation, Columbia University 1980). For comments on the Dutch book trade to New York, see Maria Keblusek, 'New York, Amsterdam, Leiden: Trading Books in the Old and New Worlds', in George Harinck and Hans Krabbendam (eds), *Amsterdam-New York: Transatlantic Relations and Urban Identities Since 1653* (Amsterdam, 2005): 117–24; and A. Gregg Roeber, '[Middle Colonies, 1720–1790] German and Dutch Books and Printing', in Hugh Amory and David D. Hall (eds), The *Colonial Book in the Atlantic* World (Cambridge, 2000): 298–313. For background on the English book trade to New York, see James N. Green, 'Book Trade in the Middle Colonies, 1680–1720' and '[Middle Colonies, 1720–1790] English Books and Printing in the Age of Franklin', in Amory and. Hall (eds), *Colonial Book in the Atlantic World*, 199–223, 248–97.
3. Hendrik Edelman, *Dutch-American Bibliography 1693–1794: A Descriptive Catalog of Dutch-Language Books, Pamphlets and Almanacs Printed in America* (Nieuwkoop, 1974).
4. Hendrik Edelman, *The Dutch Language Press in America: Two Centuries of Printing Publishing and Bookselling* (Nieuwkoop, 1986): 20–21.
5. John Z. C. Thomas, 'Printing in Colonial New York, 1693–1763' (unpublished Ph.D. dissertation, University of Tennessee, 1974).
6. On books in New Netherland, see Jaap Jacobs, *New Netherland* (Leiden and Boston, MA, 2005): 417–20; and Donna Merwick, *Death of a Notary: Conquest and Change in Colonial New York* (Ithaca and London, 1999): 67, 118, 219.
7. Joyce D. Goodfriend, *Before the Melting Pot: Society and Culture in Colonial New York City, 1664–1730* (Princeton, NJ, 1992).
8. Joyce D. Goodfriend, 'Archibald Laidlie and the Transformation of the Dutch Reformed Church in Eighteenth-Century New York City', *Journal of Presbyterian History*, 81 (2003): 149–62.
9. A. J. F. van Laer (ed. and trans.), *Correspondence of Jeremias Van Rensselaer 1651–1674* (Albany, NY, 1932): 403. For criticisms of English writing by literary men in seventeenth-century Netherlands, see Cornelius

W. Schoneveld, *Intertraffic of the Mind. Studies in Seventeenth-Century Anglo-Dutch Translation with a Checklist of Books Translated from English into Dutch, 1600–1700* (Leiden, 1983): 119–20.

10. On the literacy of New Yorkers, see David E. Narrett, *Inheritance and Family Life in Colonial New York City* (Ithaca and London, 1992): 222–7; and Merwick, *Death of a Notary*, 227.

11. The quoted text is a translation from Dutch. Henricus Selyns to Ameloveen, New York, 30 Oct 1696, Manuscript letter, Special Collections, University of Utrecht Library, MSS 996 (6k4), 2: 133r.

12. Kenneth Scott, 'Jacob Goelet: Translator of Dutch for the Province of New York', *de Halve Maen*, LV: 4 (Winter, 1981): 1–5, 20–21. The catechism was Gualtherus DuBois, *Kort-Begryp der Waare Christelyke Leere...* (New York, William Bradford, 1712). On the complicated printing history of this book, see Edelman, *Dutch-American Bibliography*, 25 [no. 3], 28–9 [no. 5].

13. Joseph Anthony Loux, Jr. (ed. and trans.), *Boel's Complaint Against Frelinghuisen* (New York, 1970): 48.

14. The quoted text is a translation from Dutch. *Verdeediging van D. Bernardus Freeman wegens HET gene hem voornamelyk ten Laste gelegt word in zeeker BOEK, genaamt KLAGTE, &c* (New York, Gedrukt by J. Peter Zenger, 1726), final page (unnumbered). Edelman notes 'Freeman apologizes for printing errors, the printer Zenger being still young and not very skilled in the Dutch language.' Edelman, *Dutch-American Bibliography*, 34.

15. The quoted text is a translation from Dutch. Lambertus De Ronde, *Gekruicigde Christus, Als Het Voornamste Toeleg van Gods Getrouwe Kruisgesanten, in Hunne Prediking, Onder den Dag, Des Nieuwe-Testaments Voorgestelt in Een Kerkreede...* (Nieuw York, Gederukt by Hendrikus De Foreest, 1752): 4–5.

16. The quoted text is a translation from Dutch. Lambertus De Ronde, *De Ware Gedagt'nis, Gelovige Navolging, en Salig Uiteinde, van Getrouwe Voorgangers, Verklaart en Toegepast, in Ene Lykrede...* (Nieuw York, Gederukt by Hendrikus De Foreest, 1752).

17. Alice P. Kenney, 'Neglected Heritage: Hudson River Valley Dutch Material Culture', *Winterthur Portfolio*, 20 (1985): 49–70 (67); Alice P. Kenney, 'Hudson Valley Psalmody', *The Hymn*, 25 (1974): 15–26.

18. For the catechism by Gualtherus Du Bois, see above n. 11, and for the catechism by Justus Falckner, see below n. 46. The textbook was Pieter Venema, *Arithmetica Of Cyffer-Konst, Volgens de Munten Maten en Gewigten, te NIEU-YORK, gebruykelyk Als Mede Een kort ontwerp van de Algebra* (New York, Gedruckt voor Jacob Goelet, by de *Oude* Slip by J. Peter Zenger, 1730).

19. New York State Archives, Albany, NY (hereafter NYSA), inventories of Abraham De La Noy, 1702; Samuel Mynderts, 1702; and Gertye Splinter, 1722.

20. Quoted in Joyce D. Goodfriend, 'Incorporating Women into the History of the Colonial Dutch Reformed Church', in Renee S. House and John W. Coakley (eds), *Patterns and Portraits: Women in the History of the Reformed Church in America* (Grand Rapids, MI, 1999): 26.

21. Philip L. White, *The Beekmans of New York in Politics and Commerce 1647–1877* (New York, 1956): 122. According to David Shields, transcripts from medical books were common in the British colonies. David Shields,

'The Manuscript in the British American World of Print', *Proceedings of the American Antiquarian Society*, 102 (1993): 403–16 (409).

22. Bartlett Burleigh James and J. Franklin Jameson (eds), *Journal of Jasper Danckaerts 1679–1680* (New York, 1913): 81–2.

23. Linda Briggs Biemer, *Women and Property in Colonial New York: The Transition from Dutch to English Law 1643–1727* (Ann Arbor, MI, 1983), appendix C, 'cargo aboard the *Charles*', 95.

24. Biemer, *Women and Property in Colonial New York*, 97.

25. James and Jameson, *Journal of Jasper Danckaerts*, 239.

26. Ibid., 296–7.

27. Joyce D. Goodfriend, 'The Limits of Religious Pluralism in Eighteenth-Century New York City', in Harinck and Krabbendam (eds), *Amsterdam-New York*, 74–5.

28. Lambertus De Ronde to Winoldus Budde, 13 Oct 1764, *Ecclesiastical Records of the State of New York* (hereafter *ERSNY*), Edward T. Corwin (ed.), *ERSNY*, 7 vols, vol. 6 (Albany, NY, 1901–16): 3967.

29. Classis of Amsterdam to L. De Ronde, 4 Feb 1765, *ERSNY*, 6: 3975.

30. Lambertus De Ronde to the Classis of Amsterdam, per John Kalkoen, 9 Sept 1765. *ERSNY*, 6: 4004.

31. William A. Bultmann, 'The S.P.G. and the Foreign Settler in the American Colonies', in Samuel Clyde McCulloch (ed.), *British Humanitarianism: Essays Honoring Frank J. Klingberg* (Philadelphia, PA, 1950): 51–65 (61–3).

32. *Book of Common Prayer/Het Boek der Gemeene Gebeden* (Amsterdam, John Crellius, 1711).

33. John Calam, *Parsons and Pedagogues: The S.P.G. Adventure in American Education* (New York and London, 1971): 91.

34. Bultmann, 'The S.P.G. and the Foreign Settler', 62.

35. The Classis of Amsterdam to Consistory in New Netherland, 26 May 1656, *ERSNY*, 1: 349. Despite the opposition of the Classis, this catechism was printed in the Netherlands and was in use in Breuckelen in 1661. For a full account of this episode, see Gerald F. De Jong, 'Dominie Johannes Megapolensis: Minister to New Netherland', *New-York Historical Society Quarterly*, 52 (1968): 7–47 (26–7).

36. Acts of the Classis, 20 Jan 1651, *ERSNY*, 1: 287.

37. Evert Pietersen to Rev. Hendric Ruilieus, minister in Amsterdam, 12 Aug 1657, *ERSNY*, 1: 402.

38. David William Voorhees (ed. and trans.), *Records of the Reformed Protestant Dutch Church of Flatbush, Kings County, New York vol. 2 Midwood Deacons' Accounts 1654–1709* (New York, 2009). My thanks to David Voorhees for this information.

39. Letter from the Rev. Jacobus Fabricius to the Amsterdam Consistory, 25 Apr/5 May 1669, Arnold J. H. vanLaer (trans.), *The Lutheran Church in New York 1649–1772. Records in the Lutheran Church Archives at Amsterdam, Holland,* (New York, 1946) (hereafter *LCNY*): 71–2.

40. Letter from Rev. Bernhard Arenzius to the Amsterdam Consistory, 19 Dec 1671, *LCNY*, 85.

41. Letter from the Rev. Justus Falckner and the Consistory of the Lutheran Church – New York, to the Amsterdam Consistory, 10 Nov 1705, *LCNY*, 99–100.

42. Letter from the Elders of the Lutheran Church at Amsterdam to the Rev. Justus Falckner, 8 Jul 1712, *LCNY*, 104.
43. Letter from Rev. Justus Falckner to the Amsterdam Consistory, 9 Jun 1713, *LCNY*, 105–6.
44. Letter from the Rev. Justus Falckner to the Rev. Bernhardus Henrich Empsychoff, pastor of the Lutheran Church at Amsterdam, 23 Oct 1713, *LCNY*, 107.
45. Letter from the Rev. Justus Falckner to the Rev. Bernhardus Henrich Empsychoff, pastor of the Lutheran Church at Amsterdam, 23 Oct 1713, *LCNY*, 107.
46. Report of Rev. W. C. Berckenmeyer to the Amsterdam Consistory, 21 Oct/1 Nov 1725, *LCNY*, 140.
47. Letter from the Elders of the Lutheran Church at Amsterdam to Rev. Justus Falckner, 17 Feb 1713, *LCNY*, 104.
48. Letter (from the Rev. Wilhelmus C. Berkenmeyer) to Messrs. Laasbye and Nieuwgaard (at Amsterdam 12 Oct. 1730). Simon Hart and Harry J. Kreider (trans.), *Protocol Book of the Lutheran Church in New York 1702–1750* (New York, 1958) (hereafter *PBLC*): 198.
49. Minutes of the Church Council, 29 Aug 1715, *PBLC*, 8. In October 1715, Justus Falckner expressed his gratitude to the Amsterdam consistory for 'the splendid generous present of 24 psalters and two church agenda'. Letter from Rev. Justus Falckner to the Amsterdam Consistory, 3 Oct 1715, *LCNY*, 109.
50. Justus Falckner, *Grondlycke Onderricht van Sekere Voorname Hoofd-Stucken,der Waren, Loutern, Saligmakendam, Christelycken Leere* (Fundamental Instruction in Certain Principal Articles of the True, Pure and Saving Christian Doctrine) (New York, W. Bradfordt, 1708).
51. Letter (from the Rev. Wilhelmus C. Berkenmeyer) to Messrs. Laasbye and Nieuwgaard (at Amsterdam. 12 Oct 1730). *PBLC*, 198.
52. This book was H. G. Masius, *Kort begrip van het onderscheyt der waare Evangeliksch Lutherse en der Gereformeerde Leere, enz* (Brief Summary of the difference between the true evangelical Lutheran and the Reformed doctrine, etc.) *PBLC*, 117, n. 13.
53. Letter (from the Rev. Wilhelmus C. Berkenmeyer) to Messrs. Laasbye and Nieuwgaard (at Amsterdam 12 Oct 1730). *PBLC*, 144–5.
54. Letter (from the Rev. Wilhelmus C. Berkenmeyer) to Messrs. Laasbye and Nieuwgaard (at Amsterdam 12 Oct 1730). *PBLC*, 197.
55. On this book, see Edelman, *Dutch-American Bibliography*, 50, n. 23.
56. James and Jameson, *Journal of Jasper Danckaerts*, 62–3; *De Trappen des Geestelycken Levens* (The Gradations of the Spiritual Life) was written by Theodorus a Brakel (1608–99); Edelman, *Dutch-American Bibliography*, 63, n. 1.
57. Scott, 'Jacob Goelet', p. 1.
58. Ibid., 5; see also above, n. 11.
59. Scott, 'Jacob Goelet', 1–3.
60. *Collections of the New-York Historical Society for 1893*, 72. Gunsmith Garrit Harsin left his 'Large Dutch House Bible' to his 'well-beloved son Bernardus' in 1753. *Collections of the New-York Historical Society for 1896*, 24.
61. *Collections of the New-York Historical Society for 1895*, 136.

62. Goodfriend, *Before the Melting Pot*, 189.
63. Kevin L. Stayton, *Dutch by Design: Tradition and Change in Two Historic Brooklyn Houses* (New York, 1990): 119. This Bible includes a register of the births and deaths of the Ditmars family in Dutch until 1781.
64. Stayton, *Dutch by Design*, 127, n. 45.
65. Goodfriend, *Before the Melting Pot*, 280, n. 68.
66. One must assume that all of New York's Dutch ministers brought books with them from Europe. The importance a colonial minister attached to his books is evident in the account of Johannes Gutwasser, who arrived in New Amsterdam only to find that Director-General Petrus Stuyvesant would not let him conduct public worship for the local Lutherans. He related that 'through the shipwreck of the ship *De Wasbleecker*, at the English island of Barbados, I lost both bodily necessities and the most and better part of my books, which damage I estimate at 250 fl[orins] Holland money.' 'Letter from Rev. Johannes E. Gutwasser to the Consistory at Amsterdam, 30 Jul, 1659, *LCNY*, 44. In a letter written shortly after his arrival in New York Sept. 1725, Lutheran minister Wilhelmus Berckenmeyer, made reference to 'payment of [the freight] on my books.' Pastor Berkenmeyer's Account of his Arrival in New York..., Sept. 1725, *PBLC*, 24. Archibald Laidlie, the city's first English-speaking minister, shipped two boxes of books from Europe to New York when he assumed his new post in 1764. Given that he had just served in Vlissingen, the Netherlands, the contents of the boxes must have included some Dutch volumes. Goodfriend, 'Archibald Laidlie', 159.
67. *Collections of the New-York Historical Society*, 1893, 394.
68. Theodore G. Tappert and John W. Doberstein (trans.), *The Journals of Henry Melchior Muhlenberg*, 3 vols, vol. 1 (Philadelphia, PA, 1942–58): 283. In 1713, when Anglican chaplain John Sharpe was formulating plans for a public library in New York City, he noted that 'a considerable addition may be made [to the collection] by buying in the best books of the Reverend Mr. Lydius deceased, Mr. Selyns, the Rd. Mr. Beys'. Sharpe, 'Proposals for Erecting a School, Library and Chapel at New York', *Collections of the New-York Historical Society for 1880*, 348.
69. Franklin Bowditch Dexter (ed.), *The Literary Diary of Ezra Stiles*, 3 vols, vol. 3 (New York, 1901): 240.
70. Westerloo Family Papers, Box 2, Folder 5, Albany Institute of Art and History, Albany, New York (trans. from the Dutch).
71. NYSA, inventory of the Estate of Margarita Van Varick, 1695.
72. *Collections of the New-York Historical Society for 1895*, 422–3.
73. *New-York Weekly Journal*, 4 Feb 1744.
74. *Collections of the New-York Historical Society for 1895*, 20–21.
75. *Collections of the New-York Historical Society for 1895*, 419–20.
76. Lending books was a customary practice among both Dutch and English New Yorkers, and there is no reason to believe that ministers did not engage in it as much as or even more than laymen. In 1744, the executors of the estate of Flatbush minister Vincentius Antonides requested those who 'have borrowed any Books of the deceased are desired to come and pay or return the Books to the Executors', *New-York Weekly Journal*, 4 Feb 1744.

77. The quoted text is a translation from Dutch. Utrecht University Library Special Collections. Mss, Henricus Selyns to Ameloveen, New York, 30 Oct 1696.

78. [Another Incident is Experienced by the Rev. Wilhelm C. Berckenmeyer... 28 Oct–2 Nov 1727], *PBLC*, 114.

79. Philip Livingston advertised Dutch Bibles in the *New-York Mercury*, 6 Nov 1752 and thereafter. Robert Crommelin advertised Dutch Bibles and Testaments in the *New-York Mercury*, 28 Aug 1758 and thereafter; on the other merchants mentioned, see below.

80. Daniel James Meeter, *'Bless the Lord, O My Soul': The New-York Liturgy of the Dutch Reformed Church, 1767* (Lanham, MD, and London, 1998): 70.

81. Cornelius Clopper, Jr., Account Books, Manuscript, New-York Historical Society.

82. *New-York Mercury*, 12 Aug 1765.

83. Goelet's trade in books remains shadowy, since no catalogues or advertisements of the titles he imported from the Netherlands or acquired locally survive.

84. Edelman, *Dutch-American Bibliography*, 83, n. 66; according to Edelman this broadside was advertised in the *New York Gazette, or Weekly Post-Boy*, 8 Nov 1756; an obituary of Curtenius appeared in *The New-York Mercury*, 1 Nov 1756.

85. 'GOELET & CURTENIUS, who have lately taken the store of Mr. John Dies, at the Golden Key, in Hanover Square, have just imported...' *New-York Mercury*, 17 Jun 1764. Prior to joining in partnership with Curtenius, Isaac Goelet advertised an assortment of second-hand books, most of them in English. One title was *sewel's dutch and English dictionary*. *New-York Mercury*, 29 Oct 1763; see also Howard S. F. Randolph, 'Jacob Boelen, Goldsmith of New York, and His Family Circle', *New York Genealogical and Biographical Record*, 72 (1941): 282.

86. 'PETER T. CURTENIUS, At the Sign of the Golden Anvil and Hammer, opposite the Oswego Market, has just imported...', adv., *New-York Mercury*, 1 Sept 1760.

87. *New-York Mercury*, 7 Dec 1761.

88. *New-York Mercury*, 9 Jan 1764; *New York Gazette*, 23 Jan, 30 Jan, 12 Mar 1764.

89. *New-York Mercury*, 30 Sept 1765.

90. Ibid., and cf. *New York Gazette or Weekly Post-Boy*, 17 Oct 1768.

91. *New-York Journal, or, the General Advertiser*, 16 May 1771. This advertisement also lists several titles in English.

92. *Rivington's New-York Gazeteer*, 10 Jun 1773, Supplement.

93. Paul F. Hoftijzer, 'Metropolis of Print: The Amsterdam Book Trade in the Seventeenth Century', in Patrick O'Brien, Derek Keene, Marjolein 't Hart and Herman van der Wee (eds), *Urban Achievement in Early Modern Europe: Golden Ages in Antwerp, Amsterdam and London* (Cambridge, 2001): 249–63; Lotte Hellinga, Alastair Duke, Jacob Harskamp and Theo Hermans (eds), *The Bookshop of the World: The Role of the Low Countries in the Book-Trade 1473–1941* ('t Goy-Houten, The Netherlands, 2001).

94. Wijnand Mijnhardt, 'The Construction of Silence: Religious and Political Radicalism in Dutch History', in Wiep van Bunge (ed.), *The Early Enlightenment in the Dutch Republic 1650–1750* (Leiden and Boston, MA, 2003): 231–62 (249).

95. P. G. Hoftijzer, 'The English Book in the Seventeenth-Century Dutch Republic', in Hellinga et al. (eds), *Bookshop of the World*, 89–107 (91).

96. Wynkoop: *New-York Mercury*, 2 Nov 1761; Bamper: *New York Gazette*, 4 Apr 1763; see also 20 Sept 1762; Low: *New York Mercury*, 12 Aug, 26 Aug 1765; Curtenius: *New-York Mercury*, 9 Jan 1764; *New York Gazette*, 30 Jan 1764; numerous few great family Bibles printed in various places in the Netherlands in the eighteenth century are extant, many with provenance.

97. Robin A. Leaver, 'Dutch Secular and Religious Songs in Eighteenth-Century New York', in Harinck and Krabbendam (eds), *Amsterdam-New York*, 99–124.

98. On Dutch schoolbooks, see William Heard Kilpatrick, *The Dutch Schools of New Netherland and New York* (Wasshington, DC, 1912).

99. This book is in the collections of the Museum of the City of New York; see Jean Parker Waterbury, *A History of Collegiate School* (New York, 1965): 49–50. It was one of the books advertised by Peter T. Curtenius, *New York Gazette*, 23 Jan 1764.

100. Low: *New-York Mercury*, 12 Aug, 26 Aug 1765; Curtenius: *New-York Mercury*, 9 Jan 1764; *New York Gazette*, 30 Jan 1764.

101. The 'parcel of old Dutch books about 30 in number' found among Samuel Mynderts's goods in 1702 and the 140 small Dutch books in the shop goods of Peter Jacobs Marius in 1702 likely included a variety of titles; NYSA, inventories of Samuel Mynderts, 1702, and Peter Jacobs Marius, 1702.

102. Bamper: *New York Gazette*, 20 Sept 1762; Low: *New York Gazette*, 6 May 1765; 3 Jun 1765; Bogart: *New-York Journal and General Advertiser*, 17 Mar 1768.

103. Low: *New-York Mercury*, 12 Aug, 26 Aug 1765; Curtenius: *New-York Mercury*, 9 Jan 1764; *New York Gazette*, 30 Jan 1764.

104. On Vitringa, see Ernestine van der Wall, 'The Religious Context of the Early Dutch Enlightenment: Moral Religion and Society' in van Bunge (ed.), *Early Enlightenment in the Dutch Republic*, 39–57 (50, n. 18).

105. On the *Nadere Reformatie*, see Fred A. van Lieburg, 'From Pure Church to Pious Culture: The Further Reformation in the Seventeenth-Century Dutch Republic', in W. Fred Graham (ed.), *Later Calvinism: International Perspectives* (Kirksville, MO, 1994): 409–29; Francis Ridderus, a Rotterdam minister, wrote 'one of the first full-length anti-atheistic treatises to have been published in the early Enlightenment Dutch Republic'. Van der Wall, 'Religious Context of the Early Dutch Enlightenment', 44–5.

106. Meeter, *'Bless the Lord, O My Soul'*, 71–2.

107. Ruth Piwonka, *A Portrait of Livingston Manor 1686–1850* (Germantown, NY, 1986): 33.

108. On the works of Jacob Cats, see Benjamin B. Roberts and Leendert F. Groenendijk, ' "Wearing Out a pair of fool's shoes": Sexual advice for Youth in Holland's Golden Age', *Journal of the History of Sexuality* 13 (2004): 139–56 (139–40).

109. *New York Gazette Revived in the Weekly Post-Boy*, 4 May 1747.

110. N. E. Osselton, *The Dumb Linguists: A Study of the Earliest English and Dutch Dictionaries* (Leiden and London, 1973): 59, n. 5.

111. *New-York Mercury*, 29 Oct 1763.

112. See above, chapter 3.

113. Thomas Noble to Daniel Henchman, New York, 12 May 1735, Thomas Noble Letterbook, Thomas Noble Collection, Moravian Archives, Bethlehem, PA.
114. Thomas Noble to Daniel Henchman, New York, 25 Aug 1735.
115. Ibid., 1 Sept 1735.
116. *The Christian's Great Interest* by William Guthrie, a Scottish Puritan, was first published in London in 1658. Seven seventeenth-century Dutch edns of this work have been identified; Schoneveld, *Intertraffic of the Mind*, 203. References to the Dutch translations of sermons by George Whitefield and Jonathan Edwards are in Edelman, *Dutch-American Bibliography*: 55 [no. 29], 56 [no. 30] and 74 [no. 57].
117. P. G. Hoftizer, 'English Book in the Seventeenth-Century Dutch Republic', 93–6; Schoneveld, *Intertraffic of the Mind*.
118. For the many seventeenth-century Dutch trans. of works by Bunyan, see Schoneveld, *Intertraffic of the Mind*, 184.
119. Leonard W. Labaree, Ralph L. Ketcham, Helen C. Boatfield and Helen H. Fineman (eds), *The Autobiography of Benjamin Franklin* (New Haven and London, 1964): 72.
120. Tom Glynn, 'The New York Society Library: Books, Authority, and Publics in Colonial and Early Republican New York', *Libraries and Culture* 40 (2005): 493–529 (522, n. 48).

8
Classical Transports: Latin and Greek Texts in North and Central America before 1800

James Raven

On 28 August 2008 Senator Barack Obama delivered his acceptance speech as Democratic candidate for the presidency of the United States. At that convention, three months before his election as the first African-American president of his country, Obama addressed his party in the stadium of the Denver Broncos. He stood in front of a newly minted classical façade, part temple, part theatre with a portico and a double rank of columns. Obama risked ridicule. As Simon Schama wrote of the event, 'Architrave alert! Fluted columns! Cecil B. DeMille Doric! What a gift to satirists who could lampoon Obama as a wannabe Demosthenes, so self-monumentalised that he seemed to be presumptuously rehearsing the inaugural oath on the Capitol steps.'[1]

Yet commentators widely acclaimed the speech, and the classical staging worked to bolster rather than undermine Obama's image. His speech, in Schama's words, upheld 'the American reverence for classical oratory'. Obama's Greco-Roman set echoed the classicism not just of the White House frontage and the Capitol backdrop of his inauguration, but also, more seductively, that of ancient and European civilization and civil politics. The Denver staging recalled the Enlightenment edifices and rhetoric of the Founding Fathers.

The use of classicism to reassure, to provide justification and to validate the new and inexperienced has a centuries-old history. Classical texts and architecture were translated and engineered in the Renaissance and transported with enthusiasm to the colonial New World. Formative studies by Richard M. Gummere, Meyer Reinhold and others have charted the influence of classical learning in the North American colonies and the early United States.[2] More recently, Caroline Winterer has recovered the history of classical scholars in North America and has argued that 'next to Christianity, the central intellectual project in America before the late nineteenth century was classicism'.[3] Susan Ford Wiltshire and Carl J. Richard have examined the classical reading of the Founding Fathers and their circle, as well as the theories of rights (including property rights and the influence of Roman law) derived from classical learning.[4] Numerous American histories are enlivened by examples of actions impelled by 'classick pages'. Among the most repeated cameos are John Adams enlisting Aristotle, Cicero and Polybius in his protests against the Stamp Act of 1765, and John Dickinson using Sallust to rally rural opposition against the Townshend Acts in 1767.[5]

On both sides of the Atlantic, but especially in the New World, usage of Greek and Latin was various. Authors and orators mined classical literature for examples and allegories of corruption, for pastoral idyll, and for the means to understand what a 'new world' was. Richard has even argued that in North America, 'social conditioning left many unable to imagine the teaching of virtue independent of the teaching of the classics'.[6] This might be an overly secular interpretation, but, certainly, for successive generations, classical languages retained a trans-national allure as the key to $\pi\alpha\iota\delta\epsilon\iota\alpha$ or the realisation of a man's full potential through education. Essentially or ornamentally, writers depended upon the ancients in romantic verse and political theory. In the arts and sciences as a whole, Françoise Waquet has chronicled the reach and endurance of the 'European sign' – to use Joseph de Maistre's mid-nineteenth-century phrase – until the end of the eighteenth century.[7] The subject is far from exhausted, however, and, in particular, might profit from further consideration of the volume, range and origin of the transatlantic traffic in classical texts.

This chapter offers a reassessment drawn from the author's research in the history of book production, importation and circulation in North America.[8] What were the characteristics and strengths of communities created across the Atlantic by the shared use of and interest in the classical languages (and hence classical inheritance)? Some comparative observations also suggest similarities and differences between transatlanticism in the classics as it was practised in different parts of the New World, including the perception of 'literary currency' in colonial North America and the early national United States. How did the demand for works of antiquity – and for editions that were themselves antique – affect the developing concern for the acquisition (with all possible speed) of the latest, most fashionable literature – a concern so central to European book production and demand by the mid-eighteenth century? Although Benedict Anderson, in his hugely influential

Imagined Communities, asserted that the 'universality of Latin never corresponded to a universal political system' and therefore that 'Latin's authority never had a true political analogue',[9] could it not be that exactly because of that Latin's reach and its transatlantic power in both temporal and geographical scope was the more insinuating and effective?

One initial comparative perspective is enlightening, even though it is almost entirely absent from the major studies of classicism in British and French North America. When Hernán Cortés reached the Yucatán in 1519, he encountered an Andalucian priest who had been shipwrecked and then enslaved in Mexico since 1511.[10] Foremost among the priest's belongings – and the means by which he was identified – was a Latin breviary. Latin might well have struck the coast of the Americas before any other written European language, and, more certainly, became embedded, both by importation and by local production, in the emergent secular and religious literature of Nueva España. Although the term 'Latin America' (América Latina) appeared only in the late nineteenth century,[11] it is not an inappropriate tag for certain cultural developments of earlier centuries.

After Cortés, several more conquistador expeditions penetrated the Mexican heartlands before the great 1540–42 expedition of Francisco Vasquez de Coronado whose friars took hundreds of Latin Bibles, missals and other religious books to the 'new Kingdom of St Francis' (New Mexico and Arizona).[12] Franciscans arrived in Mexico in 1523, Dominicans in 1526, Augustinians in 1533, Jesuits in 1572 and Carmelites in 1585. The missionary activity laid the foundation for two centuries of Latin-based writing from New Spain that was far from a simple extension of conquest religiosity but embraced literary, scientific and political publication, both printed and manuscript. In the early modern period before 1800, Latin was written in many places outside Italy, Spain, France and England, and notably including Mexico and Central America. The mid-sixteenth-century 'Controversy of the Indies', conducted in Latin, debated the rights of indigenous Americans[13] and included appeals to classical sources that were to reappear in North American theories of rights arguments in the eighteenth century. In Central America, the recoveries and creativities of the Italian Renaissance informed a tradition of humanism or 'Latin culture' that reached maturity during the eighteenth century and also contributed to debate about *hispanidad* or Spanish identity.[14] Foremost among the indigenous neo-Latinists of the New World was the Guatemalan-Mexican poet, Rafael Landívar (1731–93), descriptor of the natural world and wild life of his native lands in a language shared by Virgil, Cotton Mather, Isaac Newton and Linnaeus.[15]

For all its travels, Latin (and sometimes Greek) operated in different registers. Latin remained the favoured language of scientific, medical and scholarly texts, ensuring circulation and discussion among the learned and the interested irrespective of their sometimes obscure vernacular tongue. Britain was no exception. The physician Nathaniel Hodges (1629–88), for example, wrote his opinionated treatise on the cause of the 1665 Great Plague as *Loimologia, sive, Pestis nuperæ populum Londinensem grassantis narratio historica*. The book was published in 1672 and only later translated into English in a revised edition in 1720 (and then because of the topicality of the plague which had recently devastated Marseilles).[16] Similarly, Archbishop William King's *De origine mali* of 1702 typifies scholarly Latin publication, one also given new and different life by translation into English (in 1731), and which, in this case, forms the subject of a modern essay on the techniques of citation and reference.[17]

In the otherwise contrasting colonies of the Americas, both Church and State sanctioned and perpetuated use of the ancient languages. In the churches and homesteads of the North, the word of God was manifestly heard in the vernacular, and liturgical practice was in part founded on the rejection of Romish patterns. Yet the reading and appropriation of classical literature and images were as pervasive in New England as they were in Nueva España. The mediation of Italian humanist influence in promoting the classics proved particularly enduring and fruitful in the lands of the Spanish Crown,[18] but it was also a potent support for neoclassical scholarship and arts in the north. Even in the settlements adhering to Protestant, vernacular-based religion, an illiterate ministry was held to be one unschooled in Greek and Latin (and even Hebrew).

Practice, nonetheless, is different to aspiration, and one further difference between the Hispanic and the Anglo-Saxon territories determined the history of Latinity and especially of the *writing* in Latin in the New World (and its transport back to Europe). Latin, rather than the vernacular Spanish, dictated (or at least remained central to) the conversion crusades in Hispanic America. By contrast, the suppression of indigenous peoples and languages in North America left the vernacular of the colonizers, whether English, German, French or Dutch, as the main languages of the Church and of popular instruction. The classical languages served in the often idealized training of the Northern clergy, and, incidentally, make such productions as the Eliot 'Indian' Bible of 1663 seem exotic, marginal and ephemeral in comparison with the various Mexican parallel texts in Latin, Spanish or Nahuatl.[19]

In Central America, as led by immigrant friars, Jesuits and a locally Latin-trained clergy, the *latinismo* of incantations and instructions extended over a populous native people whose indigenous languages were various and active. The production of new practical works in Latin supplemented the Latin offices of the Catholic colonial Church. At a more rarefied level, Central American Latin publications buttressed study of the classical texts that fashioned, in the words of Gabriel Méndez Plancarte, 'a human humanism, vital and alive, that gave great pride of place to consideration of the human individual'.[20] Certain classic texts, including Cato, were translated into Nahuatl by indigenous *latinistas*.[21] The universality of the Latin also created some marked cultural transpositions. In the Catholic – or at least Catholicizing – territories of Mexico and Central America, modern Latin authorship proved variously transatlantic. The cast of practition-ers included the Wexford-born and Jesuit-educated adventurer William Lamport (1615–59), who during his imprisonment by the Inquisi-tion wrote in Latin 918 psalms and numerous hymns and devotional poems.[22]

The inherited tradition of humanism in the Northern colonies also echoed the Latin usage of their European homelands. Latin served as an entry-language to higher learning and as a (declining) discourse for the-ology, philosophy, science and medicine, but translations from the Latin to the vernacular further advanced classical ideas, narratives and images. Consideration of the transport of the classics across the Atlantic is not, therefore simply a question of texts published in the ancient languages. As in Latin America, the pervasive influence of classical civilization in North America extended across art, architecture, literature and politi-cal thought. Three general periods have traditionally been outlined.[23] The first of these is the century before about 1735 when knowledge of classical languages remained fundamental to the training of servants of both Church and State, both in formal and moral instruction. The sec-ond period comprises the remainder of the eighteenth century when the use of the classics – both Latin and Greek – was more dominant in political debate.[24] By contrast, in the third period, for 80 years or so after 1800, Latin (accompanied by a revived interest in Greek and German-led Hellenism[25]) remained the basic liberal arts training in elite education – an educational foundation that has left a very material mark on American university and college buildings and libraries, and other structures such as the Greek-letter fraternities and sororities.[26]

Other aspects of classical influence appear across a range of both intellectual and material forms. These are often found in ways that might now surprise us. Obama's set-designers might have savoured the irony that in the early South (as also in Britain and in the French Caribbean, but apparently less frequently in South America[27]) one of the most striking contributions that the classics made was to provide names for slaves – Caesar, Polydore, Scipio and the like. Inventories of slaves in Saint-Domingue commonly included Neptune, Thélémaque, Phoebus, Appolon, Bacchus, Titus and Hyppolite.[28] Some of these names, it has been suggested, represented a linguistic transport from African originals to near-sounding Roman and Hellenic equivalents: Herakles from the Mende 'heke', Cato from the Yoruba 'keta' and others. Once given, the names persisted. In modern times, Muhammad Ali renounced the classical slave name he shared with his father, Cassius Marcellus Clay.

A less controversial heritage roll-call ranges across colonies, states and towns: Virginia, Carolina and Pennsylvania, Athens, Troy, Rome, Sparta, Ithaca and dozens of others. The subtlety continues. Few, perhaps, pause to consider the naming of the fictional Americans Homer Simpson and, doubly, Hannibal Lector. In the eighteenth century, up and down the 13 colonies many gentlemen adopted equally playful (and sometimes all too earnest) classical disguises and pseudo-classical nametags when writing to the local newspapers.[29] Near the close of the century it was indeed one 'Philonaus' who proposed the setting up of the Baltimore Library Company (founded 1795), to be 'similar to the Philadelphia Library Company'.[30] Latin and Greek terms were similarly used to pepper and enliven invective. In Charleston, the printer and patriot Timothy Stephen was so incensed by the Stamp Tax that he imported a complete Greek font in order to denounce the tax the more colourfully in his newspaper.[31]

All this represented a change in the balance of respect for and usage of Latin between North and Central America (not that there was sufficient communication between these two regions for anyone to offer commentary upon this at the time). As Latin usage slowly declined in the southern New World following the expulsion of the Jesuits from Hispanic lands, Anglo-Saxon America embraced classicism – and so pervasively that it triggered a reaction that seems absent from the golden age of Latinity in Hispanic America. Northern Americans engaged in fierce debate about not simply the value of the classics in the New World, but also the value more generally of translation from the classics. Purists led campaigns to stamp out translations but many Americans also made successful interventions to extend access to the classics via the vernacular.[32] The publications of the Yorkshireman John Clarke (1687–1734) proved highly influential books on the educational use of translations from the Latin in the colonies.[33]

Classicism, as transported and traded across the Atlantic, was regarded by many North American commentators (but not apparently by their counterparts in Central America) as exclusionary and unhelpful. And contemporary debate about the relative merits of the ancients and moderns has been echoed by debates among historians about the commercial and political significance of New World classical learning. Bernard Bailyn famously dismissed classical influences on revolutionary thinking as highly marginal (and his comments are echoed by others[34]). According to Bailyn, participants exhibited amateurish and superficial learning and the pervasive classical citations are in fact 'illustrative, not determinative, of thought'.[35] Much repeated is the literary tactic of the American revolutionary poet Philip Freneau who had his 1788 'Indian Student' escape from Harvard 'Where learned men talk heathen Greek,/And Hebrew lore is gabbled o'er.' In similar vein, David Shields quotes John Seccomb's much earlier 1728 poem published in a Boston newspaper:

> At Ten this Morn. Dear Friend, *Your Most,*
> Receiv'd your Packet by the Post,
> Kiss'd the out-side, broke up the Seal-o,
> And promis'd Fi'pence to the Fellow,
> Then try'd to read – But hah! what is't?
> O vile! the Language of the Beast!
> *Chinese?* or *Syriac?* – let me see, –
> – *Amice selectissime* –
> Magick! of which thy old Acquaintance
> Knows not a Page, or Word, or Sentence,
> But stands with Horror Half a Headful,
> And cries, O terrible! O dreadful![36]

Critics surfaced even from within. One John Wilson, who taught at the Friends' Latin School in Philadelphia, declared in 1769 that classical learning was 'the grossest absurdity that ever was practiced.'[37] Other North American protests about the superficialities and redundancies of the classics abound, but more broadly, the impact of the classics on the elite is well attested in the intellectual and political history of eighteenth-century America (and there are many historians who line up against Bailyn and the anti-classicists[38]).

The ambivalence was also contemporary. Benjamin Franklin – often a critic of the influence of the classics – fondly recalled reading Plutarch in his father's small library – 'Plutarch's Lives there was, in which I read abundantly, and I still think that time spent to great advantage'.[39] Thomas Jefferson's correspondence with Joseph Priestley (in exile in America) confirms their mutual admiration of Homer.[40] Homer became from early days a routine text of colonial grammar schools, along with what James Madison called 'the common list of School classicks': Cato's *Distichs*, Aesop's *Fables*, Ovid's *Metamorphoses* and *Tristia*, Cicero's orations, letters and *De Officiis*, Florus, Eutropius and Justin, Virgil's *Aeneid*, Horace, Terence, Isocrates, and Xenophon's *Memorabilia*.[41] If (where we know of it) length of borrowing from early American 'society' or proprietary libraries is any guide to the popularity of the holdings, then we might attend to the notice inserted in the *South Carolina Gazette* for the first three months of 1756. It listed some 49 titles of books (together with 'a great number of pamphlets') overdue.[42] Among these were works by Bolingbroke and Locke, together with Demosthenes, Caesar and Longinius. Some titles were, by inference from *ESTC*, recent editions that were the first appearance in English of standard classical works.

Schooling and college education generated these classical enthusiasms (and their condemnation). Although little acknowledged between the different communities, it was a training that was widespread in the New World. At the college of Santa Cruz de Tlatelolco, Mexico (founded 1536), which has good claims to be the first university in America, instruction was in Latin and Nahautl. Latin similarly dominated the college of San José de los Naturales (1527), the Royal and Pontifical University of Mexico from 1553, and the network of Central American colleges founded by the Jesuits after 1572.[43] Some 2,000 miles north, but with very different liturgical and scholastic emphases, nine grammar schools teaching Latin had been established in Massachusetts by 1647,[44] and the principal colleges of British America, like older British and European foundations, required a strict entrance examination in Latin (and sometimes in Greek).

The eighteenth century has been called 'the Golden Age of Mexican Latin',[45] but it was a literary century that effectively ended soon after the expulsion of the Jesuits from all Spanish realms in 1767. It was exactly at this time that Latin gained new authority in the North American colleges, culminating with the 'Yale Report' of 1820 strengthening the requirements in the classical languages. From their establishment and through the nineteenth century, the colleges required all entrants to be literate in the classics – young men 'found able Extempore to Read, Construe and Parse' in the words of the Harvard College laws of 1655 and echoed by the Yale Laws (or 'Rubrique') of 1745 and the King's College, New York (later Columbia) Laws of 1755. In approving the rules of the University of Virginia, Jefferson wrote that 'it should be scrupulously insisted on that no youth can be admitted to the university unless he can read with facility Vergil, Horace, Xenophon and Homer; unless he is able to convert a page of English at sight into Latin; unless he can demonstrate any proposition at sight in the first book of Euclid, and show an acquaintance with cubic and quadratic equations'.[46]

A classics department was established at the university of Pennsylvania by 1786 when German language classical teachings were also very evident.[47] In later reflections upon their classical studies, many American gentlemen (through translations or not) averred that Seneca and Cicero had provided the fundamental models for great letter-writing. In the words of Ward Briggs, 'classics remained stubbornly at the core of the [United States] standard school and college curriculum (or was at least a common element in it) until the middle of the twentieth century.'[48]

Certainly up to 1820, classical texts – in the original and in translation – dominated the college shelves in a way rarely seen in domestic collections. In general terms, colonial institutional library development was slow but sure. By 1735 Harvard boasted 3,000 volumes. The Yale catalogue of 1743 listed 1,100 short author entries, with 804 entries (for 789 titles) in the College of New Jersey (Princeton) in 1760. Yale boasted 2,700 volumes by 1791 and Harvard 9,800 by 1790.[49] Of the Yale 1743 catalogue entries, 511 (or 46 per cent) comprised publications in Latin or (much more rarely) Greek.[50] In the 1760 Princeton catalogue 327 of the 789 titles (or 41 per cent) were in Latin or Greek, and this, quite besides the numerous volumes in English and other modern languages, devoted to Roman and Greek history, literature or philosophy.[51]

Of the *private* collections there can be no doubt that James Logan's library at Philadelphia contained the greatest number and quality of classical texts, but also distinguished, if smaller, were the earlier libraries of John Harvard, Cotton Mather, the Virginian John Carter II and Robert 'King' Carter, and then the libraries of Ralph Wormeley II, Richard Lee I, William Byrd of Westover and James Bowdoin of Massachusetts. Some 13 per cent of Logan's volumes were classical; about 5 per cent of Edwin Lloyd IV's 2,250 title library when catalogued in 1796. This was about the same proportion of classical holdings in the library

of William Munford of Virginia, the translator of Horace, in his catalogue of 1802. By contrast, only one in one hundred of the volumes
in George Washington's library in 1810 were classical works. As Walter
Edgar confirms, most of the classic literature held in most inventoried
libraries in South Carolina (but true, one suspects, for most domestic
libraries in British North America as a whole) were in English translation, and of these the most popular were Caesar's *Commentaries*, Cicero's
Offices and *Orations*, Seneca's *Morals*, works by Ovid, Horace, Terence
and Homer, all variously in translation by Ruddiman, Chapman, Clark
and, above all, Pope.[52] Short-cuts to histories and the classics proved
the 'bestsellers' of early American libraries.[53] In 1761 the Charleston
bookseller Robert Wells proudly advertised the library of James Michie,
early president of the local library society. Michie's library was to be
auctioned and ranged over law books, classics, epic poets, and histories 'in general in very good condition, many of them in elegant
bindings'.[54]

William Byrd's Westover library in Virginia – with 2,345 titles shortly
after his death in 1744 – has recently been examined in print by
Kevin Hayes, and he makes it clear how much the collecting originally derived from Byrd's days at Felsted School, Essex (the school of
Oliver Cromwell's sons, and of several Mayflower voyagers). When Byrd
left Felsted in 1690, he was, in his words, 'pretty much acquainted
with the Latin and Greek tongues, having read divers Authors therein
and was pretty accurate in the Grammars of both.'[55] Byrd's schoolmaster, Christopher Glasscock, ensured that Felsted school library was well
stocked with recent classical editions – with particular emphasis on
Sallust, Caesar, Livy and Justin.[56]

Even more noteworthy in the development of Byrd's own library was
his engagement with the late seventeenth-century 'battle of the books'.
This extended to energetic debate about the superiority of ancient learning and science compared to modern advances. Ranked among the
moderns were numerous literary advocates of 'progress' and numerous
Fellows of the Royal Society (of whom Byrd himself was one), with the
arguments distilled in the aggressive disputes between Richard Bentley
and Charles Boyle.[57] Byrd bridged both parties – or at least wanted to
appear to do so. His 'Secret Diary', compiled between 1709 and 1712,
gives detailed records of his reading, and attests to his early morning
Greek and Hebrew, with Lucian and Homer his favourites. He also gives
the impression, however, of being something of an intellectual boor,
whose dinner guests were often imprisoned by his earnest readings. Yet
he was a determined reader, recording on one day, for example, 'the

wind blew very cold at northwest. In the afternoon I took a walk again with my friend Horace.'[58]

Gentleman's libraries, such as Byrd's, remained demonstrably private rather than public, but many of their owners also shared their collections with likeminded friends, neighbours, scholars and correspondents. Many correspondents wrote from across the ocean. These letter-writers, as Nicholas Wrightson showed in an earlier chapter,[59] included fellow bibliophiles as well as associates and friends interested in particular books, writers, arguments and discoveries. In the colonial settlements themselves, informal membership of such circles remained as guarded and as honoured as membership of a proprietary library and the honour required appropriate recognition. An appreciation of literary and classical traditions and allusions, even of a particular architectural vocabulary, certainly extended to the design of the library or book parlour, and, in many of these, to their cases, ornaments, furniture, and even ceiling designs. Allegorical library fitments were suitably designed to impress and reassure.[60]

North American gentlemen's societies, edifying publications, and official and civic institutions offered representations of an enlightenment iconography that pivoted on classical allusion. Private and subscription library bookplates, and library society seals and certificates displayed various classical gods and goddesses and Latin tags and mottos. Athena–Minerva reigned as the most replicated classical image, although Ceres. Mercury and Columbia also appeared frequently. Even a shining eye featured very widely in mid eighteenth-century representations of pyramids and among other Masonic symbols and devices.[61] In the early bookplates of the New York Society Library, Minerva, in full regalia, appears in the library on a cloud. Kneeling before the goddess, an abased Native American discards his tomahawk in return for a book.[62] The oldest surviving seal of the Charleston Library Society depicts the goddess of Reason who is probably also to be taken as Minerva, resplendent in classical dress. Encircled by a banner, and with an open book resting on her lap, the goddess presides on a throne of books and scrolls, and carries a sceptre with a shining eye in the finial. The eye, representing the light of reason, was, again, commonly associated with ancient Egyptian hieroglyphs. The device, derived from the influence of the *Treatise on Hieroglyphics* of Horapollo Nilous, claimed to date entirely from later antiquity, and was popularized by various early sixteenth-century editions and compilations.[63] Reprinted editions of British publications copied or adapted the icons, as did newly minted American productions. In the frontispiece to *The Self-Interpreting Bible*, published in New York in 1792, for example, a benevolent Minerva-like goddess, replete with a Phrygian cap of liberty on a spear stands before a seated America (with feathered headdress) all set against a gigantic Grecian temple.[64]

Much of the print ordered for colonial libraries and sent from England offered cumulative lessons in the relationship between books, civility and useful knowledge. The *Universal Magazine* (first published in 1747) ranks among the most popularly ordered periodicals in British North America, and the frontispiece to its first volume portrays an imposing library with two sides open to a world in which ships set out from harbour. The bookshelves and the ships dwell beneath a banner flown from Mercury's caduceus. Readers became familiar with an adaptable repertoire of classical emblems. Many were based on engravings in Pierce Tempest's 1709 reprint of Caesar Ripa's *Iconologia*. As Tempest introduces Ripa, 'these images are the Representatives of our Notions; they properly belong to Painters, who by Colours and Shadowing, have invented the admirable Secret to give Body to our Thoughts, thereby to render them visible.'[65] In successive frontispieces, Minerva, goddess of wisdom and learning, alluded to in the Charleston Library seal, and the vehicle of the book transaction in the New York Library Society bookplates, is once again the crucial emblem of bibliographical benevolence.

It might appear that masculine interests predominate in this book world, and study of the history of classical influences in the seventeenth and eighteenth centuries often serves to heighten this impression. Nevertheless, in elite colonial circles women were often far from marginalized. Few large private libraries were established by women, and women were not, at least at first, to be members of the library societies (although several became early shareholders). Indirect access by women to books in the collection was not usually denied, however – at least in terms of borrowing as part of a household membership – and many of the great book collectors were also keen advocates of women's learning. William Byrd, for example, despite his refusal to let his wife read his books at will, gave his wife her own volumes, including a marked-up Antoninus. There is a debate here about women's involvement, and not all advocacy of advanced female participation seems entirely convincing.[66] Byrd, the great colonial bibliophile, did at least respect women translators, notably Mme. Dacier and her French translations of Homer's *Odyssey* and *Iliad*, Terence's Comedies, and her editions of Florus, Dictys Cretensis, Sextus Aurelius Victor and Eutropius, all of which Byrd owned. Byrd, also, incidentally, did much of his courting in the classic languages. After a disastrous series of liaisons, he was delighted to encounter the young Maria Taylor, to whom he wrote, in Greek, 'when I thought you knew only your mother tongue, I was passionately in love with you: but when indeed I learned that you also spoke Greek, the tongue of the Muses, I went completely crazy about you.'[67] In 1724 he married her.

Another celebrated case of female participation was that of Eliza Lucas Pinckney, the pioneer indigo grower, wife of Charleston grandee planter Charles Pinckney (d. 1758), and mother of future United States presidential candidate and general, Charles Cotesworth Pinckney. George Washington, as president, was a pall bearer at her funeral. In 1740 Eliza reported that 'I have a little library well-furnished (for my papa has left me most of his books).' She had also asked her father to order music books from London, and her future husband lent her Virgil, allegedly providing the inspiration for her own cedar grove. Eliza read several other classical writers for their contemporary utility, but it was of Virgil, that she rather marvellously decided that, 'tho' he wrote in and for Italy, it will in many instances suit Carolina.' Notably, Eliza had requested the loan of Virgil despite the warnings of 'an old lady in our Neighbourhood' who 'has a great spite at my books and had like to have thrown a volume of my Plutarchs lives into the fire the other day.... and begs most seriously I will never read father Malbrauch' [Nicolas Malebranche].[68] The marked-up Demosthenes that Pinckney lent to Eliza is now in the Thomas Cooper Library at Columbia, South Carolina.

The search for validation was as true in North America as it was in the southern continent. In some respects, the parading of a classical heritage responded to colonial crises of confidence. This can be given a positive hue – Timothy Breen, among others, has pointed to the critical role of intellectual and cultural ritual[69] – of which classical literary allusion was part – in constructing a political authority in the absence of traditional hierarchical structures. More negatively – but also more usually – elite learning and classical heritage were wielded to try to dispel hostile critiques of colonial society. By the mid-eighteenth century a new consumerism was identified as one sign of decline. In New York, Philadelphia, and Boston newspapers warned of the dangers of modernity, and in Charleston commentary on the town's fragile literary aspirations also reflected acute awareness of its perilous position in the moral geography of the empire.[70]

It is certainly true that we may discern an eclecticism in the reading of the classics in British America that corresponded to practical needs. A primary interest in the prose authors – the moralists and the historians – derives from their perceived value in promoting moral and practical guidance. The imported *belles-lettres* were little stocked in the serious private and society libraries, where the holdings of ancient poetry were also limited except where the imaginative writing of Virgil and Horace (most notably) offered moral instruction.

The library stocking of classics was, indeed, by the second half of the eighteenth century, hardly uniform. Such collecting, however various, was also increasingly challenged by those (from the north to the south) who regarded classical learning and allusion as a distraction – and even as a positively damaging force – to the colonies and then to the young United States. In 1728 John Seccomb, publishing a satiric pseudo-Latin verse in the *New England Weekly Journal* had already parodied the vanity of elite classical learning in the college. Many voices questioned the literary learning most appropriate for great colonial trading centres.[71] In the *Gentleman's Magazine* of 1776, its editor wrote that 'a classical education, the sole basis of sound learning, is in the present wise age, become obsolete and unfashionable.' It was a voice seemingly dismayed by the trend (even if its irony might have been missed by Reinhold[72]), but which nevertheless testifies to the challenges to the educational and literary primacy of classics. From the Revolutionary era onwards the debate centred upon the construction of 'useful knowledge' – and classics could be wheeled on for both defence and prosecution. Benjamin Rush, the famed doctor of Philadelphia and signatory to the Declaration of Independence, was a stern critic of classical reading; while John Muir, principal of the Academy of Alexandria in Virginia, distinguished between solid American learning, both modern and ancient, compared to the 'ornamental' learning of Europeans.[73]

It is also the case that the gravest incident in the early history of the Charleston Library Society was a dispute in the 1760s about the importance of promoting the classics in the town. The earliest Charleston Library collection, as we can now see from the surviving 1750 *Catalogue*, already included editions of Cicero, Cornelius Nepos, Herodotus, Horace, Justin, Livy, Ovid, Sallust, Tacitus, and Virgil. At the general meeting of June 1764, however, Christopher Gadsden proposed the establishment of a new committee charged with preparing a list of the best editions of classics down to the fourth century to be sent for from London.[74] The suggestion was approved, together with an allocation of £70 of the annual book-buying budget of £100. At the next meeting, however, the librarian, William Carwithen, objected that few of the classics in the library were read (and left mouldering on the shelves), while the £30 residue from the purchase was far too little to cover the pamphlets and books already on order. Gadsden's resolution was duly rescinded, and the proposal was rejected by the autumn general meeting. In protest, Gadsden resigned from the Society. During the following year debate continued at the meetings of April and October, but a compromise was reached whereby the regular order was modified to include the classics. Gadsden rejoined the Society, and, it might be argued, was entitled to claim victory. In February 1766 the secretary, William Mason, wrote to James Fletcher, the new bookseller, enclosing a 'List of Classick's' to the value of £70, and followed this with a further list for £30 worth in May 1767.[75]

Others were more severe in their opposition. Shortly after the Gadsden debate, one of the most influential leaders of the Carolinian elite, Henry Laurens, declared serious doubt about the value of the classics in what he called a 'commercial Country'. As he wrote, 'hundreds of Men have their Mouths fill'd with jabbering Latin, while their Bellies are empty.'[76] William Livingston of New York, and first Governor of New Jersey, argued in 1768 in the *Independent Reflector* that a new country was being built in which 'we want hands...more than heads. The most intimate acquaintance with the classics, will not remove our oaks, nor a taste for the *Georgics* cultivate our lands. Many of our young people are knocking their heads against the *Iliad*, who should employ their hands in clearing our swamps and draining our marshes. Others are musing, in cogitation profound, on the arrangement of a syllogism, while they ought to be guiding the til of a plow.'[77]

In ordering other practical publications, many town library members followed interests in both agrarian science and domestic horticulture and cultivation. Theirs was the frontier commercial and agrarian world pictured by Henry Laurens. Here was the progressive optimism of an Eliza Lucas Pinckney, promoting agrarian advance, and a climate in which the advocacy of improvement – both agricultural and mental (at least for the elite) – found no dissent.

It is important to note, in this respect, that many library societies were also established with the direct intention of supporting a college (when one could be afforded). Thus in Charleston, ever anxious to prove itself the greatest town of the overseas empire, John Mackenzie, radical Patriot (of Broom Hall, Goose Creek), bequeathed the Society Library a fine collection of the learned ancients 'for the use of a college when erected'. When printed in 1772, the *Catalogue* of the bequest included 861 volumes including some 125 folio editions, and 135 classical titles.[78]

The key consideration here, however, is that almost all such literature was imported from London. During the first century of American printing only 12 titles pertaining to classical literature were printed in the British colonies – all in Philadelphia – and before 1776 the only American written and published classical aid was the school text on Latin grammar by Ezekiel Cheever.[79] Other important texts, notably Clarke, were brought across by the ships. As imported to the English-speaking world, 'polite letters' were built upon the translation of the classics from Brome's Horace of 1666 then Dryden's Ovid of 1680, his Juvenal of 1697 and his Virgil of 1697, followed by l'Estrange's Aesop (1692–99) and then Pope's *Illiad* (1715–20) and *Odyssey* (1725–26).

Again, the historic comparison with Hispanic America is illuminating. Vast quantities of Bibles and religious books in Latin arrived with the friars and the great printing houses of Spain – and most notably the Crombergers of Seville – sent huge cargoes to Vera Cruz, port of entry for Mexico. The Cromberger exports included large numbers of Latin primers, school books and editions of the classics.[80] Such arrivals in Central America continued during the seventeenth and eighteenth centuries, but they supplemented and helped to inspire Mexican printed and scribal publication in Latin.[81] The importations of classical literature in North America (both in Latin and in English translation) fed a voracious demand from colleges, students, would-be students, schoolchildren and sympathetic gentlemen. Without inspiring the same sort of neo-Latin literary endeavours apparent in Central America, the trade might, in fact, be considered as more attentively and determinedly transatlantic in its focus. In a rare glance southwards, Wolfgang Haase and Meyer Reinhold briefly acknowledged this point: from this age of fundamental decisions, classical education emerged in a stronger position in the United States than in the countries of Latin America, in which it had partly, in the second half of the eighteenth century already suffered grave setbacks from the politically motivated expulsion of the Jesuits.[82]

Any bibliometric exercise to assess, however generally, the texts and print that fed British colonial and North American users, readers and defenders of the classics, certainly involves looking at production and dispatch on both sides of the Atlantic. We immediately enter a bibliographical minefield. It is one familiar to those who work on early modern and eighteenth- and nineteenth-century publishing history, but one which is even more complicated by the different locations we need to consider. As already noted in the introduction to this book, simple use of *ESTC* and other *STCs*[83] counting items by title alone disguise variations in edition sizes. It is also the case that the earlier the year of publication, the more likely that other publications of that year have not survived in any remaining copy. We also need to be wary of literary categorization – some texts were in mixed languages, and also offered translation of and advice from classical authors in English or another modern language. The best estimates to date (again based on *ESTC*) suggest the publication of almost 700 book-length translations into English of classical authors first published in Britain between 1550 and 1790, and of which nearly 350 titles went through further editions (including 38 with more than 6 editions). Some of these titles were pamphlets, but most were larger publications, most single-volume and some multi-volume.[84]

As also detailed in this book's introductory chapter, basic *ESTC* title counts demonstrate the enduring dominance of London, but also the striking relative advance of American publication after 1750.[85] The new printing from Boston, Philadelphia, New York and several other North American towns includes the 188 editions printed before 1801 in North America in French (188), in German (1,213), a few dozen in Dutch, a handful in Spanish and even fewer in Swedish and Italian. At the same time, the market for classical translation in Britain *relative* to the overall expansion in publication actually fell during the eighteenth century,[86] a trend replicated across Europe.[87] It is within that context that an assessment might be made of colonial printing of texts in Latin and Greek. Of the roughly 2 million items currently recorded in *ESTC* after 1473, 15,514 are in Latin, and of these, 7,634 (or about half) are printed after 1700 (but more than half of the *ESTC* 2 million total is printed after 1760). Such trawls exclude, of course, the hugely popular classic authors available in English translation, led (in terms of reprints of titles and only counting sole authorship) by Aesop, followed by Cicero, Ovid, Horace, Virgil, Homer, Terence, Plutarch, Xenophon, Sallust and Euclid. In the eighteenth century, absolute totals of Latin texts, by edition title, are fairly consistent across the century (although not totals relative to total publication of course) 100 in 1700, 95 in 1750, 98 in 1780, 121 in 1800. Of these only a handful were published in the colonies. *ESTC* records 40,807 items printed before 1800 in North America; of these 494 were in Latin, 435 after 1700. Not a single North American text wholly printed in Greek is recorded. In addition to the limited publication of Latin and Greek in North America (and with dedicated Greek texts, apart from extracts, non existent), American publication of classics in English translation also remained very modest before about 1820. As a result, those requiring the classics continued to depend on imports – and more so than readers of most other texts.

Latin printed in early North America consisted exclusively (from their first known appearance in 1643) of lists of graduates and theses from Harvard. Not until 1712 did a piece of printed Latin appear that was not a college list – a one-sheet poem by Nehemiah Hobart. College lists continued to predominate until 1717, however, when John Charmion published his one-sheet verse epitaph in memory of Ebenezer Pemberton (also published in English). The first Latin sheet not from Cambridge or Boston was printed the next year, 1718: namely, another college list from Yale. Graduating lists from both colleges together with reports of doctoral interrogations continued to make up the Latin North American textual corpus (if it can be so-called) until the publication in 1723 of the Harvard Library *Catalogue*. Here was native printing of Latin in the service of academic utility, and one bearing a very poor comparison with the neo-Latin printing of New Spain. A New York printing of a one-sheet Latin publication in 1732 by Alexander Campbell on the necessity of maintaining frequent elections, widened the scope beyond college use of printed Latin, but it was similarly issued in the service of enhanced authority rather than to appeal to an engaged Latin readership.

The first large Latin work printed in North America was published in Boston in 1735, a treatise on logic, *Compendium logicae*, by William Brattle, brother of a leading merchant, pastor of Cambridge, and a former Harvard tutor. His treatise was used at Harvard as a textbook until 1765, following an American reprinting by John Draper in 1758.[88] The college lists and a few funeral elegies continued to the end of century, but in 1742 the first Philadelphia Latin printing appeared when Franklin reprinted Count Zinzendorf's eight-page plea for church unity.[89] Nicolaus Ludwig, Graf von Zinzendorf, born in Dresden in 1700, and founder of Bethlehem Pennsylvania, was very much part of the Pietist movement in Germany, which emphasized personal piety and an emotional component to the religious life. On his visit to America Zinzendorf sought to unify the German Protestants of Pennsylvania, even proposing a cooperative 'council of churches'. His address in Latin was surely intended as a further bridge between speakers of different languages and dialects. Its printer, Franklin, revelled nonetheless in his scepticism of the utility of the classic, but it was paid work – and he even, despite his further concerns, printed an edition in German.

In the same city in 1765 William Bradford printed John Beveridge's *Epistolae familiares et alia quaedam miscellanea* (Familiar epistles and other miscellaneous pieces), an 88-page collection of original Latin poetry. A Scottish schoolteacher, Beveridge arrived in New England from Scotland in 1752. In 1758 he was appointed professor of languages in the College and Academy of Philadelphia, and included in his volume were English translations done by his students. Many of the pieces are on American subjects, notably Governor William Shirley and the French and Indian Wars, and are set in such American locales as Florida, the Schuylkil, Maine, Halifax and Ontario. Various of the students' Latin poems were written 'for their own improvement or amusement' and a list of 310 subscribers suggests that this was no high-risk publication. Subscribers included Benjamin Rush, William Smith, and, again, Benjamin Franklin.

During the second half of the eighteenth century, Latin textbook publication in North America began a modest advance, and included Myles Cooper's *Ethices compendium* printed in New York in 1774 and an American edition of Edward Wettenhall's Latin and Greek grammar, printed in Philadelphia in 1776. A few student exercises were also published, probably all at their own expense. The Latin translation of Young's *Night-Thoughts* from Charlestown, Massachusetts, in 1786 was also more than simple vanity, offering an obsequious dedication to John Hancock. Paralleling the increase in Latin aids and outcomes of college learning were further Latin religious commentaries, including the first South Carolina, Latin printing in 1775, the *Exercitatio theologica de nuptiis virginis superadultæ* by John Joachim Zubly. A Presbyterian minister of Swiss birth, Zubly arrived at Charleston, South Carolina, in 1744. During a turbulent political life he moved between Charleston and Savannah, Georgia, where he died in 1781 before the liberation of the city from the British. It is likely that he wrote his pamphlet in Latin to appeal to multiple language groups. In another example of Latin in the service to religious utility, the first Latin printings in Baltimore, in 1794, were Catholic liturgies. Some 250 years after the first Latin printing in the Americas, Maryland Catholics introduced clerical Latin printing to the former British domains.

Medical treatises represented the other useful contribution made by North American Latin printing. Medical dissertations in Latin began in 1771 with Jonathan Potts's short medical text, printed like almost all the rest in Philadelphia. Franklin's city published, indeed, a greater diversity of printed Latin texts than did any other North American town, and if the total was very modest it encompassed religious, pedagogical, academic, medical and the occasional exotica. Sixteen pages of Latin verses were printed in 1782, for example, in celebration of the birth of the first son of Louis XVI and foretelling a glorious future for the Bourbons. Such rarities made little impact beyond a small and interested circle, but the medical and educational texts buttressed and extended specific communities of Latin readers, and ones which spanned the Atlantic. The medical texts of Potts or those such as William Brown's *Pharmacopoeia*,[90] at least as based on surviving copies were held widely (even though later publications bearing the title *Pharmacopoeia* were very largely written in English).

Such native printing in Latin *was* very limited (especially in comparison to that of New Spain), but, in addition, what we should really note are the omissions. Most notable for their absence were the classical texts themselves. It was not until 1788 that an American printing of the classics was available – a Boston Livy – and a further five years before a Philadelphia printing of selections from Cicero. It is here, together with an even greater freight of the grammars and textbooks needed for scholarly and gentlemanly literary pursuits, that we see the real reliance on the importation of publications from Europe.

What needs to be stressed is the key role of intermediaries – the merchants and shipmasters, the financing arrangements, and, above all, the book collecting agents and the correspondents of booksellers in London. Trading in the classics carried prestige, but booksellers often found themselves tested because of it. In 1768 James Fletcher, noted bookseller of St Paul's Churchyard, narrowly escaped dismissal as supplier to the Charleston library, after which he was informed that members 'were highly Offended at your remissness in Several Particulars (*especially* in sending out the Classics unlettered contrary to the full and clear Instructions given you by their late Secretary)'.[91]

Inevitably, all private and society library book orders reflected the particular wants of collectors and library members at any given time. In many library societies, certain leading members exerted disproportionate influence in ballots, suggestion books and open meetings. The Gadsden debate about the classics, for example, raised issues beyond the extent to which members were informed about new editions or the simple idea of cultural 'lag'. When writing to London bookseller James Fletcher in early 1766 the library secretary reminded him that he must keep 'strictly to the Editions particularly specified in the List' and that 'many of them are only to be had at Second hand and some of them very scarce'. The expertise of particular committees, secretaries and correspondents was a key component in advising – and correcting – the bookseller. The other formative and often constraining feature was the book ordering process itself.

To this extent the library societies conformed to what might be termed an 'autodidactic' purchasing policy. The choice of books originated with the members themselves, within the bounds of their accumulated purchasing funds. By their design, and by what we can tell of their practices, very few American library societies built their collections under the instructions of administrators or donors, as did many colonial and British college and ecclesiastical libraries.[92] The Library Company of Philadelphia (LCP) became famous for its tin suggestion box of about 1750, painted with a lion's head and with a slot in the middle where 'Gentlemen are requested To deposit in the Lion's Mouth the Titles of such Books As they may wish to have Imported.'[93] By contrast, although still 'autodidactic', the Charleston Library Society offered no such anonymity, or, despite its lengthy procedural rules, much obvious consistency in practice.

In part, library members' demands for Latin and antique texts were also legal and political, particularly for a cluster of fundamental legal texts in the midst of colonial conflict over the Townshend duties and other complaints against the British Parliament. Bracton (or Bratton), the great classical Latin treatise on English laws and customs from the thirteenth century, represented a foundation work, a standard for the shelves. *De laudibus legum Angliæ* written in about 1468 by Sir John Fortescue, Chief Justice of the King's Bench under Henry VI, attempted to explain the advantages of English law, contrasting this with Roman law, and described the benefits of limited monarchy compared to despotic government – with clear implications for the American revolt. Published in parallel Latin and English texts from 1616, followed by editions in 1660 and 1672, a new translation with a Latin text was issued in 1737. Also making up these library reading-lists on Englishmen's rights was the 1672 edition of William Hakewill's *Modus tenendi parliamentum; or, The Old Manner of Holding Parliaments in England* (first published in 1659). Such demands by library members confirm the place of Bracton, Glanville, Fortescue and others in the modern intellectual histories of Wiltshire and Richard,[94] yet the link has not been made with their appearance on so many important library shelves where, to many library historians, they have appeared anomalous.

In the early nineteenth century the literary tastes of many collectors and of American library society members changed. In most libraries, biography and history, together with religion and philosophy, comprised nearly a third of all titles held. The other, substantial, holdings of classics, law and politics, medicine and science, literature, and practical works, were relatively evenly stocked, each with about a tenth of all titles. The earlier and later holdings of imaginative literature provide the surest and most obvious contrasts. At the Charleston Library, 'Literature' comprised 10 per cent of the total by title in 1770 but 23 per cent in 1811, confirming the new enthusiasm of library members in the early nineteenth century for novels and romances – a trend shared in astonishing regularity with all American society libraries with surviving records. By comparison, the stock of classical literature diminished slightly over these 40 years, law and politics remained roughly constant, but the proportion of travel writing doubled (from 4 to 9 per cent).[95] In Baltimore, the Library Company's founding committee decreed that acquisitions were to 'consist chiefly of books in general demand' and 'of general utility'.[96] From its foundation in 1809, the Savannah Library Society also bought large quantities of fiction, and novels comprised the main category in its first printed catalogue of 1838 – 16 per cent of the total (20 per cent including novels and belles-lettres), compared to just 3 per cent theology.[97]

In the American social libraries of the early nineteenth century, enthusiasm for the classics was apparently drying up. The partial eagerness of an earlier generation to read classical authors appears to have waned, but there are also qualifications to this perception. First, the quality of the basic collection of classics should not be ignored, and second, the provision of new titles included numerous distinguished and rare volumes. When subject divisions were introduced in Charleston in the 1806 and 1811 Catalogues, the sections headed 'Greek and Latin Authors and Translations' included all texts in Latin and Greek, modern works as well as the classics. The collection was an impressive one, ranging from the restocking of classical authors after a 1778 fire that destroyed the original list of classics so hotly debated in the 1770s, to neo-Latin texts of the sixteenth, seventeenth and eighteenth centuries. The Library Society's continued collection included English translations of Cornelius Nepos, Caesar, Cicero, Livy, Justin and Petronius, as well as Latin editions of Tacitus and Tertullian (the latter in a 1624 Paris edition). An order for the English Petronius followed a request for a Latin edition in 1761.[98] This Burman edition of Petronius, with notes also in Latin, was certainly a scholarly addition to the Library shelves, but it also offered convenient sanction of lewd material. The poems of Catullus were similarly held in both Latin and English. Many of the volumes were valuable acquisitions, notably the Stephanus Latin thesaurus, although the 1572 Greek thesaurus, set to cost the Library £25 in 1807 was deemed too expensive. Other items such as Polyaenus's *Strategems of War*, were rare or esoteric, suggesting the interests of particular members.

Apart from scientific and legal manuals and treatises written in Latin, the Library also held a strong selection of modern classics ranging from Erasmus's *Colloquies* to the *Stradae Prolusiones*. Notable among other neo-Latin compositions were mid-eighteenth-century verses by

Etonians (*Musae Etonenses*), while Melchior de Polignac's *Anti-Lucretius* (ordered by 1811) was most definitely an example of suspect 'polemical divinity', albeit in the cause of Christianity against paganism. Creech's elderly translation of Lucretius *de rerum Natura* had been available in the Charleston Library by 1806. Interest in Greek texts extended to Gilbert Wakefield's *Dio Chrysostom*, and, intriguingly, a copy of Charles Boyle's controversial 1695 edition of *Phalaridis Epistolae*, an attack on Richard Bentley's (now fully vindicated) dismissal of the text.[99] This was despite, or perhaps because of, the notable absence of Bentley editions in the classics section of the Charleston Society Library – and in contrast to the acquisition of several works by his late seventeenth-century foe, Charles Boyle.

Many of the re-ordered classics might also suggest a collection intended to support basic instruction in Latin and the classical authors. In addition to standard editions of Horace, library societies from New York to Charleston purchased various of the beautifully produced Delphin (or Dauphin's) editions of the classics, and a notably large number of volumes of the lighter authors including Lucian and Petronius. Another indication that the collection assisted guided studies in Latin was the acquisition of the *Gradus ad Parnassum*, widely used for verse composition. In Charleston, in further testimony to continued interest in reading and writing in Latin, Thomas Mills, Library member and Rector of St Andrews, undertook the unusual and laborious task of composing a *Compendium of Latin Grammar*. It was the first classical work published in South Carolina, printed and sold by Timothy and Mason in Charleston in 1795, followed by a much shorter *Compendium of Latin Syntax* later in the year.[100] By these standards, the Society's librarian required certain assistance; the catalogues he was charged with compiling contain various muddles in the Greek and Latin Authors section, including confusion between the elder and younger Pliny, and numerous typographical errors (although some were corrected in the 1811 version).

At about the same time the primacy of classics in the colleges began to be questioned – and although the battle was not lost until the end of the nineteenth century, in certain respects hostilities had begun from the 1760s and 1770s. At Yale under the presidency of Thomas Clap, English replaced Latin as language of primary instruction once students were admitted, and similar changes were observed at the College of New Jersey (Princeton) after 1765 under the leadership of John Witherspoon.[101]

For all the stirrings of opposition, classical influences, it must be repeated, ran deep. Over the century, as David Shields has written, 'learning became less a marker of gender and more one of gentility' and Latin provided status for many.[102] Native imitations increased. Productions were not as rich or influential as the equivalent indigenous Latin literature of seventeenth- and eighteenth-century Mexico (some of which was published or republished in Europe following the exile of the Hispanic Jesuits[103]), but some colourful pieces appeared. Richard Lewis, for example, master of the Latin school at Annapolis and correspondent to the Royal Society had memorably announced the reign of civility in Maryland with his *Muscipula, sive Kambromyomachia*, a poetic narrative about battles between the ancient Welsh and mice. Aquila Rose offered *Poems on Several Occasions* – imitations of Ovid's elegies of Scythian exile – and represented a 'fascination with Ovid's elegies of exile [as] out of the provincial situation of cosmopolitan intellectuals who understood themselves as living in rude backwaters'.[104] Here was read Horace, planter-hero of the georgic and of achieved civility; Virgil, oracle of expanding empire; and then Livy, eulogizer of the glory days of the Roman republic. But the sympathies of these readers and library builders and book collectors were also, this chapter argues, enmeshed in a complex – and changing – series of notions about currency and the immediate which made engagement with the imported classics – and engagement with the London agents and booksellers, a fraught and delicate relationship.

Françoise Waquet writes of an 'empire' of Latin that stretched across boundaries and across oceans whereby the dead language offered a pervasive storehouse of social and intellectual power. Yet the transatlantic Latin and classical 'community' was not homogenous but divided according to national colonialisms, albeit deployed in similar (as well as some different) cultural, educational and political practices. Today 46 million 'Hispanics' or 'Latinos' live in the United States (some 15 per cent of the 305 million population), and of those of them who voted, two-thirds supported Obama in the 2008 presidential election. Whether or not Obama's classical stage-set in Denver had much appeal for voters without Anglo Saxon roots (paradoxical as that might seem), it is certainly the case that the modern United States with its diverse population shares and takes for granted classical allusions and legacies in daily life. In the years when classical texts had to be imported to maintain pedagogical, clerical and intellectual demands for 'the classics', however, the Hispanic and the British (and French) New Worlds created divergent as well as shared 'empires' of transatlantic Latinity. As the classically trained Benedict Anderson observed,[105] Latin was determinedly a language of bilinguals, where Latin was always secondary to the vernacular tongue, and where, by the nineteenth century in Europe 'Latin had been defeated by vernacular print-capitalism for something like two centuries.'[106] But the power of Latin's reach was remarkable – the Cicero, Horace, Virgil and Ovid imported for Central American Jesuits also supplied, in very different editions, the needs of New England schoolmasters. The same authors contributed to the rote memorization in schools and colleges in the Spanish, Portuguese, British and French empires. The extension of classical influence was arguably greater in the North at the very time that its textual appreciation diminished in the South; and just as there continued the great divisions in the clerical and religious use – and non-use – of Latin texts and liturgies. Where such divisions existed in the Americas, however, the importation and exchange of Latin continued to support genuinely transatlantic connections and communities.

Notes

1. Simon Schama, 'Mile High Stadium', *The Guardian*, 30 Aug 2008, 34.
2. Richard M. Gummere, *The American Colonial Mind and the Classical Tradition* (Cambridge, MA, 1963); Meyer Reinhold, *Classica Americana: The Greek and Roman Heritage in the United States* (Detroit, 1984); Wolfgang Haase and Meyer Reinhold (eds), *The Classical Tradition and the Americas*, vol. 1 (Berlin and New York, 1994); and notably, John W. Eadie (ed.), *Classical Tradition in Early America* (Ann Arbor, MI, 1976); Susan Ford Wiltshire (ed.), *The Usefulness of Classical Learning in the Eighteenth Century* (University Park, PA, 1976); Susan Ford Wiltshire (ed.), *The Classical Tradition in the South,* special issue of *Southern Humanities Review* (Fall, 1977); Roger G. Kennedy, *Greek Revival America* (New York, 1981); Wendy A. Cooper, *Classical Taste in America 1800–1840* (New York, London and Paris, 1993).
3. Caroline Winterer, *The Culture of Classicism: Ancient Greece and Rome in American Intellectual Life, 1780–1910* (Baltimore, MD and London, 2002): 1.
4. Susan Ford Wiltshire, *Greece, Rome and the Bill of Rights* (Norman, OK and London, 1992); Carl J. Richard, *The Founders and the Classics: Greece, Rome, and the American Enlightenment* (Cambridge, MA, 1994).
5. Both are considered in Ward Briggs, 'United States', in Craig W. Kallendorf (ed.), *A Companion to the Classical Tradition* (Oxford, 2007): 282; Dickinson (as 'Fabius') was a later enthusiastic quoter of Polybius, Richard, *Founders and the Classics*, 111.
6. Richard, *Founders and the Classics*, 10.
7. Françoise Waquet, *Le Latin ou l'empire d'un signe XVIᵉ-XXᵉ siècle* (Paris, 1999).
8. James Raven, 'The Importation of Books to Colonial North America', *Publishing History* 42 (1997): 21–49; James Raven, *London Booksellers and American Customers: Transatlantic Literary Community and the Charleston Library Society, 1748–1811* (Columbia, SC, 2002); James Raven, 'Commodification and Value: Interaction in Book Traffic to North America,

c. 1750–1820', in Bill Bell, Philip Bennett, and Jonquil Bevan (eds), *Across Boundaries: The Book in Culture and Commerce* (Winchester and New Castle, DE, 2000): 73–90; James Raven. 'The Export of Books from London', in Hugh Amory and David Hall (eds), *The Colonial Book in the Atlantic World: The History of the Book in North America*, vol. 1 (New York, 1999): 183–98; James Raven, 'Social Libraries and Library Societies in Eighteenth-Century North America', in Kenneth E. Carpenter and Thomas A. Augst (eds), *Institutions of Reading: The Social Life of Libraries in the United States* (Boston, MA, 2007): 24–52.

9. Benedict Anderson, *Imagined Communities: Reflections on the Origin and Spread of Nationalism* (London, 1983, reprinted London 1991): 40, 41.

10. Andrew Laird, *The Epic of America: An Introduction to Rafael Landívar and the 'Rusticatio Mexicana* (London, 2006): 9; the priest, Aguilar, had survived alongside one other Spaniard, Andrew Laird, 'Latin in Cuauhtémoc's Shadow: Humanism and the Politics of Language in Mexico after the Conquest', in Yasmin Haskell and Juanita Feros Ruys (eds), *Latinity and Alterity in the Early Modern World* (Tempe, AZ, 2010): 169–99; I am most grateful to Andrew Laird for his suggestions for the further reading that informs this chapter.

11. 'América Latina' first gained currency in the 1890s, inclining 'Spanish Americans to lay claim to origins that pertained to Europe more generally, than to Spain in particular', Laird, *Epic of America*, 3.

12. See James Raven, 'Sent to the Wilderness: Mission Literature in Colonial America', in James Raven (ed.), *Free Print and Non-Commercial Publishing since 1700* (London and Vermont, 2000): 135–61 (135–9).

13. See David Lupher, *Romans in a New World: Classical Models in Sixteenth-Century Spanish America* (Ann Arbor, MI, 2003).

14. Andrew Laird, 'Renaissance Emblems and Aztec Glyphs: Italian Humanism and Mexico (I): 1520–1590', *Studi Umanistici Piceni: Atti dei Congressi* 26 (2006): 227–39; and 'Pagan Symbols and Christian Images: Italian Humanism and Mexico (II): 1590–1750', *Studi Umanistici Piceni: Atti dei Congressi* 28 (2008): 167–81.

15. See Laird, *Epic of America*, chs. 2 and 3.

16. Nathaniel Hodges and John Quincy (eds), *Loimologia: or, an Historical Account of the Plague in London in 1885* (London, 1720).

17. Marina Frasca-Spada, 'Compendious footnotes', in Frasca-Spada and Nick Jardine (eds), *Books and the Sciences in History* (Cambridge, 2000): 173–89.

18. Laird, 'Renaissance Emblems and Aztec Glyphs', and 'Pagan Symbols and Christian Images'.

19. John Eliot's, *Mamusee Wunneetupanatamwe Up-Biblium God* (Cambridge, MA, 1663), a Bible in Algonquian, was begun sometime between 1650 and 1658 and was later accompanied by *The Indian Grammar* of 1666.

20. The quoted text is a translation from Spanish. 'Un humanismo humano, vital, vivo e itegral, que eleva al primer plano in consideración de la persona humana', Gabriel Méndez Plancarte, *Humanismo Mexicano del Siglo XVI: Introducción, selección y versions* (Mexico City, 1946): xi.

21. Laird, 'Latin in Cuauhtémoc's Shadow'.

22. Fabio Troncarelli, 'The Man Behind the Mask of Zorro: William Lamport of Wexford', *History Ireland* 9 (2001): 22–5; Gabriel Méndez Plancarte, 'Don

Guillén de Lámport y su Regio Salterio, Manuscrito de 1655: estudios, selección, versión y notas', *Abside* 12 (1948): 2–3.

23. See, notably, Gummere, *American Colonial Mind*, and Reinhold, *Classica Americana*.

24. See Susan Ford Wiltshire (ed.), *The Usefulness of Classical Learning in the Eighteenth Century* (Philadelphia, PA, 1976).

25. See Winterer, *Culture of Classicism*, ch. 2.

26. Its final and subtle demise is chronicled by Winterer, *Culture of Classicism*, ch. 4, 'Classical Civilization Consecrated, 1870–1910'.

27. Among notable British examples, Cesar Picton (c. 1755–1836), a slave from Gorée Island, Senegal, died at Kingston upon Thames, a successful businessman; Caesar Shaw, freed slave and servant, features in two eighteenth-century portraits in the Spencers' Althorp House, Northamptonshire; Scipio Kennedy, freed slave, served at Culzean Castle, Ayrshire; cf. Michael Craton, *Searching for the Invisible Man: Slaves and Plantation Life in Jamaica* (Cambridge, MA, and London, 1978). For Caribbean references I am grateful to Matthias Röhrig Assunção.

28. Jacques de Cauna, *Au temps des isles à sucre: Histoire d'une plantation de Saint-Dominigue au XVIIIe siècle* (Paris, 2003): 92.

29. Cf. also James McLachlan, 'Classical names, American identities: Some Notes on College Students and the Classical Tradition in the 1770s', in Eadie, *Classical Tradition in Early America*: 81–98.

30. *Baltimore Daily Repository*, 29 Jan 1793.

31. Gummere, *American Colonial Mind*, 4.

32. The debate is analysed by Winterer, *Culture of Classicism*, 30–43.

33. Winterer, *Culture of Classicism*, 38.

34. Notably, Howard Mumford Jones, *O Strange New World: American Culture: The Formative Years* (New York, 1952); and see Briggs, 'United States', 282–8.

35. Bernard Bailyn, *Ideological Origins of the American Revolution: Enlarged Edition* (Cambridge, MA, and London, 1992): 23–6 (26).

36. Cited in David S, Shields, *Civil Tongues and Polite Letters in British America* (Chapel Hill, NC, and London, 1997), 215.

37. Reinhold, *Classica Americana*, 235; Winterer, *Culture of Classicism*, 15.

38. Notably, Gordon S. Wood, *The Creation of the American Republic 1776–1787* (Chapel Hill, NC, 1969): 23–6; see also Richard, *Founders and the Classics*, arguing that a classical canon was so *restrictively* influential that it inhibited the founders' critical instincts (10).

39. Edwin Wolf II, *Book Culture of a Colonial American City: Philadelphia Books, Bookmen, and Booksellers* (Oxford, 1988): 90.

40. Reinhold, *Classica Americana*, 25.

41. Ibid., 26.

42. Raven, *London Booksellers and American Customers*, 154.

43. Laird, *Epic of America*, 11–14.

44. Winterer, *Culture of Classicism*, 11.

45. Laird, *Epic of America*, 19, with a summary of the achievement, 20–30.

46. Cited in Gummere, *American Colonial Mind*, 57.

47. A. Gregg Roeber, 'German and Dutch Books and Printing', in Amory and Hall (eds), *Colonial Book in the Atlantic World*, 298–313 (312).

48. Briggs, 'United States', 279.

49. Robert B. Winans, *A Descriptive Checklist of Book Catalogues Separately Printed in America 1693–1800* (Worcester, MA, 1981).
50. *A Catalogue of the Library of Yale-College in New-Haven* (New London, CT, 1743).
51. *A Catalogue of Books in the Library of the College of New Jersey, January 29, 1760*, reprinted edn (Princeton, NJ, 1949).
52. Walter B. Edgar, 'The Libraries of Colonial South Carolina' (unpublished PhD dissertation, University of South Carolina, 1969): 32.
53. H. Trevor Colbourn, *The Lamp of Experience: Whig History and the Origins of the American Revolution* (Chapel Hill, NC, 1965): 199–232.
54. Raven, *London Booksellers and American Customers*, 77.
55. Kevin J. Hayes, *The Library of William Byrd of Westover* (Madison, WI, 1997): 5.
56. Ibid., 6.
57. See Ibid., 25–35.
58. Louis B. Wright and Marion Tinling (eds), *The Secret Diary of William Byrd of Westover 1709–1712* (Richmond, VA, 1941): 104–5.
59. See chapter 6 above, esp. pp. 115–17.
60. James Raven, 'From Promotion to Prescription: Arrangements for Reading and Eighteenth-Century Libraries', in James Raven, Helen Small, and Naomi Tadmor (eds), *The Practice and Representation of Reading in England* (Cambridge, 1996): 175–201; James Raven, 'The Representation of Philanthropy and Reading in the Eighteenth-Century Library', *Libraries and Culture* 31, 2 (Spring 1996): 492–510.
61. Raven, *London Booksellers and American Customers*, 44.
62. Reproduced and discussed in James Raven, 'I viaggi dei libri: realtà e raffigurazioni', in Maria Gioia Tavoni and Françoise Waquet (eds), *Gli spazi del libro nell'Europa del XVIII secolo* (Bologna, 1997): 47–86; and Raven, 'Representation of Philanthropy and Reading in the Eighteenth-Century Library'.
63. Raven, *London Booksellers and American Customers*, 43–4.
64. Reproduced in Rollo G. Silver, *The American Printer, 1787–1825* (Charlottesville, VA, 1967), plate XV; I am grateful to James Green for this reference.
65. P[ierce] Tempest, *Iconologia: Or, Moral Emblems, by Caesar Ripa* (London, 1709): i.
66. There is debate here between Hayes, *Library of William Byrd*, 45ff. and Daniel Blake Smith; see Wright and Tinling (eds), *Secret Diary of William Byrd*, 26, 136, 140, 295.
67. Cited in Hayes, *Library of William Byrd*, 62.
68. Memo of letter from Eliza Pinckney to her father, Jan 1741–42, and letter to Mary Bartlett (1742) in Elise Pinckney (ed.), *The Letterbook of Eliza Lucas Pinckney 1739–1762* (Chapel Hill, NC, 1972): 24, 35–7.
69. T. H. Breen, *Tobacco Culture: The Mentality of the Great Tidewater Planters on the Eve of the Revolution* (Princeton, NJ, 1985).
70. Raven, *London Booksellers and American Customers*, 46–7.
71. See Meyer Reinhold, 'Opponents of Classical Learning during the Revolutionary Period', *Proceedings of the American Philosophical Society* 112 (1968): 221–34.

72. Meyer Reinhold cites it at the opening of his edited *The Classick Pages: Classical Reading of Eighteenth-Century Americans* (University Park, PA, 1975).

73. Reinhold, *Classica Americana*, p. 35.

74. Edgar C. Reinke, 'A Classical Debate of the Charleston, South Carolina, Library Society,' *Papers of the Bibliographical Society of America* 61 (1967): 83–99.

75. Raven, *London Booksellers and American Customers*, 105–6, 220.

76. Philip M. Hamer (ed.), *The Papers of Henry Laurens*, 13 vols, vol. 8 (Columbia, SC, 1968–): 141, Laurens to John Rose, 28 Dec 1771.

77. *Independent Reflector*, 1768, 172, cited in Reinhold, *Classica Americana*, 30.

78. *A Catalogue of Books, given and devised by John Mackenzie Esquire, to the Charlestown Library Society* (Charleston, Robert Wells, 1772).

79. Reinhold, *Classica Americana*, 24.

80. Clive Griffin, *The Crombergers of Seville: The History of a Printing and Merchant Dynasty* (Oxford, 1988): 56–7, 63–97, 146, table IV.

81. Some indication of the range of imports can be gleaned from J. Yhmoff Cabrera, *Catálogo de Los Impresos Europeos del Siglo XVI que Custodia la Biblioteca Nacional de Mexico*, 3 vols (Mexico City, 1996).

82. Haase and Reinhold, *Classical Tradition and the Americas*, xii–xiii.

83. As detailed above, *ESTC* aims to record every surviving title, by edition, of letterpress items printed in England or any of its dependencies, in any language, 1473–1800, or printed in English anywhere else in the world during that period.

84. Stuart Gillespie, 'The Developing Corpus of Literary Translation', in Peter France and Stuart Gillespie (eds), *The Oxford History of Literary Translation in English vol. 3 1660–1790* (Oxford, 2005): 123–46 (143–4; cf. also figs. 1 and 2, pp. 133, 134).

85. See above, pp. 6–7.

86. Gillespie, 'The Developing Corpus of Literary Translation,' 134.

87. Henri-Jean Martin, *The French Book* (Baltimore, MD, 1996): 25–7.

88. William Brattle, *Compendium logicae secundum principia D. Renati Cartesii plerumque efformatum, et catechistice propositum* (Boston, MA, 1735).

89. Nicolaus Ludwig Zinzendorf, *Ludovici a Thurenstein in antiqvissima fratrum ecclesia ...* (Philadelphia, PA, 1742).

90. William Brown, *Pharmacopoeia simpliciorum & efficaciorum, in usum nosocomii militaris* (Philadelphia, PA, 1781).

91. Full text given in Raven, *London Booksellers and American Customers*, 254–5.

92. Wolf, *Book Culture of a Colonial American City*, 31–2.

93. Edwin Wolf, revised edn by John C. Van Horne and James Green, '*At the Instance of Benjamin Franklin*': *A Brief History of the Library Company of Philadelphia* (Philadelphia, PA, 1995), with illustration, 9.

94. See above, note 4.

95. For the similarities between libraries, see Raven, *London Booksellers and American Customers*, 199–200.

96. Stuart C. Sherman, 'The Library Company of Baltimore, 1795–1854', *Maryland Historical Magazine* 39 (1944): 6–24 (9).

97. Directors' Report, cited in Sherman, 'The Library Company of Baltimore', 16.

98. John Remington, Secretary CLS, to David Wilson, London bookseller, 14 Aug 1761 (Raven, *London Booksellers and American Customers*, 242–3).

99. David Money, *The English Horace: Anthony Alsop and the Tradition of British Latin Verse* (London and Oxford, 1998): ch. 4.
100. Raven, *London Booksellers and American Customers*, 190.
101. David D. Hall, 'Learned Culture in the Eighteenth Century', in Amory and Hall (eds), *Colonial Book in the Atlantic World*, 411–33 (419).
102. David S. Shields, 'Eighteenth-Century Literary Culture', in Amory and Hall (eds), *Colonial Book in the Atlantic World*, 434–76 (451).
103. Laird, *Epic of America*, 20; Italian publications included the *Rusticatio Mexicana* of the expelled Landívar.
104. Shields, 'Eighteenth-Century Literary Culture', 447–8.
105. Anderson read classics at Cambridge.
106. Anderson, *Imagined Communities*, 42, 77.

9

'A Small Cargoe for Tryal': Connections between the Belfast and Philadelphia Book Trades in the Later Eighteenth Century

Michael O'Connor

This chapter considers the possibility that print formed a transatlantic community by means of connections between the Belfast and Philadelphia book trades in the eighteenth century.[1] The essay will explore the nature of these connections, examining the reasons for such interaction and assessing the impact of such bonds on the status of Belfast printing.[2] While recent studies have mentioned the various connections between Irish booksellers and their counterparts in North America, primarily in places such as Philadelphia and New York – for example, the extensive work of Richard Cargill Cole[3] – attention has tended to fall upon the impact of such contacts on the American book trade and the emergence of a native reprint tradition. As such, there has been little consideration given to assessing the implications of these bonds upon Irish printing, especially printing outside of Dublin. This chapter will examine the balance of power between printing in Dublin and the Irish provinces and its subtle shift during the Revolutionary period because of these important colonial connections.

The absence of copyright legislation in Ireland until 1801 was both a blessing and a curse for the Irish book trade. Freed from having to pay the price of copy, or of having to be subject to the exclusive publication rights set down by copyright, Irish printers were able to reprint London editions of texts, which in England only the copyright holder was permitted to print. This led to a thriving reprint industry in Ireland in which reprints were sold to both a domestic and international market, but it also created a book trade in which few original publications were published. Printing in Dublin – the centre of the Irish book – was consequently regarded as deficient when compared to London and its printers were viewed suspiciously, sometimes antagonistically, by their counterparts in London. Mary Pollard gives the following synopsis:

> Considered merely as a reprinter of London books, the Dublin book trade looks like a pale and inferior reflection of that of London. As something of a phenomenon in its very rapid development in the eighteenth century, however, it deserves study in its own right, not in spite of its reprints but because its prosperity was largely based on them.[4]

With these words Pollard began her landmark study on Dublin printing in 1989, a study in which she defended the Dublin book trade against the established charges of piracy, marginality and of being fundamentally unsophisticated. In rejecting these commonly held assumptions of eighteenth-century Dublin printing, she traced the negative representation of the Irish book trade as having arisen from the complaints of mid-century English publishers, such as Samuel Richardson, whose vociferous criticism of Dublin printers as dishonest bootleggers passed largely unchallenged into history.[5] She contested these accusations of piracy through giving examples of collaboration between the Dublin and London trades.[6]

Without Pollard's work modern scholarship on the history of the Irish book would certainly have been poorer. She has made scholars sceptical of the inflated claims of British publishers, such as William Strahan and John Murray, with regards to the Irish trade and the impact of Irish reprints within an international context. For example, in October 1781 Strahan complained to the leading Edinburgh publishing-bookseller, William Creech about the damaging effects of Dublin reprints on his copyright profits: 'The Irish immediately reprint upon us in a cheap size and not only run away with the whole American Trade, but even import them, with Impunity, into all the Western Coast of Britain. Nor are we able, as you well know, to prevent this.' In the following month he stressed the dangers of Dublin reprinting, deeming it an 'illicit trade, which tears up our Property by the very Roots'.[7] While Irish reprints were sold for the most part to a domestic audience, they were sold also in Britain and in North America. It was with these latter two locations that British publishers such as Strahan were particularly concerned and it is with regard to the colonial context that this chapter is chiefly focused.

British publishers, particularly those at work in the London trade, were keen to preserve the monopoly that they exerted upon the colonies in terms of the supply of books, a monopoly which was the result of a combination of factors.[8] Trading legislation in the form of the Navigation Acts (which ensured that colonial commerce occurred with colonial and English vessels) and printing rights (exercised through legal monopolies on the publication of Bibles, prayer books, psalters and law books, which could only be undertaken by designated printers in England) resulted in the colonies being limited from the outset in terms of what they could print and with whom they could trade. Having little recourse other than to trade with English merchants and order books under patent from English suppliers, colonial contact with Britain from the seventeenth century onwards was a necessity. The fledging state of colonial printing for the greater part of the eighteenth century, the result of a shortage of capital and resources, was yet another important reason explaining colonial dealings with the English book trade.

To begin with, colonial printers suffered from a range of difficulties, such as weak markets, tight credit, restive labour, poor transportation and a dispersed readership.[9] The single greatest problem was the difficulty of obtaining basic manufacturing material. This resulted in high capital costs for printing in America.[10] Generally, it proved less of a gamble for printers in North America to order books from abroad than to expend the capital in reprinting a work and run the risk of not recouping all costs involved in its publication. This was especially so if colonial printers were offered attractive discounts by London wholesalers.

Drawn by the potential for profit in supplying a colonial trade that was reliant upon it for the provision of books, booksellers and publishers in England actively sought out trading connections with colonial booksellers with the result that 'during the third quarter of the century, London wholesaling booksellers pursued the American market with great zeal'.[11] While there is little doubt that the predominant source for books in America was England, book exportation did occur throughout the century in Scotland and Ireland.[12] Books exported from Ireland were especially a source of concern for English booksellers. Since Irish printers were under no obligation to pay copyright fees, Irish reprinted editions sold more cheaply than the originals, significantly undercutting the prices of London editions. This was further compounded by the fact that they were produced on less expensive paper and in smaller sizes such as duodecimo, which required less paper than the larger sizes.[13] Unsurprisingly, London booksellers and publishers grew alarmed at the ability of Irish printers to penetrate the colonial market with inexpensive reprints which could threaten their monopoly. The anxieties of Strahan mentioned above are emblematic of this alarm.

Strahan's claims that Irish reprints were doing untold damage to London publishers appear, however, to be exaggerated, which leads one to evaluate the actual significance of Irish reprints within an international context, of which the example of Belfast's connections with Philadelphia serves as a very useful case study. In his investigation of transatlantic publishing, Richard B. Sher has conveyed a more tempered picture, arguing that, contrary to the assertions of Murray and Strahan, British books were not always reprinted in Ireland, but he concedes that the opinions of London publishers and booksellers, while overstated, were nonetheless 'grounded in reality'. He insists that the reprint trade carried out in Dublin was in fact the axis upon which the transmission of Scottish Enlightenment texts – by authors such as David Hume and Adam Smith – across the Atlantic pivoted.[14] He writes:

> Dublin was the hinge on which the Atlantic dissemination for Enlightenment books turned. Whether they were making cheap editions or attempting to surpass the British originals they were copying, and whether their products were ultimately bound for readers in Ireland, the Americas, Britain or the Continent, the Dublin reprinters were above all else appropriators of culture.... their actions contributed almost as much as ... [the] other major publishers of new books in London and Edinburgh to the creation and diffusion of the Scottish Enlightenment as an Atlantic cultural phenomenon. The Scottish Enlightenment was crossing the Atlantic, and Irish booksellers were among its principal agents.[15]

In offering this assessment of the Irish trade in its transatlantic dimension, he makes a case, rather convincingly also, that those at work in Dublin were not simply 'copy-and-paste' printers, hastily copying the latest London edition of a text, with no regard for what was contained therein or how it was presented, but were actually vital cultural agents for the promulgation of the Scottish Enlightenment within America.

Such a reading tends to endow Dublin booksellers with a vast and impressive impact upon the North American colonial market. This is not, however, revealed by the official Irish statistics of its book exports to America throughout the eighteenth century: Ireland was prohibited from selling books and other goods across the Atlantic for the first 80 years of the century. There is, however, evidence that books were sent from Ireland as early as the 1720s. Custom House records consequently only reveal a fraction of the picture and the data does not account for the lively invisible trade that occurred in the smuggling of books throughout the century.[16]

Since Irish books sent to North America prior to 1780 were subject to seizure, the smuggling of books was not without its own risks. Illegal books subsequently incurred added expense and delay and required notable vigilance for the colonial bookseller attempting to circumvent detection of the contraband cargo by the authorities. Such obstacles notwithstanding, colonial booksellers were evidently enthusiastic about ordering cheap Irish reprints. And in the aftermath of 1780 when Irish book exports were made legal, books were shipped across the Atlantic from Ireland with increased regularity and vigour.[17]

Both Boston and New York featured prominently in the Irish book trade to North America, but the most significant and sustained connections were with booksellers in Philadelphia. The David Hall correspondence presents one case study of such print networks. Hall was probably the single most important importer of books in the colonies by mid-century. Between 1748 and 1772 his imports, it is estimated, exceeded £40,000 sterling.[18] While the main source of his supply was from London, Hall also imported material from Dublin and Belfast. Richard C. Cole's work has made irrefutable the vigour of such trading connections between booksellers in Philadelphia with those in Ireland. In *Irish Booksellers and English Writers 1740–1800* he has shown that printers and booksellers in Dublin disseminated the works of the major British writers of their time and enhanced the audience for these writers not only in Ireland and Britain but in America in places such as Philadelphia and New York.[19] The research of Sher and Cole has shown that Irish booksellers were *the* most significant distributors of English and Scottish authors and were responsible for the diffusion of this material to an American audience within the second half of the century. J.D. Fleeman has observed that Irish booksellers 'contributed to the dissemination of Enlightenment ideas and judgments, by distributing books to readers on both sides of the Atlantic, and it is particularly as the distributors of books that the Irish trade warrants close attention'.[20] The connections that were created and fostered as a result of this trade enabled the distribution of books; they also ensured that Enlightenment ideas were transmitted to the shores of America.

While the connections between Philadelphia and Dublin booksellers have been noted in some detail – for example, in the studies by Cole and Sher – there has been little attention given to the transatlantic links between Belfast and Philadelphia. This chapter seeks to redress this imbalance by taking as its chief case study the relationship between the Belfast and Philadelphia book trades in the period 1763–76. Studies by McDougall and Cole have referred briefly to Belfast's links with Philadelphia, with the latter emphasizing the economic advantages of such transactions.[21] Cole has represented the purposes of such links as an opportunity for colonial booksellers to have acquired quality Irish reprints at affordable prices. The cheapness of Irish reprinted editions would easily have appealed to the business sensibilities of colonial booksellers who, if David Hall is representative, demanded of their London agent that books be priced 'as reasonable as you can', citing the scarcity of money in Philadelphia and the cheapness of Irish and Scottish books imported into the city as making low-cost prices from suppliers a necessity.[22]

While this economic consideration was undoubtedly an important reason why colonial booksellers ordered Irish printed books, the cultivation of such links was actually heavily influenced by and utilized for other reasons than the cheapness of Belfast reprints. Philadelphia booksellers imported Belfast books seeking to appeal specifically to pockets of Ulster-Scottish communities in the colonies who wished to retain cultural links with home. And, in turn, Belfast printers and booksellers wished to supply that market, all the while utilizing contacts with Philadelphia booksellers to access political and polemical material which was unavailable outside North America and which would augment the capabilities of Belfast printing. This was especially important during the years of the Revolution when Belfast supported the cause of America, and when having access to the newest American tract and pamphlet offered printers in the town a distinct edge over their Dublin competitors. The associations with Philadelphia, therefore, during this period were partly driven by the demands of the Belfast book-buying public and by their insatiable appetite for political matter relating to the American conflict.

The outcome of such interaction was thus quite significant. Indeed, these connections meant that the supremacy of Dublin printing was in small ways changing in tandem with Belfast contacts with Philadelphia. Moreover, colonial booksellers sought to exploit the links with Belfast not simply to access books but newspapers also, as the foreign news sections of colonial newspapers were vitally important. The result therefore was the utilization of the Atlantic as a communication 'superhighway' in this period and the cultivation of linked print communities in the two locations.

Firm ties between Belfast and Philadelphia had been established by the 1760s. During this decade books printed in Belfast, the most important town in the north of Ireland, were available in Philadelphia and were requested by booksellers there. These connections, however, are not revealed in the names of subscribers of Belfast editions but disclosed in booksellers' correspondence. From the available evidence, it is apparent that the connections uniting the two book trades were created in four ways: (1) by relatives of Belfast printers working in Philadelphia; (2) by apprentices who had formerly worked in Belfast moving to Philadelphia to work in its book trade; (3) by Philadelphia booksellers with no established connection with Belfast but who were keen to initiate trade; and (4) by emigrants bringing cherished books printed in Belfast with them to the New World. Chronologically, the first three phases occurred in quick succession, whereas the impact of emigrants upon the creation of such trading connections is difficult to gauge and therefore can only problematically be placed within this timeline of events. The presence of Irish emigrants is indeed likely to explain how Belfast-printed books were available in North America before Belfast printers had made connections with colonial booksellers. By 1770 four Belfast reprints, three of which were works of religious devotion, had been obtained by the Library Company of Philadelphia. These four texts were John Bunyan, *Grace Abounding to the Chief of Sinners...* (Belfast, [s.n.], 1714); *The Gazetteer; Or the Newsman's Interpreter* (Belfast, Francis Joy, 1740); Edward Fowler, *The Design of Christianity* (Belfast, Samuel Wilson & James Magee, 1741); and Jacques Bénigne Bossuet, *An Introduction to, or a Short Discourse Concerning, Universal History* (Belfast, Wilson & Magee, 1742).[23] These examples demonstrate that Belfast books found themselves in Philadelphia possibly before Magee (and indeed other Belfast printers) had established firm contacts with booksellers there. It is probable that these works had been transported by Belfast men and women who had come to settle in the New World, which was not an uncommon means by which new books arrived in the colonies. From the available evidence, the initial contact that was established appears to have involved Belfast printers and their relatives at work in Philadelphia.

This was the case with James Magee (1707–97). Magee, whose career spanned 1735–91, was the chief Belfast printer, bookseller and publisher throughout the century, being the foremost printer in the town of plays, sermons, chapbooks and political tracts and pamphlets. Throughout the period of Volunteer associations in the 1780s he became the chief Irish printer of Volunteer sermons. He was a pivotal figure in terms of the printing and supply of books throughout the north of Ireland; his publications also retailed in Dublin and some sold as far as Philadelphia. The sale of his texts in North America occurred in the 1760s, although it is likely to have begun in the previous decade, and involved two of James's blood relations who lived there. Magee's brother Thomas worked in Philadelphia as a publisher and bookseller from 1764 to 1769. He worked at the Bible-in-Heart in 1769 and acted

as the administrator of Andrew Steuart's estate when Steuart died trag-
ically in 1769.[24] Nathaniel, possibly another brother, who lived near
Thomas in Arch Street in 1753, was commander of the ship *Alexander* of
Philadelphia that in August 1757 sailed from Belfast to the American city
carrying passengers, servants and redemptioners. Nathaniel's name also
appeared on the 'outwards' and 'inwards' entries for the Custom House,
Philadelphia in that year.[25] His role in the process of importing Belfast
books appears more ambiguous than Thomas but it seems likely that he
was transporting books to Philadelphia, as well as indentured servants,
in 1757. Unfortunately, no papers or accounts exist for James Magee,
so it is not possible to know the precise details of his arrangement with
Thomas and Nathaniel, or indeed to know the actual titles that were
sent from Belfast. But the arrangement was certainly upon solid foundations given the family connections between the Magees, confirming
Raven's assertion that in terms of the transatlantic trading of books 'the
strongest bonds were familial'.[26]

Belfast's initial trading connections with Philadelphia may have been
instigated by means of such important fraternal bonds, but the links
with booksellers in that city soon operated beyond the established network of family contacts. Former employees of the Belfast print trade,
who worked in Philadelphia as printers and booksellers, were next
utilized as a means of penetrating further into the colonial market.
Magee was well placed to do this. He trained at least two apprentices,
Andrew Steuart and Hugh Gaine, both of whom established themselves
as important printers, in Philadelphia and New York respectively. Steuart
worked in Philadelphia in the 1760s: he produced 140 imprints between
1758 and 1769. Steuart established Laetitia Court in 1758 and moved
into various premises in the seven years that he lived in Philadelphia.
Thomas notes that about 1764, Steuart went to Wilmington, North
Carolina, leaving some types and his bookshop in the care of Thomas
Magee and that of his apprentice Joseph Cruikshank.[27] James Magee
supplied Steuart with chapbooks throughout this period and the links
with his former apprentice remained long after Steuart had emigrated
from Ulster.[28] This is a view supported by Neuburg, who argues that
Magee was the source of much of Steuart's imported chapbook material.[29] Magee's other apprentice also preserved his connections with
Belfast. Hugh Gaine (1726–1807), who arrived in New York in 1745 and
worked in that city as a printer, reprinted a Belfast publication in 1776
(*The Young Clerk's Vade Mecum: Or, Compleat Law-Tutor*) and was a substantial retailer of Irish-printed publications. His catalogue of 1792 lists
more than 500 titles published in Ireland.[30]

In addition to Steuart, there were other members of the Philadelphia print trade who had formerly worked in Belfast. These contacts potentially created rich possibilities for individuals such as Magee who wished to enter the colonial market. John Dean, for example, who learned bookbinding in Belfast and Dublin and practised that trade along with bookselling in Philadelphia in 1765 and from 1775 until 1779. Also, John Reader, an English papermaker who worked in James Blow's firm in Belfast before he joined the Philadelphia book trade in 1768.[31] It would certainly have been commercially advantageous for booksellers in North America, such as Steuart or Gaine, to buy cheap Irish reprints. Copyright legislation did not apply to the colonies and in this respect mirrored the Irish trade.[32] If we consider that it was more practical and cost effective to import books, especially if a colonial bookseller knew that he had a small and select number of buyers, it appears logical that Steuart should request books from his former master. Indeed, colonial booksellers often imported single titles of works for individual customers, indicating the potential losses that they would incur through reprinting a work for such a low readership.[33] Rosalind Remer has argued such, observing that 'colonial markets were not highly developed or diverse, and importing a few copies of a book cost less than producing a whole edition locally.'[34] Moreover, since bookbinders were scarce in the colonies and binding was even more expensive there than in London – David Hall gave explicit and repeated instructions to his British agents always to send books bound – cheap Irish editions, which were sent bound to the American colonies, offered a number of economic advantages for the colonial bookseller.[35] Colonial booksellers, particularly those who had contacts with printers in Ireland, are thus likely to have taken advantage of those connections in order to access books at competitive prices.

While this economic explanation has been the predominant view to account for the importation of Irish books by colonial booksellers, the example of David Hall's association with the Belfast print trade complicates this straightforward perspective and confirms that colonial booksellers were involved with Irish printers and booksellers for reasons more diverse than the cheapness of Irish reprints.[36] On 4 February 1766, Hall wrote to Magee requesting a small parcel of books, 'forty or fifty Pounds Value', which he hoped would mark the beginning of business between the two.[37] In writing to Magee, Hall stipulated the titles and authors that he wanted, mainly works of religious devotion (including favourites such as Bunyan, Baxter and Fox), an assortment of chapbooks (with Hall insisting 'there should be a good Variety, and the more on the Droll and the merry strain the better'), plays, as well as 'Two or three Reams of Ballads – and any thing else you may think will answer'. Hall's choice of titles, indicating books which were perennially popular and inexpensive, was well suited to the kinds of material printed by Magee. It drew directly upon Magee's strengths as an important reprinter of chapbooks and devotional works. The titles ordered could easily have been accessed by a diverse market of readers, including those undergoing religious instruction, students and children.[38]

While the letter implies that this was the first correspondence between Hall and Magee, he was evidently familiar with Magee's publications, revealing 'I have, at different times, bought some Books of yours from your Brother here, of which a Parcel lately arrd [arrived] and shall pay him for them next Month.' Hall hoped that his acquaintance with Thomas Magee would allay any anxieties the Belfast printer might have in striking up business with someone who was unknown to him. The initial order was deliberately low, being 'a small Cargoe for Tryal', with Hall intending it as a test for how the envisaged trade with Magee would fare. Owing to the hazardous and expensive nature of oceanic transportation, Harlan notes, American buyers preferred placing infrequent and large orders to frequent and small ones.[39] Therefore, if the order placed with Magee proved satisfactory to Hall, further orders of greater amounts, one imagines, would have been requisitioned by the Philadelphia bookseller.

Magee's answer to this letter has not been preserved, so it is not possible to determine the full extent of his dealings with Hall. Prior to 1766, however, when he had first written to Magee, Hall had received shipments from other Belfast booksellers. His account books show evidence of his having received parcels of books from Belfast from 1762.[40] It is certain that consignments of Belfast Bibles from David Hay had been sent to Hall from 1761 to 1764; these had been instigated by John Balfour of Edinburgh. One of these shipments in 1763 was ill-fated – the Bibles were seized by Customs in Carlingford. Hall's letter to the Edinburgh publishing partnership of Hamilton and Balfour on 3 March expressed his chagrin. He bemoaned that this trade had caused him 'great Delay' and added expense – he had to pay £1 14s. 6d. for their seizure. The books 'were so Slender' and had been 'so ill packed' that he was surprised he 'got one Half of them'.[41]

The various nuisances and impediments caused by Hall's commerce with Belfast were, it should be noted, not unusual, for the process of book importation involved many potential difficulties. Colonial booksellers could, and did, encounter high pricing with their suppliers and errors in their orders. Financially also, booksellers had to pay costs other than the price of the books shipped, including interest upon the freight of goods.[42] The actual transportation of the material was not without its attendant dangers. Shipments could be delayed if vessels sprang a leak, and readers often had to wait for extended periods before their books had made the expansive journey across the Atlantic.[43] Poor packing and damp conditions on board caused damage to books, including mildew and harm to gilding. As a result, booksellers such as Hall gave specific and repeated instructions for care to be taken 'in getting the Books well packed up', with each work secured by having pieces of paper wrapped round it.[44] Colonial booksellers were only too aware of the potential problems that could occur, but importing Hay's Bibles from Belfast throughout this period caused particular problems. The seizure of Bibles in 1763 caused added delay and expense, and with an earlier shipment in 1761, the Bibles initially arrived with no invoice, leaving Hall 'at a Loss how to Sell them'.[45] His subsequent decision to write to Magee suggests Hall was sufficiently impressed by Magee's publications for him to seek out the Belfast printer and bookseller, despite his unfortunate experiences with the town trade in the past.

This reading of events, however, is only partially accurate since Hall's decision to order books from Belfast in 1766 was affected by a number of other factors, not least of which was the current state of his relationship with his longstanding London supplier. It cannot be regarded as accidental that Hall should have written to Magee during a period in which relations between the Philadelphia bookseller and Strahan, his London wholesaler, were extremely fraught. Hall's letters at this time document his frustration, noting his many complaints against Strahan, such as repeated errors with orders, inexact invoices and Strahan's frequent divergence from Hall's directives.[46] The latter point is a particularly salient one, with Hall feeling that his London contact was not as assiduous as he ought to be, leading him to remonstrate forcibly against Strahan in 1761 by asking 'what is the Matter you are not more Careful in finding me the Court and City Registers, and all new Pamphlets . . . I have lately told you, be more exact in these Matters.'[47] Far from improving, the situation actually worsened when in October 1763 Hall forbade Strahan 'for the future, to send any Thing but what is Ordered', insisting that 'you remember what I say' and threatening 'if you do send without Order, I shall be obliged to return them, without opening'.[48]

Feeling dissatisfied with Strahan's service, Hall sought to explore other bookselling contacts in both Scotland and Ireland in the 1760s: he wrote to initiate trade with Alexander Kincaid of Edinburgh in March

1764 and Magee of Belfast in February 1766. One can surmise that Hall was seeking a longstanding business relationship with another contact, a relationship which he intended to be more substantial than the occasional order. More than this, Hall may even have been looking to abandon his associate in London completely and switch to another connection more agreeable to his bookselling needs. By 1767 he was feeling particularly vulnerable. In a letter to Strahan in November, he complained that in his capacity both as a bookseller and as agent for the Library Company – he had been ordering their books since May 1763 – his reputation was being injured by orders which had not arrived, and he reiterated an observation which he had made formerly, that Strahan was too preoccupied with other business to tend to 'such small Matters' as him.[49]

At this extremely sensitive juncture, when Hall began reassessing his contacts and suppliers, the Philadelphia bookseller chose to instigate business with Magee, recognizing him as an attractive prospect. This was surely a transformative moment in Hall's career, at which he was willing to unfetter himself from dependence on Strahan, perhaps even forsake the relationship with him, in favour of other connections, including a printer and bookseller who worked not in London but in Belfast.

This is critically important, not simply owing to what it reveals about the fractious Hall–Strahan relationship at this period, but because it also provides a vital context stressing the significance of Magee within the international book trade. In the figure of Magee, Hall glimpsed a potential supplier who was extremely well placed to cater to his bookselling needs. Firstly, a network of contacts had hitherto been established which involved James in Belfast and his brother Thomas (and possibly Nathaniel also) in Philadelphia. This may have been established from as early as 1753 when there is evidence of both Thomas and Nathaniel living in Philadelphia, but it is certain that Magee's books were sold there from 1766. The quality of his books, moreover, may have been an added selling point. His publications were singled out for praise by the travel writer Richard Twiss in *A Tour of Ireland in 1775* (London, 1776) who remarked, 'A few books have been printed in Belfast, by one James Magee, in a much neater manner than in any other part of Ireland, both as to the beauty of the types, and the fineness of the paper.'[50] A similar point is suggested by Sher, who has argued that while Irish reprints were produced in formats smaller than the London edition, for reasons of economy, these editions were by no means 'quick and dirty'. These editions were actually seeking to challenge London editions of texts in their presentation, format and typography.[51] Given Magee's prominence as a printer and bookseller in Ireland, the diversity of material that he produced and the obvious recognition from his editions that he was a craftsman, it is not surprising that colonial booksellers – particularly those who had familiarity with his publications, such as Hall – expressed an interest in establishing business with him.

Hall had other motivations, however, in singling Magee out. This was a period in which he actively sought access to provincial newspapers from England, Scotland and Ireland in order to furnish the foreign intelligence section of his *Pennsylvania Gazette*.[52] In 1766 he asked Strahan to use his connections in order to acquire Irish newspapers for him.[53] Keen to secure papers particularly from Belfast and Derry, Hall's decision to contact Magee must have been, in some measure, driven by this desire. His eagerness to acquire provincial newspapers was foremost in these years, in which he repeatedly requested and cajoled his various contacts in order that his newspaper could be as current as possible with the latest international news.[54]

This quest for Irish newspapers, particularly newspapers from the north of Ireland, was undoubtedly related to the expanding population of Ulster-Scots settlers in North America, for whom news of Ulster, as well as publications from Belfast, would have been especially resonant. It has been estimated that in the years between 1700 and 1776 at least 200,000 Presbyterians left Ulster, the greater number of whom established themselves in Philadelphia and New York. So significant was this migration that Kerby has noted that 'both in size and in relative proportion, Ulster emigration far overshadowed all other population movements from Ireland to colonial America.'[55] This group was also the most likely to preserve its connections, both familial and cultural, with home: 'Although Anglicans, like Catholics, tended to emigrate and assimilate as individuals, Dissenters transplanted communal and familial networks, retained relatively close ties to Ireland, and remained culturally distinct.'[56] Hall's selection of Magee as a bookselling contact was an obvious means of targeting this audience since many of Magee's reprints were Scottish, and among these there was a strong emphasis on Dissenting tracts and sermons.[57] These books, moreover, were printed in a town that possessed a strong Scottish element, thereby underscoring the closeness of the connections with Scotland.[58] It would have been evident to Hall from Magee's publications that Magee could usefully target this community.

Magee's supply of Belfast-printed books to his brother in Philadelphia ought to be understood therefore in this context: as a means of supplying material to a growing audience of expatriates who wished to preserve the special bond with home. Evidently, Hall also wished to engage himself in that process, indicated by his desire to obtain Magee's publications, as well as newspapers from Ulster. But if Hall was enthusiastic about pursuing this specific market, he was not alone. Scottish and Irish reprints had been sold in Philadelphia from as early as the 1750s and, if Hall is to be believed, imported in considerable number. He spoke of 'a great many Books... from Ireland and Scotland'.[59] It is likely that Hall was not overemphasizing the situation; the demand for books from Ulster is further suggested by the incidence of American reprintings of Belfast books in the succeeding years. These texts were reprinted in Philadelphia and New York, as well as Salem, Massachusetts, in the 1770s, a persuasive indicator of the colonial market for Belfast material.[60] There was a particular emphasis on schoolbooks and works of instruction. A Belfast primer (spelling book) written by schoolmaster John Manson and printed in the town about 1760 was reprinted in Philadelphia by John Dunlap in 1770, although that date is open to question.[61] And in New York, Hugh Gaine, the former apprentice of Magee, reprinted *The Young Clerk's Vade Mecum: Or, Complete Law-Tutor* in 1776, the work being printed in Belfast.[62] In both of these cases Belfast editions were reprinted by printers who had formerly lived in Ulster (Strabane and Belfast respectively). This suggests that there were readers in North America who wished to preserve the cultural links with home.

These connections with Belfast were still being used as selling points in American reprinted editions at the turn of the century. For example, publications written by Belfast authors were reprinted in Philadelphia and Wilmington in 1795 and 1798 respectively and these American reprints highlighted the Belfast heritage of the authors. *Laws and Usages Respecting Bills of Exchange, and Promissory Notes* was printed for T. Stephens by F. & R. Bailey in Philadelphia (1795), its imprint noting that it was written by 'John Tisdall, Notary Bublic [*sic*] of Belfast'. Also, a reprint of John Gough's *Practical Arithmetick in Four Books* was printed in Wilmington by Peter Brynberg (1798) with the addition of 'an Appendix of Algebra, by the Late W. ATDINSON [*sic*], of Belfast', perhaps having been written by W. Atkinson who was treasurer of Portadown Rangers in 1795.[63] Evidently these publications sought to appeal to a market of readers for whom the mention of Belfast was a point of enticement, which suggests a likely appeal to a community of Ulster migrants.

While booksellers and printers in Philadelphia and New York responded to this demand for Belfast-printed books, first, through importing and, secondly, through reprinting Belfast texts, those at work in the Belfast book trade had their own motivations for being involved with colonial booksellers. Belfast's ties with North American booksellers were part of a wider quest for prestige and standing. Printers such as Magee used their Philadelphia connections as a means of accessing original political material which was unavailable outside North America and which had the effect of augmenting the status and capabilities of Belfast printing, at a time when Belfast was vying with Dublin for greater power in the Irish book trade.

A case in point is Magee's reprinting of American political texts throughout the Revolutionary War. Magee's American publications were not simply the latest reprinted editions from London – which were characteristic of Magee's corpus (until the 1770 period) and of the Irish trade in general – but included material that had been originally published outside London. He reprinted three texts which had been originally published in Philadelphia. These represented the culmination of his involvement with printers and booksellers there and helped to create Magee's position as Belfast's chief supplier and printer of American printed matter. During the years 1771–78 Magee published 15 publications that dealt with the highly topical subject of the deteriorating relations between the American colonies and England. Of this number, seven key texts can be confirmed as having been printed by Magee. These are Thomas Coombe's *Sermon Preached before the Congregations of Christ Church and St. Peter's Philadelphia on Thursday, July 20, 1775* (1775); William Pitt's *Speech on the 20th of January 1775* (1775); Abbé Raynal's *Sentiments of a Foreigner, on the Disputes of Great-Britain with America* (1775); Caleb Evans' *British Constitutional Liberty. A Sermon, Preached in Broad-mead, Bristol, November 5, 1775* (1776); William Smith's *Oration in Memory of General Montgomery, and of the Officers and Soldiers, who Fell with him, December 31, 1775* (1776); William Steel Dickson's collection of *Sermons* (1778?); and John Wesley's *Compassionate Address to the Inhabitants of Ireland* (1778).

The three texts which were originally published in America were Abbé Raynal's *Sentiments of a Foreigner* (1775), Thomas Coombe's *Sermon ·Preached before the Congregations of Christ Church and St. Peter's* (1775) and William Smith's *Oration in Memory of General Montgomery* (1776). Magee's Philadelphia reprints championed the colonists' cause and argued that their right to resistance was self-defence. They contended that it was their entitlement to seek political representation: 'we ask not a superiority, we only claim an equality with our brethren', as Raynal reasoned.[64] The three texts formed part of the American Revolutionary debates occurring at this time, in which the sense of interest and anxiety generated by the rupturing of Anglo-American relations was felt especially keenly in the town of Belfast. Belfast, as the centre of the Presbyterian community in Ireland, was especially sympathetic to the American colonists. Dissenters' opposition to unjust or oppressive statutes, which derived from their own experience of penal legislation, made them sensitive to the colonists' complaints concerning their lack of political voice.[65] Northern Dissenters consequently denounced the war as 'unjust, cruel, & detestable' and William Steel Dickson said in a sermon he gave in Belfast, 'there is scarcely a Protestant Family of the middle Classes amongst us who does not reckon Kindred with the Inhabitants of that extensive Continent.'[66] So enthusiastic was the level of support among Ulster Dissenters (who cited commercial, cultural and religious reasons why they opposed the war and sympathized with their colonial counterparts) that the *Belfast News-Letter* championed the rights of the colonists. These sympathies were suggested most of all by the paper's reprinting of the Declaration of Independence (the *Belfast News-Letter* was the first newspaper to report the Declaration outside America).[67] And in 1775–76 Belfast bookshops quickly filled up with texts relating to the American crisis, of which James Magee was the pre-eminent supplier in the north of Ireland.[68] In responding to this high level of interest, Magee used the contacts that he had established with the Philadelphia book trade in order to meet local demand for American political publications.

In the first instance, his contacts enabled him to reprint material that was seldom available elsewhere. For example, the Belfast reprinted edition of *Sentiments of a Foreigner* by Abbé Guillaume-Thomas Raynal was the only reprinted edition of the book outside North America. This was a text which was excerpted from Raynal's *Histoire philosophique et politique des établissemen[t]s et du commerce des Européens dans les deux Indes* (Amsterdam, 1770), first translated into English in London 1776.[69] The work was printed by James Humphrey in March 1775 and reprinted by Magee on 11 April of that year.[70] Given the shortness of the time-frame – Magee's reprint appeared less than five weeks after the work was first printed – Humphrey's text (either an advance copy or proofs) would have had to have been sent to Magee before the work went on sale in Philadelphia, since the passage across the Atlantic to Belfast is likely to have taken at least six weeks.[71] This may have been performed with Humphrey's knowledge and consent, but there is also the possibility that the sheets used by Magee as the source of his copy were surreptitiously obtained before Humphrey's edition had even appeared in bookshops in Philadelphia. Such dealings were not unfamiliar among Irish printers.[72]

In reprinting the first English translation of *Histoire...dans les Deux Indes*, albeit only in excerpted form, Magee had provided a text that was not to be available in complete translation until the following year. He had reprinted a text that had originated not in London but in Philadelphia and evidently he made use of his Philadelphia connections in order to access Humphrey's edition in advance of its sale in America. Magee was demonstrating that he had the contacts and the capabilities to produce material relating to the American crisis that was among the latest publications and that he was not a small town provincial printer, slavishly deriving material from the metropolis.

Indeed, not simply content with having established connections with the Philadelphia book trade, nor with having made use of such contacts to produce material unavailable outside North America, Belfast printers purposely disclosed on imprints their intimacy with printers there. This can be illustrated in Smith's *Oration in Memory of General Montgomery* which Magee reprinted in 1776. In his reprint the title page confidently announced that it was 'Philadelphia: printed by John Dunlap, and, Belfast: reprinted, by James Magee, 1776'. In Ireland Smith's *Oration* was reprinted in Dublin by John Beatty and in Belfast by Magee, both in 1776. The inclusion of Dunlap's name as the original printer occurred on the imprints of both these reprints. This explicit gesture of linking Magee with a specific Philadelphia printer was intended to augment Magee's status but it also reflected back upon Philadelphia printing, which was growing in significance. Throughout the years of the American Revolution (1775–83) Philadelphia printers produced an output of works that was drawing closer to the total of the Dublin trade; according to the *ESTC*, they lagged behind Dublin printers by only 25 per cent. Magee's acknowledgment of Philadelphia as the place of original publication was not remarkable, since it was common for reprinted texts to indicate where the work was first printed. His inclusion of Dunlap's name as the original publisher was, however, distinctly unusual. No other of Magee's publications, numbering 377 in total, imitated this practice.[73] In fact the word 'reprinted' occurred 415 times in pre-1801 American imprints, but only in 13 of those imprints was the first printer named.[74] Bearing in mind that Magee's imprints were often ambiguous, the explicitness of the publication detail here is especially salient.

While there is some circumstantial evidence to suggest that Dunlap's name was known in Belfast, owing most likely to family connections, it appears that Magee's naming of Dunlap was an attempt to associate his shop with Philadelphia, to affirm secure, tangible, even personal connections with the city.[75] Magee was actively engaged in selling to his readers these ties with Philadelphia, which itself was a means of indicating the American sympathies of his publications, sentiments which were felt throughout Ulster and which are likely to have translated into readership sales. Also, this reflects the bourgeoning confidence of Belfast as a town. No longer was it content to follow that which was being propounded in London; Belfast sought the example of other cities in the provinces (Philadelphia especially) that were growing in commercial and political importance and which were challenging the primacy of London.

This case study of the book ties between Belfast and Philadelphia *c.* 1763–76 is important for scholarship on the history of the book, not least because there has been no previous study devoted to investigating the interchanges between the two book trades, but also because what can be extrapolated from it challenges some of the common assumptions held regarding Irish printing and Irish reprinted editions. For example, it has been an accepted view that the dissemination of Irish books across the Atlantic to cities such as New York and Philadelphia was driven by capitalist enterprise and that the cheapness of Irish reprints, allied with the high price of printing in America, compelled colonial booksellers to import Irish books. While this might account for the sale of Belfast and Dublin printed books in North America, it offers only a partial account. The complete picture is much more nuanced. The example of Hall's order to Magee has demonstrated that economic considerations were peripheral to other more pressing issues, such as, in his case, the desire to commence a new business relationship at a time of great stress in dealings with existing contacts.

Of greater significance still was the particular kind of reader that Hall was hoping to attract by means of this material: the sale of Belfast books in Philadelphia was driven by a rising demographic of Ulster immigrants, for whom Belfast texts were eminently familiar and resonant of home. The appeal to readers of Ulster-Scots extraction is foremost among the reasons why the publications of James Magee were requested, imported and reprinted in Philadelphia. It appears that Belfast editions were actually preferred here, indicated by Dunlap and Gaine's reprinting of Belfast texts. One could argue further that colonial printers wanted to make the connections with Belfast explicit – Gaine's reprint of *The Young Clerk's Vade Mecum* emphasized its Belfast heritage: 'Belfast printed: New-York, re-printed by H. Gaine'.[76]

This chapter thus revisits the question of the importance of reprinted editions in the colonial market. In a culture in which, as Raven has noted, 'books were notable luxury goods – totems of respectability and conveyors of metropolitan thought', imported books in the colonies were much sought after commodities.[77] Indigenous publications were regarded as homespun and colonial gentlemen showed the greatest pride of possession in the imported book; London editions carried the ultimate prestige.[78] This portrayal of the high status and preference among readers for London editions must, however, be contested when we consider the demand for Belfast books in Philadelphia. While first editions and fine editions are traditionally celebrated – we imagine that readers must have sought them – reprints, it must be remembered, are actually indicators of cultural preferences. Belfast reprints that were imported to North America therefore were acquired because readers sought these particular editions. They were redolent of Belfast/Ulster by means of their content but especially in their typography and design, and thus offered an advantage over any other edition. They offered nostalgic meaning and value to a market of Ulster-Scots readers hungry to hold on to, or to recapture, the memories and identity of home. Of course, the same analysis might be applied to other Irish reprints sold in an American context; they would have had undoubted significance for the pockets of Irish migrants now living in the New World, who are likely to have been among the readers of this kind of material.

This reading of events tends to shift the focus away from the economic merit of Belfast and Dublin reprints and locates their significance rather within a cultural context. Such a view is consonant with Sher's assessment of the contribution made by Irish printers and Irish reprints in America in which he emphasized that Irish printers and booksellers, by means of their reprints, were vital agents in disseminating Scottish Enlightenment culture to America. But if we are inclined to think of printers such as Magee as being in this mould, and that by means of his reprints he was disseminating not just books but fragments of cultural and national identity to a community transposed to a new homeland, we are in danger of overlooking the other cultural significance of his reprints – namely, their impact on a Irish market. For these reprints were ultimately an expression of the rising confidence of Belfast, both as a town and as an important printing hub.

By means of his connection with the Philadelphia and (possibly) New York book trades, Magee was able to sell his books, but he was also able to access new American works. For example, in March 1775 Magee advertised an impressive consignment of polemical tracts and pamphlets, newly 'imported from America'. These imported publications, seven in total, included titles such as *Free Thoughts on the Proceedings of the Continental Congress* (1774); *The Congress Canvassed; Or, An Examination into the Conduct of the Delegates* (1774) and *A View of the Controversy between Great-Britain and Her Colonies* (1774).[79] His contacts with North American booksellers assisted him in terms not only of what he could import, but also what he could reprint. His reprinting of American political texts forged links (commercial and ideological) with the colonies and rooted Irish men and women firmly in an imperial dispute in which they, like the colonies, existed at the periphery of the empire. Moreover, by taking greater publishing risks, and reprinting material from places other than London, Magee was endeavouring to construct an image of himself as a far-reaching printer, quite literally in the case of his ties with the Philadelphia book trade. In flagging up the names of Philadelphia printers (in this way, indicating connections to his readers), Magee self-consciously moved away from the limiting provincialism of Irish town printing and consolidated his reputation as an innovative and progressive printer of Dissenting tracts and polemics. The result was that Belfast printing, by means of Magee, was moving from the margins. This increasing self-assurance can be witnessed in Magee's decision to offer competing editions to the Dublin trade at this time, including single-handedly offering a challenge to syndicate or 'conger' publications of the newly formed Dublin Company of Booksellers.[80] No longer content to issue word-for-word reprints from the metropolis and operate as a printing dependency of London, Belfast printing was renegotiating its status as a small town trade and was consciously occupying a more prominent place both nationally and internationally. Magee's connections with the colonial book trade, particularly his relationship with booksellers and printers in Philadelphia, was pivotal to this emerging confidence and offered Belfast booksellers valuable and new-found leverage within the Irish book trade.

Notes

1. I am indebted to delegates to the conference, 'Connected by Books: the Forging of Transatlantic Literary Communities', University of Essex, 2 Dec. 2007, for their various suggestions, and also to recommendations offered by Moyra Haslett.

2. In the following, 'printer' refers to those who personally, or through their employees, operated the printing press; 'publisher' alludes to those responsible, financially, for putting the book on sale although the word was not in frequent use until the nineteenth century; 'bookseller' denotes a seller of books, the individual responsible for the retail distribution of a work. The term 'bookselling' is used, however, in its eighteenth-century composite

meaning to indicate not simply the sale of an item but also the printing, publication, sale and distribution of printed matter.

3. Richard Cargill Cole, *Irish Booksellers and English Writers 1740–1800* (London, 1986).

4. Mary Pollard, *Dublin's Trade in Books, 1550–1800* (Oxford, 1989): v.

5. Ibid., 66, 88–9; see also Cole, *Irish Booksellers and English Writers*, 11; Richard B. Sher, *The Enlightenment & the Book: Scottish Authors & Their Publishers in Eighteenth-Century Britain, Ireland, & America* (Chicago, IL, and London, 2006): 444, 497.

6. Pollard, *Dublin's Trade in Books*, 66; see 97–102 for a discussion of those Dublin publishers who entered into agreements with London copyright holders for reprint rights.

7. Letters from Strahan to Creech (18 Oct and 20 Nov 1781), cited in Sher, *The Enlightenment & the Book*, 448.

8. For the international trade in books, see Giles Barber, 'Books from the Old World and for the New: The British International Trade in Books in the Eighteenth Century', *Studies on Voltaire and the Eighteenth Century*, 151 (1976): 219–24; Giles Barber, 'Book Imports and Exports in the Eighteenth Century', in Robin Myers and Michael Harris (eds), *The Sale and Distribution of Books from 1700* (Oxford, 1982): 94–95; Stephen Botein, 'The Anglo-American Book Trade before 1776: Personnel and Strategies' in William L. Joyce, David D. Hall, Richard D. Brown, and John B. Hench (eds), *Printing and Society in Early America* (Worcester, MA, 1983): 48–82; James Raven, 'The Export of Books to Colonial North America', *Publishing History* 42 (1997): 21–49; James Raven, *London Booksellers and American Customers: Transatlantic Literary Community and the Charleston Library Society, 1748–1811* (Columbia, SC, 2002).

9. John Bidwell, 'Part Two. Printers' Supplies and Capitalization' in Hugh Amory and David D. Hall (eds), *A History of the Book in America, vol. I, The Colonial Book in the Atlantic World* (Chapel Hill, NC, 2007): 163.

10. Raven, *London Booksellers and American Customers*, 6.

11. James Raven, 'Part Three: The Importation of Books in the Eighteenth Century', in Amory and Hall (eds), *A History of the Book in America*, 188.

12. For a useful discussion of the Scottish trade in books to North America, see Warren McDougall, 'Scottish Books for America in the Mid 18th Century' in Robin Myers and Michael Harris (eds), *Spreading the Word: The Distribution Networks of Print 1550–1850* (Winchester and New Castle, DE, 1990): 21–46.

13. See Colm Lennon, 'The Print Trade, 1700–1800' in Raymond Gillespie & Andrew Hadfield (eds), *The Oxford History of the Irish Book vol. 3 The Irish Book in English 1550–1800* (Oxford, 2006): 84; Pollard, *Dublin's Trade in Books*, pp. 110–18; James Phillips, *Printing and Bookselling in Dublin, 1670–1800* (Dublin, 1998): 285–86.

14. Scottish Enlightenment texts were reprinted extensively in Ireland. This needs to be offered with the caveat, however, that Scottish Enlightenment books made up only a small fraction of the total amount of books reprinted in late eighteenth-century Dublin. Sher, *The Enlightenment & the Book*, 448.

15. Sher, *The Enlightenment & the Book*, 502.

16. Cole, *Irish Booksellers and English Writers*, 4; Pollard, *Dublin's Trade in Books*, 140–3.

17. Pollard, *Dublin's Trade in Books*, 149.
18. James Green, 'Part One: English Books and Printing in the Age of Franklin', in Amory and Hall (eds), *A History of the Book in America*, 278.
19. Cole, *Irish Booksellers and English Writers*, ix.
20. J. D. Fleeman, 'Book Review: Irish Booksellers and English Writers 1740–1800 by R. C. Cole', *The Review of English Studies*, New Series, 38, 152 (Nov, 1987): 568.
21. Cole, *Irish Booksellers and English Writers*, 41; McDougall, 'Scottish Books for America in the Mid 18th Century', 31.
22. David Hall, letter to William Strahan, 21 Mar 1752 in Letterbook 4, Commencing Anno 1750 (1750–1755), American Philosophical Society, B. H142.1–3: David Hall Papers (hereafter DHP).
23. *The Charter, Laws, and Catalogue of Books, of the Library Company of Philadelphia* (Philadelphia, PA, B. Franklin & D. Hall, 1757): 112; *The Charter, Laws, and Catalogue of Books, of the Library Company of Philadelphia* (Philadelphia, PA, Joseph Crukshank, 1770), 'Books in Duodecimo G', nos. 150 & 527; 'Books in Octavo U', no. 128.
24. Glenn H. Brown and Maude O. Brown, *A Directory of the Book-Arts and Book Trade in Philadelphia to 1820* (New York, 1950): 79; *Pennsylvania Gazette* (hereafter *PG*) 19 Oct 1769.
25. *Belfast News-Letter* (hereafter *BNL*), 1 Jul 1757; *PG*, 5 Apr 1753; 3 Mar 1757; 17 Nov 1757.
26. Raven, 'Part Three', 189.
27. Cole, *Irish Booksellers and English Writers*, 44; Brown and Brown, *A Directory of the Book-Arts and Book Trade in Philadelphia to 1820*, 114; Marcus A. McCorison (ed.), Isaiah Thomas, *The History of Printing in America with a Biography of Printers & an Account of Newspapers* (New York, 1970): 386.
28. A catalogue of chapbooks, sold by Steuart and placed as an advertisement leaf in one of his publications (Robert Russel's *Seven Sermons*, 1763), offers a list of titles that are strikingly similar to the chapbooks printed and sold by Magee, and which he also advertised in his reprint of *Seven Sermons*, possibly in 1750. The chapbook titles that are common to both are considerable, adding force to the view that Steuart was selling material which had been imported from Magee.
29. Victor E. Neuburg, 'Chapbooks in America: Reconstructing the Popular Reading of Early America', in Cathy N. Davidson (ed.), *Reading in America Literature & Social History* (Baltimore, MD and London, 1989): 87–8.
30. Cole, *Irish Booksellers and English Writers*, 43.
31. Ibid., 45, 46.
32. Copyright was extended to Ireland in 1801, while the American Copyright Act of 1790 protected only American writers and British writers were not protected until the Chace Act of 1891.
33. For an example of this practice, see David Hall, letter to William Strahan, 3 Sep 1764 in Letterbook 3, Commencing Anno 1764 (1764–7) DHP.
34. Rosalind Remer, *Printers and Men of Capital: Philadelphia Book Publishers in the New Republic* (Philadelphia, PA, 1996): 12.
35. Robert D. Harlan, 'David Hall's Bookshop and its British Sources of Supply', in David Kaser (ed.), *Books in America's Past: Essays Honouring Rudolph H. Gjelsness* (Charlottesville, NC, 1966): 6.

36. The cheapness of Irish reprints has been regarded as the main motivation as to why colonial booksellers imported this material. For example, see Pollard, *Dublin's Trade in Books*, 163; Cole, *Irish Booksellers and English Writers*, 191, 198.

37. David Hall, letter to James Magee, 4 Feb 1766 in Letterbook 3, DHP.

38. For a useful discussion of the kinds of books read by children and students in colonial America, see E. Jennifer Monaghan, *Learning to Read and Write in Colonial America* (Amherst, MA, 2005): 302–332.

39. Robert D. Harlan, 'William Strahan's American Book Trade, 1744–76', *The Library Quarterly*, 31 (1961): 240.

40. See David Hall, Account Current Book, Commencing Anno 1748–[1768] DHP.

41. David Hall, letter to Hamilton & Balfour, 3 Mar 1763 in Letterbook 2, Commencing Anno 1759 (1759–64) DHP; letter to Balfour, 20 Nov 1764 in Letterbook 3, DHP.

42. David Hall, letter to Johnson and Unwin, 9 Aug 1759 in Letterbook 2, DHP.

43. Ibid., 21 Aug 1759; letter to Hamilton and Balfour, 2 Jul 1760 in Letterbook 2, DHP.

44. For example, David Hall, letter to Hamilton and Balfour, 22 Dec 1760 in Letterbook 2, DHP; letter to William Strahan, 2 Apr 1761 in Letterbook 2, DHP; letter to Alexander Kincaid, 17 Dec 1765 in Letterbook 3, DHP.

45. David Hall, letter to Hamilton and Balfour, 20 Jul 1761 in Letterbook 2, DHP.

46. See David Hall, letters to William Strahan, 9 Aug 1759; 6 Dec 1760; 2 Apr 1761; & 4 Nov 1761 in Letterbook 2, DHP.

47. David Hall, letter to William Strahan, 2 Apr 1761 in Letterbook 2, DHP.

48. Ibid., 11 Oct 1763.

49. Ibid., 14 May 1763 in Letterbook 2 and 16 Nov 1767 in Letterbook 3, DHP.

50. Richard Twiss, *A Tour in Ireland in 1775* (London: printed for the Author; and sold by J. Robinson, in New Bond-Street; J. Walter, at Charing-Cross; G. Robinson, in Paternoster Row; & G. Kearsley, in Fleet-street, 1776): 78.

51. Sher, *The Enlightenment & the Book,* pp. 497–502.

52. See for example, letter to Alexander Kincaid, 17 Dec 1765 and letter to William Strahan, 7 Jun 1766 in Letterbook 3, DHP.

53. David Hall, letter to William Strahan, 7 Jun 1766 in Letterbook 3, DHP.

54. For example, David Hall, letter to Alexander Kincaid, 17 Dec 1765 in Letterbook 3, DHP; letter to William Strahan, 7 Jun 1766 in Letterbook 3, DHP.

55. Kerby A. Miller, *Emigrants and Exiles: Ireland and the Irish Exodus to North America* (New York and Oxford, 1985): 137, 153.

56. Ibid., 150.

57. For example, throughout his career Magee consistently reprinted sermons by the Scottish Seceding brothers, Ralph and Ebenezer Erskine, doubtless resonating with Dissenters and Seceders in Ulster who looked to Scotland as their mother church.

58. W. H. Crawford, 'Ireland: Small Towns in Ulster' in Peter Borsay and Lindsay Proudfoot (eds), *Provincial Towns in Early Modern England and Ireland: Change, Convergence and Divergence*, Proceedings of the British Academy, 108 (Oxford, 2002): 116–17.

59. See David Hall, letter to William Strahan, 21 Mar 1752 in Letterbook 2, DHP.

60. For example, John Nelson's *A Letter to the Protestant Dissenters in the Parish of Ballykelly*, which had been printed for Belfast printer John Hay in 1766 and reprinted by Magee in 1770, was reprinted in Salem, Massachusetts, in 1771 and 1772 (although the latter is likely to have been a reissue) and in Newburyport (1798).
61. David Manson, *A New Primer; Or, Child's Best Guide* (Philadelphia, PA: John Dunlap, 1770?).
62. *The Young Clerk's Vade Mecum: Or, Compleat Law-Tutor* ([New York]: Belfast printed: New-York, re-printed by H. Gaine, 1776).
63. *BNL*, 16–19 Oct 1795.
64. Raynal, *The Sentiments of a Foreigner, on the Disputes of Great-Britain with America* (Belfast: James Magee, 1775), 19.
65. James E. Bradley, *Religion, Revolution, and English Radicalism: Nonconformity in Eighteenth-Century Politics and Society* (Cambridge and New York, 1990): 7.
66. William Campbell, 'Sketches of the History of Presbyterians in Ireland' (1803), Presbyterian Historical Society of Ireland, Campbell MSS, p. 235; William Steel Dickson, *Sermons on the Following Subjects. I. The Advantages of National Repentance. II. The Ruinous Effects of Civil War. III. The Coming of the Son of Man. IV. The Hope of Meeting, Knowing, and Rejoicing with Virtuous Friends, in a Future World* (Belfast, James Magee, [1778?]): 45.
67. See *BNL*, 20–23 Aug 1776.
68. For Ulster Dissenters' support of the American colonies, see Ian McBride, *Scripture Politics: Ulster Presbyterians and Irish Radicalism in the Late Eighteenth-Century Ireland* (Oxford, 1998): 113–123.
69. It was translated by J. Justamond and printed for T. Cadell in London in 1776. Hereafter, I use *Histoire dans les Deux Indes* as its short title. For a list of English translations of *Histoire dans les Deux Indes*, see Appendix 2, 'French Books connected with the French Enlightenment Published in Ireland, 1700–1800' in Graham Gargett and Geraldine Sheridan (eds), *Ireland and the French Enlightenment, 1700–1800* (Basingstoke, 1999): 268–9.
70. The dating of Humphrey's text has been ascertained by the advertisement, pp. [iii]–iv, which is dated 17 Mar 1775. Magee's reprint was printed and available for sale on 11 Apr, see *BNL*, 11–14 Apr 1775.
71. A journey between Larne and New York was a passage of 32 days, while the passage between Derry and Philadelphia took six weeks. *BNL*, 24–7 Nov 1778; Stephen A. Royle and Caitríona Ní Laoire, ' "Dare the Boist'rous Main": The Role of the *Belfast News Letter* in the Process of Emigration from Ulster, 1760–1800', *The Canadian Geographer/Le Géographe Canadien*, 50, 1 (2006): 58.
72. There is the famous example of the Dublin pirated edition of Richardson's *Sir Charles Grandison* in 1753. See Pollard, *Dublin's Trade in Books*, 88–9; Cole, *Irish Booksellers and English Writers*, 11.
73. I have calculated that Magee produced 377 works. It is certain, however, that Magee printed more titles than this. In this study however all calculations respecting Magee's career only take into account texts whose dating is certain. Publications where questions remain about the dating are not included in my calculations.
74. This information was ascertained by performing a search of Early American Imprints (Evans & Shaw Shoemaker online). I am grateful to James Green of the Library Company of Philadelphia for this information.

75. Despite leaving his home in Strabane when he was a boy there were still extant family members of the Dunlap family in Ulster with whom John communicated from Philadelphia. This is revealed in the Dunlap letters held in Public Records office of Northern Ireland (PRONI). Local connections would explain this familiarity with Dunlap's name as Dunlap would not have been known as the printer of the Declaration of Independence at this point.
76. See note 59.
77. Raven, *London Booksellers and American Customers*, 8.
78. Barber, 'Book Imports and Exports in the Eighteenth Century', 95–6.
79. *BNL*, 7–10 Mar 1775.
80. For details of this challenge to the Dublin trade, see Michael O'Connor, 'James Magee (1707–1797) and the Belfast Print Trade, 1771–1781' (unpublished PhD thesis, Queen's University Belfast, 2007): 164–69.

10
From the French or Not: Transatlantic Contributions to the Making of the Brazilian Novel

Sandra Guardini T. Vasconcelos

> Nothing is foreign to us, because everything is.
>
> (Paulo Emilio Salles Gomes)[1]

In an interview given in 1977 to a Brazilian periodical, Roberto Schwarz, one of Brazil's leading literary critics, resumed a debate initiated by his 1973 essay 'Misplaced Ideas', in which he argued that not only do ideas travel but, in the case of Brazilian nineteenth-century literature, they travelled by boat, 'coming from Europe every fortnight, on board steamships, in the shape of books, magazines and newspapers'.[2]

The suspension of censorship in 1821 resulted in a more regular and free circulation of books, magazines and newspapers in the bookshops, libraries and circulating libraries of Rio de Janeiro, the majority of which had been established in the 1820s and 1830s. Among these books, available for either purchase or loan, were both novels and romances. The books came mostly from Lisbon and Paris and were mainly Portuguese or French. Until recently, we could advance little evidence of the existence of British novels among the books sent to Rio de Janeiro. The term 'British novel' is used in this chapter in preference to 'English novel'; these were novels all originally written in English and a few were later translated into French and/or Portuguese. They were published either in the British Isles (the great majority in London) or, if in translation, in France, Belgium, Germany (Leipzig) and Portugal. Brazilian literary historians and critics tended to consider this British presence and its impact on Brazilian novel writing and novelists as small and irrelevant. However, a more thorough investigation of those books reveals that Britain and British novelists were much more prominent and played a far more important role in the making of the Brazilian novel than was previously recognized. Indeed, a considerable number of the novels that reached Rio de Janeiro actually concealed their place of origin, a fact that challenges the claimed primacy of French novels and novelists in the making and consolidation of the Brazilian novel.

A wealth of evidence, much contained in the advertisements found in newspapers and circulating library catalogues, suggests that the small Brazilian reading public had at its disposal a considerable number of British authors and novels. This chapter is an attempt to reconstruct the history of the circulation of those novels in Brazil in the context of the importation of books from Europe.

Throughout the colonial period, Brazil was challenged by structural obstacles to the circulation of books in its territory. It was a country without its own press, with few booksellers and a recent history of censorship. Rubens Borba de Moraes informs us that Swift's *Gulliver's Travels* (1726) and Sterne's *A Sentimental Journey Through France and Italy* (1768) could only be read by special licence, because they had been included in the list of books forbidden by the Real Mesa Censória (the Portuguese censorship committee).[3] Even after the opening of its ports in 1808, Brazil depended on the illegal trade carried out by the British, French and Dutch, and on the few individuals publishing books in Portuguese in London and Paris, which supplied its small consumer market. Napoleon's invasion of Portugal was imminent, and the Portuguese monarchy was under threat. The Prince Regent Dom João had been convinced by Great Britain's diplomatic envoy Lord Strangford to flee to his Brazilian colony. Shortly after his arrival in January 1808, Dom João complied with the clauses in the treaties he had signed with the British Government, through the facilitation of trade between Brazil and Britain and also by conferring upon Britain and its citizens advantages and privileges granted to no other foreign country. The opening of the Brazilian ports to trade with foreign nations in 1808 resulted therefore from British force, but was, in terms of the history of the book, fortunate.

British merchants wasted no time in offering this tropical outpost of the Portuguese monarchy a regular supply of merchandise and manufactured goods, which included chinaware, glass, pots and pans, cutlery and tools, all of which found their way onto the shelves of shops and warehouses in the city of Rio de Janeiro. It was not only hardware and utensils that were made available to the inhabitants of the still small and provincial Brazilian capital. Books, periodicals and, in particular, novels also found their way into the country. Even today, these accompaniments to the new habits of consumption, new fashions and certain refinement of manners, are attributed to the British presence in Rio de Janeiro's everyday life from 1808.

The foundation of Impressão Régia (Royal Press), also in 1808, the cessation of censorship in 1821 and the growing settlement of French booksellers in Rio de Janeiro, all contributed to the wider availability of books. Gradually, advertisements began to announce the sales of 'novels' at the 'Gazeta shops'. By the 1820s these shops adjacent to the daily newspaper offices offered books for sale and loan. In the 1830s circulating libraries, similar to those in France and Britain, were founded as commercial enterprises responsible for making available throughout the province the packages of novels sent from the metropolis. Booksellers and circulating libraries assumed responsibility for the dispersal and circulation of novels, and they played a central role as shapers and mediators of taste, as had their counterparts in France and Britain. Nelson Schapochnik records the existence of Cremière's circulating library on the Rua da Alfândega, and those of Mongie, Dujardin and Mad Breton on the Rua do Ouvidor.[4] It was not only bestsellers but also remainders and editions specially made for the French circulating libraries that were destined for the readerships of Lisbon and Rio de Janeiro. Some of these works had already been translated into Portuguese.

British novels crossed the English Channel throughout the eighteenth century and France was taken by storm. Fashionable and popular among French readers, it was unsurprising that British novels (almost always in translation) became a common fare of French circulating libraries and booksellers. French catalogues of that time abound with novels described as '*traduit de l'anglois*', a phrase that became close to a cliché in book-lists and advertisements. Their translation into French allowed them to acquire what was believed to be an extra layer of varnish and sophistication. This was how dozens of books arrived in Brazil, and it was the origin of the common critical mistake of taking them for what they were not, that is, of French origin. The fascination for and 'exceptional receptivity towards the ornaments of French culture', which, according to Laurence Hallewell, were seen by Brazilians as tokens of modernity and progress,[5] may be a reasonable explanation as to why French versions and editions of British novels were favoured. It was a tempting commercial strategy to make the books easier to lend and sell. The phrase 'translated from the French', which appeared in a great number of novels that circulated in Brazil, is often a false clue, disguising their British origin.

A. N. Pigoreau's *Petite bibliographie biographico-romancière*[6] and Harold Streeter's compilation, found in *The Eighteenth-Century English Novel in*

French Translation,[7] are very useful sources in the search for the true origin of many of the novels listed in the catalogues of circulating libraries in Rio de Janeiro. The comparison between the bibliographical information available, which includes the translator's name or initials, shows that often the edition that came to Brazil, or the text that served as the original for translation into Portuguese, was exactly the same as one of those held by a French circulating library. This is the case, for example, with *L'Italien, ou le confessional des pénitents noirs*, by Ann Radcliffe, and *Alberto, ou o deserto de Strathnavern* by Mrs Helme.[8] Hence Marlyse Meyer's claim that the novelistic paradigms which came to Brazil were always English, although mediation was French.[9]

The *Gazeta do Rio de Janeiro,* from its foundation on 10 September 1808 until 22 June 1822, when its publication was discontinued, adopted the habit of announcing in its section 'Loja da Gazeta' (Gazeta shop), the arrival in Brazil of what it described as 'moderníssimas e divertidas novellas' (very modern and amusing novels). These novels included anonymous works together with old favourites such as Le Sage's *Diabo Coxo*[10], Bernardin de Saint-Pierre's *Paulo e Virgínia, A Choupana Índia*, Chateaubriand's *Atala, ou Amores de Dois Selvagens* and Marmontel's *Belizário*. British fiction shared space with the French: Mrs Elizabeth Helme's *Luiza, ou o cazal* [sic] *no bosque* (21 September 1816), Jonathan Swift's *Viagens de Guliver* (15 March 1817), Daniel Defoe's *Vida e Aventuras admiráveis de Robinson Crusoe* (9 April 1817), Henry Fielding's *Tom Jones, ou O Engeitado* [sic] (10 May 1817), the anonymous[11] *Vida de Arnaldo Zulig* (4 July 1818) and the complement to *Historia da infeliz Clarissa Harlowe* in eight volumes, by Samuel Richardson (8 March 1820).[12]

The *Jornal do Comércio,* founded by the French editor Pierre Plancher-Seignot in Rio de Janeiro in 1827 also followed the practice of advertising recent imported fiction. In addition, it resumed the habit of advertising the novels and romances available for sale at the apothecaries and bookshops that had become part of the townscape of Rio de Janeiro. Although bookshops and circulating libraries took rather longer to reach the other provinces of the empire, it was not impossible for novels to be discovered in the interior of the country. They were, however, only found in the greater homes and private libraries. Typical of those novels on the domestic shelves were the Portuguese translations of Defoe, Scott and Radcliffe mentioned by Gilberto Freyre in his *Ingleses no Brasil.*[13]

British novels were, obviously, the common fare of the Rio de Janeiro British Subscription Library, a circulating library with a good supply of new European publications that opened in 1826 to serve the British community of the city. In the British Subscription Library could be found most British novels in the original, in editions that are also recorded in the catalogues of the Real Gabinete Português de Leitura do Rio de Janeiro (founded in 1837) and the Biblioteca Fluminense (founded in 1847). Generally, however, the novels that reached Rio on the packet boats had already been translated into Portuguese, usually from versions in French. An additional source of publications were the French bookshops that from the 1820s clustered around the Rua do Ouvidor, the centre of elegant life in the city. The proprietors of these bookshops, Villeneuve, Didot, Mongie, Crémière, Garnier, Plancher and Dujardin, rented and sold novels to a very small literate population, for whom novel-reading became part of a general code of good manners, which they aspired to follow and imitate.

In reality, therefore, it appears that consignments of British novels arrived at Rio de Janeiro harbour from the first three decades of the nineteenth century. Most were translated from the French and travelled to Brazil via Paris or Lisbon. The novels continued to flow in throughout the century, as records in circulating library catalogues testify. The volumes still extant on the shelves of the Real Gabinete Português de Leitura in Rio de Janeiro are, for example, evidence of the popularity and longevity of these novels. In addition to the works of the founding fathers of the British novel, Defoe, Richardson, Fielding and Sterne, imported novels included a full range of the different types of novels current in eighteenth- and nineteenth-century Britain. These included both Horace Walpole's *The Castle of Otranto* and Ann Radcliffe's Gothic novels, dozens of novels of 'sentiment', Frances Burney's novels of manners, novels by William Godwin, the complete works of Walter Scott and many of Charles Dickens's novels. These were accompanied by many less famous or anonymous works which were of little literary standing. The originals had been destined to feed the market for novels and meet the demands of the reading public in Britain and, no doubt, in France, the destination of a significant proportion of the output of British novelists at that time. This is the range of novels that, together, came to constitute the collections of the imperial capital's circulating libraries.[14]

Once its ports were opened to the free trade of European goods and censorship was abolished, Brazil was invaded by novels; perhaps not so much in the number of copies, since there were few readers, but in the wide variety of titles and authors, to which the catalogues bear testimony. The impact upon existing Brazilian readers and men of letters of the arrival of these books and the virtually simultaneous contact they provided with everything the British and the French had taken around two centuries to produce can be imagined. In the matter of a few years, Brazil received Defoe, Richardson, Sterne, Radcliffe, Scott, Dickens, Charlotte Brontë, and Bulwer-Lytton. Such reading was quite in addition to Le Sage, Chateaubriand, Marivaux, Dumas (père and fils), Fénelon, Paul de Kock, Rousseau and Eugène Sue. The sudden availability of such a diversity of authors and texts reduced the sense of the long period during which they were originally written and presented a variety of themes, forms and techniques sufficient to amaze any reader or aspiring author. There was little delay before booksellers, merchants and circulating libraries began to disseminate both the latest publications and the works of famous novelists in addition to those of popular authors. This move helped to shatter the centuries-long isolation of Brazil and brought the country within the nineteenth-century literary market.

Against the general absence of the records of readers and reading in Brazil in this period, one testimony stands out: that of José de Alencar (1829–77), novelist and politician, who played a central role in the consolidation of the novel in Brazil. His reminiscences can help us to move beyond the evidence of the mere availability of these novels and investigate the potential modes of appropriation of these models, a process described by Machado de Assis as 'external inflow'.[15] Alencar was one of those for whom the reading of European novels contributed to 'imprint on [his] spirit the moulds of this literary structure'[16]. The novels read by Alencar crossed the oceans, and carried within them recurrent themes – marriage, private and domestic life, usurpation of rights and inheritance – all of them imbued with powerful, heightened emotions. Many were expressed in the ornate, elevated language characteristic of the period.

Similarly, the different novel genres current in eighteenth- and nineteenth-century Britain now circulating in Brazil offered inspiration to the country's first fiction writers. If the distinction between *novel* and *romance* made by Clara Reeve in *The Progress of Romance* (1785) is considered, it can be seen that a romance repertoire was undoubtedly present in the first novels produced by early Brazilian authors: unbridled passion, seduction, kidnappings, betrayals, frightful villains, disrepute, last-minute revelations, an absence of restraint, the lack of a causal link between events, stereotyped characters (depicted as either extremely good or extremely evil) and so forth. In line with the more modern insistence of the 'novel', however, certain authors began to give greater importance to realism and plausibility to bring the narrative closer to the life of the 'middling' people who were, supposedly, the novel's primary material. It appeared that with the *embourgeoisement* of manners and the changes in the role of women in Brazilian society, there was a corresponding growth in the power of the novel. The new genre of the novel appeared to usurp the romance, although the latter continued to influence the work of Romantic novelists.

In addition to the works of widely recognized novelists and of their lesser-known brethren, a survey of British novels in circulation in Brazil has indicated the presence of a group of female novelists who had become well known and widely read in Britain in the eighteenth century: Frances Burney, Elizabeth Inchbald, Sophia Lee and Ann Radcliffe. To these can be added Regina Maria Roche, with *Amanda e Oscar* (*The Children of the Abbey*, 1796), and Elizabeth Helme with *Sinclair das Ilhas* (*St Clair of the Isles, or The Outlaws of Barra*, 1803).[17] The number of circulating libraries established in several regions of Brazil, mainly in the second half of the nineteenth century, indicates that the habit of reading novels became increasingly widespread. A study by Ana Luiza Martins, *Gabinetes de Leitura da Província de São Paulo: A Pluralidade de um Espaço Esquecido (1847–90)*, surveyed around 20 circulating libraries scattered throughout the province of São Paulo, in whose collections novels predominated, especially feuilletons. Martins's findings corroborate the significant presence of foreign authors in translation. Scott and Dickens were among those identified.

One other consequence of these developments links Brazil to the social history of the novel in Europe. The expansion of reading sites and the greatly facilitated access to books in general, and novels in particular, became, unsurprisingly, a matter of concern. This was especially so given the seclusion of Brazilian women, the paucity of their education and the limited world in which they lived. All this made the reading women a privileged public as far as the consumption of feuilletons and popular novels was concerned. This condition, so very similar to that of eighteenth-century French and British women, might explain the complaints of late nineteenth-century novelist Júlia Lopes de Almeida regarding the pernicious effects that the reading of novels could have on women. She warned against 'detrimental, unwholesome novels, filled with romantic adventures and dangerous heroes', recommending instead works of moral edification.[18]

Here, then was a transatlantic community of aversion to novel-reading and of moral panic inspired by the increasing influence of (much translated) popular fiction. It appeared that in Brazil there was the same need to justify the lack of theoretical dignity of the new genre.

This, according to Antonio Candido, made seventeenth-century French writers and, one might suggest, eighteenth-century British novelists as well appropriate the artifice of the 'sweet remedy' (Horace's *utile et dulci*) in order to disguise the inferiority complex that romances and novels suffered in the face of the classical tradition of the tragedy and the epic. The novel arrived in Brazil as a genre that had already been consolidated in Europe. It did not struggle long to achieve recognition and Brazilian novelists were able to progress rapidly. Indeed, in comparison to its British counterpart, the Brazilian novel quickly dropped its 'state of ashamed shyness'[19] and erased the taint of being regarded as a minor and bastard genre. Similarly, it was quicker in accepting the 'validity in itself of mimesis' and the 'free play of creative fantasy'.[20]

Marlyse Meyer has indicated that 'the fictions imagined by eighteenth-century ladies and spinsters lulled Brazilian nineteenth-century imaginations',[21] a comment appropriate to writers and readers alike. In her extraordinary study of the feuilleton, Meyer demonstrated the remarkable penetration of the '*romance-folhetim*' (or *roman-feuilleton*, a counterpart of the popular British novel) in Brazil in the nineteenth century and the consequences this had for later melodrama and soap opera. The formula is similar to that found in the most popular British novels: kidnappings, treachery, dishonour, virtue in distress, horrifying villainy, seduced and abandoned heroines. The dramatic events of the *romance-folhetim* were accompanied by the realistic description of everyday life, together with appraisal of both domestic space and the new role of women in the bourgeois family as educators and as the reformers of manners and morals.

In Brazil, as in Britain, interest in novels and romances was related to the changes that were taking place within society. In his writing on the 1860s, Nelson Werneck Sodré stressed that:

if the great majority of the public was constituted by marriageable young ladies and students, and the privileged literary theme must be, exactly because of that, marriage, a little blended with the old love motif, and the press and literature, closely connected then, advanced to meet this demand. Women began to free themselves, little by little, from colonial confinement and submitted themselves to the patterns of European fashion, appearing in the drawing rooms and a little on the streets.[22]

Despite the deficiencies of Brazil's education system and the results of the first official literacy survey in 1872, which indicated that only one-fifth of the free population could read, the custom of reading aloud at family evening reunions should not be overlooked. The concept of 'circles of listeners' must be added to the numbers of those who were occasionally able to take advantage of the circulation of books in the country. The oral audience included Brazilian women whose lack of education was frequently remarked upon by the foreign visitors who travelled throughout the country. The writing of the English traveller Maria Graham, however, presented an alternative version and testified to the existence of a few women who were habitual readers of even philosophy and politics. Such was the case of a Dona Maria Clara, mentioned by Graham. Similarly, the publication of periodicals aimed specifically at the 'fair sex' suggests a female readership. It is necessary, therefore, to caution against the myth of women's illiteracy in colonial Brazil and to offer more relative analysis. According to Delso Renault, for example, the *Gazeta do Rio de Janeiro* in 1813 already published advertisements which announced the establishment of the first lay boarding schools for girls, established by one Dona Catharina Jacob.[23]

The frequency and regularity of these advertisements, which announced the opening of schools for young women, with sewing, embroidery, languages, dancing and music on the curriculum, indicate that there was a clientele for the services they offered. Even so, it is true that the level of education was probably minimal, since many girls appeared to give up their studies before their conclusion. The warnings against the dangers of reading fiction, however, clearly indicates that there was a female reading public for those novels that arrived on board the European steamboats. At the same time, the insistence upon the supply of edifying or instructive reading suggests the existence of an educational project that was aimed at preparing Brazilian society for a European-inspired future. An Enlightenment project, similar to that which had taken place in Britain and France throughout the whole of the eighteenth century, was now, in Brazil, embodied in the foundation of colleges, in the increased role of the press and in the growing interest in the diffusion of knowledge.

The press played a major role in the instruction of its readers. The newspapers and periodicals, with their sections on anthologies, miscellanies, and feuilletons, seem to have constituted 'a kind of local version of the *Encyclopédie*'.[24] By this activity, the newspapers and periodicals decisively contributed to the formation of a reading public. The opportunity to publish edifying stories appeared to have been an obvious course. What was new was that, alongside the enduring habit of the translation of foreign narratives to fill the leisure hours of a readership eager for European novelties, there was also a desire to create a national literature, embodied in the experiments of the forerunners of Brazilian fiction and published in several periodicals.

In the wake of the independence movement and with the desire of Brazilians to build a nation and create a national literature, foreign novels and novelists were a source of inspiration. Texts from across the Atlantic suggested paths presented themes and literary forms and offered potential solutions to those who first ventured into the territory of fiction. However, while it is true that the appropriation by Brazilians of the European novel tradition did not function merely as 'imitation' or 'mechanical reproduction' but as 'participation in the resources which became common assets by means of our dependency, contributing to make it into an interdependency',[25] it is also true that the historical conditions which had engendered the invention of the novel were completely different from those of colonial Brazil.

This chapter in this volume of collected essays gives particular attention to the presence of the British novel in the intellectual and artistic life of Brazil.[26] The corollary of that investigation is to understand the role of such transatlanticism in the making of the Brazilian novel. In doing so, we broach the conceptual and historical problem of the relationship between literary form and content. In other words, the novel rose in Europe as a response to the need to embody changes which could no longer be represented by existing literary forms. But what were the consequences of the adoption of a European literary form – the epic of the bourgeoisie in Georg Lukács's formulation – by a country where production was still based on slavery and where there was not yet a bourgeoisie on the complex scale of Europe. The restricted nature of the bourgeoisie in Brazil is confirmed by scholars such as Nelson Werneck Sodré and Wanderley Guilherme dos Santos. The latter remarked that

> until recently, there was not in Brazil an organized bourgeoisie, aiming to mould the State apparatus and structure society according to the logic of the market. Of course there were the bourgeois, there were the capitalists, but there was not a bourgeois class as a political actor approximately from 1850 to 1950, when a peculiar market society was, in any event, in the process of constituting itself at the mercy of the logic of circumstances.[27]

In addition, Sérgio Buarque de Holanda claimed that the novel only 'rose and prospered naturally where bourgeois society rose and could prosper'.[28] This situation presents a problem. How did the novel genre behave when transplanted to the periphery of the capitalist system, as was the case with its export to Brazil? The challenge faced by prospective writers was significant: it entailed the absorption of European models and their reworking for local conditions. Brazil's first prose fiction writers embarked upon this process in the 1830s, albeit with very unsatisfactory and somewhat rudimentary results. Indeed, their initial productions might be described, almost without exception, as mere exercises in fiction. The pioneers did, however, admit to the level of difficulty they faced. It is again Sérgio Buarque de Holanda who offered an explanation for such fragile attempts. He believed that the provincial milieu of Brazil offered little raw material for the novel; that is, the country lacked the forms of everyday life that were characteristic of European societies. The first Brazilian prose fiction writers were unable to develop a literary form that actually matched the materials they had at their disposal, whether through lack of talent or social conditioning. Indeed, it may have been that the lack of complexity in Brazilian society produced insufficiently stimulating material to enable writers to produce works of literary significance.

The desire to write Brazilian fiction outran the possibilities available and the mismatch between form and content in the work of its early apprentices is evident. In spite of their limitations, however, these minor, secondary writers paved the way for their successors, and, as such, decisively collaborated in the making of the Brazilian novel. The authors frequently resorted to the same artifices used in the British novel, in order to emphasize the moralizing nature of, and lend an air of veracity to, their stories. Given the different historical conditions and the miniscule Brazilian reading public, it remains to be explained why the forerunners of Brazilian fiction made the claims that they did. It might be supposed that in a nation still in the making, whose material base was founded on slavery, with a society still in the process of structuring itself, the recourse to what were borrowed, imported, literary strategies must have served other purposes. After all, there is nothing more distant from the European bourgeois family than the organization of the manorial houses in Portuguese America, where masters, relatives, slaves and dependents all lived under the same roof. On this side of the Atlantic there was a general lack of education and the tyrannical power of patriarchs remained unchallenged. The women remained confined to the domestic space and subject to rigid morality and exemplary punishment, as witnessed by the foreign travellers who traversed the country. Earlier, in eighteenth-century France and, even more so, in eighteenth-century Britain, various impediments to the refashioning of the role of men and women within the family had been removed and women had begun to enter the world of education. Certainly, fierce controls remained over what young women and the working class read, but in Europe the novel had been consolidated as a genre and, hence, had become more widely accepted. In Brazil the novel had only just begun to penetrate the educated circles of Rio de Janeiro.

The adoption of European standards in the imperial capital during the reign of Dom João VI demonstrated the need to introduce still more civilized customs. It brought about significant changes in people's ways of life, modified colonial habits and made available to the growing political, economic and cultural elite better education, theatres, books, bookshops and printing presses, along with the arrival of the latest tokens of European civilization in the shape of manufactured goods and commodities. The settlement of the Portuguese Court in the small colonial capital, and its transformation into first a viceroyalty and subsequently the capital of the Brazilian Empire (following Brazil's independence in 1822), brought a visible investment in the urbanization of the city. Much to the fore was a conscious campaign to polish manners, refine habits and normalize conduct, with the clear intention to educate the Brazilian people and build a national culture.[29]

Literature proved pivotal in both the advance of civility and in the building of a national consciousness in Brazil. Of particular importance were the several literary periodicals and miscellanies that were launched and then unceremoniously discontinued, together with the production of prose fiction in the country. This civilizing mission battled against the rudeness, ignorance and closed nature of Brazil's reactionary colonial society, and aimed to shape a civilized world and nation. The novel, as a matter of course, engaged in these movements, albeit relatively late. The first Brazilian novel, Teixeira e Souza's *O Filho do Pescador*, was not published until 1843. The British novel, in terms of content, placed an emphasis on the confrontation of moral values and played an important role as an imaginary site of both conflict and reconciliation between bourgeois and aristocratic interests and values. Both were soon allied against a new historical force – the industrial and urban working classes. By contrast, in Brazil the nineteenth-century novel functioned as an instrument of discovery and interpretation of the country,[30] its people, history, geography, customs and regions. In addition, the infant Brazilian novel served, in the hands of the ruling class, as a tool to build an idea of a nation. The elite who wrote the novels treated with arrogant cynicism and prejudice the other sections of this country in the making: the free, but impoverished, workers and the slaves. The moralizing intent, although present and clearly directed towards the elite, was less pervasive than in the British (and French) novel and shared the readers' interest in the development and stimulation of feelings of patriotism and the dissemination of knowledge of the country. The precept *utile et dulci*, that is, a common maxim of 'profit and delight', which guided the writing of books, was translated in different ways by British and Brazilian novelists. Patrick Brantlinger reminds us of how mass literacy was considered a 'menace' and as medicine that could very easily turn into poison.[31]

Given the usual delay with which ideas arrived and circulated in Brazil, it should be of little surprise that nineteenth-century Brazilian men of letters still defended classical precepts and norms that had already been discarded in Europe. Notions such as decorum and the *utile et dulci* maxim were familiar to educated Brazilians because the sons of wealthy families studied and received a classical education in Europe. They were what Fernando de Azevedo called 'an intellectual elite of importation'. Brazilian education, at least until the end of the eighteenth century, also included the classical humanities, with an emphasis on grammar, rhetoric and philosophy. Virgil, Cicero, Homer and Horace were not unknown to students and readers and could be studied in the dozens of handbooks on rhetoric and poetics, as well as many other textbooks, and in compendiums. The importation, sale and circulation of these books were not restricted, in spite of censorship.[32] However, the same Fernando de Azevedo considered them 'a thin minority of men of letters, which floated, alien to and above the social milieu'.[33] These were the 'minorities' which, when Dom João VI and his Court arrived in Rio de Janeiro, assumed the task of embarking upon the 'civilizing crusade'.[34] Their intention was to introduce more civilized and urbane habits to replace those of the old local patriarchal society.

This has been a transatlantic cultural history of similar procedures, different ends and very diverse histories. As transplanted to Brazil, the European bourgeois novel found an agrarian and pro-slavery country. In the place of the European bourgeoisie, which had become economically powerful and socially prestigious, there was a Brazilian oligarchy, supported by vast estates and slavery. This oligarchy with neither tradition nor nobility defined itself in terms of the size of its property, the number of its slaves, and its leisure and ostentation. The coffee barons did eventually succeed the sugar mill masters of the seventeenth and eighteenth centuries, but this did not represent a real change in the socio-economic structure of the country. Whether they lived in rural manorial estates or in urban mansions, this moneyed aristocracy retained its slaves, who lived in slave quarters on the farms or in shanties in the towns. Between these two extremes of the social scale, there was a population of free men, composed of merchants, peddlers, officials and civil servants. This was a social structure so unlike that in which the novel rose and flourished in Europe that it could be asked whether the genre, once transplanted to Brazilian soil, did not itself seem a 'misplaced idea'.

The relevance of France as a model and reference point for Brazilian culture is not denied. The British, in contrast, were less famous for their cultural contributions and better known for their manufactured goods and their involvement in the political and economic affairs of the Brazilian Empire. It was this that resulted in the almost total erasure of the British presence from the history of the nineteenth-century Brazilian novel. Notwithstanding the admiration many entertained for the British political system and the debates around its laissez-faire policy, the often uneasy and notoriously tense relations between the Brazilian and British Governments in economics and politics produced, to say the least, a degree of ambiguity in the way that Britain was viewed in Brazil.

The intensification of British moral pressure and, indeed, violence against the slave traffic from 1839 only reinforced the Brazilian people's revolt against the British, a feeling openly acknowledged by the scholarly Justiniano José da Rocha in his newspaper *O Brasil*: 'if there is today in the country a common and eminently popular idea, that is that England is our most deceptive and tenacious enemy' (1 October 1843). The convoluted nature of this relationship and the source of its ambiguity are highlighted by José Murilo de Carvalho:

> Considered as the leading country of the civilized world, as the richest, strongest, as the nation of civil, political and economic liberties, it [England] could not but be seen as a model by whoever judged these characteristics indisputable values. To begin with, the very condition of England as a more economically powerful country and, in particular, the history of its relations with Portugal and later with Brazil, placed it in a very dubious position. If there was admiration for its material progress and political system, there was also, on the other hand, a unanimous condemnation of its superiority in relation to Brazil.[35]

It may appear contradictory to discuss the borrowings of literary forms and techniques from the British novel in a period so ostensibly marked by these frictions. It is also important to understand the strong and continuing presence of French culture, which was always viewed as a token of refinement and civilization by Brazilians. These cultures of importation co-existed with a clear struggle in support of national values and a sense of nationality waged by intellectuals, politicians and men of letters, who strove vigorously to shape and define the contours of a national consciousness. The process of acclimatization of the novel in Brazil took place during a turbulent period, characterized by political turmoil, rebellions in the provinces, internal conflicts and the circulation of republican and federalist ideas. In the same way that a drama might be viewed as a 'school of manners', the novel became imbued with a clear pedagogical and, to some extent, political mission. The novel, as brought across the Atlantic, became a tool for debate about the national question, with a special relevance for the themes of the aggrandizement of Brazil's natural beauties, of the contest between foreign and national interests and the discussion of what being Brazilian really meant.[36]

With these concerns in mind, novelists who were conscious of their mission to build a *Brazilian* literature were much less prone to engage in the usual moral justification, so common in the works of their French and British counterparts. In a weak form only can moral apologetics be detected in the prefaces, in the intrigues of the narratives, in the discourse of the narrators, and in the opinions and criticism of journalists who commented on the developing novel. The higher levels of literacy in Britain were significant in the eighteenth century, but literacy did advance in nineteenth-century Brazil. Although calculations are controversial, in 1790 Burke estimated that there were 80,000 readers in a population of almost 8 million (1 per cent). Nearly a century later, the 1872 Brazilian census counted 1,575,912 literate people in a free population of 8,490,910 inhabitants (18.56 per cent). Here, the gradual inclusion of the previously marginalized women and working classes into the reading public impelled the Government to attempt greater surveillance of the types of reading in circulation.

A common strategy among British novelists, the 'true narrative' ploy also made its appearance, both in the short novels by the earliest Brazilian authors and in the works of better-known novelists, who insisted upon authenticity, didactic purpose and moral appeal in their stories. The intent of the Brazilian writers seems to have been to conquer the readers' resistance and lend an air of seriousness to fiction-reading. However, the tone of these works is neither as angry nor as conservative as that found in British periodicals and in the correspondence of British readers. In an atmosphere that was less uncomfortable with the liberties of fiction, this defensive attitude, the evident need for self-justification and reactions against the dangers posed by novel-reading were more timid and restricted to the very limited circle of authors and critics. Horace's *Omine tulit punctum qui miscuit utile dulci* is quoted, for example, in an article published in *Minerva Brasiliense*.[37] The citation reminded novelists of their pledge to offer readers 'the image of virtue (...) and the horror of vice'. For many of these critics, this ideal would be the noble mission of a bastard genre, whose redemption could be achieved through the relentless defence of moral principles wrapped in an interesting and entertaining story – just as the classical precepts had advocated.

Very little is known of what ordinary readers thought of this new genre that had begun to make its first appearance on Brazilian soil. Surviving testimonials are rare and the responses produced by the novel now virtually invisible. In Britain, on the contrary, novel-reading mobilized readers who, in letters and diaries, exercised what could be described as amateur criticism. The newness of the genre and its inclination to probe the private lives of common men and women no doubt explained the interest generated. Contemporary debate moved beyond the limits of official criticism, and discussions invaded everyday lives. Among Brazilians, warnings of the dangers of novel-reading were much more muted and circumscribed. Perhaps that is why Horace's precept often sounds like a cliché. The mistrust and prejudice directed against the novel in Britain appeared conventional and empty when transferred and made explicit in Brazilian texts. Criticism appeared weaker because of its disconnection from any historical imposition. For local elites morality was often a façade, and for the population of free and poor men and women a certain relaxation of customs and the slippage between the world of order and disorder,[38] as shown in Manuel Antonio de Almeida's *Memórias de um Sargento de Milícias*, could make any moral exhortation or edifying lecture both misplaced and pointless. Even so, appeals to virtue, moderation and moral principles were very convenient in a country where, since the beginning of colonization, the Portuguese settlers had taken black and Indian lovers, and where the traces of racial mixture were visible everywhere, and the consequences of miscegenation feared.

Brazilian critics did not confine themselves to the demand that fiction should assume an edifying role, but also engaged in a discussion of formal problems and directions. In addition, they demanded that novelists wrote stories that were plausible and faithful to reality. José de Alencar's *Lucíola*, for example, refers to his protagonist's correspondence, as did

Richardson in his *Pamela*. In the prologue to another of Alencar's novels, *Senhora*, readers are told that the story is true and the narrative comes from a person who had been trusted with the details of the circumstances and their confidences by the main actors of 'this curious drama'. This is unsurprising when it is noted that although Alencar never claimed to have read Richardson, he had been an avid youthful reader of the English novelist's followers, including women writers such as Elizabeth Helme and Regina Maria Roche. There are, nevertheless, certain notable differences in the fictional treatment of edifying example on each side of the Atlantic. In a society concerned with the notions of decorum, appropriateness, modesty and virtue, as was the case of eighteenth-century and nineteenth-century Britain, it was unthinkable for any heroine of Richardson's or those of his followers to permit herself to be touched, however slightly, by a stranger inside a coach. But this is exactly what happens to Carlota in *Cinco Minutos*, one of Alencar's early works.

A general moral concern was important to the new Brazilian novelists, however. Although Alencar was less guarded in defining his heroines' virtue and modesty, he was still very concerned about the consequences of their behaviour and its impact upon their marriage prospects. In the wake of so many British sentimental novels, marriage also became a crucial topic to Alencar, particularly in his later novels when the commodification of human relations, in the form of marriages of convenience or prostitution, became a central element of his plots. *Senhora*, for example, deals with the complications and conflicts arising when a poor girl becomes an heiress and, literally, purchases a husband, the man who had previously jilted her because of his ambition. By 1875, when this novel was published, the genre had become sufficiently mature to engage with themes familiar to the European bourgeois world, and Brazil had reached a stage of social, political and economic development that had enabled the writing of a realist, bourgeois novel.[39]

From the initial exercises of the forerunners of Brazilian fiction, so intent on the creation of a national literature, to the works of the two most important nineteenth-century Brazilian novelists, José de Alencar and Machado de Assis, Brazilian fiction travelled a great distance. If such travel was not in temporal terms, it certainly was in terms of the knowledge that was absorbed and incorporated thanks to the availability and circulation of foreign literary models, among which British novels (often in translation) played a prominent role. It fell to Alencar and Machado to resolve and overcome the difficulties of form and of the mismatches that had been the trademark of their predecessors. These initial maladjustments were the inevitable result of the adoption of techniques and procedures that had evolved in response to different social structures and historical processes. However, they represented initial, important groundwork that enabled succeeding novelists to take the decisive step, which left imitation behind and gradually reduced this 'variance between representation and what [...] we know to be its context'.[40]

If, as Roberto Schwarz claimed, 'ideas are in their place when they represent abstractions of the process they refer to',[41] the novel progressed from being a misplaced idea in Brazil to its remaking to reflect local conditions. It laid the foundations for what Machado de Assis would eventually accomplish in his greatest novels. Schwarz acknowledged that Alencar represented an important and decisive move in that direction, but, as part of the traffic in the novel across the Atlantic, the contribution of British novels as mediated by French translators and by French, Portuguese and British merchants, should not be minimized.

Notes

1. Paulo Emílio Salles Gomes, *Cinema, trajetória no subdesenvolvimento* (Rio de Janeiro, 1980): 77. This chapter, first translated by the author, has been further interpolated by James Raven and Rachel Duffett. The chapter also presents the preliminary results of a research project still in progress, sponsored by two Brazilian funding agencies, FAPESP and CNPq.
2. Roberto Schwarz, *Movimento*, 26 Jul 1977. The original essay was published as 'As idéias fora do lugar' in 1973 and later included in *Ao Vencedor as Batatas* (São Paulo, 1977).
3. See *Livros e Bibliotecas no Brasil Colonial* (Rio de Janeiro, 1979).
4. See 'Contextos de Leitura no Rio de Janeiro do século XIX: salões, gabinetes literários e bibliotecas' in Stella Bresciani, *Imagens da Cidade. Séculos XIX e XX* (São Paulo, 1993): 147–62.
5. Laurence Hallewell, *O Livro no Brasil (sua história)* (São Paulo, 1985): 117.
6. A. N. Pigoreau, *Petite bibliographie biographico-romancière, ou Dictionnaire des romanciers tans anciens que modernes, tant nationaux qu'étrangers; avec un mot sur chacun d'eux et la notice des romans qu'ils ont donné, soit comme auteurs, soit comme traducteurs, précédé d'un catalogue des meilleurs romans publiés depuis plusiers années, et suivi de tableaux propres à en faire connaître les différents genres et à diriger dans le choix des ouvrages qui doivent faire la base d'un cabinet de lecture* (Paris, Pigoreau Librarie, 1821–8, including supplements).
7. Harold W. Streeter, *The Eighteenth-Century English Novel in French Translation: A Bibliographical Study* (New York, 1941).
8. Ann Radcliffe, *The Italian, or the Confessional of the Black Penitents*, 3 vols (London, 1797) and Elizabeth Helme, *Albert, or the Wilds of Strathnavern*, 4 vols (London, 1799); for further details, see 1797: 70 and 1799: 47, respectively, in, James Raven and Antonia Forster, *The English Novel 1770–1799:*

A Bibliographical Survey of Prose Fiction Published in the British Isles [vol. 1 of Peter Garside, James Raven and Rainer Schöwerling, *The English Novel 1770–1829*] (Oxford, 2000).

9. See Marlyse Meyer, 'O que é, ou quem foi *Sinclair das Ilhas?*', *Revista do Instituto de Estudos Brasileiros*, vol. 14 (São Paulo, 1973): 37–63.

10. First novel published by Impressão Régia (the Imperial Press founded in Brazil), in 1810, from the original *Le diable boiteaux*. See Rubens Borba de Moraes, *Livros e Bibliotecas no Brasil Colonial* (Rio de Janeiro, 1979).

11. In fact by Eliza Kirkham Mathews, *Arnold Zulig: A Swiss Story by the Author of Constance, Pharos, and Argus* (London, 1790); Raven and Forster, *English Novel 1770–1799*, 1790: 56.

12. Respective original titles in French and/or English: *Le Diable Boiteaux* (*The Devil on Two Sticks*); *Paul et Virginie* (*The History of Paul and Virginia; or The Shipwreck*); *La Chaumière Indienne* (*The Indian Cottage*). *Atala* (*Atala; or The Love and Constancy of Two Savages in the Desert*); *Bélisaire* (*Belisarius, A Tale*); *Louisa or the Cottage on the Moor*; *Gulliver's Travels*; *Robinson Crusoe*; *Tom Jones*; *Arnold Zulig: A Swiss Story* (attributed to Eliza Kirkham Mathews); *Clarissa Harlowe*. The information between parentheses refers to the dates when the novels were first advertised in the newspaper.
   Since 1801, there is evidence of license requests made by the bookseller Paulo Martin, Junior, to the Portuguese Real Mesa Censória for the shipment of the French versions of Defoe's and Richardson's novels: *Aventures de Robinson Crusoe* (Paris, 1799); *Histoire de Clarisse* (Venice, 1788); *Histoire de Grandisson* (Amsterdam, 1777). For the circulation of books in the colonial period, see Márcia Abreu, *Os Caminhos dos Livros* (Campinas and São Paulo, 2003): 95–7.

13. Gilberto Freyre, *Ingleses no Brasil: Aspectos da influência britânica sobre a vida, a paisagem e a cultura do Brasil* (Rio de Janeiro, 1948); both Freyre and Hallewell state that already by 1832 the Tipografia Pinheiro, Faria and Cia published the novel *A Caverna da Morte* (*The Cavern of Death*) in Olinda; but both Frevre and Hallewell wrongly attribute its authorship to Ann Radcliffe; it remains anonymous and with no copy of the original English edn apparently surviving – see Raven and Forster, *English Novel 1770–1799*, 1794: 6.

14. The complete list of novels can be accessed at http://www.caminhosdo romance.iel.unicamp.br.

15. Machado de Assis, 'A nova geração', in Machado de Assis (ed.), *Obra completa*, 3 vols, vol. 3 (Rio de Janeiro, 1992): 813.

16. José de Alencar, 'Como e porque sou romancista', *Obra Completa*, 4 vols (Rio de Janeiro, 1965), vol. 1; Marlyse Meyer draws our attention to references to *Sinclair of the Isles*, by Mrs Helme, not only in Alencar but also in Machado de Assis and Guimarães Rosa; see Meyer, 'O que é, ou quem foi *Sinclair das Ilhas?*'.

17. See Raven and Forster, *English Novel 1770–1799*, 1796: 78; and Peter Garside and Rainer Schöwerling, *English Novel 1800–1829: A Bibliographical Survey of Prose Fiction Published in the British Isles* [vol. 2 of Peter Garside, James Raven and Rainer Schöwerling, *The English Novel 1770–1829*] 1803: 34. It was Marlyse Meyer who first recognized Helme's and Roche's work, by drawing out comments by Alencar and Machado.

18. Júlia Lopes de Almeida, *Livro das Noivas* (Rio de Janeiro, 1895): 36 ['novelas prejudiciais, insalubres, recheadas de aventuras românticas e de heróis perigosos'].
19. In the original: 'estado de timidez envergonhada'. The phrase is Antonio Candido's, in his essay, 'Timidez do romance', in Antonio Candido (ed.), *Educação pela noite e outros ensaios* (São Paulo, 1987): 82–99.
20. Candido, 'Timidez do romance', p. 88. In the original: 'validade em si mesma da mimese' and 'livre jogo da fantasia criadora', respectively.
21. Marlyse Meyer, 'Mulheres Romancistas Inglesas do Século XVIII e Romance Brasileiro', in Marlyse Meyer (ed.), *Caminhos do Imaginário no Brasil* (São Paulo, 1993): 47–72. In the original: 'as ficções imaginadas por senhoras e solteironas inglesas do século XVIII embalaram as imaginações novecentistas brasileiras'.
22. Nelson Werneck Sodré, *História da Imprensa no Brasil* (Rio de Janeiro, 1966): 227–8. In the original: 'Se a parte mais numerosa do público era constituída pelas moças casadouras e pelos estudantes, e o tema literário por excelência devia ser, por isso mesmo, o do casamento, misturado um pouco com o velho motivo do amor, a imprensa e a literatura, casadas estreitamente então, seriam levadas a atender a essa solicitação premente. A mulher começava a libertar-se, a pouco e pouco, da clausura colonial e subordinava-se aos padrões da moda européia exibindo-se nos salões e um pouco nas ruas.'
23. Delso Renault, *O Rio Antigo nos Anúncios de Jornais (1808–1850)* (Rio de Janeiro, 1969).
24. Flora Süssekind, *O Brasil não é longe daqui. O narrador. A viagem* (São Paulo, 1990): 79.
25. Antonio Candido, 'Literatura e subdesenvolvimento', in Antonio Candido (ed.), *A educação pela noite e outros ensaios* (São Paulo, 1987): 19.
26. I refer the reader once more to the complete list of British novels available in nineteenth-century Brazil; see above, note 14.
27. Wanderley Guilherme dos Santos, 'A práxis liberal no Brasil: propostas para reflexão e pesquisa', *Ordem burguesa e liberalismo político* (São Paulo, 1978): 65–117 (110).
28. Sérgio Buarque de Holanda, 'Melville', in Antonio Arnoni Prado (ed.), *O espírito e a letra: ensaios de crítica literária (1948–59)*, vol. 2 (São Paulo, 1996): 266; article originally published in *Diário Carioca*, 8 Oct 1950.
29. See Jean Marcel Carvalho França, *Literatura e Sociedade no Rio de Janeiro oitocentista* (Lisbon, 1999), where these arguments are developed and to whom I owe the ideas in this paragraph.
30. The phrase is Antonio Candido's in *Formação da Literatura Brasileira* (São Paulo, 1959).
31. Patrick Brantlinger, *The Reading Lesson: The Threat of Mass Literacy in Nineteenth-Century British Fiction* (Bloomington, IN, 1998).
32. See Abreu, *Os Caminhos dos Livros*.
33. Fernando de Azevedo, *A Cultura Brasileira: Introdução ao estudo da cultura no Brasil*, 4th edn (São Paulo, 1964): 278.
34. The phrase can be found in França, *Literatura e Sociedade*, 10.
35. José Murilo de Carvalho, *Teatro de sombras: a política imperial* (Rio de Janeiro, 1988): 116.

36. The issue has a long history; in 1873 Machado de Assis was discussing the problem in his essay *Instinto de Nacionalidade*.
37. A. F. Dutra e Mello, 'A Moreninha', *Minerva Brasiliense*, 1–2, 2 (1844): 24; 2 (15 Oct 1844): 747.
38. The reference is to Antonio Candido's essay 'Dialética da Malandragem', in Antonio Candido (ed.), *O Discurso e a Cidade* (São Paulo, 1993).
39. One should, however, recall Roberto Schwarz's reading of *Senhora*, pointing out its misfits, which of course does not diminish the interest it arouses; see his *Ao Vencedor as Batatas* (São Paulo, 1977).
40. Schwarz, *Ao Vencedor as Batatas*, 21.
41. In the same interview in *Movimento*, 26 Jul 1977, referred to at the beginning of this chapter; see above, note 2.

11
'Learning from Abroad?': Communities of Knowledge and the Monitorial System in Independent Spanish America

Eugenia Roldán Vera

The book trade between Western Europe and Spanish America increased dramatically during the first third of the nineteenth century. The various American independence movements (1808–24) generated a revolution in reading habits which coincided not only with the end of Spain's commercial monopoly over the continent, but also with the consolidation of Britain and France as mass producers and exporters of print. Between 1815 and 1830, Britain and France were actively engaged in the export of printed materials, in various languages, to Spanish American countries, especially to Mexico, Argentina, Chile, the Colombian confederation (today's Colombia, Ecuador and Venezuela), Peru, and some of the Central American states. A significant amount of this was related to educational matters. France was to remain the chief exporter of French and Spanish literature to Spanish America during most of the nineteenth century, but Britain was, for a short period, the main centre from which instructive, political and economic texts arrived. These printed items, in addition to literature from other European countries published and sent by French and British entrepreneurs and philanthropists, had an eminently didactic role for Spanish Americans in their struggle for independence from Spain and in their efforts towards nation-building.[1]

This chapter provides an examination of the relations established in this period among British, French and Spanish American learned communities, educators, intellectuals and statesmen concerning one particular kind of didactic material that was conveyed through the networks of print: literature related to the monitorial system of education.[2]

This method of schooling, devised within the British Empire by the missionary Andrew Bell in Madras, India, and the elementary schoolteacher Joseph Lancaster in a London working-class neighbourhood, and strongly promoted in Restoration France, was disseminated throughout many countries in five continents during the first half of the nineteenth century, including many in Spanish America. Its distinctive feature was the principle of pupil tuition: children were meant to teach other children in a 'mutual' fashion. This system was intended to enable the instruction of a large number of pupils through few teachers, in a short time, and at low cost. The system was extremely appealing to Spanish America because, thanks to its low cost and its ease of replication, it seemed to offer the possibility of universal elementary instruction, which was essential for the creation of citizens in the new independent order.[3] Introduced in the region around 1817, the system spread rapidly in the following years, and by 1828 virtually all Spanish American countries had issued laws institutionalizing it, either partially or totally.[4] Its popularity declined after the mid-1830s, when it began to be replaced by more teacher-centred forms of education, but it survived as an alternative method for some elements of schooling in various countries until the 1880s.

The following chapter offers an analysis of the communication of the monitorial system in print, manuals, newspapers and correspondence published in the contemporary press. I will suggest that the network through which knowledge of the system was conveyed played an important role in the manner in which that knowledge was conceived and reformulated, not only in the Spanish American countries but also in the European centres from which most of the information came. The focus will be on the initial introduction of the monitorial system, which was foundational for the very definition of this pedagogical innovation. Indeed, this is the period in which transatlantic communications gained a new intensity. At issue is the centrality of print for the dissemination and implementation of the method in Spanish America, and will then examine the composition of the networks of people through which the circulation of printed information about the monitorial system was made possible. Finally, the third and longest part of this chapter will be devoted to the study of the dynamics of the communication established between the communities of promoters of the monitorial system in Spanish America, France and Britain.

From 1816, British, French and Spanish editions of monitorial system manuals became available in several Spanish American countries. Foreign manuals were often reviewed in articles in the periodical press, where some of the first Spanish translations were published in serial form. Between 1816 and 1824 Spanish Americans had access to a number of significant documents, including a revised version of Lancaster's plan published in English by the British and Foreign School Society (BFSS); Joseph Lancaster's *Improvements on Education*; a French translation of Lancaster's *The British System of Education*; Alexander Laborde's combined plan of Bell and Lancaster in French, and also several Spanish editions of the same work; the French manual by the Count de Lasteyrie; the French edition of Joseph Hamel's report on Lancaster's system (originally published in Russian and in German); the French manual of Mme Quignon on monitorial schooling for girls, and a similar one published in English by the BFSS.[5]

These manuals provided a thorough – and multinational transatlantic – guide for the environment and conduct of a monitorial school. The reading of the manuals was supposed to be sufficient for the creation, or the conversion, of a regular school into a monitorial one. They contained detailed descriptions of the physical arrangement of the classroom, the division of levels of learning, the hierarchy of the teaching children, called monitors or instructors, and the role of the teacher, as well as the technique, form and content of the teaching itself. This method was intended to be standard and uniform in a variety of contexts, and the manuals left the teachers with very little freedom to improvise. Indeed, in a monitorial school it was the method more than the skills or even the knowledge of the teacher that was key to the successful functioning of the teaching process. Teacher requirements were reduced to a minimum. As a monitorial manual put it, 'Such is the excellence of the plan of the British system that if the organization of the school be exactly maintained, even a moderate degree of learning on the part of the master, provided he possesses the higher qualifications, will be sufficient'.[6]

The monitorial school drew inspiration from the rationalized factory work of industrial England. It aspired to be a perfectly regulated environment in which every activity was planned and programmed in advance. Everything was structured around a sophisticated and pervasive choreography of movements and exercises that were intended to guarantee the full attention and the individual progress of each pupil. A large group of students (500–1,000) was divided into small classes of six to ten students, according to their level of learning, each of which was led by a monitor. Monitors were pupils with a slightly higher level of knowledge and they, in turn, answered to a general monitor responsible for order, who was under the direct command of the teacher. The students were ranked within their small classes according to their performance, and with every exercise they moved up and down the ranking. Whoever reached the highest level of his class at the end of a given lesson was either promoted to the next class or became monitor of the same one. A complex system of registers of school attendance, of ascending and descending order of pupils within their classes or across classes, and of individual prizes and punishments, all contributed to the control of the pupils' behaviour. The school day was divided into short units of exercises that were different for every class, and each class performed its individual exercises conducted by its own monitor. These exercises by the different classes took place simultaneously together in one large classroom. The manuals provided the sequence of lessons for each class and the tasks were performed on the commands issued by the general monitors of each of the subjects taught. The teacher simply had to supervise the correct functioning of the whole classroom.[7]

It is clear that the most important requirement for teachers of monitorial schools was that they had a detailed understanding of the method. Given that normal (model) schools for the training of teachers were merely a further step in the implementation of the system, the printed manuals of the monitorial system were fundamental to its introduction and initial expansion in areas as distant from Britain as Spanish America. In theory, a pupil who had completed his education in a monitorial school could start teaching in any other one. Manuals constituted a direct guide for teachers, for benefactors and for administrators of the Lancasterian Societies who ran some of the monitorial schools, and for members of the municipal authorities who supervised or administered others. The manuals were also an important medium by which to publicize the method and to ensure that public opinion was favourable to its implementation. Even so, manuals were not the only printed element necessary for the teaching process. The monitorial system spared the need for individual textbooks for the students, but tables for the teaching of reading and arithmetic were essential in the classroom, as well as printed instructions for the monitors (when the latter were not available, manuscript copies were used). The tables were normally printed locally, although there is evidence that British and French Lancasterian Societies sent to Spanish America copies of tables printed in Spain. Moreover, in Spanish American monitorial schools catechisms of religion and civic catechisms were also often employed in the classroom, but it was not essential that each child had his or her own book.

How did these manuals make their way from Europe to Spanish America? In a period in which the book trade between the Spanish

American countries and France and Britain was not formally established, the shipment of books occurred in a variety of ways. Although the end of the commercial monopoly of Spain over her colonies meant that large quantities of French and British books began to arrive in Spanish America in the 1810s and 1820s, this flow of print was not uniform and did not develop its own channels of trade but depended on contingent agents. With a few exceptions, before 1840 it was not customary for European publishing houses to send their shipments directly to selected booksellers, nor were these houses used to opening branches in the region.[8] This particular kind of instructive literature had its own specific channels of circulation, the human component of which was very important. Indeed, networks of print were also networks of individuals, in this case a relatively small number of individuals, and an analysis of the interaction of those individuals is essential to understand the further development of monitorial schooling on both sides of the Atlantic.

There were three different channels of the transatlantic book trade that were particularly relevant to the introduction and circulation of material relating to the monitorial system. The first channel comprised the groups of British and French merchants who arrived in Spanish America in search of opportunities for trade and investment. In general, these were not professional booksellers, but mainly individuals involved in diverse activities that ranged from trade in manufactured goods and luxury items to engagement in agricultural, mining or colonization companies. Most of the merchants interacted with the local elites and some joined the civic associations that began to emerge in the post-independence era. Such associations were created for the development of sport, music, theatre, 'good taste' and knowledge. They included societies for the promotion of the monitorial method, especially in port cities like Buenos Aires. As part of their business, these foreigners transported a number of books that were left on consignment in local shops, only some of them bookshops. Most of those books were cheap literature, but there were also instructive texts, including manuals of the monitorial system.[9]

A second, very different channel for the importation of European books into the region resulted from the network of Spanish American diplomats, politicians and émigrés resident in Europe during the 1810s and 1820s. South Americans in Europe included representatives of Spanish American governments to the Spanish Cortes, who also used the opportunity to travel around France and Britain; chargés d'affaires, who sought acknowledgement of the independence of their countries from the governments of the European powers; and official envoys, who had a mission to contract loans and recruit investors for mining or agricultural enterprises. The émigrés also included independence-fighters in exile, who gathered money or purchased weapons for the cause. Together, these Spanish Americans formed a relatively small group of highly cosmopolitan individuals who were extremely active in the conveying of information and print between the European centres and the New World.[10] Most of what they chose to send to their superiors, friends, relatives, or for the enrichment of their own libraries had a didactic, enlightening purpose, as its intention was to assist the ruling elites involved in the design and organization of their new nations.

It is therefore not surprising that evidence suggests that a great deal of the printed information on the monitorial method arrived in Spanish America through this channel. Of various examples, the Mexican politician Lucas Alamán obtained the French translation of a text by Joseph Hamel about the system while he was travelling in France after taking part in the Spanish Cortes of 1820. Alamán used that manual as the basis for an abridgement of the method he published on his return to Mexico.[11] During the trip, Alamán also came across French texts of Laborde and de Lasteyrie, and apparently visited a monitorial school in England. Similarly, Andrés Bello, a prominent Venezuelan intellectual exiled in London, sent a number of books to Caracas with the specific purpose of facilitating the introduction of the monitorial system there. In one of his regular shipments to his brother he included the following texts: the New Testament in Spanish for use in monitorial schools (a Spanish translation published by the British and Foreign Bible Society (BFBS) in London); the BFSS *Manual of the System of Teaching* in English; the directions of the BFSS for the organization of Lancasterian Societies; and de Lasteyrie's *Nouveau systéme*.[12] These books enabled Carlos Bello to operate one of the first monitorial schools in Venezuela in 1823, a role to which he was appointed by the local municipality. A further example of this personalized flow of information was that of Manuel Codorniu: a Spanish delegate to the Spanish Cortes in 1820, he travelled afterwards to Mexico and brought with him the French translation of a work of Lancaster by de Lasteyrie (1815), which served as the basis for the manual published by the Mexican Compañía Lancasteriana in 1824.

Finally, a third channel for the shipment and distribution of Lancasterian manuals was that provided by the British and French societies devoted to the promotion of monitorial teaching, that is the BFSS and the Société pour l'Instruction Élémentaire (SIE). As will be argued below, both societies were engaged in publishing, translating and sometimes shipping books and tables of school lessons, either through their agents in different countries or in response to specific requests from teachers.

The arrival of the first British, French and Spanish editions of the manuals for the monitorial system formed the basis for the further production of monitorial manuals in the Spanish American countries themselves, a process through which the method underwent significant variations and was imbued with new values.[13] This initial moment of arrival of information about the monitorial system is significant, for it was then that a particular dynamic of exchange on educational matters was established between learned communities on both sides of the Atlantic. Indeed, in a book trade that was not subject to the rules of the free market, the role of the political and cultural Spanish American elites in the selection and transportation of printed material was decisive. These elites established close relations with European travellers and investors as well as with the British and French educational societies. Together, these three kinds of agents not only mobilized information about the monitorial system, but they also helped to shape the knowledge itself.

The introduction of printed manuals and their translation and reprinting in the Spanish American countries contributed to the rapid expansion of the monitorial system in the first half of the 1820s. Yet, for all their detailed content, the manuals were not completely self-explanatory to many of their promoters. Indeed, the first information about the system in the form of manuals or newspaper articles generated a desire to learn even more about it. Accordingly, individuals in Spanish America and members of the local Lancasterian Societies began to write to the European societies which had published the manuals and who were involved in the promotion of the system both at home and abroad. It was through the interaction of these parties, united by their interest in monitorial schooling, that distinct learned communities were formed on both sides of the Atlantic. As suggested below, the particular dynamic of the relations established between these communities both defined the role of each of the parties involved in the communication, and shaped the production of educational knowledge in general. Moreover, because the majority of their correspondence was published in the contemporary press, and because some of these printed materials were sent to further interested parties, this exchange can also be regarded as embedded in the networks of print, and shaped by the conditions that affect a printed object.

The two main British and French societies devoted to the local promotion of the monitorial system developed an overseas orientation almost simultaneously in the mid-1810s. The London-based BFSS, founded in 1808,[14] set up a foreign fund in 1817 for the dispatch of books and teachers abroad.[15] For its part, the French SIE created in 1818 a committee for foreign schools with the intention of the propagation of this 'great, liberal and useful [mutual] method'; that is, for the shipment of books, tables, slates and teachers abroad.[16] The other British society committed to the monitorial system, the National Society for Promoting the Education of the Poor on the Principles of the Established Church (founded on the teachings of Andrew Bell, and a rival of the BFSS) also had a missionary dimension, but was apparently not active in independent Spanish America.

In line with its international orientation, the BFSS sent two teachers to Spanish America, James Thomson (between 1818 and 1825) and Henry Dunn (in 1831). The BFSS also certified a third, Anthony Eaton, at the request of the Chilean legation. Of these three, only Thomson was successful in his mission, and he became a key figure in the foundation and expansion of monitorial schools and schools for teachers in several cities throughout Argentina, Uruguay, Chile, Peru and Colombia.[17] Through Thomson, the BFSS also introduced timetables of lessons (from both England and Spain), slates and other school materials. Thomson was also an agent of the BFBS and in this capacity he introduced a considerable number of Bibles and New Testaments in Spanish and in some indigenous languages. The BFSS and the BFBS were sister societies. Most of their members belonged to both associations and both oriented themselves by a non-denominational principle, in contrast to the parallel societies sponsored by the Church of England with similar purposes. The distribution of the Bible and the creation of elementary schools were related missionary activities: only literate societies would be able to read the Bible, and the mere availability of Bibles in societies of a limited culture of print would promote the desire to learn to read. As noted above, the BFSS intended that its schools used excerpts of the New Testament for the teaching of religion. There is also evidence that the SIE sent timetables of school lessons (in French), slates and other materials to Argentina and Chile, mainly at the request of French teachers running private schools in those countries. The SIE was, however, mainly active in the non-Spanish-speaking countries of the region, such as Haiti and Brazil. The SIE had closer links with Spain, especially as it trained Spanish teachers resident in Paris who were later sent back to found schools in their own country.[18]

In fact, rather than a direct involvement in the appointment of teachers, an area in which both the BFSS and the SIE were far more proactive in other regions of the world, a more important dimension of the activities of both societies in the American continent was the exchange of correspondence and materials between these European societies and the politicians, intellectuals and members of Lancasterian Societies in various Spanish American countries.

The correspondence between the British and French societies and the Spanish American promoters of the monitorial method was regularly published in the monthly edition of the *Journal d'Éducation* of the SIE and in the *Annual Reports* of the BFSS. In addition, excerpts of the correspondence were often published in Spanish American journals. Moreover, copies of the British and French journals were sometimes sent by the societies themselves, or by diplomatic envoys, to the Spanish American countries. The fact that this correspondence was printed, both in the centres that were distributing the information and in the places that were receiving it, gave the communication a public dimension, and contributed to making discussion about the mutual method an open one.

Between 1818 and 1828, the SIE maintained regular correspondence with a number of significant individuals: the Central American and Colombian envoys in London, Marcial Zebadúa and José María Restrepo; the Guatemala-based politician and intellectual José Cecilio del Valle; the secretary of the Philanthropic Society of Bogotá, José María Esteves; the Mexican politician Lucas Alamán; the Argentinian envoy in London (later president of his country) Bernardino Rivadavia; and the Italian resident in England Joseph Pecchio, who acted as a conduit between certain Spanish Americans (Zebadúa and Valle) and the SIE. The SIE's sphere of influence overlapped with that of the BFSS, which also had direct contact with Alamán, Zebadúa and Rivadavia, especially during their period of residence in London but also after they had returned to their own countries. The BFSS was also in contact with the Mexican envoy in London, Vicente Rocafuerte (later president of his native Ecuador), and with his Chilean counterpart José Irisarri, as well as with two independent British teachers, John Armstrong in Buenos Aires and James Watts in Colombia. Many of its correspondents had formed part of the circle of Spanish American diplomats and émigrés in London, and it was during their English residence that they made contact with the BFSS for the first time. The BFSS also had a strong connection to Spanish America through the abundant correspondence of its agent in the region, James Thomson.[19] Thomson regularly sent the BFSS lists of Spanish Americans with whom the society could communicate directly; the lists included the names of high-ranking politicians and clergymen involved in the promotion of public instruction.[20]

Letters came to and from both sides of the ocean usually accompanied by books, pamphlets or newspaper cuttings about the monitorial system. There was, however, a fundamental difference in what was received in each continent. The Spanish Americans, who usually initiated the contact, almost always requested experienced teachers, timetables of lessons, teachers' manuals, school textbooks, school materials, and books of general knowledge for a wider audience. Valle even suggested that the SIE should sponsor the creation of a 'popular library' in the city of Guatemala.[21] When the European societies replied, they did indeed send timetables of lessons, school materials (although these normally had to be purchased), and occasionally a manual on the monitorial method. However, instead of teachers, popular books or financial sponsorship for local libraries, European societies sent certificates of membership for their own society, copies of their internal regulations and instructions for the creation of Lancasterian Societies modelled upon their own.

The SIE and the BFSS received from the Spanish Americans (or from Thomson in the latter's case) a number of newspaper cuttings, which described the local progress of monitorial schools and the most recent laws that institutionalized the monitorial method, as well as the printed regulations of local Lancasterian Societies and monitorial schools. The latter were usually accompanied by a note requesting observations and advice from the societies on the improvement of the organization of their work. On only a few occasions did Spanish American correspondents send a book from their own country to the SIE in the hope of obtaining comments and approval from the organization: Valle sent his own *Memory on Education* to the SIE and requested in return one or two copies of elementary books in French that he would translate 'for the instruction of his people'.[22] Alamán sent a copy of a *Civic Catechism* by Miguel Busto, which was reviewed by the SIE's Spanish correspondent José Mariano Vallejo and stored in its library.

In this exchange it is evident that Spanish Americans were looking for validation of their local policies from those whom they regarded as the authorities in educational matters. It appeared to be an essential element in the process of converting the educational system, inherited from the Spanish, into a modern programme that was free of the vices of the old order. By sending information about their local activities leading Spanish Americans expected to be evaluated and to receive approval that would legitimate their work. Yet the BFSS and the SIE were also seeking validation for themselves in these exchanges. Local benefactors were easier to attract if the societies could prove that they worked for the international expansion of the method and that their engagements abroad were fruitful. In that sense, the SIE often advertised with pride that it counted Valle, Zebadúa and Restrepo among its foreign correspondents in America. The BFSS, through its success overseas, obtained local recognition and was in a position to compete for importance with the Anglican National Society for Promoting Education. In the case of the SIE, overseas membership meant not only an increase in favourable public opinion and the securing of local benefactors,[23] but through the export of the mutual method the SIE contributed to the assertion of France's 'civilizing mission'.[24]

The dissemination of the mutual method was especially important for the SIE's identity; it allowed the society to recover for France ground that had been lost in not having actually *invented* this endeavour. Indeed, whatever resistance there was in France to the mutual method, or *enseignement mutuel,* was mostly related to its *English* origin. For those who thought of the method as beneficial, the fact that such a source of enlightenment and civil improvement was not a French invention was hard to swallow: 'The [mutual] method has been accused of being English (and we believe it!), that is taken to be a mistake, an unforgivable mistake for some spirits', wrote the Duc de La Rochefoucauld in 1819, and, 'I could, like many of my countrymen, claim this invention to my own homeland, and that would not lack foundations.'[25] It was in response to this preoccupation that many French manuals attempted to locate the innovators of the mutual method in their own country. Regardless of whether this claim of invention was convincing or not, the concern regarding France's role was played out and partly resolved in the relations established between the SIE and other countries who wished to implement the method. For the leading members of the SIE it was, after all, not disastrous that the system was not a French invention, provided that France knew how to take advantage of it and was able to turn it into something positive for itself and for others. It was evident that France had the 'spirit of invention' and that it *could* have created the method.

France had an even loftier ambition: that of 'taking advantage of all discoveries and inventions from wherever they came as long as they were useful to the welfare of mankind'.[26] France, 'the most enlightened of all nations in the progress of the arts and sciences' had not only to 'live up to its reputation', but also to 'get ahead of Europe' by perfectly implementing the monitorial method.[27] It was through this process that France would be able 'to contribute to the welfare of the people, to achieve national glory and prosperity, and to be prepared for the sweetest and most honourable conquests'.[28] Therefore, in its mission to perfect the monitorial method for the benefit of mankind, it is clear that the SIE was keen to extend its sphere of influence into other continents, to establish correspondence with influential individuals abroad, and to send them certificates of membership and copies of its internal regulations in order for them to replicate its organizational model. However, this did not mean that the SIE was willing, or indeed able, to meet the concrete demands for books, materials and teachers that it received from its foreign correspondents.

For the Spanish Americans involved in Lancasterian Societies or in government educational policy, their relationship with the European educational societies also meant more than an external legitimation of their internal reforms, or merely the possibility of obtaining schoolbooks, materials and skilled teachers. Those with access to the societies' materials and the exchange of local information about the monitorial system might regard themselves as members of a higher community of learned men. Most Spanish Americans defined themselves as youthful and in a state of receptivity after three centuries of Spanish-forbidden access to the enlightened part of the world; contact with other learned men was for them a way to prove their 'civilized' status whether as a society or a group. In fact, the most frequently cited justification for the adoption of the system in the Spanish American manuals was that it had already been adopted by the most 'civilized' nations in 'the most cultured nations of Europe'.[29] Thus, the monitorial method itself was not only a vehicle for the enlightenment of society, but a direct link to civilization. In some cases the argument employed in the French manuals regarding the need to catch up with a system that could be perfected locally was enthusiastically transplanted to Spanish America: '[Although] we have started late with this kind of teaching', wrote one of the founders of the Lancasterian Company of Mexico City, 'thanks to the positive influence of a society made of a large number of wise and patriot citizens, soon we will get ahead of the countries that adopted it much earlier than us.'[30]

Valle, a man of letters who never travelled to Europe but who maintained a fervent correspondence with a number of European intellectuals, took this line of argument even further to express his hope for what the 'family' of learned men in both continents could achieve together for the benefit of the rest of the world. In a letter to Pecchio, translator of a manual of the monitorial system into Italian and his main link with the SIE, he wrote:

I deeply cherish the correspondence with men who, like you, cultivate the letters with success. I pray God that similar relations may be established between the European friends of sciences and the Americans who share that interest!... [Through this communication] the universal improvement of the human species will make immense progress; the friends of the sciences will be interested in the bonds that unite them, and together they will form one family with which, in happy harmony, the united children of Europe and America can contribute to the welfare of the people of Africa, Asia and Australasia.[31]

Passages like these make the Spanish American understanding of the monitorial system appear closer to that of the French rather than the English, its original invention in France being a system aimed at giving some instruction to the children of the poor, as well as inculcating them with notions of subordination. After all, in their embrace of the system as an instrument for mass instruction that would prevent the repetition of the excesses of the Revolution, it was the French promoters of the *enseignement mutuel* who first attributed to the monitorial method the capacity to provide a full education 'intellectual, moral and religious'.[32] In addition, it was the French who considered it appropriate for a variety of subjects beyond the three Rs and religion, and even deemed it suitable for 'the first classes of society'.[33] These were all approaches adopted wholeheartedly by the Spanish Americans, who extended the French interpretation even further. It cannot simply be concluded that such concerns were 'imported' to the Spanish American countries, for the latter had their own political agendas and cultural conditioning. However, it is undeniable that the French mediation in the communication of knowledge about the monitorial method from Britain to Spanish America, through the reading of French manuals and through the exchange of correspondence with French educational officials, significantly influenced the ways in which the method was appropriated on the other side of the Atlantic. Moreover, in terms of the system's characteristics as a vehicle of 'social happiness', Spanish Americans took a step forward from the French. In newly independent Spanish America, the monitorial method was strongly associated with very concrete political concerns: it was not only the universal education promised by the cheapness and efficiency of the method that the new ruling elites found exciting, but, as argued above, the actual educational techniques of the method were given particular republican meanings.[34]

It was not only the information and the items exchanged between Spanish Americans and European societies that played an important role in the definition of the nature of the mutual method. The very terms on which that exchange was based affected the manner in which the method was appropriated and developed. Although knowledge of the monitorial method was regarded as an element that united communities of enlightened men on both sides of the ocean, from the beginning, the language used in this communication shaped the features of a relationship between parties who were essentially unequal.

The texts and correspondence regarding the mutual method are rich in metaphors of commercial exchange and exploitation of natural resources. The French Count de Lasteyrie fully embraced his country's civilizing mission and described the 'export' of the method to the Americas as follows:

> The New World, which seems to have been discovered only to fulfil the bloody greediness of the Europeans, has just received from their hands a treasure [the mutual method of education] which is much more precious than the products which have caused, during a considerable time, so much injustice, wars and devastation.[35]

In drawing upon the 'black legend' with which the European powers condemned Spain's colonial rule in the region, and thus reasserting France's 'righteous' position in that respect, de Lasteyrie seemed to imply that the monitorial system could somehow compensate for past ravages. For the agent of the BFSS in South America, James Thomson, such ravages had not necessarily disappeared with the end of the colonial period, but he too presented the monitorial method as a European gift that could counterbalance centuries of exploitation. In a letter to the BFSS, he commented:

> Your Committee rejoice that the advantages of education, and the superior excellence of the British System are duly appreciated in the States of South America. And it affords them high gratification to reflect, that while by speculation and commerce so many are aiming to acquire the wealth of the New World, the efforts of enlightened zeal are employed, in conveying to the inhabitants those truths which an inspired writer declares to be 'more precious than gold'.[36]

In spite of his criticism of foreign speculators, Thomson regarded the monitorial method as a fair payment for the natural wealth that Europeans were extracting from this territory. The transaction was thus presented as an exchange of European knowledge for American natural resources; while the Europeans were extracting natural richness, the Americans were receiving the better part of the deal: enlightenment. In a typical reproduction of colonial dynamics, these were exactly the terms in which the Spanish Americans framed their relationship with the British and French educational societies and with other influential European intellectuals. For Valle, an avid reader and prolific writer, the exchange of educational knowledge outranked that of agricultural products and precious metals. In the same letter to Pecchio, who forwarded it to the SIE, Valle expressed his desire: 'With great joy I expect to see the establishment of a communication of thoughts which will be more important than the exchange of products from the land or the mines; an exchange more useful than the trade of vanilla, of cochineal and of indigo!'[37]

In the same way that the export of natural produce in return for the import of knowledge could not be of equal value, neither could the exchange of information between Spanish American politicians and European educational societies. Valle himself offers a notable example of the terms in which that relationship between 'the friends of the sciences' on both sides of the Atlantic was framed. In his abundant correspondence with men of science such as George A. Thompson, Vicente Rocafuerte, Abbé de Pradt, Jean-Baptiste Say, Álvaro Flórez Estrada, José Joaquín de Mora, Jullien de Paris and Alexander von Humboldt, Valle often included a number of his own texts. Valle sent copies of the paper he edited, *El Redactor*, to Rocafuerte (as envoy in London), Pradt, Say, Flórez Estrada, Mora and Humboldt; the articles he wanted the Europeans to read were those entitled 'Descripción de la República de Centroamérica', 'Noticia de los cinco estados que forman Centroamérica y de la Constitución de cada uno de ellos, 'Discurso sobre la importancia de la República Centroamericana para mantener el equilibrio y asegurar la paz en las otras de América', 'Descripción de Suchitepeques, departamento de Guatemala', 'Descripción de Quetzaltenango, departamento de Guatemala', 'Arancel provincial de los derechos de importación y exportación', 'Proyecto de una Expedición científica' and 'Pensamientos sobre el Congreso de Panamá', among others. To the editors of *Biblioteca Americana*, a Spanish magazine published in London by a group of Spanish American exiles and envoys, Valle sent his 'Noticias y datos que puedan dar nombre a Guatemala'. And to Jullien de Paris, editor of the

French *Revue Encyclopédique*, he sent his 'Exposición sobre la libertad de comercio' and a 'Memoria sobre agricultura, industria y comercio'.

While Valle sent particular texts on the history, nature, politics and education of his native Central America, he asked his correspondents to send him different kinds of works. Typically, he wrote to Álvaro Florez Estrada, a Spanish exile in London who had written an influential treatise on political economy:

> I wish that every wise man of Europe devotes his talent to design the Plan that the American Republics should follow in their internal and external affairs...[38] You, who have put together in a book the most useful that to date has been written in England, France, Italy and Germany, would make your work more useful if you united the theory with precise indications as to what is best for the Spanish American states to achieve wealth and prosperity. Your work would then have a double value in the new world, and your soul would enjoy the satisfaction of having shown the way to emerging societies that need a guide or preceptor.[39]

Although Valle's letters were both factual and deeply philosophical, the Honduran placed himself, vis-à-vis 'the wise men of Europe', in a position of inferiority in terms of knowledge production. Thus, while he was providing specific information about his country and clearly seeking approval for the policies he was introducing locally, he requested that the Europeans should use this information to make plans and instructions for improving the organization of the emerging Spanish American states. A similar dynamic was established in the relationships between a number of prominent Spanish American statesmen, Rivadavia, Bolívar, Santander and their British mentor Jeremy Bentham, who was also an advocator of the monitorial method in the Americas. The Spanish Americans would send Bentham copies of local legislation and projects for government administration, trade, education or prison reform, expecting to obtain from the English thinker not only validation but also rules, methods and general plans for the government of their countries. This was exactly the pattern of exchange established between the Spanish Americans and the British and French educational societies. By sending their regulations, lists of schools and catalogues of achievements, the Spanish Americans were giving particular information about the introduction and development of the monitorial method in their countries. In return, the European societies provided the methods, plans and models that could best serve the Spanish American nations in the organization of their schools. The secretary of the Philanthropic Society of Bogotá described his expectations in this exchange with the SIE in 1827:

> You are an illustrious body devoted to the prosperity and welfare of the new republics, after doing so much for the public instruction in your own soil. Indeed [you] deeply know the nature of our limitations and our needs, and [you] are going to help us in the most open and generous way to destroy in our country the evils of ignorance...This society [of Bogotá]...expects to receive from the experience of the enlightenment of the most celebrated men who form the SIE, information about the books, methods and instructions that are most appropriate to expand and improve public education in Colombia.[40]

The botanical metaphor well illustrates the way in which the production and flow of information between Europe and Spanish America was perceived. Valle's correspondence with the Europeans and Bentham's with the Spanish Americans is littered with references to the gathering and classification of plants. Both authors urge their correspondents to participate in a botanical collaboration aiming at the correct identification of American species. Yet in both cases it is clear that the role of the Spanish Americans was merely to collect exotic species for dispatch to Europe, where professional botanists would classify them and integrate them into the general body of knowledge. Bentham concluded a letter of educational advice to Rivadavia by requesting an introduction to any Argentine willing to start a botanical relationship with him:

> Should any such [man interested in botany] fall in your way, to whom it would be matter of amusement to communicate to this quarter of the globe specimens of the natural riches of the vegetable kingdom in your Republic, I would with all due gratitude in the character of trustee for the fraternity of European Botanists accept, in that shape in which I ever receive payment for any such little service as it may be in the power of my labours to render to the species of animals to which I belong.[41]

Valle even suggested that it was necessary for the great naturalists and geographers to go to America, following the example of Alexander von Humboldt, in order to gather information and the biological or mineral samples necessary for the grand scientific theories that the Spanish

Americans were not yet able to formulate. The land was rich but the people were not able to cultivate this richness:

> The natural resources of this republic are immense. The country has a happy geographical location: the land is fertile, the temperatures are diverse, the vegetation is prodigious, the mountains are rich, nature is great and majestic. But this nature has not been yet cultivated by the powerful hand of art. We do not have men, and the enlightenment that gives life to the peoples is still missing.[42]

The dynamic of this communication was that America supplied the raw materials and Europe the theory and science. America was rich in nature, it was the region of political revolutions and of social transformation. It was a territory that could serve as a source for the elaboration of European theories, plans and models. These same theories, plans and models would, in turn, provide guidance for the Spanish American republics in the process of their reinvention as independent, modern states. Yet a very important aspect of this flow of information was that both interlocutors understood their relationship as a collaborative one. Botany, by definition, required a local process of sample gathering, and a process of classification that could be done, or *had to be done*, elsewhere, by someone who had the necessary scholarly apparatus to integrate the findings into the established body of knowledge. Botanical knowledge was produced through the interaction of two worlds with different resources and ways of thinking. Similarly, although on a different scale, the flow of information across various parts of the globe *produced* a particular kind of educational knowledge, knowledge that was being constructed on both sides of the Atlantic through the very process of the exchange.

In the process of internationalization of any kind of educational knowledge, the networks of communication play a fundamental role. As this chapter has argued, not only do such networks allow the transmission of information, but they also affect the very process of the production of knowledge and its meaning. The study of the exchange of information between European and Spanish American societies for the promotion of monitorial teaching reveals flows in both directions. All parties expected and received something in the exchange. France frequently acted as an intermediary in communications between Great Britain, where the method first originated, and Spanish America, and this partly explains the civilizing power attributed to the model in the New World. The values with which the method was endowed in Spanish

America were developed through the association of its pedagogical techniques with local concerns and the particular political projects of the receiving countries.

In their relationship with the European societies, the Spanish American elites sought validation for the introduction of a system that was previously unknown in the region, as well as a more general legitimation within the new political order. However, the European societies also sought legitimation as an objective of the exchange. The issue of the origin of the method, which was problematic for France, was resolved by the SIE through the act of establishing relations with other countries for the dissemination of the benefits of this educational innovation. By contrast, the widespread missionary activities of the BFSS allowed it to compete for prominence with the Anglican National Society for Promoting Education in the promotion of the method. It also made the work of the BFSS's sister society, the BFBS, viable. Moreover, the language in which the communication between the European and Spanish American societies was framed, with its metaphors of commercial and natural exchange, gave shape to an epistemological relationship based on the 'extraction' of local produce. Unprocessed fragments of information about the political and educational characteristics of the countries were paid for with knowledge, methods, plans and directions for the new members of the ruling elites. Study of the networks of communication through print, understood not only as the means for the transmission of certain knowledge but also as constitutive of that knowledge, assists in the understanding of the internationalization of educational and other kinds of knowledge. By focusing on the complexity and multi-directionality of the communication process we may move away from static notions of the production and reception of ideas, and instead move closer to the relational dimension which is present in any process of the production of knowledge.

Notes

1. Research for this paper was originally carried out during the course of a Humboldt postdoctoral fellowship at the Comparative Education Centre of the Humboldt University, Berlin, funded by the Alexander Humboldt Foundation. I am most grateful to the Department of Educational Research at CINVESTAV, Mexico City, for institutional support in the process of writing and submitting this chapter.
2. In Spanish America, the system was known indistinctly as 'monitorial', 'mutual', or 'Lancasterian', terms which are used as synonymous below.

3. On the development of the monitorial system of education in the different Spanish American countries, see, among others, Domingo Amunátegui Solar, *El sistema de Láncaster en Chile i en otros países sudamericanos* (Santiago, Imprenta Cervantes, 1895); Myriam Báez Osorio, 'La escuela lancasteriana en Colombia', *Revista de Ciencias de la Educación* 155 (1993): 381–97; Rafael Fernández Heres, *Sumario sobre la escuela caraqueña de Joseph Lancaster* (1824–27) (Caracas, 1984); Marcelo Caruso, 'The Persistence of Educational Semantics: Patterns of Variation in Monitorial Schooling in Colombia (1821–1844)', *Paedagogica Historica* 41, 6 (2005): 721–44; Claudina López y Mariano Narodowsky, 'El mejor de los métodos posibles: la introducción del método lancasteriano en Iberoamérica en el temprano siglo XIX', in María Helena Cámara Bastos and Luciano Mendes de Faria Filho (eds), *A escola elementar no século XIX: o método monitorial/mutuo* (Passo Fundo, 1999): 44–72; Eugenia Roldán Vera, 'The Monitorial System of Education and Civic Culture in Early Independent Mexico', *Paedagogica Historica* 35, 2 (1999): 279–331; Eugenia Roldán Vera, 'Order in the Classroom: The Spanish American Appropriation of the Monitorial System of Education', *Paedagogica Historica* 41, 6 (2005): 655–75; Dorothy Tanck, 'Las escuelas lancasterianas en la ciudad de México', *Historia Mexicana* 32, 4 (1973): 494–513.
4. On the introduction and early expansion of the monitorial system in Spanish America, see Eugenia Roldán Vera and Thomas Schupp, 'Bridges over the Atlantic: A Network Analysis of the Introduction of the Monitorial System of Education in Early-Independent Spanish America', *Comparativ – Leipziger Beiträge zu Universalgeschichte und vergleichenden Gesellschaftsforschung* 15 (2005): 58–93.
5. Charles Philibert de Lasteyrie, *Nouveau système d'éducation pour les Écoles primaires, adoptée dans les quatre parties du monde* (Paris, Deterville, 1815; Paris, L. Colas, 1819); Joseph Lancaster, *Système anglais d'instruction, ou Recueil complet des améliorations et inventions mises en pratique aux écoles royales en Angleterre, par Joseph Lancaster*, tr. par le duc de La Rochefoucauld-Liancourt (Paris, Mme Huzard, 1815); British and Foreign School Society, *Manual of the System of Teaching Reading, Writing, Arithmetic, and Needle-Work* (London, 1816); Alexandre Louis Joseph de Laborde, *Plan d'éducation pour les enfans pauvres, d'après les deux Méthodes combinées du docteur Bell et de M. Lancaster* (Paris, L. Colas, 1815, 1816, 1819); Alexandre Louis Joseph de Laborde, *Plan de enseñanza para escuelas de primeras letras, según los métodos combinados del Dr. Bell y del Sr. Lancaster: adaptados á la religión católica* (Paris?, 1816; Mallorca, Imp. Real, 1819); *Lecciones de enseñanza mútua segun los métodos combinados por Bell y Lancaster, ó Plan de educación para los niños pobres* (Valencia, Manuel Muñoz y Compañia, 1818); Joseph Hamel, *Der gegenseitige Unterricht; Geschichte seiner Einführung und Ausbreitung durch Dr. A. Bell, J. Lancaster und andere* (Paris, Bey Firmin Didot, 1818); Sociedad económica gaditana de amigos del país, Cádiz, *Manual practico de método de mutua enseñanza: para las escuelas de primeras letras* (Cádiz, Hércules, 1818); Mme. Quignon, *Manuel des écoles élémentaires pour les filles, ou Précis de la méthode d'enseignement mutuel appliquée a la lecture, a l'écriture, au calcul et a la couture* (Paris, L. Colas, 1819). For a study of the manuals used as sources for each of the Spanish American manuals published in the 1820s and 1830s, see Eugenia Roldán Vera, 'Internacionalización pedagógica

y comunicación en perspectiva histórica: la introducción del método de enseñanza mutua en Hispanoamérica independiente', in Marcelo Caruso and Heinz-Elmar Tenorth (eds), *Internacionalización: Semántica y sistemas educativos en perspectiva comparada* (Buenos Aires, 2008).

6. BFSS, *Manual of the System of Teaching Reading, Writing, Arithmetic, and Needle-Work, in the Elementary Schools of the British and Foreign School Society* (London, 1816).

7. Andrew Bell, *Instructions for Conducting a School, through the Agency of the Scholars Themselves: Comprising the Analysis of an Experiment in Education, Made at the Male Asylum, Madras, 1789–1796* (London, J. Murray, 1808).

8. See Eugenia Roldán Vera, *The British Book Trade and Spanish American Independence: Education and Knowledge Transmission in Transcontinental Perspective* (Aldershot, 2003).

9. For the role of this kind of agent in the distribution of the books published by the house of Rudolph Ackermann in the 1820s, see Roldán Vera, *The British Book Trade and Spanish American Independence*, ch. 3.

10. The most comprehensive study of the political and educational activities of these individuals considered as a group is Karen Racine, 'Imagining Independence: London's Spanish-American Community, 1790–1829' (unpublished Ph.D. dissertation, Tulane University, 1996); see also María Teresa Berruezo León, *La lucha de Hispanoamérica por su independencia en Inglaterra* (Madrid, 1989).

11. Lucas Alamán, 'Instrucción para el establecimiento de escuelas, según los principios de la enseñanza mutua, presentada a la Excma. Diputación Provincial de México', *La Sabatina Universal* (México), 16–18 (Sept–Oct 1822).

12. Carlos Bello to the municipality of Caracas, 16 Aug 1824, cited in Fernández Heres, *Sumario sobre la escuela caraqueña*, 62.

13. On these variations, see for example, Roldán Vera, 'The Monitorial System of Education and Civic Culture'.

14. Originally founded with the name of 'Lancasterian Institution for Promoting the Education of the Labouring and Manufacturing Classes of Society of Every Religious Persuasion', the society was re-founded in 1814 as the 'British and Foreign School Society' after it distanced itself administratively from Joseph Lancaster.

15. See George F. Bartle, 'The Teaching Manuals and Lessons Books of the British and Foreign School Society', *History of Education Society* 46 (Autumn 1990): 22–33.

16. Raymond Tronchot, 'L'enseignement mutuel en France de 1815 a 1833: les luttes politiques et religieuses autour de la question scolaire', 3 vols, vol. 1 (unpublished PhD thesis, University of Paris, 1970): 440.

17. See James Thomson, *Letters on the Moral and Religious State of South America, Written During a Residence of Nearly Seven Years in Buenos Aires, Chile, Peru, and Colombia* (London, James Nisbet, 1827). On James Thomson, see Amunátegui Solar, *El sistema de Lancaster*; Webster E. Browning, 'Joseph Lancaster, James Thomson, and the Lancasterian System of Mutual Instruction, with Special Reference to Hispanic America', *The Hispanic American Historical Review* 4 (1921): 49–98; Arnoldo Canclini, *La Biblia en la Argentina: su distribución e influencia hasta 1853* (Buenos Aires, 1987); López and

Narodowsky, 'El mejor de los métodos posibles'; Eugenia Roldán Vera, 'Export as Import: James Thomson's Civilising Mission in South America (1818–1825)', in Marcelo Caruso and Eugenia Roldán Vera (eds), *Imported Modernity in Post-Colonial State Formation: the Appropriation of Political, Educational and Cultural Models in Nineteenth-Century Latin America* (Frankfurt am Main, 2007): 231–76.

18. Tronchot, 'L'enseignement mutuel'.
19. A number of those letters are printed in Thomson, *Letters on the Moral and Religious State of South America*.
20. Among them, Father Bartolomé Muñoz in Buenos Aires, and General Freire, Rafael Echevarria, Camilio Henríquez and Manuel Salas in Chile. It is not clear whether the BFSS established correspondence with them or not.
21. Valle to SIE, Guatemala, 19 Oct 1829, in *Cartas autógrafas*, 421–2.
22. Ibid.
23. *Journal d'Éducation*, May 1828, 198.
24. On the modus operandi of the British societies that promoted the monitorial system, see Patrick Ressler, 'Nonprofit-Marketing im Schulbereich. Die weltweite Verbreitung des Bell-Lancaster-Systems in der ersten Hälfte des 19. Jahrhunderts' (unpublished PhD dissertation, Institut für Erziehungswissenschaften, Humboldt University, Berlin, 2008).
25. 'On accuse cette méthode d'être anglaise, et (le croirait-on!) on lui en fait un tort, un tort impardonnable pour certains esprits. Je pourrais, comme plusieurs de mes compatriotes, revendiquer cette invention pour ma patrie, et ce ne serait pas sans fondemens', François-Alexandre-Frédéric de La Rochefoucauld-Liancourt, *Discours de M. le duc de La Rochefoucauld à la Assemblée générale de la Société pour l'enseignement élémentaire, tenue le 28 avril 1819* (Paris, L. Colas, 1819): 7.
26. 'Personne, je crois, ne contestera a la France l'esprit d'invention. Elle en a un supérieur encore, celui de croire qu'elle s'honore elle-même, en mettent à profit toutes les découvertes, toutes les inventions, de quelque lieu qu'elles viennent, si elles sont utiles au bonheur des hommes', La Rochefoucauld, *Discours*, 7.
27. 'La France s'est illustrée dans la carrière des sciences et des arts plus que toute autre nation; il est de son intérêt, non-seulement de soutenir cette réputation, mais elle doit même devancer l'Europe. L'Enseignement mutuel, appliqué aux sciences en Angleterre, produira dans ce pays des avantages que nous ne devons pas négliger. La gloire de la patrie et le bonheur des Français nous commandent donc impérieusement de faire usage d'un instrument dont nous sommes les premiers inventeurs: profitons des améliorations que le temps lui a données, conduisons-le a sa dernière perfection, et ne négligeons pas les grands avantages qu'il nous offre', Lasteyrie, *Nouveau système*, 121.
28. '…la belle mission de s'enquérir dans tous les pays des inventions, des méthodes, des institutions qu, apportées en France, pourraient y contribuera bonheur du peuple, accroître la gloire et la prospérité nationales, et préparer ainsi a la France les plus douces, les plus honorables conquêtes. Et ne doutons pas que, sous le prince qui nous gouverne, ces vœux ne soient réalisés', La Rochefoucauld, *Discours*, 7.
29. Alamán, 'Instrucción para el establecimiento de escuelas', 16.

30. '[Aunque] hemos empezado tarde este genero de enseñanza, con el influjo tan eficaz de una sociedad compuesta de un crecido numero de ciudadanos sabios y patriotas, en breve adelantaremos á las naciones que lo adoptaron mucho antes que nosotros', Manuel Codorniu y Ferreras, *Discurso inaugural en la abertura de las escuelas mutuas de la Filantropia* (México, Martín Rivera, 1823): 29–30.

31. Valle to Pecchio, Guatemala, 3 Apr 1827. 'J'attache le plus grand prix à correspondre avec les hommes qui, comme vous, cultivent les lettres avec succès. Plut à Dieu que de pareilles relations pussent s'ouvrir entre les Européens amis des sciences et les Américains qui partagent ce goût.!... Le perfectionnement universel de l'espèce humaine ferait des progrès immenses; les amis des sciences, resserrant les liens qui les unissent, formeraient une seule famille, où réunis dans une heureuse harmonie les fils de l'Europe et de l'Amérique pourraient contribuer au bonheur des habitans de 'Afrique, de l'Asie et de l'Australasie', *Journal d'Éducation*, Jan 1828, 94.

32. Laborde, *Plan d'éducation*, 2.

33. Lasteyrie, *Nouveau Système*, 112–13. On the appropriation and development of the monitorial system in France, see Tronchot, 'L'enseignement mutuel'.

34. Roldán Vera, 'Monitorial System of Education and Civic Culture'.

35. 'Le Nouveau-Monde, qui semblait n'avoir été découvert que pour assouvir l'avarice sanguinaire des Européens, vient enfin de recevoir de leurs mains un trésor bien plus précieux que cet or et ces produits qui ont occasionné, pendant un laps de temps trop considérable, tant d'injustices, de guerres et de ravages'; Lasteyrie, *Nouveau Système*, 19

36. *BFSS Annual Reports*, May 1825, 30.

37. 'Avec quelle joie ne verrai-je pas s'établir une communication de pensées plus importante que l'échange des productions du sol ou des mines; bien plus utile que le commerce de la vanille, de la cochenille et de l'indigo!' Valle to Pecchio, Guatemala, 3 Apr 1827, in *Jorunal d'Éducation*, Jan 1828, 94.

38. 'Deseo que todo Sabio de Europa dedique sus talentos á designar el Plan que deben seguir las Repúblicas de América en sus relaciones interiores y exteriores...sepa que indudablemente será protegido por los Gobiernos', Valle to Álvaro Florez Estrada, Guatemala, 7 Oct 1828, in *Cartas autógrafas*, 399–402.

39. 'Yo quisiera que V. que ha querido reunir en un libro lo más útil que se ha escrito en Inglaterra, Francia, Italia y Alemania, diese más importancia a sus trabajos uniendo con la teoría indicaciones oportunas de lo que conviene hacer á los Estados americanos para su riqueza y prosperidad. Su obra tendría entonces doble precio en el nuevo mundo, y su alma gozaría la satisfacción de haber señalado el camino á Sociedades nacientes que necesitan guia ó preceptor', Valle to Florez Estrada, Guatemala, 9 Jun 1827, in *Cartas autógrafas*, 401–2.

40. '[Vous êtes un illustre corps que se dévoue à la prospérité et au bonheur des nouvelles républiques, après avoir tant fait pour perfectionner l'instruction populaire sur son propre sol. En effet la Société pour l'Instruction Élémentaire de Paris connaît à fond le nature de nos privations et de nos besoins, et elle veut nous aider de la manière la plus franche et la plus généreuse à détruire, dans notre pays, le mal de l'ignorance...Cette Société aura grand plaisir et s'honorera de toute manière, en entrant en communication

avec la Société d'Instruction Élémentaire de Paris, et celle de Bogota espère recevoir de l'expérience des lumières des hommes célèbres qui en font partie, d'importants reseignemens sur les livres, les méthodes et les instructions les plus propres à répandre et à perfectionner, dans la Colombie, l'éducation populaire, à la quelle donne des soins particuliers.]', Esteves to SIE, Bogotá, 7 Feb 1827, in *Journal d'Éducation*, Sept 1827, 287–9.

41. Bentham to Rivadavia, 13–15 Jun 1822, in *The Correspondence of Jeremy Bentham*, ed. by Catherine Fuller, vol. 11 (Oxford, 2000): 118.

42. 'Hay inmensidad en los recursos naturales de esta república. Es feliz su posición geográfica: son fecundas las tierras, diversas las temperaturas, prodigiosa la vegetación, ricas las montañas, grande y majestuosa la naturaleza. Pero todavía no la ha cultivado la mano poderosa del arte. No tenemos hombres, y falta la ilustración que da vida a los pueblos', Valle to José Joaquín de Mora, Guatemala, 3 Jul 1826, 328–9.

12
Business and Reading Across the Atlantic: W. & R. Chambers and the United States Market, 1840–60

Aileen Fyfe

In autumn 1853, the Edinburgh publisher William Chambers made a tour of British North America and parts of the United States. Although he had been doing business with Canada since the mid-1830s, and with the United States since the mid-1840s, this was his first trip across the Atlantic. Officially, it was a holiday timed to coincide with the New York Great Exhibition. He visited the Crystal Palace on 19 November, and recorded in his diary that he 'Admired the American machinery and tools' and saw 'Good American sculpture, few American pictures'.[1] But Chambers was too much interested in the cause of education and literature to refrain from using his travels to call upon publishers and literary men, and to pay careful attention to the publications he encountered. In a series of articles later published in *Chambers's Edinburgh Journal* (*CEJ*), he explained how amazed he was to see newspapers 'everywhere in the hands of the labouring as well as the wealthy classes... In the streets, at the doors of hotels, and in railway-cars, boys are seen selling them in considerable numbers... Newspapers, in a word, are not a casual luxury, but a necessary of life.'[2] Chambers was exceedingly impressed with the prevalence of education, the ubiquity of print, and the taste for reading that he encountered in the United States.[3]

Back in Britain, Chambers's own firm was one of a few pioneers struggling to increase the availability of print, and particularly print which could compensate for the inadequate national provision of education. *Chambers's Edinburgh Journal* formed the basis of the now extensive operations of W. & R. Chambers, which specialized in steam-printing large runs of very cheap works, often published in parts. All its works were intended to be instructive and improving for the working and lower-middle classes, though some (including the *Journal*) also incorporated a measure of entertainment which assisted their sales figures. In Britain, William Chambers often felt he was fighting an uphill battle, hindered by prejudices against cheap print and the taxation on paper, and by poor educational provision. He saw the American market as an ideal opportunity, full of just the readers he hoped to reach.

Existing studies of the transatlantic book trade in the mid-nineteenth century have tended to focus on the problems faced by famous novelists and their publishers in the absence of an international copyright agreement.[4] British publishers and authors routinely saw American publishers as pirates, reprinting publications without permission or payment. Yet, in fact, the famous novelists were fortunate in wielding some bargaining power. Their works were in such demand that even without copyright, they had a reasonable chance of getting some payment from the United States, usually for access to advance sheets. The situation was rather different for the publications produced by W. & R. Chambers. Many of these were anonymous, most were by professional literary men of the middling sorts, and they were almost all non-fiction. These were not the kinds of works for which the Harper Brothers would be meeting the incoming steamer at New York docks, but they could nevertheless expect substantial sales in the highly literate and keenly self-improving literary marketplace of the United States.

This chapter investigates how W. & R. Chambers conducted its North American business. Ideally, the transatlantic community of readers was to be reached by the same products and methods used for Britain and its colonies. But the reality was import taxes, lack of copyright, the constant threat of possible 'piratical' reprinting, the difficulty of assessing the character of distant business partners, misunderstandings about books ordered and payment schedules, and, moreover, customers with different experiences and expectations of print. An introduction to the Chambers firm and its experience of long-distance business is followed, below, by discussion of the ways in which Chambers's publications could enter and circulate in the United States. This leads to an assessment of the significance of the threat of reprinting, and of its impact on the firm's methods. Finally, the chapter examines the ways in which Chambers's works were transformed, occasionally editorially but usually physically, in order to make them more attractive to the American market. The evidence reveals both the difficulty of trying to create a transatlantic business community, and the problems of assuming a similarity between customers on opposite sides of the Atlantic.

William Chambers launched the 1½d. *Chambers's Edinburgh Journal* of instruction and amusement in February 1832, shortly ahead of the *Penny Magazine*.[5] Within months, W. & R. Chambers was formed when William's younger brother Robert joined the enterprise.[6] By February 1833, the *Journal* was claiming sales of 50,000 copies a week, with half the run selling in England.[7] This success encouraged the brothers to experiment with other types of publication, and they built up a business that included departments for publishing and editorial work, and for composition, stereotyping and steam-printing. By 1845, they had ten steam-printing machines and a staff of at least 80 at their Edinburgh headquarters, had already opened a branch office in Glasgow, and would soon add one in London.[8] All their publications were rooted in the inadequate education and literacy of the British lower classes, and sought to provide solid information, written in a suitable style and published at a much lower than usual price. When these publications began to reach America, they had to circulate in a very different context, where literacy, education and print were much more democratically dispersed.

The first of the new Chambers projects was the *Information for the People* (1833–34), a series of instructive pamphlets explaining 'the most important branches of science, physical, mathematical, and moral, natural history, political history, geography, and literature'.[9] For three halfpennies [or 1½d.], readers received eight large triple-columned pages each forming an encyclopaedia-type article on, for instance, the United States, the steam engine, or the history of Britain. The 50 pamphlets appeared fortnightly, and had initial sales of around 16,000–18,000 per number.[10] Chambers went on to launch other series of cheap pamphlets, although, as the titles indicate, the later series made more provision for amusement: the *Miscellany of Useful and Entertaining Tracts* (1844–47), *Papers for the People* (1850–51) and the *Repository of Instructive and Amusing Tracts* (1852–54).

In Britain, steam-printing at this time was used exclusively for high-circulation newspapers and periodicals, but Chambers quickly decided to try its machines on books as well. The firm began to issue its 'People's Editions' in 1836, offering cheap reprints of out-of-copyright works. Other publishers could offer Paley's *Natural Theology* and Butler's *Analogy* for 5 or 6s., but Chambers could offer them at just 1s. 6d., and its sales were consequently much higher.[11] The 'Educational Course', which the firm started in 1835, eventually provided textbooks, readers, dictionaries, grammars and copybooks for every stage of education, from learning to read and write, through arithmetic and geography, to science, Latin and German.[12] Most of the Educational Course books were priced around 2s., but the most basic readers and introductory level works cost just 6d. or 10d., and it was these which became the best-sellers of the series: the *Introduction to the Sciences* (1836) and the *First Book of Reading* (1838) had both sold around 70,000 copies by 1843.[13]

By that time, Chambers had already expanded from lowland Scotland into a national British market, and it also had a limited number of regular arrangements with British colonies in North America, the West Indies, Australia and New Zealand. The firm's experience with these markets coloured its expectations of the United States. Within three months of the *Journal*'s launch, its success in England necessitated the printing of a separate edition in London (from stereotype plates), and the appointment of an agent, William Somerville Orr, to oversee it.[14] Orr also acted as distributor to English retail booksellers. Cases of books and serials were dispatched to Orr by coastal steamer, and he sent out packages to towns all over England by stagecoach and railway. This particular method of dealing with distant markets, however, proved undesirable in the long run: Orr's own complicated and occasionally improvident business relationships were a constant worry to Chambers. In 1853, they finally replaced his agency with a London branch office run by younger brother David Chambers. William Chambers believed that his firm had lost several tens of thousands of pounds over the years of its connection with Orr.[15]

In consequence of the Orr debacle, William Chambers became wary of forming new agencies, and very conscious of the difficulty of accurately assessing and controlling potential partners from a distance. Nevertheless, the company did form successful connections with firms such as A. & W. McKinlay in Halifax, Gilchrist & Alexander in Sydney and A. Crombie in Hobart, some of which lasted for many years. From the late 1830s, these booksellers received a box or two of books once a year, shipped – initially by sail – from Leith (for Australia and Tasmania), and Greenock or Liverpool (for Nova Scotia).[16] These firms were retail booksellers, and typically placed orders for specific books and sent payment with the order. Orr in London, and his counterpart in Dublin, held Chambers's stock 'on sale', with accounts settled either quarterly or six-monthly, but transit times were too long and ships too infrequent to permit such arrangements to be extended overseas.

Trying to do transatlantic business with the United States was intriguingly different, from both British and colonial operations. The United States levied import taxes on British goods, and provided no legal protection for British copyrights. On the positive side, the development of the United States publishing trade meant that Chambers could try to make arrangements for distribution with other publishers, rather than connecting directly with retail booksellers. The extensive reading audience in the United States also seemed to provide a particularly fertile field for its wares. Furthermore, the improvements in transatlantic shipping by the mid-1840s meant that letters and goods could cross the ocean by steamship in 10–14 days, meaning that Boston or Philadelphia (and, indeed Halifax) no longer seemed as distant as they had in the 1830s. Monthly shipments, rather than yearly consignments, were quite possible. Nevertheless, this could still be painfully slow when time-critical arrangements – such as synchronous issuing of new titles on both sides of the Atlantic – were being negotiated. Whereas letters from Edinburgh to London took a day and, by 1854, instructions could be telegraphed to the London branch office in a matter of hours, it was not until the mid-1860s that the transatlantic telegraph cable was laid, and the physical transatlantic journey time would not be significantly reduced until the advent of air travel.[17]

Because most of Chambers's contacts in the United States were with publishers, rather than retail booksellers, the relationships differed from those with the colonies. Colonial booksellers were subordinate to Chambers and the other British publishers on which they depended for supplies. When Charles S. Sterns set up as a bookseller in Pictou, Nova Scotia, he petitioned to secure a stock of Chambers's publications by enclosing a letter from James Dawson (who had already done business with Chambers) recommending his former apprentice and expressing himself willing to act as guarantor.[18] American publishers, in contrast, expected to be treated as equals in their relationship with Chambers. When Gould, Kendall & Lincoln of Boston, and Lea & Blanchard of Philadelphia contacted Chambers, they simply sent copies of their trade catalogues (rather than letters of introduction) to indicate their standing.[19] Such a manner of forming a business acquaintance, followed (as it was in Gould's case) by several months of negotiations by monthly transatlantic letter, was an imperfect way of getting to know someone. It was not until 15 October 1853 that William Chambers met Charles Gould in person; six weeks later, in Philadelphia, he also met Joshua B. Lippincott, who was not just a publisher but carried on 'the peculiar business of book-merchants' for 'retail-booksellers coming from every part of the States'.[20] The outcome of these two personal meetings was that Lippincott quickly replaced Gould in Chambers's business affections.[21]

William Chambers was critical of businesses which over-extended themselves, or opened themselves to risk by accepting or granting credit carelessly.[22] He tried to ensure that his firm paid in cash as far as possible, and extended credit carefully. The colonial booksellers usually sent bills with their orders, which could thus be treated almost as cash transactions. American publishers, however, were used to a system of extensive credit.[23] Gould was unusual in sending a bill of exchange, drawn on a Liverpool bank, as an advance deposit on its order.[24] Lea & Blanchard read Chambers's proposed terms of settlement as a slur on its credit standing, and referred Chambers to Longman & Co. in London.[25] Even after several years of dealing with Lippincott, problems still arose about when payment was due. The absence of a system of international banking entailed complicated debates about whether the three months that it took for British banks to negotiate Lippincott's American bills into sterling currency should be additional to the period of credit Chambers was allowing Lippincott, or calculated as part of it.[26]

Even once agreements had been formed, and methods of payment arranged, there could still be problems relating to the different technological practices on opposite sides of the Atlantic.[27] Selling stereotype plates to America, for instance, turned out to be more complicated than expected. Gould was aware that there might be problems, for it specified to Chambers that it would like the back of the plates to 'be shaved, if you have the machinery to do it', rather than 'turned'.[28] Even with this advance warning, Gould still found 'many of your plates quite difficult to work'; among other things, 'all the plates were too large & we have been obliged to take them to the Foundry & have them trim'd'.[29] In Edinburgh, brass rules were fixed to the stereotype plates to produce a border to the text; but Gould had to explain that in Boston, such practices 'are unknown', and although 'We have consulted our best printers...they are ignorant of any process by which it can be accomplished.'[30] All of these problems could be corrected, with time, effort and inclination, but the problems illustrate vividly that Chambers and Gould were operating in distinct technical communities.

In the mid-nineteenth century, W. & R. Chambers was hardly the first nor the only British publishing firm attempting to negotiate the American market. In the first half of the century, the vast majority of books available in the United States were written by British authors.[31] There were therefore already plenty of routes, both well established and more recent, for getting books across the Atlantic and Chambers used most of them. This section outlines the various options, demonstrating that there was more to the transatlantic book trade than the question of 'imports or reprints'.

By the mid-1850s, Chambers had formed two long-term relationships with publishers in the United States: the dwindling relationship with Gould, Kendall & Lincoln, and the recent but thriving relationship with Lippincott. With these publishers (and a few others) Chambers made agreements for the bulk importation of its publications in the form of printed sheets – usually in quantities of 500 or 1,000 copies – which were then folded, stitched and covered or bound in the United States, to meet local needs and preferences. This arrangement was Chambers's preferred option, since it kept production under its control and ensured that the firm received payment for every copy of the work circulated in America. It was only attractive to the American publishers, however, if Chambers could offer a substantial discount off the usual trade price. If this was enough to balance out the cost of transatlantic freight and Customs charges, then it was possible for the works to be available in America at a similar price as if they had been reprinted locally. It was unlikely that the American publisher would make more money by importing than by reprinting, but the risk of tying up capital in reprinting would be removed. This arrangement could work for Chambers's publications because, unlike most British publications, they were already very cheap, and thus similar in price to American works. For instance, Lea & Blanchard reprinted the Latin section of the Educational Course: its Cicero, Virgil and Caesar readers were priced at 50c. and 75c. (or 2s. and 3s.), which was not significantly different from the retail price of the original Chambers's editions at 2s. and 3s. 6d.[32] Other British publishers, particularly those which specialized in original literary fiction, would find that even with a discount their publications would seem expensive to American customers.

Chambers also sometimes made agreements to sell stereotype plates for certain publications. In this case, the firm received a single payment, which bore no relation to the number of copies subsequently printed from the plates. The payment could not be particularly high, since the American publisher could always threaten to make his own plates by resetting type from an imported copy of the book. This was the preferred option of most American publishers which wished to work with Chambers, since it saved the cost of resetting, and gave the American publisher complete control over production, binding, distribution and profit. Gould's initial approach to Chambers was an enquiry regarding 'at what price you will sell us the plates, or a duplicate set of same', for the *Cyclopaedia of English Literature* (edited by Robert Chambers, 1846), which it believed 'might sell in this country'.[33] Chambers subsequently (though without success) offered Gould plates for the German schoolbooks and Robert Chambers's four-volume *Life and Works of Robert Burns* (1851–52).[34] From Chambers's point of view, however, the low payment and lack of remuneration per copy sold made this arrangement less than ideal. It was only willing to sell plates for its book publications, and not for the *Journal* or other serials, which were high circulation, high income publications.

In addition to these agreements with other publishers for bulk importation, substantial numbers of Chambers's publications entered the United States via other trade channels, usually as bound books. Chambers would, for instance, fill orders placed (and paid for) by individual American retail booksellers, as long as these would not interfere with the sales of publications sent to Gould or Lippincott. Thus, Edmond Barrington of Philadelphia ordered several hundred of each of the Latin and German schoolbooks direct from Chambers in 1855, but H.H. Derby of Cincinnati's order was declined, since Chambers had 'considerable transactions with Messrs Lippincott of Philadelphia in regard to the books you refer to'.[35]

Yet more books went to America through trade channels over which Chambers had less control. The New York publisher Francis & Co. used its contact with the London publisher Baldwin as a means of obtaining British books for its customers. Thus, until his retirement in 1854, Baldwin supplied Francis with W. & R. Chambers's publications which he had presumably purchased (at trade prices) from William Orr's agency, or, most recently, from David Chambers's branch office.[36] More books may have travelled via the services of a specialized import agency: in the 1840s, George Putnam was based in London and made arrangements with London and Edinburgh publishers for their books and periodicals to be stocked in Wiley & Putnam's New York store.[37]

In the late 1840s, New York auction houses (and also several transatlantic freight companies) began advertising in the *Publishers' Circular* to attract consignments from British publishers.[38] In October 1847, for instance, Bangs, Platt & Co. claimed that its sales offered 'means superior to any other for the introduction to the notice of the American Trade both of surplus and new stock adapted to circulation in the United States', and that they were unique in being 'fully attended by the dealers of the United States and Canadas'.[39] By the following March, the firm was announcing a 'Special Sale of Contributions from Great Britain early in the month of May next', suggesting that there was indeed interest from British publishers.[40] Chambers appears to have used this channel for the first (and probably only) time with the 1853 spring trade sales. The letter announcing the dispatch of its consignment was extremely deferential to whatever Messrs Bangs might 'deem...advisable' and ended, 'We leave the matter however to your discretion.'[41] Whether this discretion failed, or whether Chambers had sent far too many publications in the first place, part of the lot remained unsold a year later and was passed on to Lippincott.[42]

Bangs, Brother & Co. (as the firm became) became increasingly involved in the transatlantic trade and, by the mid-1850s, it had set up an 'English Book Depot', to provide a permanent facility for the sale of British books, in addition to the twice-yearly trade sales. Several major British publishers, including Chambers, sent stock to this Depot, and during the financial panic of 1857 (in which Bangs looked likely to fail), these publishers were sufficiently concerned about the quantity of their stock, which was imperilled, and the necessity of continuing such a useful channel as the Depot, that they sent Sampson Low, Jnr., to New York with power of attorney to ensure their interests were protected.[43] There is, however, no surviving evidence of whether Chambers continued to use the new Depot established under Charles Scribner's control.

In addition to these trade channels, Chambers's publications could also circulate in the United States in ways beyond the control of their publisher. Perhaps a relatively insignificant option was the trade in second-hand books, which was not limited to the antiquarian books sought by bibliophiles. Even relatively recent publications might have crossed the Atlantic only in small numbers. One of Putnam's other roles during his years in London was to undertake commissions for individuals seeking such hard-to-find books.[44] He visited auctions and antiquarian book dealers, and sometimes placed advertisements in the London *Publishers' Circular* for books he had yet to locate. In July 1848, the agent then working for Wiley in London sought to purchase titles as varied as Pierre Gassendi's *Life of Epicurus* (1647), Joseph Priestley's *Address on church discipline...and the corruption of it* (1770) and Robert Chambers's *Biographical Dictionary of Eminent Scotsmen* (1835), as well as a complete run of the *Microscopic Journal*.[45] It is possible that some of the earlier Chambers publications went to America through this route, although the back numbers of the *Journal* and serials were kept in print.

Rather more significant are the ways in which Chambers's publications might circulate as copies reprinted without permission in the United States. The lack of an international copyright treaty made this perfectly legal, and for highly desirable titles (such as the latest novel by Dickens or Bulwer-Lytton) most of the American copies in circulation were reprints, rather than imports. Reprinting was certainly a concern for Chambers, but few of its publications were in high enough demand to attract reprinters the way the famous novels did. The next section will focus on how the few attempts to reprint Chambers's publications affected its attempts to make arrangements for importation, but suffice it to say here that an American reprint of the *Journal* was tried on several occasions, but was always short-lived. The *Journal* might, however, have been known by reputation, since excerpts from it regularly appeared in the pages of the successful weekly eclectic *Littell's Living Age* (LLA) (or '*Littell's*' – see Chapter 13) throughout the late 1840s, and also in the short-lived *The World as It Moves* (New York, 1849).

The *Information for the People* was reprinted in Philadelphia, as 'the first American edition', but the only other works that appear to have been reprinted in significant numbers were the textbooks of the Educational Course. David Page's *Rudiments of Geology* (1836) reappeared in a Philadelphia edition in 1846, with additional notes by David Meredith Reese, and then formed part of A.S. Barnes of New York's series of scientific textbooks with the title *Elements of ...* in 1849.[46] And, as we have already seen, Lea & Blanchard of Philadelphia reprinted the Latin textbooks, and were quite open about doing so. The firm announced to Chambers in May 1850 that, 'we are republishing your Series of Classical Educational Books, & propose continuing them.'[47] It wished, however, to purchase stereotype plates for the next title in the series, the Latin-English dictionary. Dictionaries were complex works to reset, involving two languages, several sizes of type and plenty of opportunity for errors to creep in. Thus, Lea & Blanchard was keen to buy the dictionary plates (and Chambers agreed, for £175), but had no desire to purchase plates of any of the other titles Chambers offered since it could reset those cheaply and easily itself.[48] The fact that it was the Educational Course which seems to have been most preyed upon by American reprinters reiterates the importance of textbooks as reliable steady sellers on both sides of the Atlantic.

The publications whose circulation as imports or reprints caused Chambers most concern were *Chambers's Journal* and the several series of instructive pamphlets. These were the ones which sold in the largest numbers in Britain, and might be expected to sell best in the United States. For these publications, selling stereotype plates was not a good option, since the fee was not related to the subsequent circulation – which Chambers assumed would be high. This section, therefore, looks at how the firm tried to improve the circulation of its serials in the United States, and how the desire to increase imports through Gould and Lippincott was negotiated in the context of potential 'piratical' reprints.

In the mid-1840s, expansion into the United States seemed an important strategy for rebuilding the circulation of *Chambers's Journal*, which was being hit by a wave of new penny periodicals, full of fiction, gossip and illustrations.[49] In 1847, circulation had fallen from 90,000 to 75,000 copies per week, and it would fall further in the early 1850s.[50] *Chambers's Journal* seems to have been relatively little known in America at this point in time, for in 1846 Gould, Kendall & Lincoln reported that, 'We have not seen your "Journal" for some years & cannot find one here now.'[51] There was, therefore, ample room for improvement in the American circulation figures, and Chambers would have seen the fact that the *Journal* had been several times reprinted in New York as evidence of demand from the American public, even though the last such attempt had lapsed in 1840.

In February 1833, an editorial in the *Journal* announced that a reprint of its 'principal articles' was appearing in New York.[52] In fact, the reprint by R.J. Richards had already ceased, though a Mr Hobart was clearly interested in continuing it, and would negotiate with Chambers over the possible sale of stereotype plates later that year.[53] These negotiations stalled, since Hobart reckoned he could make his own plates at a lower cost than Chambers was offering to sell them. Acknowledging that 'we cannot oppose your choosing to do so', Chambers offered instead to supply quantities of the *Journal* at a discount price, but Hobart seems not to have been tempted.[54] Eighteen months later, however, the *Journal* reported that it was again being 'regularly reprinted in New York'.[55] In addition to the sporadic attentions of New York printers, A. Waldie of Philadelphia used its contents as the basis for his fortnightly *The Portfolio, and companion to the select circulating library* (1835–36). In 1838, Chambers contacted William Jackson of New York, who had been the authorized reprinter of the *Penny Magazine* of the Society for the Diffusion of Useful Knowledge since 1833. Jackson was offered a duplicate set of stereotype plates, and printed the *Journal* until 1840, at which point he seems to have gone out of business.[56] The *Penny Magazine* was continued by another printer, but *Chambers's Journal* was not.[57]

The tone of the *Journal*'s reports of its own reprinting in New York suggests that in the 1830s Chambers was naively delighted at the extended circulation of the periodical and keen to improve it even further, even by selling stereotype plates for a small, one-off payment. By the 1840s, though, the firm was starting to perceive reprinters – even authorized ones – as taking profits that should belong to it. Once alerted to the *Journal*'s existence, Gould expressed its willingness to purchase plates but, unfortunately, Chambers was no longer willing to sell them.[58] The key problem was British North America. Chambers was exporting relatively few copies of the *Journal* to the United States, so a payment from Gould for the plates would have more than made up for any loss of orders when American readers chose to buy the local edition instead. But the *Journal* had been selling increasingly well in the Canadian colonies, and William Chambers (or someone writing on his behalf) told Gould that the firm feared an American edition would 'inevitably compete with ours' in Canada.[59] Chambers wished to extend the audience for the *Journal*, not compete for the existing readers.

The damage that an American reprint could do to the Canadian sales of *Chambers's Journal* was demonstrated in 1854, just months after William Chambers had congratulated himself, while in New York, that his journal had not yet 'yielded to its destiny' of 'an unauthorised transatlantic impression'.[60] By the time Chambers wrote up his travels for the *Journal*, the New York printer Peter D. Orvis had started reprinting it.[61] The Edinburgh and New York editions had the same retail price (3c. or 1½d.), but for the Canadians, the cost of shipping was clearly lower from New York.[62] Although the 1842 Copyright Act had made it illegal for the Canadians to import foreign reprints of copyright works, the 1847 Foreign Reprints Act re-allowed such importations, on the condition that a tax was levied to compensate the copyright holders.[63] In reality, few British authors or publishers received payments from the Canadians, and many American reprints crossed the border. In December 1854, William Chambers explained to a correspondent in Nova Scotia that 'pirate reprints of our Journal' were being admitted into Canada, that 'nothing has ever been paid to us', and that as a consequence, 'our exports to the British American colonies is rapidly lessening [*sic*], and we anticipate that it will soon reduce to nearly nothing.'[64] Fortunately, Orvis's reprint had ceased by 1856.

Despite its position on stereotype plates, Chambers still hoped to increase the *Journal*'s circulation in the United States. Its compromise was to offer reductions for the bulk importation of printed sheets of the *Journal*. In 1833, it had offered a rate of £4 per thousand if a 1,000 were taken, but to Gould in 1847 it offered a rate of £3 7s. 6d. per thousand, if at least 5,000 were taken.[65] For context, the standard price offered to the British trade was £4 6s. 6d. per thousand, and the selling price was £6 5s. 0d.[66] The discount offered to Gould was substantial, but it does not seem to have tempted it.[67]

Seven years later, J.B. Lippincott did include sheets of the *Journal* in his first order from Chambers. Yet despite Lippincott's enthusiasm and activity, he could not make the publication viable as imported sheets.

The problem lay in the cost of shipping for a weekly publication, exacerbated by the arrival of Orvis's New York reprint. Lippincott's initial order was for the *Journal* in weekly numbers, and he also issued it in monthly parts with a cover printed in Philadelphia.[68] By June 1854, however, he was receiving it only monthly, to save on shipping charges.[69] In Britain, the *Journal* had a substantial sale in its monthly parts, and if American readers showed a similar preference, the absence of the weekly version in Philadelphia would not harm circulation. Unfortunately, once Orvis began issuing his New York edition, there was direct competition between the Orvis weekly reprint and the Lippincott monthly import. There was nothing Chambers could do to help Lippincott beat off this competition for priority without returning to weekly dispatches – 'but you probably find this too expensive'.[70] Orvis's edition hit Lippincott's sales badly, and the Philadelphia firm sought further discounts from Chambers to enable it to undercut the opposition. In April 1855, knowing that Lippincott was likely to stop taking the *Journal*, Chambers reduced the price to £3 per thousand 'in the hope of inducing you to continue it'.[71] This was, in fact, virtually cost price, but it was not enough.[72] The following month, Chambers was 'sorry the Journal cannot be made to pay, but there seems to be no remedy for it, and we shall now discontinue sending any more'.[73] Shipping costs versus the need for priority conspired against the success of an imported *Chambers's Journal*.[74]

Some idea of the extent of the *Journal*'s potential circulation in the United States may be gained from its aggregate circulation figures (these were always expressed as weekly averages even if sales were in monthly parts). When Lippincott began taking the *Journal*, the aggregate figures increased for the first time in over a decade, with weekly sales rising from 49,000 in 1853 to 65,000 in 1854. The analysis of those extra sales is complicated by the fact that Lippincott's order coincided with the latest relaunch of the *Journal*, which would also be expected to increase sales. But by 1856, when Lippincott had ceased to order any copies, the circulation figures had returned to 1853 levels. Those extra sales of 16,000 a week during 1854 give us a ballpark figure for how valuable the American market could be for Chambers.[75] Meanwhile, the 1855 figures suggest the impact of Orvis's reprint upon Lippincott's import. Average sales over the whole year were just 4,000 per week above the 1853 level. That represents Lippincott's sales for just five months, suggesting that his sales for those months had fallen from 16,000 to around 9,600. Some falling off is common after the first few issues of any new periodical, but a large part of the reduction must have been due to readers (or booksellers) switching to the Orvis reprint.

The case of *Chambers's Journal* demonstrates how difficult it was for British publishers to promote their periodicals in the United States. As the publishers of the big quarterlies had already discovered, if there was a reprinter interested in the periodical, then it was virtually impossible for imported copies, however discounted, to compete. Hence, Murray, Longman, Blackwood and Chapman agreed to help the reprinters by supplying advance sheets, for a fee, as this seemed to be the only way they were likely to receive any compensation.[76] Orvis did, in fact, offer to purchase advance sheets from Chambers, but his offer could not have been accepted without threatening Chambers's recent agreement with Lippincott.[77] Chambers might have been able to beat off Orvis if it had been willing to supply Lippincott with stereotype plates (and if Lippincott had been willing to import them weekly), but concerns about the Canadian market militated against such an option. If it had not been for Orvis's timely arrival on the reprinting scene, it is possible that *Chambers's Journal* would have succeeded as a discounted import. Yet Lippincott's lack of enthusiasm to recommence imports, once Orvis had disappeared, suggests that he was wary lest all the effort that he would put into promoting the *Journal* should, again, be poached by an upstart rival – for it was never possible to know where or when someone might decide to start a reprint.

The American fate of the various instructive serials produced by Chambers demonstrates that offering discounts for bulk importation of works was a viable option. Among its series publications, only the *Information for the People* attracted the attention of American reprinters. It was originally reset and stereotyped (from the revised 1841–42 edition) by the Philadelphia firm of G.B. Zieber, a short-lived house specializing in reprints, and it was re-issued virtually every year through the 1850s by a group of other Philadelphia firms, including J.L. Gihon, one of the key subscription publishing firms.[78] Chambers's other series – the *Miscellany of Tracts*, the *Repository of Tracts* and the *Papers for the People* – all appear to have circulated in the United States solely as imports, primarily through Gould and Lippincott, and to have done so successfully.[79]

Despite Gould's unwillingness to take the *Journal* (and indeed, the *Information*), it did take the *Miscellany of Tracts* as printed sheets with apparent success. Gould continued to place orders for the *Miscellany of Tracts* – usually for 250 complete sets at a time – throughout the late 1840s and into the 1850s. Indeed, there seems to have been a continued demand for it in Boston long after British sales had died away. By 1855, Chambers was letting the work go out of print, so Gould's continued requests for complete sets were impossible to fill without reprinting a few numbers specially.[80] As Chambers explained: 'the cost of printing these small impressions much increases the expense of production.'[81] Despite a 25 per cent increase in costs, and fears that its sales were being damaged by Lippincott's importation of the same work, Gould continued to find customers for the *Miscellany* until at least 1857. Lippincott took 1,000 of each volume of the then-issuing *Repository* in 1854, and was confident enough to place an order for 1,000 of the *Papers for the People* several years after the series was concluded.[82] In addition to the absence of local competition, the advantage that these serials had over the *Journal* was that they were not date-stamped or time-limited. The *Journal* did not carry news (since it was an unstamped periodical), but it did note current events. This was why Orvis's ability to be first on the market with the most recent issue offered a substantial competitive advantage over Lippincott's import. The other serials had a more timeless appeal, as is witnessed by their continued sale years after their first publication, on both sides of the Atlantic. For the same reason, several of Chambers's book publications – of which there were increasing numbers by the 1850s – were also successfully imported into the United States as printed sheets.

These examples illustrate how Chambers used a variety of different approaches to enable its publications to circulate in the United States. For certain book publications, preferably where the firm could identify a publisher known to be interested, Chambers was willing to sell stereotype plates. It preferred to make such an arrangement ahead of publication, so that the duplicate plates could be made at the same time as the originals – making duplicates after publication (as had to be done with the *Cyclopaedia of English Literature*, for Gould) was expensive, time-consuming and annoying. For other books, for which there was no obvious American partner with whom to make a pre-publication arrangement, and for the instructive serials, Chambers was willing to offer discounts on bulk purchases of printed sheets. This tactic failed with *Chambers's Journal*, which was sufficiently attractive to encourage American reprinters and whose time-stamped quality gave those reprinters an advantage over the authorized importers. The problem of *Chambers's Journal* appears only to have been solved in the mid-1860s, when Chambers finally allowed a set of plates to be used for a New York printing.[83]

Once Chambers's publications had crossed the Atlantic they still had to find customers, and that depended upon the contents, appearance and price being attractive to American readers. When they started negotiating with American publishers in the mid-1840s, neither William nor Robert Chambers had yet been to the United States. Indeed, in 1837, an article in *Chambers's Journal* had appealed for more news from the United States, since the British were currently 'very much in the dark as to American enterprise' and, indeed, all things American.[84] This unfamiliarity meant that Chambers was entirely reliant on its American contacts to advise it on what would sell. Negotiations about which titles should go to America were usually initiated by Chambers, which suggested particular publications to Gould or Lippincott for acceptance or rejection. Gould frequently refused suggestions: it had bought the plates of the *Cyclopaedia of English Literature*, and it took sheets of the *Miscellany of Useful and Entertaining Tracts*, but declined plates of the German schoolbook series and the *Life of Burns*,[85] as well as sheets of the *Journal* and of a revised *Information for the People*.[86] Gould's pattern of refusals to take Chambers's works appears to indicate that it was happy with the two steady selling early choices, but did not want the effort (or expense) that it suspected would be needed to seek customers for works untested in America.

The surviving correspondence gives the impression that Chambers regarded Gould as over-cautious, and that the firm felt more comfortable with Lippincott, who seems to have shared the brothers' desire to spread large numbers of printed works as far afield as possible. It must also have helped that Chambers and Lippincott forged their relationship personally in Philadelphia, rather than through correspondence. Lippincott's very first order in January 1854 had included not just the *Journal*, but also the *Repository of Tracts*, the *Miscellany of Tracts*, the *Papers for the People* and some unidentified books.[87] The firm appears not to have taken the Educational Course books, but it did take other books – again, in sheets. If Lippincott agreed to take enough copies of a particular new book, Chambers was willing to issue those copies with an alternative title page. Thus, William Chambers's account of his trip to Canada and the United States, *Things as they are in America* (1854), circulated in the United States with Lippincott's imprint, even though the sheets were printed in Edinburgh.[88] Of his subsequent *American Slavery and Colour* (1857), 500 copies bore the imprint of Dix, Edwards & Co. of New York, with which Chambers was just beginning a relationship (one that failed shortly afterwards amid recriminations).[89] With these arrangements, Chambers would send copies only to the particular publisher. In many other cases, though, the books kept their Chambers imprint and were sent to several American contacts. Bangs, Brother & Co. found 'so ready a sale' for George Dodd's *Pictorial History of the Russian War* (1855–56) in the English Book Depot in New York that it ordered more copies, even though it was also being sold by Dix, Edwards & Co. and by Gould in Boston.[90]

It is surely significant that, of the titles mentioned above as being successfully imported, several had a direct American reference, and the *Russian War* was clearly cashing in on recent events in the Crimea. Lippincott also imported at least 500 copies of Chambers's *Hand-book of American Literature* (1855) by Joseph Gostick.[91] Equally, the works about which Lippincott appears to have been less than enthusiastic were those that lacked either topical or American reference. Despite Lippincott's lack of enthusiasm, Chambers sent 500 of the first numbers of its re-issue of Charles Knight's *Pictorial History of England* and the *Pictorial Bible* to Philadelphia, in the hope that their successful sale would encourage Lippincott to order more. Chambers added the reassurance that 'that portion of Pictorial History of England which refers to the American Revolution will be considerably improved'.[92] Nevertheless, Lippincott declined to place orders for the further parts. Chambers now changed tack, and tried to persuade Lippincott to sell the works in volumes – sending the extra numbers and the covers needed to make up the first volume of each work at its own expense.[93] Sales did not improve, and Lippincott eventually returned 'the whole stock of it by first sailing vessel [i.e. cheaply] to Liverpool' in autumn 1857.[94] Presumably a history of England, however discreetly edited, was not of intrinsic interest to American readers, while Bibles were already available in all sorts of formats – including cheap illustrated ones – from a range of American publishing houses.

Chambers increasingly came to realize that American readers had different preferences from the British lower-middle and working-class readers that it was used to targeting. Since most Chambers publications circulated in America as sheets printed in Edinburgh, only limited changes could be made. An alternative title page was one option; part-works could be given new covers (Gould requested that references to prices in shillings and pence were removed, and that the title of the *Miscellany of Useful and Entertaining Tracts* should replace the word 'Tracts' with 'Knowledge'[95]); and Lippincott or Gould could insert their own advertising material while binding the works. But compared with the opportunities available to reprinters, these were very minor changes. For instance, some of the early efforts to reprint the *Journal* had reprinted only selected articles of particular interest to American readers. Similarly, when articles from the *Journal* were reprinted in *Littell's Living Age*, they appeared in a completely new context, alongside poems, tales and reviews originally published in the *Athenaeum*, the *British Quarterly Review* and the *Christian Witness*.[96]

The changes which could be made by reprinters can be illustrated by examining Zieber's Philadelphia 'American edition' of *Information for the People*. Although it claimed to have 'numerous additions', these were limited to suggestions for further reading added to some of the articles near the start of the first volume.[97] Yet, although the text of the articles remained unchanged, the preface was transformed for American readers. Chambers's preface to the 1841–42 revised edition had been firmly couched in terms of the British social system, in which only a privileged few had access to education, information and print. It explained that most encyclopedias were unsuitable for 'a large portion of the middle and the whole of the working classes', and presented the *Information* as something which might be '*really* within the reach' of those classes, and could 'send down light into the lower regions of society'. It mentioned the necessity of publishing in 'detached sheets, and these bearing a very small price', while implying that this was an unusual tactic, and ended with a clarion call for the introduction of a national education system in Britain.[98] The (shorter) preface to the American edition, in contrast, drew upon the British preface's description of the content of the *Information*, but did not comment on the physical format of the work, omitted the plea for an education system and recast the potential audience in carefully democratic terms, presenting the *Information* as an important work for 'all classes of the people' and 'the people generally'.[99] Moreover, Zieber's edition rearranged the order of the entries, moving the block of geographical and historical description of nations (which had a heavy emphasis on Britain and the British Empire) from the start of Volume 1 to the end of Volume 2, and moving the articles on the physical sciences and their applications ahead of the articles on zoology. The result was to de-emphasize the Britishness of the work, and to emphasize its practical utility.

The main area where Gould or Lippincott could alter the Chambers works they imported was in the physical format used to issue them. The books and serials arrived as sheets, which could be stitched between paper covers, bound in boards or lavishly bound in leather and gilt. The Chambers brothers were themselves firm believers in the utility of part-works: the *Information for the People*, the *Cyclopaedia of English Literature* and the other instructive serials appeared first as tracts, and were subsequently collected for re-issue in parts, volumes and complete sets.[100] Readers could, for instance, purchase the *Repository of Tracts* in 1d. numbers over 108 weeks, or in monthly parts for 5d., or wait until the end of the issue for the more attractive library option of six thick volumes in cloth gilt, for 2s. 6d. each.[101] They could choose how to purchase their reading material, in a way that best suited their personal circumstances.

Chambers initially assumed that its American partners would wish to use the same range of formats. But the correspondence makes clear that the Americans preferred to issue nothing smaller than a volume, and ideally only complete sets. This first came to light during negotiations over the plates of the *Cyclopaedia of English Literature* in 1846. When Chambers offered to send plates in monthly batches of six sheets, Gould was 'much disappointed in learning the length of time proposed' (about 15 months), for 'we intend to issue the work complete & not in numbers as you suppose, and therefore wish to receive all the plates at the earliest day possible.'[102] A few months later, Gould was still prevaricating over whether to get started on publication, even if it did mean issuing in parts, or to wait for all the plates to arrive and issue the work 'in two handsome volumes'. In Gould's judgement, the *Cyclopaedia* would sell better in America if issued as volumes. Moreover, Gould faced competition from 'the Complete work being now for Sale in this market', and despite the higher price of that imported work ($5.50 for two volumes), Gould was convinced that issuing in numbers 'would operate unfavourably'.[103] Similarly, Gould asked for the *Miscellany of Tracts*, not in numbers or parts, but 'two volumes at a time … every two months, wh[ich] w[oul]d be as often as we should issue them'.[104] Indeed, Zieber's *Information for the People* appeared in two volumes, with all indications of the original part-work format removed, indicating that Gould was not alone in his preference for volumes.

Part of the reason for Gould's prejudice against part issues was the extremely small profit margin on such short cheap works. For Chambers, this was a necessary part of the mission to improve the working classes, and simply meant that very large numbers had to be sold to yield a respectable profit. Gould, however, was not dealing with very large numbers, but only with several hundred copies. Given the 'expense of advertising &c to create a demand', Gould preferred to work with bound volumes, on which it could charge a price which 'would remunerate us for the trouble & outlay'.[105] But it may also have been part of the reaction against the extreme cheapening of print in the United States in the early 1840s, when entire novels were printed as supplements to newspapers and sold for just 12½c.[106] Although very cheap print had become widely available, it had also tended to be low-quality print, and once the American book trade restabilized, mainstream publishers used the higher quality of their products to justify their slightly higher prices. As Gould explained to Chambers, 'the public are tired of Nos'.[107] This was quite a contrast from Chambers's usual situation in Britain, where there was still a great shortage of very cheap print and numbers were still welcome.

In 1856, when Chambers suggested that Lippincott try selling the *Pictorial History of England* in volumes, we can see that it was coming to recognize the existence of different transatlantic preferences. Indeed, the decision to publish a *Hand-book of American Literature* in 1855 (despite having turned down Gould's suggestion for such a volume nine years earlier[108]), and the firm's willingness to include many articles on American topics, with at least some written by Americans recruited by Lippincott, in the company's next major project, the *Chambers's Encyclopaedia* (1860–68), demonstrates that Chambers had now acquired a deeper respect for American literature, its authors and its readers.[109]

The absence of copyright, and the licence that gave to the activities of reprinters, was certainly a problem to be faced by all those trying to work within a transatlantic book trade community in the mid-nineteenth century. Even though no reprint of *Chambers's Journal* was successful in the long term, the ever present threat of a reprint severely limited the viability of the imported edition. Yet, it was only the *Journal* and some parts of the Educational Course which were seriously affected by the activities of reprinters. The viability of Chambers's other books and serials as imports demonstrates that British and American publishers could find mutually constructive ways of doing business, even without the legal protection of copyright.

In the late 1840s and 1850s, W. & R. Chambers was still getting to know the United States, and experimenting to find out what methods of distribution worked and what products were marketable. Even as it built up what would become a long relationship with Lippincott, it continued to supply retail booksellers direct, offer stereotype plates for particular titles to other publishers, and send consignments to the English Book Depot in New York. The firm also gradually came to realize that, just as the ideal of smooth transatlantic trade was hampered by the lack of a fully integrated banking and business community, so too, readers in the United States were distinct from those in Britain. Chambers appears to have made only limited efforts to change the contents of its works to appeal to an American readership, but its partners in Boston and Philadelphia did what they could with the physical format of the publications to make them successful in their new market.

The 1850s seems to have been a time of growing interest in the American market among British publishers. The belief that an international copyright treaty was about to be signed was no doubt part of that, but it was far from the only factor. Steamship services were becoming reliable and frequent, carrying goods, letters, people and bills of exchange across the Atlantic. In the mid-1840s, Chambers and its contacts had still been making careful choices about when to use expensive steamer services and when to use sailing ships. By the late 1850s, the cost of freight on the steamers had come down several times, and the use of steamers was almost routine. This ease of communication did a great deal to increase knowledge of the markets and the methods of reaching them on both sides of the Atlantic, while the ease of personal travel meant that increasing numbers of publishers had either crossed the Atlantic themselves, or had a friend, relative or colleague who had. Some British publishers even started to open branch offices in New York in the mid-1850s. When Robert Chambers made his first trip to the United States in 1860, therefore, he was visiting a much more familiar country than had his brother, seven years earlier.

Notes

1. Entry for 19 Nov 1853, in W. & R. Chambers Archive, National Library of Scotland, deposit 341 (hereafter WRC) item 35 (American Notebook).
2. [W. Chambers], 'New York Concluded', *Chambers's Edinburgh Journal* (hereafter *CEJ*) (10 Jun 1854): 358. The articles were later collected and issued as W. Chambers, *Things as they are in America* (Edinburgh, 1854).
3. On these issues, see Ronald J. Zboray, *A Fictive People: Antebellum Economic Development and the American Reading Public* (New York, 1993); Richard D. Brown, *Knowledge Is Power: The Diffusion of Information in Early America, 1700–1865*, chs. 6–9 (New York, 1990); David M. Henkin, *City Reading: Written Words and Public Spaces in Antebellum New York* (New York, 1999).
4. James J. Barnes, *Authors, Publishers and Politicians: The Quest for an Anglo-American Copyright Agreement, 1815–1854* (London, 1974); Simon Nowell-Smith, *International Copyright Law and the Publisher in the Reign of Queen Victoria* (Oxford, 1968); Meredith L. McGill, *American Literature and the Culture of Reprinting, 1834–1853* (Philadelphia, PA, 2002).
5. On *Chambers's Journal*, see Sondra Miley Cooney, 'Publishers for the People: W. & R. Chambers – the Early Years, 1832–50' (PhD dissertation, Ohio State University, 1970); chs. 2–3; Robert Scholnick, ' "The Fiery Cross of

Knowledge": *Chambers's Edinburgh Journal*, 1832–43.' *Victorian Periodicals Review*, 32 (1999): 324–58; Robert Scholnick, 'Intersecting Empires: W. & R. Chambers and Emigration, 1832–1844', *Bibliotheck* 24 (1999): 5–17 and Laurel Brake, 'The Popular "Weeklies" ', in Bill Bell (ed.), *Edinburgh History of the Book in Scotland vol. 3 Ambition and Industry 1800–1880*, (Edinburgh, 2007): 359–69.

6. For the early history of the firm (and of the brothers), see William Chambers, *Memoir of Robert Chambers with Autobiographical Reminiscences* (New York, 1872), esp. chs 1–5; *The Story of a Long and Busy Life* (Edinburgh, 1882); and Cooney, 'Publishers for the People', 218–34.

7. 'Chambers's Edinburgh Journal', *CEJ*, 2 Feb 1833, 1. Circulation figures for the period to 1849 are cited in Cooney, 'Publishers for the People', 96–8. Detailed circulation figures from 1844 onwards can be found in WRC 275 (Publication Ledger 2, 1845–67, hereafter PL2), fols. 4–5.

8. Chambers own account is in 'Address to Readers', *CEJ*, 4 Jan 1845, 1; though see also Cooney, 'Publishers for the People', 214–5.

9. Preface, *Information for the People*, vol. 1 (1841–42 edn): [iii].

10. 'Chambers's Journal' *CEJ*, 1 Feb 1834, 1. The series had sold 62,500 sets by the time it was revised and expanded (to 100 pamphlets) in 1841–42, see figures in WRC 274 (Publication Ledger 1842–45, hereafter PL1), fols. 261–2. It was revised again in 1848–49 and 1857–58.

11. *Natural Theology* (People's edn, Nov 1837) sold 13,500 copies in four years, yielding a profit of £220, see WRC 274 (PL1), fol. 352.

12. The Educational Course is discussed in detail in Cooney, 'Publishers for the People', ch. 4.

13. Cooney, 'Publishers for the People', 207.

14. It was originally reset from advance sheets, but Chambers were soon sending stereotype plates to London. See 'Mechanism of Chambers's Journal', *CEJ* (1835, vol. 4): 150.

15. For Chambers's public comments on Orr's agency, see Chambers, *Memoir of Robert Chambers*, ch. 13. Also, S. M. Cooney, 'William Somerville Orr, London Publisher and Printer: The Skeleton in W. & R. Chambers's Closet,' in J. Hinks and C. Armstrong (eds), *Worlds of Print: Diversity in the Book Trade* (London, 2006): 135–47.

16. Invoices for the shipping of packages to these firms in the late 1830s survive in the various files of Receipts in the Chambers archive, e.g. WRC 459–60, 470–1, and 495–6; McKinlay and Gilchrist still feature regularly in the correspondence from the 1850s (although Crombie seems to have disappeared), see WRC 163 (Letter Book 1853–67, hereafter LB).

17. For a reference to the use of telegraphy, see Chambers to Francis, 22 Dec 1854, WRC 322 (Literary Labour, hereafter LL, 1855).

18. Dawson to Chambers, 22 Apr 1858, WRC 325 (LL 1858); Chambers to Sterns, 4 Jun 1858 and Chambers to Dawson n.d., both in WRC 163 (LB).

19. Gould to Chambers, 15 Oct 1845, WRC 314 (LL 1844–7); Lea & Blanchard to Chambers, 27 May 1850, WRC 121 (Correspondence H-O, hereafter Corresp.), fol. 40.

20. [W. Chambers], 'Philadelphia', *CEJ*, 9 Sept 1854, 171.

21. Dates of meetings (though no details) from WRC 35 (American Notebook).

22. Chambers, *Memoir of Robert Chambers*, 278–80.

23. Rosalind Remer, *Printers and Men of Capital: The Philadelphia Book Trade in the New Republic* (Philadelphia, PA, 1996), esp. ch. 5.

24. Gould to Chambers, 27 Feb 1846, WRC 314 (LL 1844–7).

25. Lea & Blanchard to Chambers, 5 Jul 1850, WRC 317 (LL 1850).

26. Chambers to Lippincott, 30 Nov 1854 and 26 Jan 1855, WRC 163 (LB), fol. 70 and fol. 75.

27. Nowell-Smith, *International Copyright*, 78; Michael Winship, 'Printing with Plates in the Nineteenth Century' *Printing History*, 3 (1983), 15–27.

28. Gould to Chambers, 27 Feb 1846, WRC 314 (LL 1844–7).

29. Ibid., 31 Dec 1846, WRC 314 (LL 1844–47).

30. Gould to Chambers, 30 May 1846, WRC 314 (LL 1844–47).

31. Barnes, *Authors, Publishers and Politicians*, 49.

32. Lea & Blanchard to Chambers, 27 May 1850 (which is written on the back of their trade catalogue), WRC 121 (Corresp.), fol. 40. Note, the exchange rate was approximately $5 = £1, thus 25 cents = 1 shilling.

33. Gould to Chambers, 15 Oct 1845, WRC 314 (LL 1844–7).

34. The plates for *Life of Burns* ultimately went to Harper Brothers in New York, see Chambers to Harpers, 25 Jul 1851, and Harpers to Chambers, 13 Aug 1851, WRC 318 (LL 1851).

35. Chambers to Barrington, 31 Oct 1855, WRC 163 (LB), fol. 116; Chambers to Derby, 19 Nov 1855, ibid., fol. 121.

36. Chambers to Francis, 22 Dec 1854 (sorting out arrangements consequent upon Baldwin's retirement), WRC 322 (LL 1855).

37. Putnam's latest biographer suggests he may have met the Chamberses on his trip to Edinburgh in 1836, though there is no direct evidence and it is, perhaps, a little early for Chambers to be considered major publishers. See Ezra Greenspan, *George Palmer Putnam: Representative American Publisher* (University Park, PA, 2000): 62.

38. Clarence S. Brigham, 'History of Book Auctions in America', *Bulletin of the New York Public Library* 39 (1935): 64–7; Michael Winship, 'Getting the Books Out: Trade Sales, Parcel Sales and Book Fairs in the Nineteenth-Century United States', in Michael Hackenberg (ed.), *Getting the Books Out* (Washington, DC, 1987): 4–25.

39. *Publishers' Circular*, 1 Oct 1847, 338; Adverts also appeared from rival firm Cooley, Keese & Hill, for instance, *Publishers' Circular*, 1 Jan 1847, 24.

40. *Publishers' Circular*, 1 Mar 1848, 99.

41. Chambers to Bangs, 10 Feb 1853, WRC 320 (LL 1853).

42. Chambers to Bangs, 17 Jan 1854, WRC 163 (LB), fol. 25.

43. Low's Report on his activities in the United States on behalf of British publishers (presented at the London Coffee House), 6 Jan 1858, WRC 325 (LL 1858). Low managed to get a new Depot set up, bank-rolled by Charles Scribner, and managed by Charles Welford, who had been in charge of the now-defunct Bangs Depot.

44. He bought the first Gutenberg Bible to go to America. It was bought from him by James Lennox, see 'Selected Correspondence' reprinted in Ezra Greenspan (ed.), *The House of Putnam, 1837–1872: A Documentary Volume* (Detroit, 2001). See also Greenspan, *George Palmer Putnam*, chs. 3–6.

45. *Publishers' Circular*, 1 Jul 1848, 224. Robert Chambers was author, but not publisher, of the *Biographical Dictionary*.

46. These imprints appear in the National Union Catalog etc.
47. Lea & Blanchard to Chambers, 27 May 1850, WRC 121 (Corresp.), fol. 40.
48. Ibid., 5 Jul 1850, WRC 317 (LL 1850).
49. Patricia Anderson, *The Printed Image and the Transformation of Popular Culture 1790–1860* (Oxford, 1991).
50. Figures from WRC 275 (PL2).
51. Gould to Chambers, 31 Dec 1846, WRC 314 (LL 1844–7).
52. 'Chambers's Edinburgh Journal', *CEJ* (2 Feb 1833): 1.
53. *CEJ* with Richards' imprint survives at the American Antiquarian Society.
54. Chambers to Hobart, 20 Jul 1833, WRC 312 (LL 1832–40).
55. 'Chambers's Edinburgh Journal', *CEJ* (31 Jan 1835): 2.
56. The offer is recorded in Chambers Transactions Notebook, 21 Jun 1838, Dep 341/414. The price was £4 10s. 0d., ten shillings less than the price offered to Hobart in 1833.
57. AAS catalogue.
58. Chambers to Gould, 30 Sept 1847, WRC 314 (LL 1844–47).
59. Chambers to Gould 30 Sept 1847, WRC 314 (LL 1844–47).
60. [W. Chambers], 'New York concluded', *CEJ* (10 Jun 1854): 359.
61. For Chambers' knowledge of Orvis's activities, see Chambers to Lippincott, 10 Mar 1854, WRC 163 (LB), fol. 45. Orvis was the printer of the *Illustrated New York Journal* in 1853–54, which became (or was merged into) *Frank Leslie's New York Journal*.
62. A poster (with price) for the New York edition survives loose in WRC 641 (Press Cuttings). Although no imprint is given, this is presumably for Orvis's edition.
63. Barnes, *Authors, Publishers and Politicians*, 147–52.
64. Memorandum to R. Noble, 19 Dec 1854, WRC 321 (LL 1854).
65. Chambers to Gould 30 Sept 1847, WRC 314 (LL 1844–47).
66. UK trade price was 1s. 1½d. per dozen, with 13 counting as 12. See, for instance, WRC 600 (1858 Trade Catalogue).
67. A hint of this may be gleaned from Gould's comments on the *Miscellany*, in Gould to Chambers, 31 Dec 1846, WRC 314 (LL 1844–47).
68. Chambers to Lippincott, 10 Mar 1854, WRC 163 (LB), fol. 45.
69. Chambers to Lippincott, 5 Jun 1854, WRC 163 (LB), fol. 30. It is not clear if he received the monthly parts as issued in Britain, or if he still printed his own covers.
70. Chambers to Lippincott, 5 Jun 1854, WRC 163 (LB), fol. 30.
71. Chambers to Lippincott, 13 Apr 1855, WRC 163 (LB), fol. 82.
72. In 1847, when Chambers established the rate of £3 7s. 6d., the average production costs (1844–46) were just £1 1s. 7d. per thousand, giving clear profit. But by the mid-1850s, the *Journal* run was declining and paper costs were rising: production costs had become £2 18s. 0d. (1852–54 average). Production costs have been calculated from the figures in WRC 275 (PL2), fols. 4–5.
73. WRC to Lippincott, 18 May 1855, WRC 163 (LB), fol. 86.
74. In early 1854, Chambers suggested to Lippincott that they try another method of besting Orvis, following Blackwood's example some years earlier. The plan would involve an American article being inserted in the *Journal*, so that the reprinter would find himself in breach of American copyright

laws. This was how Blackwood had persuaded Scott to make a payment for advance sheets, but since Chambers did not want to come to terms with Orvis, it is not clear whether such a plan would have worked. Nor is there any indication that it was attempted. For Chambers's suggestion, see Chambers to Lippincott, 10 Mar 1854, WRC 163 (LB), fol. 45. For Blackwood, see Barnes, *Authors, Publishers and Politicians*, 37–42.

75. In contrast, Leonard Scott's New York reprint of *Blackwood's Edinburgh Magazine* had been finding around 4,000 subscribers (in 1848), see Barnes, *Authors, Publishers and Politicians*, 41.

76. Barnes, *Authors, Publishers and Politicians*, 35–45.

77. Chambers to Lippincott, 2 May 1854, WRC 321 (LL 1854).

78. Imprints appear in library catalogues. For Zieber, see *Dictionary of Literary Biography vol. 49 American Literary Publishing Houses, 1638–1899*, Peter Dzwonkoski (ed.) (Detroit, 1986). For Chambers's awareness of Zieber, see Chambers to Gould, 30 Sept 1847, WRC 314 (LL 1844–47). On Gihon and subscription publishing, see Michael Hackenberg, 'The Subscription Publishing Network in Nineteenth-Century America' in Michael Hackenberg (ed.), *Getting the Books Out*, vol. 45–75 (Washington, DC, 1987): 59.

79. Gould reported in Dec 1846 that an unspecified New York house had announced a reprint of the *Miscellany*, but no trace of such a reprint survives. Gould to Chambers, 31 Dec 1846, WRC 314 (LL 1844–47).

80. See the several letters from Gould to Chambers, 1853–57, in WRC 163 (LB). British sales are recorded in WRC 275 (PL2). By the mid-1850s, orders from Gould and Lippincott seem to have accounted for perhaps a third of all sales of the *Miscellany* in any given year.

81. Chambers to Gould, 16 Aug 1855, WRC 163 (LB), fol. 97.

82. Chambers to Lippincott, 16 Oct 1854 and 15 Apr 1856, WRC 163 (LB), fol. 49 and fol. 137.

83. Copies survive of a New York imprint from 1865, which appears to be co-published with the Edinburgh and London edition – nothing about this appears to survive in the archival material, so we do not know about the circumstances behind it.

84. 'A Few Hints about Newspapers', *CEJ* (vol. 6, 1837): 28–9.

85. Chambers to Gould, 9 Aug 1850, WRC 317 (LL 1850). Both the German books and Burns were subsequently offered to other publishers.

86. Chambers tried to reassure them that they would find sales, because Zieber 'has copied a ten year old book', something of an exaggeration, since Zieber's edition was only five years old. Chambers to Gould, 30 Sept 1847, WRC 314 (LL 1844–47).

87. The order was dispatched in several batches, mentioned in William Chambers to Lippincott, 17 Jan 1854, WRC 321 (LL 1854), and Chambers to Lippincott, 9 Feb 1854, WRC 163 (LB), fol. 24.

88. Chambers to Lippincott, 2 May 1854, WRC 321 (LL 1854). This mentions 2,000 copies for Lippincott, though this was later reduced to 1,500, in anticipation of competition from an edition reprinted by P. D. Orvis in New York. Surviving copies of this title in American libraries bear Lippincott's imprint (only one copy with Orvis's imprint has been located).

89. Chambers to Dix, Edwards, 25 Mar 1857, WRC 163 (LB), fol. 213. The contact between Chambers and Dix, Edwards appears to have been brokered

by Frederick Law Olmsted (the designer of Central Park), whom Chambers accused of having wilfully misled them about Dix, Edwards & Co's financial standing, see Olmsted to Chambers, 13 Oct 1857, WRC 324 (LL 1857).

90. For Bangs, see Chambers to Bangs, 5 Dec 1856, WRC 163 (LB), fol. 194. For Dix, Edwards, see Chambers to Dix, 5 Dec 1856, ibid., fol. 190. For Gould, see Chambers to Gould, 19 Jan 1857, ibid., fol. 207.

91. Chambers to Lippincott, 8 May 1856, WRC 163 (LB), fol. 143.

92. Chambers to Lippincott, 28 Nov 1854, WRC 163 (LB), fol. 65. Chambers's revised and updated edition of the *Pictorial History of England* (1839–41) appeared between 1855–58.

93. Chambers to Lippincott, 13 Apr 1855, WRC 163 (LB), fol. 82.

94. Chambers to Lippincott, 24 Oct 1856, WRC 163 (LB), fol. 185.

95. Gould to Chambers, 31 Dec 1846, WRC 314 (LL 1844–7).

96. *Living Age* (vol. 5) 12 Apr 1845, for instance, reprinted the February 1845 annual address to readers from *Chambers's Journal* (and four other articles from *Chambers's*), as well as items from the other periodicals mentioned.

97. Quotes from title page of *Information for the People* (1st American edn, 1848).

98. Preface, *Information for the People*, vol. 1 (1841–42 edn): iii.

99. Preface, *Information for the People*, vol. 1 (1st American edn, 1848): 1.

100. For their subsequent *Chambers's Encyclopaedia* (1860–68), which also appeared in parts, see Sondra Miley Cooney, 'A Catalogue of *Chambers's Encyclopaedia* 1868', *Bibliotheck* 24 (1999): 17–110.

101. See WRC 600 (1858 Trade Catalogue): 9.

102. Gould to Chambers, 27 Feb 1846, WRC 314 (LL 1844–47).

103. Gould to Chambers, 30 May 1846, WRC 314 (LL 1844–47). Gould mentions the imported edition and its price in Gould to Chambers 1 Jan 1846, WRC 314 (LL 1844–46).

104. Gould to Chambers, 31 Dec 1846, WRC 314 (LL 1844–7).

105. Gould to Chambers, 31 Dec 1846, WRC 314 (LL 1844–7).

106. Barnes, *Authors, Publishers and Politicians*, ch. 1.

107. Gould to Chambers, 30 May 1846, WRC 314 (LL 1844–47).

108. The idea is referred to in Gould to Chambers, 31 Dec 1846, WRC 314 (LL 1844–47).

109. On the *Encyclopaedia* articles and contributors, see Cooney, 'A Catalogue of *Chambers's Encyclopaedia* 1868'. For Lippincott's recruitment of contributors, see Chambers to Lippincott, 11 Oct 1859, WRC 163 (LB), fol. 350.

13

'The Power of Steam': Anti-slavery and Reform in Britain and America, 1844–60

Robert J. Scholnick

In his 'Address...on...Emancipation of the Negroes in the British West Indies', delivered 1 August 1844 in Concord, Massachusetts, Ralph Waldo Emerson asserted that for moral vision and political energy the American anti-slavery cause had come to depend on the British, who on 1 August 1838 had completed the process of emancipating all the slaves in their possessions:

> We are indebted mainly to this movement, and the continuers of it, for the popular discussion of every point of practical ethics, and a reference of every question to the absolute standard. It is notorious, that the political, religious, and social schemes, with which the minds of men are now most occupied, have been matured, or at least broached, in the free and daring discussions of these assemblies. Men have become aware through the emancipation, and kindred events, of the presence of powers, which, in their days of darkness, they had overlooked.[1]

Only seven years earlier, in 'The American Scholar', Emerson had boasted that 'our day of dependence, our long apprenticeship to the learning of other lands, draws to a close',[2] but now he acknowledged an ironic reversal: if the United States were to realize the principles of human rights that ostensibly had justified its violent separation from Britain, the nation must now follow the lead of the British, who, he claimed, had created a 'moral revolution' by 'add[ing] a new element into modern politics, namely the civilization of the Negro'.[3]

Emerson apparently overlooked the fact that members of the Boston African-American community had long since entered 'modern politics', as it were, in their campaign to end slavery and secure their rights as citizens, including that of attendance at integrated schools. For members of this community, Britain had long been an essential resource. As David Walker asserted in his subversive 1829 *Appeal to the Colored Citizens of the World*, 'the English are the best friends the colored people have on earth. They have done one hundred times more for the melioration of our condition, than all the other nations of the world put together.'[4] The historian James Brewer Stewart wrote that 'from its inception by Garrison and Walker, Boston's abolitionist crusade was thus irrevocably anglophile, subversively patriotic, and based on an African-American view of history's moral direction set in transatlantic terms.'[5]

Better than anyone else, Frederick Douglass came to embody this principle. On his return from two years of anti-slavery campaigning in Britain, where his *Narrative of the Life of Frederick Douglass, an American Slave* was something of a sensation, he told a New York audience on 11 May 1847 that 'I went to England, Monarchical England, to get rid of Democratic Slavery, and I must confess that, at the very threshold, I was satisfied that I had gone to the right place.'[6] In a speech in London on 22 May 1846, Douglass credited new technologies in the inexpensive reproduction and distribution of information with bringing the voice of British anti-slavery to America. 'You have an influence on America that no other nation can have', he asserted:

> You have been brought together by the power of steam to a marvelous extent; the distance between London and Boston is now reduced to some 12 or 14 days, so the denunciations against slavery uttered in London this week, may be heard on the streets of Boston, and reverberating amidst the hills of Massachusetts. There is nothing that is said here against slavery that will not be recorded in the United States.[7]

In the famous 1852 address 'What to the Slave is the Fourth of July?', he spoke of the potential of internationalism to promote social justice: 'Nations do not now stand in the same relation to each other that they did ages ago.' Whereas 'long established customs of hurtful character could formerly fence themselves in, and do their work with social impunity,' now, 'oceans...link nations together....Space is comparatively annihilated. – Thoughts expressed on one side of the Atlantic are distinctly heard on the other.' He called the new internationalism one of the 'obvious tendencies of the age'.[8] Paul Giles has remarked that 'a sense of estrangement from American institutions impelled [Douglass] intellectually and politically toward transnational perspectives in the middle part of his career.'[9]

What were the material mechanisms that 'annihilated' space and brought the two English-speaking democracies together? How were British denunciations of slavery heard in America and what is known of their impact? In addition, what was the influence of such conservatives as Thomas Carlyle, who, as we will see, would call for something very much like the reinstitution of slavery in the West Indies? The purpose of this chapter is to explore the network that enabled Americans and Britons to communicate in the ante-bellum period about the paramount issue of slavery. Despite the efforts of Carlyle and other reactionaries to shield American slavery from criticism, even such Tory periodicals as the *Quarterly Review* joined with their progressive rivals to condemn the institution. The powerful voice of British anti-slavery forced Americans to confront a difficult, painful subject, one that they would just as soon have ignored.

Eliakim Littell's *The Living Age* (or *Littell's Living Age* or simply *Littell's*, as it was familiarly known) was a Boston 'eclectic' or miscellaneous weekly made up of pieces drawn primarily from the British periodical press.[10] Established in May 1844, *The Living Age* (as noted above in Chapter 12) published within a month or so essays that had appeared in British quarterlies, monthlies, weeklies of opinion and newspapers. Littell also occasionally republished articles from American newspapers, including William Cullen Bryant's New York *Evening Post* and the anti-slavery Washington *National Standard*.[11] A reading of *The Living Age* enables us to see just how the British periodical press became a strong and consistent voice in the promotion of the anti-slavery cause in America. However, both as a matter of journalistic fairness and to give his readers an accurate sense of shifting British opinion, Littell included a sampling of conservative and even reactionary essays from British periodicals. Such pieces encouraged American apologists for slavery to hope that Britain might well come round to their side. On balance, however, the powerful voice of British anti-slavery provided precisely the sort of support that the abolitionist community found essential. In turn, American progressives 'wrote back' to the Mother Country, particularly in support of the working class. The resulting alliance of progressives on both sides of the ocean achieved notable success, first in advancing the anti-slavery cause, and, once the Civil War began, in keeping Britain from recognizing the Confederacy, thereby contributing significantly to the Union victory. That victory in turn made possible such progressive measures in Britain as the Reform Bill of 1867. As the British writer and politician John Morley put it in the *Fortnightly Review* in 1870, 'The triumph of the North...was the force that made English liberalism powerful enough to enfranchize the workmen, depose official Christianity in Ireland, and deal the first blow at the landlords.'[12] *The Living Age* served as an essential transatlantic arena, a place where fundamental questions could be debated.

Littell, like Douglass, was a fervent internationalist, writing in 1848 that, since 'the steamship has brought Europe, Asia, and Africa, into our neighborhood...and will greatly multiply our connections as Merchants, Travelers, and Politicians, with all parts of the world,' it 'now becomes every intelligent American to be informed of the conditions and changes of foreign countries....Nations seem to be hastening through a rapid process of change, to some new state of things, which the merely political prophet cannot compute or see.'[13] Littell's life's work was to promote that change by bringing high-quality, low-cost reading materials from abroad to Americans. Born on 2 January 1797 in Burlington, New Jersey, he became a general publisher in Philadelphia in 1818, and the next year established the *National Recorder*, a weekly, to publish the 'cream of foreign literature'. The *Recorder* later became the *Saturday Magazine*, which merged with *The Museum of Foreign Literature*. In January 1843, Littell purchased *The American Eclectic*, which appeared every two months and which he combined with *The Museum* under the name of *The Eclectic Museum*, which he edited from New York. An obituary notice published in *The Living Age* after Littell's death on 17 May 1870 describes *The Museum* as 'a monthly publication [which] included nearly everything that was really worthy of reproduction in the periodical literature of Great Britain', a periodical that 'for twenty-one years...had a brilliant reputation, and held foremost rank'.[14] In January 1844, Littell sold his interest in *The Museum* to begin *The Living Age* in Boston. He would skilfully negotiate the sectional politics of the antebellum period, survive the challenges of Civil War publishing and set the direction of a magazine that, remarkably, would last until 1941.[15]

The Living Age came into being at a time when, despite heated conflicts over the Oregon boundary and the annexation of Texas, Britain and America were growing closer together. In 1846 Congress passed the Walker Tariff, which opened the American market for British manufactures, even as Britain reduced tariffs on agricultural products, a boon to American farmers. Emigration from Britain to America was on the upswing. The nations managed to settle their dispute over the Oregon boundary – prompted by the 'friendly address movement in the press of both countries' initiated by Elihu Burritt, the American pacifist and

peace activist who spent a great deal of time in Britain calling attention to the desperate condition of the working class.[16] Littell regularly
drew from the British press to report on Burritt's efforts in Britain to
build transatlantic understanding, not least through adoption of penny
postage. In an essay on 'Great Britain and the United States', reproduced
by Littell in August 1851, *The Times* claimed that Britain was 'far more
closely united' with the United States

> than [with] any one of our colonies, and while these communities are
> colonies in name, but in reality, either prisons, garrisons, or indepen-
> dent communities, the United States keep up a perpetual interchange
> of the most important good offices; indeed, the relations between the
> parent and the child, separated as they are in politics, are unparalleled
> in their intimate nature as they are in their enormous extent.[17]

American anti-slavery leaders such as Burritt, Douglass, Emerson and
Garrison drew inspiration from the British anti-slavery movement,
even as British liberals cited the progressive example of the United
States in such areas as education, voting rights, treatment of workers and separation of Church and State. The fate of liberal democracy
hung in the balance as the two nations sent ideas of all sorts, scientific, economic, social, political and literary, back and forth across
the Atlantic through books, periodicals, newspapers, personal contacts,
letters, visiting journalists and lecturers.

It is not known what motivated Littell to create a new periodical in
Boston. Perhaps it was that Boston was the first American port for the
new steamers operated by the British and North American Royal Mail
Steam Packet Company, which came into service in 1840, when the first
ship, the *Britannia*, sailed to Halifax in 12 days and then on to Boston in
two days more. Littell's prospectus speaks of the 'cordial approval and
encouragement' of such leading progressives as John Quincy Adams,
who entering Congress in 1832 championed the anti-slavery cause.
Littell thereby signalled his own opposition to slavery.[18] He would add at
the bottom of the Table of Contents page a commendation from Adams:

> Of all the Periodical Journals devoted to literature and science which
> abound in Europe and in this country, this has appeared to me to
> be the most useful. It contains indeed the exposition only of the cur-
> rent literature of the English language, but this by its immense extent
> and comprehension includes a portraiture of the human mind in the
> utmost expansion of the present age.[19]

Littell did not publish material that was otherwise unavailable. In the absence of international copyright, as Frank Luther Mott has written, 'all the more prominent English magazines and reviews were regularly republished on this side of the water'.[20] The absence of international copyright, along with the mechanization of printing, speedy steamship service and improved distribution through the expanding railway network, made *The Living Age* possible, since there was no need to pay for contributions. It sold for only 12½c. per copy or $6 per year, and offered readers a diverse sampling from British periodicals – with special attention to British comment on America.

When Littell launched *The Living Age*, British periodicals dominated the domestic market; American editors could not compete with their British cousins in cosmopolitan range, intellectual depth, quality, humour or comprehensiveness. So widely read were British periodicals in America that, according to an essay on 'The United States of America' from the *North British Review* reproduced in *The Living Age* on 14 December 1844:

> The more intelligent and educated classes [in America] ... do not trust to newspapers for information about European literature and politics, but are much in the habit of reading our reviews and other periodicals of a higher class. Most of the leading British reviews are republished in America, and are sold much cheaper than in this country; our half-crown magazines being generally sold for nine-pence, and our six shilling quarterlies for two; and we have reason to believe, that about as large a proportion of men connected with the learned professions are in the habit of reading four or five of our leading reviews as are to be found even among ourselves.[21]

Through the great Victorian periodicals, which were reprinted and sold inexpensively in America, American readers could participate in an ongoing transatlantic conversation. Given the extensive circulation of their periodicals in America, British writers were well aware that they were simultaneously addressing readers on both sides of the water. Significant in its own right, *The Living Age* helps us today, as it did its original readers, in identifying the range of comment on America that appeared in British periodicals.

The British press could not possibly ignore the United States, which in the 1840s emerged as both ally and rival. 'In the whole range of political and social questions there are none surpassing in speculative interest and practical importance those involved in the relations between Great

Britain and the United States; and these have rarely been more critical or more interesting than at the present moment', *The National Review* asserted in 'The Political Tendencies of America', a discussion of five books about America republished in *The Living Age* on 28 June 1856. 'There is no nation on earth whom it so much imports us to study and read aright as the American', the periodical continued. However, standing in the way of even closer relations was America's 'special "domestic institution" ', slavery, which 'we regard with condemnation and abhorrence, and which they themselves in secret feel to be a danger, an embarrassment, and a reproach, but in public think it necessary to defend with the vehemence and anger with which men always defend their vulnerable points.'[22] By publishing just such essays, Littell compelled Americans to confront a subject that they would have preferred to avoid.

In 1844 where else could the struggling American abolitionist movement have turned for support but to Britain? While the 'average northerner', as Martin Duberman has written, may well have thought himself opposed to slavery, he 'certainly did not think it an evil sufficiently profound to risk, by "precipitous action", the nation's present wealth or future power.'[23] Most Americans would just as soon have ignored the troubling reality and discredited those who campaigned for abolitionism, a movement associated with Boston, where William Lloyd Garrison had his headquarters. Aware that his move to Boston might alienate readers elsewhere, Littell opened *The Living Age* on 11 May 1844 with an appeal to the 'Southern and Western' readers of his former publication, *The Museum*, not 'to give up on us because we have *annexed* New England. We cannot agree to the dissolution of the union that has subsisted between us for so many years'.[24]

Talk of 'annexation' was everywhere; the previous month Secretary of State John C. Calhoun had sent a letter to the British Minister to Washington, Sir Richard Pakenham, in justification of the American annexation of Texas. Ostensibly the letter was a reply to one from Lord Aberdeen, the British Foreign Secretary, which stated that while the British would continue to work for the elimination of slavery throughout the world, they had no designs on Texas. Calhoun responded that since it was England's 'settled policy, and the object of her constant exertion, to procure the general abolition of slavery throughout the world', America would continue to protect an institution sanctioned by American law.[25] On 22 April, President Tyler sent an annexation treaty, along with Calhoun's letter, to the Senate with the instruction that the matter be considered secretly. However, on 27 April Senator Benjamin

Tappan of Ohio sent the documents to his brother Lewis, the abolitionist leader, with the request that they be 'published in the [New York] *Evening Post'*. Lewis complied, which created a sensation and forced a delay in the ratification of the treaty. However, Calhoun evidently achieved exactly what he intended: the denial of the Democratic nomination to former president Martin Van Buren of New York in favour of a slave-holder, James K. Polk of Tennessee, a 'national imperialist who might diffuse the North's resentment of the slavepower'.[26] The South's success in bringing Texas into the Union as a slave state forced anti-slavery Americans to confront a new reality: slavery would not simply wither away; they must mount a campaign to root it out.

Just as Littell was launching his venture, a wave of Anglophobia spread throughout the country as a result of suspected British meddling in Texas. Would *The Living Age*, created to bring Britain to America, be destroyed by the furore? Littell's challenge was to diffuse potential hostility to a Boston periodical without becoming hostage to Southern interests or compromising editorial integrity. In the first of his introductory 'Correspondence' columns, he framed the move to Boston in non-ideological terms by the assertion that proximity to Britain made Boston the best place in which to publish: 'It is to [our readers'] advantage that we should have the most favourite post for our army of observation, that is, our printing-office. We shall here receive foreign periodicals earliest.' Boston also afforded excellent postal connections with other regions. Littell's statement that 'we are as desirous of continuing and increasing our business to the west and south as ever' reflected his awareness of the threat to the venture.[27]

Littell claimed immediate success, and reported in his 'Correspondence' column the next week that 'we sold in two days the whole edition of No. 1, and have printed a second.'[28] On 1 June, he noted that a *'third edition of No. 1 is just published'*.[29] The overtures to the South and West seem to have succeeded; the weekly gained commendations from newspapers throughout the country. Bryant's anti-slavery *Evening Post* in New York remarked that *Littell's* 'contains a prodigious amount of and variety of the best periodical literature of England', and the *Southern Churchman* of Alexandria wrote that for 'variety of excellence of contents, it has, we think, no rival in this country. The frequency of its publication enables its editor to present a continuous chain of the best reading' of the foreign press. Even the *Mobile Advertiser* remarked that it is 'everywhere commended, and we trust that it may come into universal favor'. The *Mobile Advertiser* included a subscriber's letter, which claimed that *The Living Age:*

will suit all tastes, whilst it will not pander to a meretricious appetite for the false and disgusting and unreal pictures of life and manners with which the press of this country now teems. This book... is even cheaper than the cheapest of those brochures which come to us... from the north. And it contains the very best matter imaginable in all the varieties of style found in some twenty or thirty of the principal foreign reviews, magazines, and miscellanies, from the grave quarterlies to the funny Punch.[30]

Was the letter planted by Littell? In 1846 Walt Whitman praised *The Living Age* as 'a sterling weekly, containing the cream of foreign periodical literature'.[31]

In the introduction to the issue for 15 June, Littell explained that in operating *The Museum of Foreign Literature* he 'never hesitated to reprint foreign attacks on the United States, however ill-natured, or however true they might be. We have no sympathy with the very great tenderness of that patriotism which cannot hear of our *alleged* faults, and shrinks from every attack.' Should 'we... who wish to show to this country the public opinion of England and of Europe, upon all leading topics of the day, be afraid to print what may be said of our great men?' He would 'trust [his] readers' to have confidence in his professionalism in selecting articles for their significance, not because of their conformity to his own 'private opinions and prejudices'. Readers might take offence at one piece or another, but *The Living Age* would demonstrate the importance – even the necessity – of blunt criticism. Just as he would include British articles critical of America, so too would he publish material critical of the British, as with their 'annexations in India (against the *will* of the annexed by the way)'.[32]

Included in that 15 June 1844 issue under the title 'Topics of the Day' were essays from *The Spectator* and *Britannia* brilliantly skewering America as a hypocritical country that had betrayed its democratic roots by extending the reach of slavery. In 'The Moral Prospects of the United States', published in London on 11 May, *The Spectator* referred to the many 'Calhouns' of America – all those who 'look upon the occupation of Texas as nothing but a just and necessary step in defence of the sacred institution of negro slavery; and all to take pride in extending their territory by violent or fraudulent appropriations of what belongs to neighbouring powers'. Such policies threatened to debase the people at large:

[The] low swindling principles of repudiation, the callousness to human suffering of the slave-owner, and the plundering propensities of the conqueror, are not likely to be confined to the cabinet; the poison will penetrate into domestic circles. A class will be formed in every State as demoralized as the rabble of Rome under the emperors.

In 'Texas' *Britannia* condemned America for speaking of slavery as 'a "political institution," not a suffering and a misery – a sale of human beings as immortal as ourselves, and the abandonment of men, be their colour what it may, to the wretchedness, the vice, the cruelty, and the despair which must be included in all the general corruptions of transatlantic slavery'. Further,

> It is enough to excite universal disgust to know that in America human beings are actually born and reared for exportation, like pigs; that creatures capable of local attachment and natural affections are habitually dragged from the place of their birth and all their early associations, and sent into distant countries for sale... or that children are torn from their parents, never to see or be seen by them again in this world; and all this only to put money in the pocket of a ruffian with his mouth stuffed full of the verbiage of liberty and philanthropy.

Britannia thundered that 'the world [now understands] that the republic that laid down as its first principle that "all men are by nature equal," comes forward now as the formal advocate of slavery.'[33]

Such essays appeared at a time when, as mentioned, mainstream American periodicals simply did not publish such outspoken material. There is no evidence that Emerson, Douglass or other speakers at the Concord meeting of 1 August 1844 read these pieces in *The Living Age* or elsewhere, but it is likely that they did. The conclusion must be that the powerful denunciations of slavery from the British press pushed them at last to speak out, as Emerson would do at that notable anti-slavery meeting in August. It is inconceivable that they were unaware of such powerful denunciations of American slavery. British writers raised tough questions: if slavery was not integral to the American system, what was being done to eliminate it? Would America forever remain a slave-holding nation? If Calhoun did not speak for America, who did?

Remarkably, in publishing such pieces in a national periodical, Littell managed to circumvent the 'intellectual blockade' that the South sought to place on anti-slavery writings. The event that had precipitated the blockade was Nat Turner's rebellion in 1831, which 'many southerners interpreted... as proof that [anti-slavery] advocacy was taking effect. The South reacted by adopting the pro-slavery doctrine as a matter of creed.... Open discussion of slavery fell under a taboo.'[34] *The Living Age* escaped detection, at least until the middle of the next decade, when, it will be seen, the New Orleans monthly *De Bow's Review* awoke to the fact that each week Boston was sending a Trojan horse into Southern homes, reading rooms and libraries.

Once the furore over Calhoun's letter abated, the tone of British discussions of American slavery shifted, from outrage to a sense of frustration, betrayal and sad disappointment. *The Spectator* explained on 20 July 1844 that

> of all countries it is in every account most desirable to abolish slavery in the United States; has any progress been made to that end? The question is still an enigma, so dark that men refuse to hazard a guess at its solution, or even to look it in the face. Is that progress?[35]

Still, the British sought to be supportive. On 27 July 1844, the *Athenaeum*, after listing America's national flaws 'of slavery, of ruffian violence and... fatal desire for territorial acquisition', expressed the hope that the country would 'work out the noblest of all triumphs, that of self-cure and self-redemption'.[36] In the essay on 'The United States of America' which is quoted above, the *North British Review* assumed a tone of earnest concern, as when one speaks to a dear friend of a 'painful subject' which must be confronted. That subject is slavery, which

> no friend of America can contemplate without feelings of the deepest sorrow and regret. It is a topic on which, of all others, our American brethren are most sensitive, probably from a lurking consciousness that it is the deepest and darkest stain attaching to their country, and all they can adduce in explanation or palliation affords no adequate defence of it.

Admitting that, from the British perspective, the difficulties of eliminating slavery might well be underestimated, the *North British Review* urged Americans not to 'overrate them'. Addressing the silent centre, it asserted that just because they might object to certain tactics of the abolitionists, that was no reason not to act. Everyone 'should... be doing something'.[37]

In December 1845, Littell published *Fraser's Magazine's* 'England and Yankee-Land', which charged that Americans in both the North and

South supported the institution of slavery because of its financial benefits. It described slavery as 'a deep-rooted and complicated evil to which
the Americans seem already hopelessly resigned'. Therefore the author
doubted that it would be eliminated anytime soon, if at all:

> The question of abolitionism is adjourned until the dissolution of
> the Union. The north-eastern states forsook the cause of *honesty* as
> soon as they deemed it inconsistent with the *best policy*. Their feelings
> of humanity were not proof against their commercial and political
> interests; and, with the exception of a few 'ranting fanatics,' the
> anti-slavery outcry has been hushed up and the subject dropped as
> dangerous and disorganizing.[38]

That, of course, was exactly what Littell was doing: exposing what in
America had been 'hushed up'.

British writers developed the argument that the elimination of
American slavery was pivotal for the cause of reform throughout the
world. If a democracy like America persisted in holding slaves, could
reform be expected elsewhere? In 'Slavery and the Slave Trade', published by Littell on 24 May 1845, the *London Examiner* warned that
if American slavery was not abolished, 'it will be not only sad for the
negro race, but humanity, since it must throw a chill upon every kind
of political measure or policy, founded upon religious or philanthropic
sentiment.' Further, 'it will be a most melancholy and disheartening
tale, should history have to tell the failure of English efforts to put an
end to slavery and the slave trade.'[39]

However, the anti-slavery effort was not a one-way street. American
reformers reminded the British that the anti-slavery cause depended
upon their own efforts to improve the deplorable condition of the
working class at home. If British workers lived less well than American
slaves, why should slavery be eliminated? That was the point made by
Horace Greeley, editor of the *New York Tribune*, in a speech to the British
Anti-Slavery Society and published by Littell in 1851. While welcoming anti-slavery agitation from the British, Greeley insisted that such
efforts could not be a substitute for the desperately needed improvement in the lot of 'the depressed laboring class here at home'. He
called for 'determined efforts for the eradication of those social evils
and miseries *here* which are appealed to and relied on by slaveholders and their champions everywhere as justifying the continuance of
slavery'.[40]

Equally, if not even more detrimental to the American anti-slavery cause, was the apparent failure of British emancipation. In 1833, the Colonial Secretary, Edward Stanley, had presented emancipation to Parliament as a 'mighty experiment', one that would conclusively prove that, as Adam Smith had predicted, free labour was more productive than slave labour.[41] In 1838, after the intermediate 'apprenticeship' period during which slaves had still been obligated to work about 40 hours per week for their masters had ended, production of agricultural staples in the West Indies had fallen precipitously. Prices to British consumers rose, and British planters faced ruin. Yet, such slave-holding territories as Cuba and Brazil managed to increase output. Despite the British blockade, they stepped up the importation of slaves from Africa.[42] Paradoxically, even as they attacked American slavery, British writers had to confront the apparent failures of their own policies. For instance, in a June 1844 essay (not published by Littell), *Blackwood's Magazine* summarized the situation in 'Africa – Slave Trades – Tropical Colonies':

> Instead of supplying her own wants with Tropical produce, and next nearly all Europe, as she formerly did, it is the fact that, in some of the most important articles, she has barely sufficient to supply her own wants; while the whole of her colonial possessions...are at this moment supplied with [in the article of sugar] foreign slave produce.... Such a state of things cannot continue, nor ought it any longer be permitted to continue, without adopting an effectual remedy.[43]

Parliament was considering the question of whether the protective tariffs on sugar should be increased or eliminated; Littell had no choice but to report on these issues.

When Emerson delivered his Address on Emancipation on 1 August 1844, only 11 issues of *The Living Age* had been published, but already five substantial pieces on the apparent failure of emancipation in the West Indies had appeared. On 20 July, Littell included an essay from *The Spectator*, published in London on 8 June 1844, which criticized 'the anti-slavery people' for:

> shutting their eyes to the disastrous results of their own errors; and the consequence is, that the slave-trade continues, more cruel and profitable than ever; emancipation of the slaves in the countries

where they most abound is as distant as ever... and the only large community that they have succeeded in forcing to abolish slavery – that of the West Indies – is threatened with consequent ruin. Is that encouraging?

Another *Spectator* essay appearing that week in *The Living Age* detailed the costs to the British public of a 'perplexed and mismanaged business'. The public has purchased 'at any price the luxury of sentiment – in shedding tears over the name of slavery, getting up projects to quash it, and consenting to blink the fact, that, for all the outlay, there is as much slavery as ever.' *The Spectator* opened the essay by calling emancipation:

a badly-fulfilled bargain. The public has paid long for 'slave-trade sup-pression', as the fruitless and costly *efforts* to suppress the slave-trade are called; it pays a high price for sugar, to protect the West Indies from ruin, which is not done; it pays all round, and purchases – what? Nothing but mortification.[44]

Pro-slavery American journals such as *The Southern Quarterly Review*, in an essay on the 'Annexation of Texas', published in October 1844, drew on such reports to conclude that 'The experiment of emancipation of the slaves, held in the British colonies, has not succeeded.... As an economical experiment, it resulted in total failure.... This was not the beneficial "experiment" she proposed to present to the world.'[45]

That same month, *The Living Age* included a pointed essay from *The Colonial Magazine* exposing a fundamental inconsistency in British prac-tices: that 'England, as the chief purchaser of slave-labour produce, is also indirectly the great cause of slavery in many parts of the world, especially in North and South America.'[46] Here was the dark side of globalization: nations might be tied ever more closely together through networks of trade and communication, but these new relationships, far from promoting human rights, were responsible for an increase in the amount of slavery in the world. Paradoxically, the world's leading anti-slavery nation might be seen as slavery's leading supporter through its imports. Whither globalization? While British journals did not as yet retreat from their anti-slavery crusade, they spoke of the limits of such endeavours. *The Spectator* commented in an article published by Littell on 22 August 1846, of a

truth that has been creeping on the conviction of all unbiased observers – that the pertinacious attempt of this country forcibly to suppress the slave-trade carried on by other countries, alien to our laws, is impractical. Our devices to effect it, our resources to disguise the ruinous cost to ourselves, are exhausted.[47]

The appearance in *Fraser's Magazine* in December 1849 of Carlyle's 'Occasional Discourse on the Negro Question' introduced an ugly, racist dimension to the subject. He spoke out ostensibly on behalf of the hard-working British citizens who were forced to pay for the misguided policies of liberating a race incapable of assuming the responsibilities of freedom. 'Black Quashee' is pictured lounging about the pumpkin patch, working but half an hour a day while valuable crops lie rotting. Carlyle warned that 'the idle black man in the West Indies had not long since the right, and will again if it please Heaven, have the right...to be *compelled* to work as he was fit, and to *do* the Maker's will'. By way of introduction, *Fraser's Magazine's* editors commented that 'as the colonial and negro question is still alive, and likely to grow livelier for some time, we...give [the essay] publicity without [necessarily agreeing with its] strange notions and doctrines.' This was a lame excuse for publishing such racist comments – but there was no going back.

Littell faced a difficult decision. If he elected to publish the essay, he would undermine the anti-slavery cause. But the essay was too significant to ignore, and not to publish it would be to renege a promise not to censor what he offered readers. On 9 February 1850, he introduced it as follows: 'We find the following pages in Fraser's Magazine. Are they by Mr. Carlyle? They will be a grief to many of his admirers in this region, and yet they, and others (if others indeed there be!) will think it desirable to read whatever the sage may write.'[48] On 9 March 1850, Littell included John Stuart Mill's response to Carlyle, also from *Fraser's Magazine*. Mill warned of the damage that Carlyle's 'abominable' essay would do, especially in America, where 'the decisive conflict between right and iniquity seems about to commence.' As he remarked,

the words of English writers of celebrity are words of power on the other side of the ocean; and the owners of human flesh...will welcome such auxiliary. Circulated as his dissertation will probably be...from one end of the American Union to the other, I hardly know of an act by which one person could have done so much mischief...and I hold...he has made himself an instrument of what an able writer in the *Inquirer* justly calls a 'true work of the devil'.[49]

In fact, Carlyle's essay provided just the sort of support from Britain that Southern intellectuals and their Northern supporters most desired. That April, New York's *Democratic Review*, a defender of the South, claimed that a decided reaction had taken place in England against the anti-slavery mania; thoughtful Britons were now coming around to support American slavery.[50] And in June 1850, *De Bow's Review* reprinted the essay, which it called 'a piece of pungent satire, upon the whole body of pseudo philanthropists who, within the last few years, have been a curse to our own country as to England.... When British writers can so speak, it is time for Northern fanaticism to pause and recollect.'[51]

Littell recognized the damage that Carlyle's notorious essay was doing and that spring he published a series of dispatches from Jamaica that had begun to appear in the *Evening Post* in March. Written by the paper's associate editor, John Bigelow, these vivid pieces of travel writing, which incorporated pointed social commentary, were later collected as *Jamaica in 1850*, released early in 1851. Bigelow forcefully argued that economic difficulties were caused not, as Carlyle charged, by lazy blacks, but rather by incompetent white plantation owners. In all, Bigelow offered an inspiring report on the progress of the former slaves to establish themselves as independent farmers, despite the determined efforts of their former owners. On 1 June 1850, the London *Examiner* published a most perceptive and supportive essay on Bigelow's series, 'Prospects of Jamaica', written, it would appear, by the paper's editor, Albany Fonblanque.[52] On 10 August 1850, Littell published this article from the progressive *Examiner*, which he used as a concluding statement following his own republication of the last of Bigelow's dispatches from the *Evening Post*.[53] In this way, Littell supplied anti-slavery forces with essential ammunition. He would also republish the London *Examiner's* excellent review of Bigelow's published volume *Jamaica in 1850*, released by Putnam.[54]

While few in Britain subscribed to Carlyle's extreme position, there is little doubt that during the 1850s the British commitment to the world-wide anti-slavery effort wavered. In an essay published in *The Living Age* on 23 July 1853, *The Economist* went so far as to ask, 'Can Slavery Be Abolished?' The issue was whether Britain should pressure slave-holding nations through boycotts. While 'our reason and our hearts call upon us to abhor [slavery] and strive against it,' the fact is that Britain has 'no...business, as a nation, to take up the cause of the abolitionist in the United States, and declare a war of opinion against southern planters', the author maintained. The article explicitly repudiated the suggestion that Britain 'give up the use of slave-grown cotton', insisting instead that, 'Immediate and unconditional emancipation is simply an impossibility.... The declaration that immediate and unconditional emancipation is the duty of the masters in the States is not to be surpassed for impracticality by any project hatched in this world inside or outside of Bedlam.'[55]

The anti-slavery forces struggled to fight back against the onslaught of negative commentary.

Even during the 1840s, Douglass did his best to convince his British audiences of their essential role in the anti-slavery struggle. In the 1846 speech at London's Finsbury Chapel quoted earlier, Douglass asserted that

I am here because the slaveholders do not want me to be here....The slaveholders felt that when slavery was denounced among themselves, it was not so bad, but let one of the slaves get loose, let him summon the people of Britain, and make known to them the conduct of slaveholders to the slaves, and it cuts them to the quick, and produces a sensation such as would be produced by nothing else.[56]

In 1849 the *Southern Literary Messenger* gratuitously mentioned Douglass in the course of a review of Charles Lyell's *A Second Visit to the United States of America*:

We are not surprised to learn that this work...has met with little favor at home, since [Lyell] in no degree sympathizes with the anti-slavery fanaticism which manifests itself...in unmeasured denunciation of the Southern States of our Union. On the contrary, while it is evident that he considers slavery an evil in the abstract, he bears willing testimony to the happy condition of the slaves, – testimony, which will be most unacceptable to the Frederick-Douglass philanthropists of England.[57]

The comment revealed just how important British opinion remained in the South, and it suggested why Southerners would look to periodicals such as *The Living Age*, which, after all, offered a convenient means to fashion a self-image as a replication of the British aristocracy. Offering a sampling of British 'culture', *The Living Age* seemed to have found a place in Southern homes and reading rooms. In July 1850, that uncompromising defender of slavery, *De Bow's Review*, praised *the Boston weekly*, remarking that it 'embraces selections from all the foreign periodical publications, and is, of course, an invaluable miscellany'.[58] The Living

Age would prove invaluable for Southern readers looking for evidence of shifts in British opinion favourable to slavery, as happened with Carlyle.

It was not until September 1856, in 'The War against the South', that the editor, J.D.B. De Bow (1820–67) awoke to the fact that the Boston weekly was not what it seemed: 'We always very highly recommended *The Living Age* and recommended it for Southern support', he confessed. He noted that *the weekly* carried testimonials on its cover from Southern papers. But now De Bow wrote in fury that:

> On the outside of the same cover, and in the most conspicuous type, appears the following from the abolition house of Jewett & Co., Boston. Thus is the leaven working. Can we not have foreign literature and science, as was customary in Littell, and be spared the nauseating doses?

As evidence, De Bow quoted in full an advertisement from the Jewett publishing firm for three books: *Friends of Free Territory, Free Men and Freemont!*; a collection of speeches by Charles Sumner; and *Six Months in Kansas*, written 'by a Boston lady', Hannah Ropes Gray. A map of Kansas was also offered for sale, and the advertisement solicited agents to sell the firm's books.[59]

The editor's angry rebuke of *The Living Age* comes as part of an essay published in the aftermath of the notorious caning of Massachusetts Senator Charles Sumner by Congressman Preston Brooks of South Carolina on the floor of the Senate on 26 May. Brooks surprised Sumner and beat him into unconsciousness in retaliation for Sumner's 'Crime Against Kansas' speech excoriating Brooks' cousin Senator Andrew P. Butler of South Carolina and Senator Stephen Douglas of Illinois for their advocacy of the Kansas-Nebraska Act. This Act repealed the Missouri Compromise of 1820. Sumner charged that the new Act opened the West to the spread of slavery. The attack on Sumner marked the hardening of positions in North and South, as reflected in the comments of DeBow, who reported that he had been collecting 'for some time past whatever papers, speeches, etc., have come within our reach, going to show the kind of feeling entertained by the men who are sweeping everything before them in the free States, and are coming nearer and nearer to the possession of Federal power.'

One such document was a letter of support to Sumner from such luminaries as Josiah Quincy, Longfellow, Sparks, Dana and Everett. De Bow also quoted from an anti-slavery speech by Emerson to his Concord neighbours attacking the South as a 'barbarous community.... I think we must get rid of slavery or we must get rid of freedom'. De Bow had not actually seen Emerson's Address, but was relying on 'an extract in *Littell's The Living Age*, 637', a reference to the number published on August 9, 1856. So incensed was the New Orleans editor at the attacks on the South from Britain and Boston carried by *The Living Age* that he could not stop himself, but quoted extensively from several articles denouncing the attack on Sumner reprinted by Littell. Paradoxically, in seeking to indict *The Living Age* for the sin of publishing incendiary material, *De Bow's* reproduced significant portions of the very material that it found reprehensible. So determined were Southerners like De Bow to isolate the region from Northern intellectual life, that reports of what was written and said in Boston and Concord first had to travel to London and then back to Boston before being sent to the South. Now, however, De Bow vowed to keep *The Living Age* out of the South, further increasing its intellectual, political and social isolation.[60]

De Bow had ample reason to be furious with *The Living Age*, which continued to publish denunciations of the South from British periodicals. For instance, on 26 July 1856 it carried *The Economist's* angry discussion of 'The Outrage in the Senate'.[61] Two weeks later *The Living Age* published three essays on this subject, from *The Economist*, the London *Examiner*, and one entitled 'United States' from *The Spectator*. This essay described an ominous turn in North-South sectional relations – for which it blamed the South:

> Of late years the Abolitionist agitation of the North has materially declined; far less pressure was put upon the South, and there did appear a possibility that the slavery question might be staved off until its settlement could be approached in the calm and prudent spirit of the late Whig senator from Kentucky, Henry Clay [1772–1852]. The South has met moderation with violence, and has resorted to extremes which appear to render a civil war inevitable, if indeed they do not bring on the long-anticipated disruption of the Union.[62]

It would appear that British writers saw the caning of Sumner, and particularly the refusal of Southern leaders to condemn it as the cowardly act that it was, as a turning point: either civil war or the dissolution of the Union as constituted would become inevitable.

Less than a year later, in July 1857, *De Bow's Review* again attacked the Boston weekly in 'The Abolitionism of Littell's Living Age – Elihu Burritt'.[63] The reference is to the *The Living Age* for 20 June 1857, where De Bow found two particularly offensive items. The first came from

England: a lengthy article from the *Quarterly Review* on two anti-slavery volumes, Harriet Beecher Stowe's novel *Dred* and a gathering of various anti-slavery items under the title *American Slavery*. The item included a 'reprint of an article on Uncle Tom's Cabin, and of Mr. Sumner's Speech of the 19th and 20th of May, 1856 with a notice of the events which followed that speech'.[64] In the latter essay, Eliakim Littell himself strongly endorsed the plan developed by Elihu Burritt, mentioned above, to end slavery gradually, through compensated emancipation. State by state, the slaves would be freed, with payments coming from the Federal Treasury to their former owners. Burritt's *A Plan of Brotherly Copartnership of the North and the South, for the Peaceful Extinction of Slavery*, followed the British precedent of providing compensation to slave owners, but was hotly contested by large segments of the abolitionist community since it would reward slave-holders with cash payments even though they held human beings in bondage.[65]

Exploding, De Bow wrote that it had been:

> some time since we warned our readers against the growing abolitionism of this once reliable journal, popular at the South as well as throughout the country. It has, at last, taken another great step, thrown off the flimsy mask, and insolently undertakes to lecture the South and Southern statesmen on their future duties. If this work has yet Southern subscribers, it should cease to have any to-day.

And he warned further that 'thus does the journal travel entirely out of its appropriate sphere, in this matter, in order that the wretched instincts for mischief, and for intermeddling in other people's affairs, which is so characteristic usually of Northern ill-regulated minds, may be gratified.'

De Bow proceeded to defend slavery as an institution sanctioned by a God who:

> has decreed orders and degrees, and subordinations, and that the institution of slavery, as practiced by [the South] is one of these, tending to the development of society and ... the elevation of a race, which, when left to itself in Africa, in Hayti, in Jamaica, falls naturally and rapidly into barbarism. This is her high function; and in the Union or out of it, she will exercise it, leaving Mr. Burritt and his friends to swap jack-knives, converse with invisible spirits, run off negroes, manufacture tooth-picks and clocks ... showing how Yankee

philanthropy may be gratified in purchasing negroes and making their masters pay for them.

De Bow concluded by quoting from Burritt's pamphlet, including the admission that 'by popular sentiment, commercial partnership, religious communion, and legislative action, the free States have lived in guilty complicity with the system of slavery from the foundation of the Republic.'[66]

Insisting that Littell's *The Living Age* be banned from the South, De Bow was in effect attempting to prove Frederick Douglass wrong in his assertion in 'What to the Slave is the Fourth of July?' that, 'no nation can now shut itself up from the surrounding world and trot around in the same old path of its fathers without interference.' If De Bow and his fellow editors could manage it, the South would indeed immunize itself from threatening thought – from Britain, Boston or anywhere else. And in this way he testified to the importance of ideas as they came to the South through *The Living Age*. On the other hand, the North allowed the free circulation of pro- and anti-slavery ideas from all sources, foreign and domestic. British periodicals continued to condemn slavery – and issued warnings that the South would have been wise to heed. But as reflected in De Bow's denunciations of *The Living Age*, the South refused even to listen. In removing itself from this transatlantic interchange, the South signaled that conflict would be preferable to dialogue.

Eliakim Littell's remarkable weekly continued to draw from British periodicals in order to challenge the 'walled cities and empires' of the South – to use Douglass's phrase. As a journalist and editor, Littell understood his function not as one of confirming or reinforcing the assumptions of his readers, but rather as challenging them by the publication of opinions that were 'worthy of their consideration, however they may disagree with them'. Only in this way, he understood, could the weekly participate meaningfully in the 'living age'. His periodical developed a global perspective that came to be essential in the anti-slavery movement. What Emerson asserted in August 1844 would be true throughout the ante-bellum years: 'We are indebted [to the British anti-slavery] movement, and the continuers of it for the popular discussion of every point of practical ethics, and a reference of every question to the absolute standard.' And in a speech delivered on 3 August 1857, Frederick Douglass stated flatly that:

The abolition movement in America, like many other institutions in this country, was largely derived from England....Mr. Garrison applied British abolitionism to American slavery. He did that and nothing more. He found its principles here plainly stated and defined; its truths glowingly enunciated, and the whole subject illustrated, and elaborated in a masterly manner.[67]

Paradoxically, to fight for the cause of human equality and democracy, Americans had to draw significantly from 'England, monarchical England', as Douglass put it on arriving back in America on 11 May 1847. Littell understood that one could not be an American citizen without renewing one's citizenship in the larger global community, a community that had at its core an open, rich, and vital transatlantic dialogue, a dialogue that took place on the pages of *The Living Age*.

Notes

1. Ralph Waldo Emerson, 'Emancipation in the West Indies', in Len Geogeon and Joel Myerson (eds), *Emerson's Antislavery Writings* (New Haven, CT, 1995): 28.
2. Ralph Waldo Emerson, 'The American Scholar', *The Collected Works of Ralph Waldo Emerson*, 7 vols. to date, vol. I (Cambridge, MA, 1971–): 52.
3. Emerson, 'Emancipation in the West Indies,' p. 23.
4. David Walker, *Walker's Appeal to the Coloured Citizens of the World* (Boston, MA, 1829; rpt. 2000).
5. James Brewer Stewart, 'Boston, Abolition, and the Atlantic World, 1820–1861', in Donald M. Jacobs (ed.), *Courage and Conscience: Black and White Abolitionists in Boston* (Bloomington, IN, 1993): 111.
6. John W. Blassingame, (ed.), *Frederick Douglass Papers, Series One: Speeches, Debates, and Interviews vol. 2 1847–54* (New Haven, CT, 1982): 59.
7. John W. Blassingame, (ed.), *Frederick Douglass Papers, Series One: Speeches, Debates, and Interviews vol. 1 1841–46* (New Haven, CT, 1979): 387.
8. Ibid.
9. Paul Giles, *Virtual Americas: Transnational Fictions and the Transatlantic Imaginary* (Durham, NC, and London, 2002): 26.
10. See also Robert J. Scholnick, 'Emancipation and the Atlantic Triangle' intro. to John Bigelow, *Jamaica in 1850* (Univ. Illinois Press edn, 2006): ix–lvi; and Scholnick, ' "The Man [and Woman] at the other End of the Lever": Douglass, Stowe, and the Perils and Promise of Living in a Global Village,' *Resources for American Literary Study*, 30 (2006): 43–75.
11. Little has been written on *The Living Age*. A sketch is to be found in Frank Luther Mott, *A History of American Magazines*, 5 vols, vol. 1 (Cambridge, MA, 1966): 747–49. Cathy Packer comments on the magazine in 'Eliakim Littell and Robert S. Littell', *Dictionary of Literary Biography: American Magazine Journalists* (Detroit, MI, 1989): 222–5. In *American Literature and the Culture of Reprinting, 1834–1853*, Meredith L. McGill briefly discusses *The Living Age*, claiming that in drawing from periodicals from all points on the political spectrum, the reprint magazine 'renders much of the cultural freight carried

by a particular article largely unrecoverable by removing it from the context in which it signified'. Further, she claims that 'Littell and other reprint publishers seem surprisingly indifferent to the carefully crafted sensibilities and political commitments of the journals from which they draw' (26–27). But as in the case of Carlyle's 'On the Negro Question', Littell went out of his way to speculate on the identity of the author – and his own prefatory comments to certain articles as well as his brief editorial introductions did provide a political frame for the articles selected for reprinting. In the case of the explosive question of slavery, if he wanted to play it 'safe', he could have largely avoided the subject. Meredith L. McGill, *American Literature and the Culture of Reprinting* (Philadelphia, PA, 2003).

12. John Morley, 'England and the War', *Fortnightly Review* I (Oct 1870): 479, quoted in R. J. M. Blackett, *Divided Hearts: Britain and the American Civil War* (Baton Rouge, LA, 2001): 5.

13. *Littell's Living Age* also known as *The Living Age* and familiarly as *Littell's* (hereafter *LLA*) 18 (15 Jul 1848): 144.

14. Ibid., 105 (18 Jun 1870): 707.

15. After Eliakim Littell's death in 1870, his son Robert edited the periodical. After his death in 1896, it was sold to Frank Foxcroft, who understandably eliminated 'Littell's' from the title. According to Mott, *History of American Magazines*, the Atlantic Monthly Company purchased the magazine in 1919, from a Colonel Du Pont. See Packer, *DLB*, 79, and Mott, for complementary accounts of the periodical's fortunes following Robert's death.

16. *Dictionary of American Biography*, vol. 3, 328–30.

17. *LLA*, 30 (28 Aug 1851): 373–4.

18. Prospectus in Mott, *History of American Magazines*.

19. *LLA*, 18 (15 Jul 1848): 144.

20. Mott, *History of American Magazines*, vol. 1, 392.

21. *LLA*, 3 (14 Dec 1844): 395.

22. Ibid., 49 (28 Jun 1856): 770.

23. Martin Duberman, *Antislavery Vanguard* (Princeton, NJ, 1965): 413; see also Leonard L. Richards, *The Free North and Southern Domination: 1780–1860* (Baton Rouge, LA, 2000).

24. *LLA*, 1 (11 May 1844): 1.

25. Quoted in William Freehling, *The Road to Disunion* I (New York, 1990): 408.

26. Ibid., p. 430.

27. *LLA*, 1 (11 May 1844): 2.

28. Ibid., 1 (25 May 1844): 66.

29. Ibid., 1 (1 Jun 1844): 130.

30. Ibid., 1, Miscellaneous Front Pages.

31. Whitman, *The Journalism*, 2 vols. ed. Herbert Bergman et al. (New York, NY, 1998), 1: 298. Article from the *Brooklyn Eagle*, 21 Mar 1846.

32. *LLA*, 1 (15 Jun 1844): 258.

33. Ibid., 1 (15 Jun 1844): 278.

34. David M. Porter, *The Impending Crisis* (New York, NY, 1976): 39.

35. *LLA* 1 (20 Jul 1844): 588.

36. Ibid., 1 (27 Jul 1844): 675.

37. Ibid., 3 (14 Dec 1844): 401.

38. Ibid., 7 (13 Dec 1845): 495.

39. Ibid., 5 (24 May 1845): 357–8.
40. Ibid., 30 (28 Aug 1851): 382–3.
41. See Seymour Drescher, *The Mighty Experiment* (Oxford and New York, 2002): 123–8.
42. In addition to Drescher, see Howard Temperley, *British Antislavery* (London, 1972); and Thomas C. Holt, *The Problem of Freedom* (Baltimore, MD, 1992).
43. *Blackwood's*, 55 (Jun 1844): 742.
44. *LLA*, 1 (20 Jul 1844): 586.
45. *The Southern Quarterly Review*, 6 (Oct 1844): 507.
46. *LLA*, 2 (12 Aug 1844): 631.
47. Ibid., 10 (26 Aug 1846): 367.
48. Ibid., 24 (9 Feb 1850): 248–54.
49. Ibid., 24 (9 Mar 1850): 465–9.
50. *Democratic Review*, 26 (Apr 1850): 289–305.
51. *De Bow's Review*, 2 (Jun 1850): 527–38.
52. *The Examiner*, No. 2: 209 (1 Jun 1850): 339.
53. *LLA*, 26 (10 Aug 1850): 251–4.
54. Ibid., 29 (31 May 1851): 426–9.
55. Ibid., 38 (23 Jul 1853): 223.
56. Blassingame et al., *Frederick Douglass Papers, Series One, Speeches, Debates, and Interviews*, vol. 1. 293.
57. *Southern Literary Messenger*, 15 (Sept 1849): 639.
58. *De Bow's Review* 9 (Jul 1850): 128.
59. Ibid., 21 (Sept 1856): 275.
60. Ibid., 21 (Sept 1856): 274–5.
61. *LLA*, 50 (26 Jul 1856): 249–51.
62. Ibid., 50 (9 Aug 1856): 379–80.
63. *De Dow's Review*, 20 (Jul 1857): 187–90.
64. *LLA*, 53 (20 Jun 1857): 705–22.
65. Ibid., 53 (20 Jun 1857): 754–65.
66. *De Bow's Review*, 20 (Jul 1857): 87–90.
67. Frederick Douglass, 'The Significance of Emancipation in the West Indies', in John Blassingame (ed.), *The Frederick Douglass Papers. Series One: Speeches, Debates, and Interviews vol 3 1855–63* (New Haven, CT, 1985): 190.

Index